FOR JACK, AND NO WONDER

Certainly those determining acts of her life were not ideally beautiful. They were the mixed result of a young and noble impulse struggling amidst the conditions of an imperfect social state, in which great feelings will often take the aspect of error, and great faith the aspect of illusion. For there is no creature whose inward being is so strong that it is not greatly determined by what lies outside it.

—George Eliot, *Middlemarch*

contents

women's monasticism and medieval society

NUNNERIES IN FRANCE AND ENGLAND, 890–1215

BRUCE L. VENARDE

Cornell University Press ITHACA AND LONDON

Copyright © 1997 by Cornell University

All rights reserved. Except for brief quotations in a review, this book, or parts
thereof, must not be reproduced in any form without permission in writing
from the publisher. For information, address Cornell University Press,
Sage House, 512 East State Street, Ithaca, New York 14850.

First published 1997 by Cornell University Press
First printing, Cornell Paperbacks, 1999

Printed in the United States of America

Library of Congress Cataloging-in-Publication Data

Venarde, Bruce L., 1962–
   Women's monasticism and medieval society : nunneries in France and
England, 890–1215 / Bruce L. Venarde.
     p. cm.
   Includes bibliographical references and index.
   ISBN 0-8014-3203-0 (cloth : alk. paper)
   ISBN 0-8014-8615-7 (pbk. : alk. paper)
   1. Convents—Europe—History. 2. Monasticism and religious orders
for women—History—Middle Ages, 600–1500. I. Title.
BX4220.E85V46   1996
271'.9'00420902—dc20   96–30260

Cornell University Press strives to use environmentally responsible suppliers
and materials to the fullest extent possible in the publishing of its books.
Such materials include vegetable-based, low-VOC inks and acid-free papers
that are recycled, totally chlorine-free, or partly composed of nonwood fibers.

Cloth printing   10 9 8 7 6 5 4 3 2 1

Paperback printing   10 9 8 7 6 5 4 3 2 1

illustrations

TABLES

pReface

historians of women and religious life in Western Europe have seen the tenth, eleventh, and twelfth centuries as a period of retrenchment for women's monasticism. In this view, although women participated in monastic and other forms of holy life from early medieval times, monastic women's status and visibility went into decline before the year 1000. Houses of nuns became few and socially exclusive; women were for the most part excluded from the reform movements of the tenth, eleventh, and twelfth centuries. Indeed, the new religious ideals of the period 900–1200, which affected everything from the tone of individual spirituality to the power of the papacy, acted as a check on women in monasticism. An index of the marginality of female participation in Christian life is the exceedingly small number of women saints, who comprised well under 10 percent of all saints in the two centuries following the millennium. The situation changed markedly around the turn of the thirteenth century, in a time of rehabilitation of the feminine in thought and practice—the rise of the cult of the Virgin Mary, many new female saints, and the religious life of the beguines. Only then did women whose needs had been largely ignored find some measure, at least, of recognition and institutional identity both within the traditional cenobitic framework and in other kinds of religious lives and associations.

Such is the story as it has been told for some decades. This book tells a different story. In a large part of the Christian West, I will show, the number of monasteries for women grew most rapidly not after 1200 but from the 1080s through the 1160s. Since most of this growth was not directly associated with contemporary reforming ideals or male-centered movements, it becomes necessary to examine the expansion of female monasticism from different historical perspectives. What follows is a study of institutions based on the conviction that ecclesiastical history is not a simple reflection of religious ideology, the playing out in the world of otherworldly ideals. Rather, the foundations of monastic communities are interesting precisely because they take place at the crossroads where ideals and realities meet. Monastic expansion reflects social and economic change as well as individual and group aspiration. The interplay of these forces provides the vocabulary for my narrative of the immense expansion of women's monasticism in the central Middle Ages. I do not question that the early thirteenth century was a time of remarkable change in the history of Christianity. But in the sphere of female monastic foundation, as in so many others, the twelfth century was the great creative era in a large part of the West.

There has been an enormous growth of scholarly interest in medieval women in the last three decades, but full-length studies on women in religious life remain few. I have taken my cue primarily from historians of female monasticism, especially Sharon K. Elkins and Penelope D. Johnson. However, it may be equally appropriate to consider my work in the context of a group of recent books on somewhat more diverse subjects, which I refer to collectively as "social history of the medieval Church." The prototype in this genre is R. W. Southern's pathbreaking *Western Society and the Church in the Middle Ages,* written with the credo that the successes and failures of the medieval Church can be understood only by placing them in the broadest social context. The model was taken up in the United States by Lester K. Little, who retold the history of religious life in the central Middle Ages in terms of the changing nature of the European economy. Since then Constance H. Berman, Lisa M. Bitel, Constance B. Bouchard, George W. Dameron, Maureen C. Miller, Barbara H. Rosenwein, and Stephen D. White, among others, have followed in the footsteps of Southern and Little in their attention to the importance of matters secular in the evaluation of ecclesiastical change. The foundation of nunneries, too, must be viewed as part of a larger story of change and growth. Here in turn I try to understand the activities and experiences of medieval Christians by focusing on issues besides institutional evolution and by describing change in realms other than the purely moral and spiritual.

This is a small book on a big subject, so it seems wise to state explicitly its goals and limits. What follows is by no means a comprehensive study of women's monasticism in the central Middle Ages. I concentrate instead on the processes surrounding the origins of monasteries for women, their foundations, and, sometimes, early histories. The chronological and geographical boundaries are suggested by the title and made more specific in Chapter 1, which also provides the statistical framework for the story I want to tell. The four subsequent chapters provide a survey of growth from the early tenth to the early thirteenth century, mostly by means of narrative and anecdote, sometimes with numerical illustration. Chapter 2 examines the largely royal and princely initiatives in the two centuries preceding the most significant growth of women's monasticism. The heart of the book is in Chapters 3 and 4. Chapter 3 describes the inspirational and practical contributions of hermits, bishops, and petty aristocrats in the multiplication of nunneries, circa 1080–circa 1170. Chapter 4 identifies some important contexts for that growth, in particular familial and marital situations, economic expansion, and the decentralization of power. The final chapter tries to account for the notable decrease of nunnery foundations in the late twelfth century. The Epilogue first sketches briefly the nature of post-1215 foundations and by way of conclusion returns briefly to the statistical mode to compare the pace of monastic foundations for men and women in the central Middle Ages.

I devote very little space to the quotidian lives and achievements of religious women. Perhaps more important, my book addresses only in passing the spirituality of religious women, a subject about which, given the relative dearth of reliable contemporary sources for the period and region concerned, fairly little can be said. Because of the scarcity of hagiographical and other devotional sources about and by monastic women in this age, what surfaces most often is the practical acumen of the nuns, as evidenced in charters (see Chapter 4). But I have worked from one very important assumption, which is argued at some length in Chapter 2 and then reprised briefly thereafter. There always were, in the time and space considered here, more women desirous of entry into the religious life than there were places for them. The motives for these aspirations were what we would called mixed, and some of the less "spiritual" contexts for female vocation are examined in some detail here. But only rarely, I think, was it a question of supply creating demand. What is remarkable is the degree to which women who wanted to enter monastic life were accommodated, especially in the years circa 1080–circa 1170, when the women themselves frequently seized the initiative.

A theme adumbrated in the first chapter and argued at greater length in the Epilogue is the coincidence of ebb and flow of monastic foundations for women with those for men in the central Middle Ages. The rest of the book also occasionally compares male and female foundation patterns and experiences (especially when monasteries housed religious of both sexes). Certainly, women never achieved anything like equality of opportunity in religious life; nunneries comprised only a fraction of the total number of monasteries in medieval Europe. Nevertheless, monastic expansion for men *and* women in the time and place under scrutiny here occurred very much on the same schedule. Historians of monks usually describe that growth in terms of self-conscious and programmatic renewal. In focusing on "reform," do we miss out on a more comprehensive understanding of the textures and meanings of medieval monasticism?

I've had a lot of help. Early guidance was provided by Thomas N. Bisson, who was careful, thoughtful, tactful, and kind. Michael McCormick offered a number of useful suggestions for revision. I owe a long-standing debt of gratitude to two superb teachers. Fredric L. Cheyette first encouraged me to study ecclesiastical charters, doubtless little suspecting I would write a book based primarily on them. Rhoda M. Schall introduced me to the world of the distant past in Latin class over fifteen years ago, and seems to have forgiven me for abandoning antiquity for the Middle Ages. Several busy scholars have taken the time to read parts of the manuscript. I thank Lorraine Attreed, Steven Biel, Steven Epstein, Penelope Johnson, and Laura Smoller for their comments, some of which I have been wise enough to heed. For information, assistance, and support at critical junctures I am grateful to Martin Aurell, Constance Berman, Lisa Bitel, Nicolas Brooks, Philippe Buc, Giles Constable, Jonathan Elukin, Theodore Evergates, Robert Favreau, Marc Forster, Patrick Geary, Katherine Gill, Jeffrey Gross, Thomas Head, Eric Hinderaker, Mary Martin McLaughlin, R. I. Moore, Mark Peterson, James Powers, Amy Remensnyder, Barbara Rosenwein, Vincent Tompkins, and David Venarde. For help with computers, I thank Iain Cockburn, Lee Davison, and especially Elizabeth Richter.

The Department of History at Harvard University made possible my research in France in 1989 and 1990. The staffs of the Archives Départementales in Angers, Caen, Marseilles, and Rouen, the Bibliothèque Municipale in Poitiers, and the Bibliothèque Nationale and Archives Nationales in Paris provided able and friendly assistance to a mangler of the French language. I am particularly grateful to Françoise Poirer-Coutansais, the director of the archives in Angers, for making my introduction to archival research such a pleasant and rewarding experience and to the Gérard family for their hospitality. Back home, the staff of the Harvard libraries, especially the reference and circulation departments in Widener Library, provided tremendously efficient and remarkably cheerful service.

All historians, indeed all people, should have friends such as mine. Some of their names have already appeared, and I would like to pay special tribute to one more. Maureen Miller has been my close colleague and good pal since we entered graduate school together in 1984, and she has read and improved versions of most of what follows. A born teacher, Maureen knows exactly how to balance acute criticism and confidence-building praise. Her contribution to this book is very great.

My experience with Cornell University Press has been wonderful. John Ackerman has answered even stupid letters with astonishing speed; Carol Betsch, Elizabeth Holmes, Kay Scheuer, and Marie-Josée Schorp have taken excellent care of the manuscript. An anonymous reader for the press gave a tremendously helpful seven-page single-spaced report that enabled me to improve the argument and form of the book.

A humanist's enterprise should honor the living and the dead. I hope this one honors five people in particular. Jack and Dell Venarde have shown astonishing generosity and forbearance over many years. It is of course largely their doing that I have been interested in books since I was able to pick them up, but few parents will unquestioningly give their children the opportunity to pursue impractical interests at such length. In her ninetieth year, my grandmother, Dell Trawick, is a shining reminder of how quickly and happily change can occur, even when you have stopped expecting it. My late grandfather, Roy J. Venarde, told stories of my ancestors in such a way as to inspire in me an abiding interest in people I could never meet. His simple accounts of birth, marriage, and death or his comical imitations of pretentious cousins could gather together for a moment many generations. In such fleeting instants great passions are born. Finally, I remember David Herlihy, under whose guidance I began the research that resulted in this book. His early death deprived the profession of a great scholar and me of a mentor whose greatest gift was an infectious delight in recovering the past. I love all these people, and I miss the last two still.

I do not know how to thank Jack Eckert. So I give him the book, in glad remembrance and joyous prospect.

BRUCE L. VENARDE

Cambridge, Massachusetts
Feast of St. Godelieve, 1995

note on terms

There is no medieval Latin word for a monastery for women. The term I usually employ is "nunnery," a word with a classical Latin root, but which did not become common until the thirteenth century, and then in English and Romance languages. Despite some unfortunate post-medieval overtones of the word ("Get thee to a nunnery"), I use it because it is precise. Less exact is "convent," which does have a medieval Latin root, but like *conventus* and the modern French *couvent*, can apply to monastic houses for men or women. I have used this term sparingly and mean it, as ordinarily in modern American, to signal a women's monastic house.

The geographical scope of my inquiry is described in detail in Chapter 1. It is a great region of Western Europe and Britain that extends from the Mediterranean to the Cheviot Hills and from the Pyrenees to the western and southern reaches of the Rhine basin. It is roughly, then, the "France and England" of the book's subtitle, but my boundaries are those of medieval dioceses, the most geographically stable institutional entities of the central Middle Ages. I sometimes refer to the entire area as "northwestern Europe," partly as convenient shorthand and partly to emphasize that I am describing a phenomenon common to a large, socially and linguistically diverse landscape.

abbreviations

ADML   Archives Départementales de Maine-et-Loire, Angers.
BN   Bibliothèque Nationale, Paris.
CS   *Cartularium saxonicum*, ed. Walter de Gray Birch. 4 vols. London, 1855–1899.
DHGE   *Dictionnaire d'histoire et de géographie ecclésiastiques.* Paris, 1912– .
GC   *Gallia christiana in provincias ecclesiasticas distributa.* 16 vols. Paris, 1744–1877.
HGL   Claude Devic and Joseph Vaissete, *Histoire générale de Languedoc.* 16 vols. Toulouse, 1872–1904.
MB   *Monasticon Belge.* 8 vols. Bruges/Liège, 1890–1993.
MGH SS *Monumenta Germaniae Historica, Scriptores.* Hanover, 1826– .
MP   Norbert Backmund, *Monasticon Praemonstratense.* 3 vols. Straubing, 1948–1956.
MRH   David Knowles and R. Neville Hadcock, *Medieval Religious Houses: England and Wales.* 2d ed. London, 1971.
OV   Orderic Vitalis, *The Ecclesiastical History of Orderic Vitalis*, ed. and trans. Marjorie Chibnall. 6 vols. Oxford, 1969–1980.
PL   *Patrologiae cursus completus, Series latina*, ed. J.-P. Migne. 221 vols. Paris, 1844–1864.
SASC   *Anglo-Saxon Charters: An Annotated List and Bibliography*, ed. Peter Sawyer. London, 1968.
VCH   *Victoria County Histories.* London, 1900– .

the expansion of female monasticism in the central middle ages

Multiplicata est sicut stelle celi et excrevit in immensum cysterciensis ordinis religio sanctimonialium. . . . Fundabantur cenobia, edificabantur monasteria, replebantur claustra.

The community of Cistercian nuns multiplied just as the stars of heaven and grew prodigiously. . . . Convents were founded, monasteries built, cloisters filled.

—Jacques de Vitry, *Historia Occidentalis*

Monasticism occupies a central but anomalous place in the history of the Middle Ages. Monks and nuns were the *religiosi*; they practiced the purest Christianity, a life of prayer and work embracing poverty, chastity, and obedience. From monastic colonies such as Canterbury and Fulda much of Europe was evangelized, and in Ireland abbots supplemented or superseded bishops in providing a framework for ecclesiastical organization. The work of teaching letters and copying manuscripts in monasteries preserved the legacy of classical culture through the political and social dislocations of the early medieval period and inspired great artistic achievements in illumination and metalwork. Abbeys became the centers of huge and widely dispersed estates whose leaders were important figures in the world they renounced.

In the great hierarchy of the church, from rural priest to pope, there is no well-defined place for monastic communities or their inhabitants. The importance of the monastic tradition rests on its manifold accomplishments, spiritual and otherwise, rather than on any circumscribed offices or roles. The abbeys scattered across early medieval Europe were autonomous units, most of them entirely free of formal relation to the institutions of what we call the secular church. And in marked contrast to the priesthood, the regular life remained open to all comers. Women were virgins and martyrs in the primitive church, and in the fourth century A.D. women peopled some of the first cenobitic communities in the Nile Valley, the birthplace of Christian monasticism. Houses of nuns appeared in the West before the year 500. The Catholic priesthood was by the sixth century the all-male preserve it has remained, but women continued to enter the religious life throughout the Middle Ages.

It is not the least of the peculiarities of medieval monasticism that it always included women. Settlements of nuns persisted and sometimes flourished within the confines of a male-dominated church and indeed a male-dominated society. Nor were these convents in any sense marginal. They existed as threads in the fabric of medieval society or perhaps in the interstices of that fabric. The importance of female monasticism lies precisely in its relationship to social, economic, and institutional organization and development. An examination of the origins of medieval women's religious communities suggests much not only about nuns, women, and monasticism, but also about the very nature of medieval society and the important changes it experienced.

METHODS, SOURCES, AND BOUNDARIES

The framework of this book is my database of nunneries founded in a large portion of Western Europe from the fifth century to 1350. Each of over 850 entries notes the name of the house and its location, dates of foundation and any subsequent destruction, restoration, or refoundation, and information about founders and important patrons.[1] The computer makes it possible to manipulate these categories in relation to one another quickly and accurately, providing a broad chronological and geographical survey, an evolving map of the world of female monasticism. It can order nunneries according to the date of their establishment, showing the pace of new foundation across the Middle Ages. The computer can also help to describe the geographical distribution of convents, marking areas of particularly dense or sparse settlement of women religious, and to note how that distribution changed over time. Such a broad survey can identify change and describe it in considerable detail. In short, the machine can help both to define a general problem, a critical period for female monasticism in the central Middle Ages, and to point

1. For a more detailed description of the database, how it was assembled, and important cautionary notes, see the introductory matter in Appendix A, which provides a handlist of women's monastic foundations in northwestern Europe, 900–1300.

toward the specific places and times that are the most important instances or components of change.

The problem with any method highlighting change is its tendency to obscure and undervalue continuity. Furthermore, many categories of human experience are simply not susceptible to numerical analysis. Still, a collection of empirical data in narrowly defined categories can at least alert us to the fact of change. Any explanation of change is left to our discretion; it must rely on our ability to ask questions of the sort a computer will not suggest and on our sensitivity to continuities and the ultimate unquantifiability of the past. Statistical analysis can identify a period of central importance in the history of female monasticism in Western Europe and direct us toward the most notable phases in the making of a new map of female monasticism; however, only examining and analyzing written records—the traditional techniques of historical research—can help to answer questions about how and why these changes came about and to flesh out the bare bones of statistics. Such research also uncovers continuities and similarities that a computer-assisted survey, best at describing change and difference, tends to obscure.

A variety of source materials illuminates the relationship of female monasticism to society on the local, regional, and pan-European scale. The most important for this study are the records of the nunneries themselves, specifically the charters that reveal the social basis of women's monasticism in a period of rapid growth. These "documents of practice" describe the circumstances of foundation, endowment, relative wealth, and sometimes even population of individual houses. Taken as a whole, such records place a monastic community in its milieu: they indicate the most important sources of patronage and support and also hint, in records of disputes and their settlement, at tensions and hostilities surrounding conventual life. Such documents show the relationship of nunneries to local secular and ecclesiastical leaders and indicate what part those people played in shaping the regular religious life of women.

The records of what is usually called institutional history, the official and public promulgations of churchmen and lay lords, provide different perspectives on the history of women's monasticism. The laws and charters of kings, counts, and dukes and the chronicles by the great monastic historians depict the forces of political order and disorder affecting the growth and life of nunneries. The records of episcopal councils, regional and ecumenical, show the concerns of ecclesiastical hierarchs about women in the religious life and the ways in which they encouraged and discouraged its growth. Materials issued from Rome suggest the attitude and degree of support for and interest in female monasticism at the papal level. Records of monastic councils cast light on the problems of incorporating women into male monastic orders and show the ambiguous attitudes toward women in the new religious orders of the central Middle Ages.

Interpreting any kind of medieval source is, of course, problematic, but special difficulties arise with hagiography and imaginative literature. Nevertheless, these materials can provide unique insights into the history of female monasticism. The life of an errant preacher such as Robert of Arbrissel shows why he became interested in increasing the opportunities for religious life for women. Biographies of female saints such as the English recluse Christina of Markyate show what kinds of pressures worked on women of religious temperament and what options they had. Imaginative literature also is suggestive about the image of holy women and the place of nuns in medieval society. Such sources are inevitably impressionistic, but they offer the most vivid and compelling portraits of religious women in an ever-evolving social and spiritual environment.

The chapters that follow narrate the growth of female monasticism, charting foundations from the end of the ninth century to circa 1215. The geographical boundaries are those of medieval dioceses. The area under scrutiny includes territories in fifteen archdiocesan provinces (Figure 1). In the north are the two English archdioceses of Canterbury and York. The Continental area encompasses eleven entire archdioceses as they existed in the central Middle Ages: Aix-en-Provence, Arles, Auch, Bordeaux, Bourges, Lyon, Narbonne, Reims, Rouen, Sens, and Tours. Also included are the non-Alpine dioceses of the archdiocese of Vienne (Die, Grenoble, Valence, Vienne, and Viviers), as well as the three suffragan dioceses of Metz, Toul, and Verdun, but not their metropolitan see of Trier, which by the twelfth century extended eastward to the Rhine and beyond.[2] The natural boundaries of this region are, moving clockwise from the north, the Cheviot Hills and lower Tweed Valley, lower Meuse, lower Moselle, western Rhine, and upper Doubs basins, the Jura, the high Alps, the Mediterranean, the Pyrenees, the Bay of Biscay, and the Irish Sea. In medieval terms, the region included the kingdom of England, Wales, all but the trans-Pyrenean counties of old West Frank-

2. The archdiocesan divisions corresponded largely to the Roman provincial definitions of late antiquity: the *provincia Lugdunensis prima* became the ecclesiastical province of Lyon, the *provincia Belgica secunda* became the ecclesiastical province of Reims, and so on. Both archdiocesan and diocesan structure and boundaries remained remarkably stable from the early Middle Ages to the fourteenth century. For the list of Gallic ecclesiastical provinces, see GC, prefatory matter to vol. 1.

FIGURE 1. Geographical scope of the study

land, plus Lorraine, Burgundy, Dauphiné, and Provence. This great region is characterized, I argue, by a distinctive and largely uniform pattern of monastic foundation for women.

A few limitations demand some explanation. Even if it were desirable, it would be impossible to examine every instance of foundation. All too often, the origins of women's monasteries are completely obscure, or the sketchy details available offer little fodder for analysis. Although my examples and data come from all corners of a large geographical area, materials concerning northern and western France and southern England are the richest. Hence my method has been to read carefully the materials concerning houses in those regions, especially the congregation of monasteries headed by the western French abbey of Fontevraud, and to extend my analysis from there. The choice of examples offers, I believe, a balanced picture.[3] Beyond the problem of selection is that of applicability. The pattern described here is *not* universal: matters were different in the Rhineland and on the other side of the Alps and the Pyrenees, where other spiritual influences and mundane realities meant that both expansion and decline of women's monasticism followed a different course.[4]

CONVENTS IN NORTHWESTERN EUROPE: AN OVERVIEW

How many nunneries were there in the West in the central Middle Ages? Like many simple questions, this one is difficult to answer. Most medieval chroniclers mention nuns or their communities only in passing, some

3. Asks one scholar of monasticism, bewailing implicit and explicit assumptions that exhaustive research on monastic institutions will lead to a scientifically accurate synthesis: "Would you ask a zoologist not to describe a sheep, for example, until he had seen all currently living sheep?" Albert D'Haenens, "Quotidienneté et contexte: Pour un modèle d'interprétation de la réalité monastique médiévale (XIe–XIIe siècles)," in *Istituzioni monastiche e istituzioni canonicali in Occidente (1123–1215)*, Miscellanea del Centro di Studi Medioevali 9 (Milan, 1980), 569.
4. In the diocese of Liège, for example, over half of all medieval foundations took place between 1210 and 1240; the early thirteenth century is also the greatest period of expansion in the archdiocesan see of Trier. Much of the emphasis on thirteenth-century opportunities for religious women is owed to traditional historiographical emphasis on Liegois and the Rhineland, the western end of the medieval Empire. For patterns of growth in regions near the one under study, see Karl J. Leyser, *Rule and Conflict in an Early Medieval Society: Ottonian Saxony* (Bloomington, Ind., 1979), 63–73, which has an excellent bibliography; Michel Parisse, "Les monastères de femmes en Saxe (XIe–XIIe siècles)," *Revue Mabillon* n.s. 2 [= 63] (1991): 5–48; Allessandra Veronese, "Monasteri femminili in Italia settentrionale nell'alto medioevo: Confronto con i monasteri maschili attraverso un tentativo di analisi 'statistica,'" *Benedicta* 34 (1987): 355–416. It is worth repeating that when I use the term "northwestern Europe," it means the territory defined in diocesan terms.

managing to omit religious women entirely. Orderic Vitalis (ca. 1070–ca. 1142), in the thirteen books of his *Ecclesiastical History*, used words meaning "nun" fewer than fifty times, and he is more informative about religious women than most of his contemporaries.[5] When narratives do address female monasticism, the information presented often is difficult to interpret. About 1150, Herman of Laon wrote that there were 1,000 religious women at Prémontré, a community of canons and canonesses in northern France, and 10,000 sisters in the monasteries affiliated with Prémontré; the figures are too large to be credible.[6] About seventy years later, Jacques de Vitry, after likening the host of new Cistercian nunneries to the stars, stated the number of such communities in the diocese of Liège: seven.[7]

It is therefore not surprising that modern historians of female monasticism cannot agree about numerical significance and often are vague in their disagreement. Brenda Bolton states that in the twelfth century, nunneries were "few in number" and that religious women of the period were "catered for erratically";[8] Jane Schulenburg concedes that in the same century there was a "great proliferation of new women's communities."[9] Such sharp differences in perception make it all the more crucial to begin any analysis of qualitative change by describing quantitative change as specifically as possible.[10]

Over 850 female monastic communities were founded in the region under study by the mid-fourteenth century. Figure 2 shows the rate of foundation of nunneries from the establishment of a convent by John Cassian at Marseille in the second decade of the fifth century to the arrival of the Black Death in Western Europe, the period spanning all

5. An *Index verborum* for the entire *History* (OV 1: 246–386) cites *monacha* 7 times and *sanctimonialis* 38 times.

6. PL 156: 994, 997. The figures are repeated but doubted by A. Erens, "Les soeurs dans l'ordre de Prémontré," *Analecta Praemonstratensia* 5 (1929): 7.

7. Jacques de Vitry, *The Historia Occidentalis of Jacques de Vitry*, ed. John Frederick Hinnebusch (Fribourg, 1972), 117.

8. Brenda Bolton, "Mulieres Sanctae," in *Women in Medieval Society*, ed. Susan Mosher Stuard (Philadelphia, 1976), 142–143.

9. Jane Tibbetts Schulenburg, "Women's Monastic Communities, 500–1100: Patterns of Expansion and Decline," *Signs* 14 (1989): 291.

10. It should be stressed that the figures given are conservative—that is, I have presumed *against* the existence of a community unless there is reliable evidence for it. The same policy has been followed for foundation dates, which are often impossible to state exactly; all estimates are *terminus ante hoc*, although there are doubtless numerous cases in which a community existed before the first mention of it. Nevertheless, I am confident that the repertory in its present form is a largely accurate description of the number and pace of foundation of nunneries in one portion of Western Christendom. For more detail and a handlist of foundations from 900 to 1300, see Appendix A.

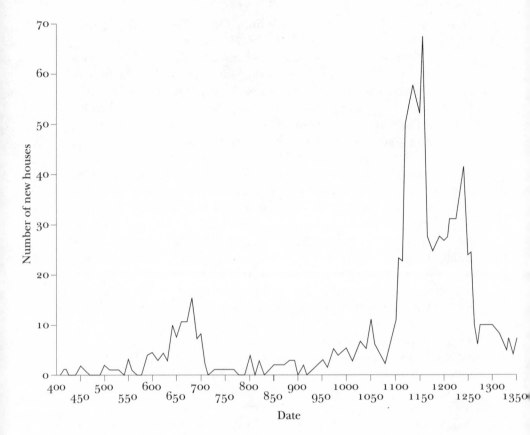

FIGURE 2. Foundations and refoundations of monasteries for women, 400–1350 (by decade)

major developments in medieval monasticism that affected women.[11] For much of this era, the pace of new foundation was slow. Three periods stand out: one in the seventh century, another lasting from the end of the eleventh century to the late twelfth, and the third in the 1220s, 1230s, and 1240s.[12] The second period is the most dramatic—the great age of expansion the present study examines.

11. Because of the caution exercised in estimating dates of foundation, it may well be that the whole curve should be displaced slightly to the left. However, there is no reason to assume its shape would change substantially, even with more precise evidence about foundation dates.

12. The first great age of female monasticism is expertly treated in recent studies. Suzanne Fonay Wemple, *Women in Frankish Society: Marriage and the Cloister, 500 to 900* (Philadelphia,

Before setting out the particulars of the growth of female monasticism, one should relate it to demographic change in Western Europe in the central Middle Ages. There is general agreement that after centuries of virtual stasis, population began to grow again around the millennium, continuing until the late thirteenth or early fourteenth century. It further appears that the most rapid growth occurred in the latter half of this period, that is, starting about 1150.[13] The appearance of new nunneries, then, was not simply a result of population expansion. Major increase in the number of convents did not begin until a century or so after new population growth, and the number of new nunneries began to fall off just as demographic expansion became most notable.[14]

PATTERNS OF GROWTH

Table 1 illustrates the multiplication of female monastic communities in the central Middle Ages. It appears that between 900 and 930 A.D. not a single nunnery was founded in the Continental portion of the area under study—the longest period since the fifth century without a new monastic foundation for women. But with the foundations of Alfred the Great in Wessex at the end of the ninth century and the establishment of the house of Bouxières-aux-Dames near Nancy in 930, a new era was at hand. In the tenth century, the small number of new foundations was confined primarily to three regions: southern England, Lorraine, and Poitou. In the eleventh century, new foundations became more frequent, especially after 1040, and spread over a wider territory, now en-

1981), 126–188, considers the role of religious women in the Merovingian and Carolingian worlds. On early England, see Stephanie Hollis, *Anglo-Saxon Women and the Church: Sharing a Common Fate* (Woodbridge, Eng., 1992). For statistical analysis and comparison with foundations for monks in France, Belgium, and England, see Schulenburg, "Women's Monastic Communities, 500–1100," in particular the tables on p. 266. (My figures for the period before 1000 differ from Schulenburg's very little.)

13. J. C. Russell, "Population in Europe, 500–1500," in Carlo M. Cipolla, ed., *The Fontana Economic History of Europe*, vol. 1: *The Middle Ages* (New York, 1976), 39; Jacques Le Goff, "Croissance et prise de conscience urbaine," in J. Le Goff, ed., *La ville médiévale* (Paris, 1980), 189. Russell thinks the key period was "1150–1200 to 1300"; Le Goff finds that most of the growth occurred "roughly between 1150 and 1300."

14. Monastic foundations and demographic developments are related, as I will argue, but the story is complex, not an easy matter of foundations increasing as overall population did.

Table 1. Number of nunneries founded or refounded, 900–1350, by region

Period	Northern tier	Central tier	Southern tier	Total
900–925	2	0	0	2
926–950	2	4	2	8
951–975	2	1	4	7
976–1000	4	4	4	12
1001–1025	1	3	2	6
1026–1050	1	12	8	21
1051–1075	0	5	3	8
1076–1100	3	9	5	17
1101–1125	4	32	29	65
1126–1150	27	79	37	143
1151–1175	62	20	22	104
1176–1200	25	27	14	66
1201–1225	11	36	23	70
1226–1250	11	55	21	87
1251–1275	3	10	24	37
1276–1300	4	4	21	29
1301–1325	0	7	9	16
1326–1350	2	4	7	13
	164	312	235	711

Note: The northern tier is defined as the archdioceses of York and Canterbury; the central tier as the archdioceses of Reims, Rouen, Sens, Tours, and Lyon and the dioceses of Metz, Toul, and Verdun; and the southern tier as the archdioceses of Bordeaux, Bourges, Auch, Narbonne, Arles, and Aix-en-Provence and the dioceses of Die, Grenoble, Valence, Vienne, and Viviers. The border between the central and southern tiers is, roughly, the Loire, flowing from its source in the Massif Central northwest and then west to the Bay of Biscay.

compassing central and eastern England as well as western, central, and northern France (including Flanders), with a few houses in the Midi.

Not until the late eleventh century, however, did the number of new nunneries begin to surpass that of the mid-seventh century. Two things characterize the most rapid period of growth, circa 1080–circa 1170. First, it began abruptly, with the number of new communities appearing in the years 1081–1110 nearly equaling the total founded in the previous century. Growth became rapid in the second quarter of the twelfth century. Second, expansion was apparent in almost every part of the area under scrutiny, absent only in isolated and thinly populated peninsular Brittany and the higher elevations of the Massif Central. Certainly, foundations were more numerous in some regions than in others. It is hardly surprising that there were fewer nunneries in Wales than in eastern England, or more in Champagne than in Languedoc, as more fertile regions could support a higher density of both lay and religious people. But the nearly universal expansion of female monasticism across an area whose component regions knew diverse political and social realities, and indeed were subject to very different influences on religious life, is quite striking.

Almost as general was the declining number of new foundations in the late twelfth century. The only important exceptions were Provence, Languedoc, and Gascony, where expansion continued at nearly the same pace as in the period 1080–1170. After 1200, female monastic communities continued to appear in the south, steadily if a bit more slowly than before, until nearly the end of the thirteenth century. The story for regions farther north was quite different. In Champagne, the Ile de France, Flanders, Brabant, and Hainault (the territory from the upper and middle Seine valley north) there was a renewed increase in foundations from the early thirteenth century, but this new boom ended decisively shortly after 1250. Elsewhere in the north of France, growth in number of convents was essentially halted after 1220. Relatively few new convents were founded in England after the reign of Henry Plantagenet (1154–1189).

The area considered experienced three patterns of expansion of female monasticism in the central Middle Ages. In England and Wales, the vast majority of convents emerged between 1130 and 1180, with notably few foundations before or after. In the Continental territories north of the Loire, the most frequent establishment of new convents was between 1080 and 1155, with an important secondary peak in the early thirteenth century, after which there were few new foundations. In the Midi, growth was never as impressive, but it continued at a fairly steady pace through the twelfth century, with a slight decline over the next century. Within a context of major and widespread expansion, then, the rate of foundation of new nunneries varied somewhat across space and time.

The aggregate result of all these new foundations is described in Figure 3. At the millennium, there were about seventy nunneries in France and England.[15] While most of these communities, and most founded after the year 1000, survived until the end of the Middle Ages, some disappeared earlier.[16] From the late eleventh century, statistics show a marked increase in the number of active monastic communities for women. Between 1080 and 1170 the number of convents rose from one

15. This is, if anything, a high estimate, as it seems important not to exaggerate the increase in the centuries that follow (see Appendix A).
16. This is especially true in the case of Premonstratensian communities for women, most of which had vanished within a century of their establishment. See Chapter 5.

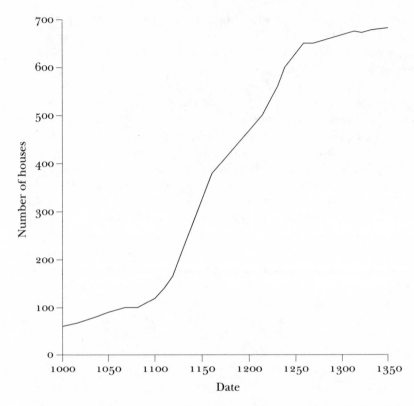

FIGURE 3. Total number of active nunneries, 1000–1350 (by decade)

hundred to over four hundred. The figure grew to approximately 525 by 1220 and reached 650 by the late thirteenth century. Few new nunneries were founded from then until the Black Death.

NUNNERIES IN AN AGE OF MONASTIC REVIVAL

This multiplication of nunneries occurred during a long period of monastic renewal in Europe usually described as having three primary phases. First, the foundation in 909 of Cluny, a Benedictine monastery in Burgundy, signaled the beginning of a new era. Cluny became the head of a great federation of monasteries noted for their independence from local lay and episcopal interference. The second phase of monastic reform, from the end of the eleventh century to about 1150, is most closely associated with the Cistercian order, named for its first house, Cîteaux, founded in 1098. This network of monasteries, which espoused asceticism and strict observance of the Rule of Saint Benedict, grew enormously, especially under the leadership of Bernard of Clairvaux. At Bernard's death in 1153, the order numbered well over 300 houses. The third great wave of reforming enthusiasm came in the early thirteenth century with the appearance of the mendicant friars inspired by Francis of Assisi and Dominic. Although they originally spurned all possessions in favor of a life of absolute poverty and mostly urban evangelism, the friars soon formed communities. Even though their mission remained different, favoring preaching over prayer, they came increasingly to resemble the more traditional monastic communities.[17]

Despite their differences, all three of these movements share a common characteristic: they were male-centered, that is, they were originally designed to accommodate the spiritual aspirations of men. Women shared in them, but their place was always secondary, in two senses. First, female "branches," as they are called, of the new monastic orders appeared after the movements were well under way. Second, there were always fewer houses for women than for men within these movements. The most striking example is the case of the Cluniacs. The first nunnery affiliated with Cluny, Marcigny, was founded in 1055, nearly a century and a half after Cluny, and there was never more than a handful of Cluniac nunneries in Western Europe, amidst hundreds of male communities associated with Cluny.[18]

It is in the context of the subject position of women in the new religious orders that historians most often study nuns and nunneries in the central Middle Ages.[19] However, such an approach ignores the continu-

17. Some historians exclude the mendicants from the history of monasticism, because the urban and evangelical activities of the Franciscans, Dominicans, and others were so markedly different from the prayer-centered lives of earlier monks and nuns. However, the mendicant movement may be seen as a continuation of the monastic tradition in the sense that it was a response to a set of perceived social needs and social ills whereby individuals pledged to devote their lives to spiritual ends for the betterment of the whole Christian community.

18. Else Maria Wischermann, *Marcigny-sur-Loire: Gründungs- und Frühgeschichte des ersten Cluniacenserinnenpriorates (1055–1150)* (Munich, 1986), 503, lists 19 European nunneries affiliated at their foundation or later with Cluny. Of these, only 5 were originally founded as Cluniac in the area under study, one of those after 1350.

19. This is the plan of analysis in Micheline de Fontette, *Les religieuses à l'âge classique du droit canon* (Paris, 1967). The study begins with a consideration of the sisters of the order of Prémontré, claiming that their story illustrates themes common to all orders. But to start by analyzing the only monastic federation that, having accepted women in its early history,

ing vitality of traditional Benedictine monasticism.[20] In addition, the twelfth century saw the birth of two monastic federations that chiefly addressed women's needs and are frequently excluded from general surveys of monastic innovation in the central Middle Ages. The abbey of Fontevraud in western France, founded in 1101, became the mother house for dozens of priories; the Gilbertine houses were the most original English contribution to medieval monasticism.[21] Both Fontevrist and Gilbertine houses were mixed, including women and men, but religious life for women was the focus of these institutions.

Nevertheless, the coincidence of the two most important eras for the foundation of female monasteries (circa 1080–circa 1170 and circa 1215–circa 1260) with the initial successes of the Cistercian and mendicant movements is worth investigating. The categories for analysis here are not only the affiliation of the house with a male-centered order, but also the place of women in individual institutions, whether the needs of women were of primary or secondary importance in these religious houses. The results are summarized in Table 2.[22]

Clearly the expansion of female monasticism in this period was not simply a reflection or imitation of male-centered reform monasticism. This is especially true for the twelfth century, during which 64 percent of all new foundations for women had no official tie to a male monastic congregation. Even in the period of most rapid growth, 1126–1150, nearly 60 percent of the new nunneries were either autonomous Benedictine or Augustinian communities or houses of the Fontevrist and Gilbertine orders.[23] Toward the end of the twelfth century, this pattern began to shift, and from 1200 to 1300 two-thirds of new women's houses

---

later excluded them entirely, is to present an unduly gloomy picture. The approach also lends itself to circular reasoning in making global evaluations: to assess acknowledged minorities will almost surely lead to the conclusion that they were less visible and influential than the majority.

20. John Van Engen, "The 'Crisis of Cenobitism' Reconsidered: Benedictine Monasticism in the Years 1050–1150," *Speculum* 61 (1986): 269–304.

21. R. W. Southern, *Western Society and the Church in the Middle Ages* (Harmondsworth, Eng., 1970), mentions Fontevraud not in the survey of medieval monasticism (chap. 6, "The Religious Orders," 214–299), but rather in chap. 7, "Fringe Orders and Anti-Orders" (in a subsection, "The influence of women in religious life," 309–317, which also considers female Cluniacs, Premonstratensians, and Cistercians). He does not mention the Gilbertines.

22. On the subject position of the Premonstratensian sisters in mixed communities, see the comments in Erens, "Les soeurs dans l'ordre de Prémontré," 13–17, including a somewhat caustic section on the life of the sisters.

23. Before 1100 there was only one nunnery, Cluniac Marcigny, attached to a male-centered order. There was no "Benedictine Order" as such before the thirteenth century.

Table 2. Number of monastic houses for women founded 1101–1300, by congregational identity

Period	a	b	c	d	e	f	Total	g (%)
1101–1125	26	25	10	1	—	3	65	78
1126–1150	59	24	39	19	—	2	143	58
1151–1175	52	16	6	27	—	3	104	65
1176–1200	35	4	2	23	—	2	66	59
1201–1225	15	3	1	45	4	2	70	26
1226–1250	27	1	1	47	8	3	87	31
1251–1275	12	—	—	7	16	2	37	32
1276–1300	10	—	—	2	15	2	29	34

Note: Column headings are as follows.
(a) Autonomous nunneries following the Benedictine or Augustinian Rule
(b) Fontevrist and Gilbertine monasteries (female-centered communities of nuns and monks)
(c) Premonstratensian houses (male-centered communities for regular canons and canonesses)
(d) Cistercian nunneries
(e) Franciscan or Dominican foundations for women
(f) Others, including Cluniac and Carthusian nunneries, or communities for which no such identification is possible
(g) Percentage of all new foundations that had no direct tie to any male-centered monastic movement or order (a+b/total)

were in fact affiliated with male-centered orders. These communities were not, for the most part, derived from the new mendicant movement, but rather affiliated with the well-established Cistercian order (in which the appearance of new monasteries for men had considerably slowed by 1200). Cistercian nunneries account for more than 40 percent of all nunneries founded in the region under consideration in the thirteenth century.[24] In short, the foundation of nunneries, although doubtless sometimes inspired by contemporary developments in male monasticism, was to a considerable degree institutionally independent of male-centered innovation. To describe the history of women's monasticism in the high Middle Ages in terms of the self-conscious reforming initiatives is relevant, but insufficient.

To sum up: nunneries in France and England multiplied almost tenfold between the millennium and 1300. The bulk of this increase came

24. The relationship of the Cistercian monks to women's houses is a complex problem that will be addressed below. For present purposes, the attitude of the male Cistercian hierarchy toward these nunneries is less important than the model of piety and practice Cîteaux provided for numerous communities of women who called themselves Cistercians.

between 1080 and 1215, which saw the establishment of about 425 new monastic communities for women, over half of all nunneries founded in the millennium before the Black Death. Although there were significant local and regional variations in the pace of nunnery foundation, the expansion of female monasticism was geographically comprehensive, encompassing all but the most isolated districts. By the end of the thirteenth century, nearly all the inhabitants of this great region were no more than a day's journey from a female monastic community, and most were closer than that.

The pattern of growth of female monasticism admits no easy explanation. It gives rise to a host of questions about the relationship of female monasticism to other developments in a period of rapid and fundamental changes in the nature of European society and calls for consideration of developments outside the purview of traditional institutional church history. As R. W. Southern argues, "It is only when we study church history as an aspect of secular history that we can begin to understand the limitations and opportunities of the medieval church."[25] What follows is one attempt to describe opportunities and limitations, especially in the late eleventh and twelfth centuries. The initial context, however, is supplied by the story of nunnery foundations in the preceding period.

25. Southern, *Western Society and the Church*, 360.

the old-fashioned way: foundations in the tenth and eleventh centuries

Aliud quoque monasterium iuxta orientalem portam Sceftesburg, habitationi sanctimonialium habile, idem prefatus rex aedificari imperavit, in quo propriam filiam suam Aethelgeofu, devotam Deo virginem, abbatissam constituit, cum qua etiam aliae multae nobiles moniales in monastica vita Deo servientes in eodem monasterio habitant.

The king ordered to be built near the east gate of Shaftesbury another monastery, suitable for the residence of nuns. In it he appointed as abbess his own daughter Aethelgifu, a virgin vowed to God, with whom live in the same monastery many other noble nuns, serving God in the monastic life.

—Asser, *Life of King Alfred*

*H*istorians of Western Europe agree that the millennium marked a key turning point in the history of the Middle Ages. By 1000 A.D., French royal authority was limited to a small area around Paris, and in turn the great princes in the old Carolingian realm faced a challenge to their authority in the form of upstart petty lords whose castles came to dominate the landscape. Around this time population started a steady increase that endured for three centuries, as the agricultural economy of Europe began a sustained, if at first slow, expansion. One recent study goes so far as to claim that it was not until the new millenium that the political, social, and economic structures of late antiquity disappeared from the European countryside and the medieval period really began.[1]

1. Guy Bois, *The Transformation of the Year One Thousand: The Village of Lournand from Antiquity to Feudalism*, trans. Jean Birrell (New York, 1992), is a vigorous restatement of a thesis first argued, with different emphases, by Georges Duby and R.W. Southern in the 1950s. New work on the subject in light of some recent dissent includes T. N. Bisson, "The 'Feudal Revolution,'" *Past and Present* 142 (1994): 6–42, and Patrick J. Geary, *Phantoms of Remembrance: Memory and Oblivion at the End of the First Millennium* (Princeton, 1994), esp. 23–26. The En-

The year 1000 often is considered as a watershed in ecclesiastical history as well. In a well-known formulation, the monastic historian Rodolf Glaber (ca. 980–ca. 1046) described the opening of a new era just after the millennium: "It was as if the world, shaking itself and throwing off its great age, were clothing itself everywhere in a white mantle of churches," many of them monasteries. Glaber doubtless had in mind the revival inspired by the example of Cluny, the famed Burgundian abbey founded in 909 by Duke William the Pious of Aquitaine, where the chronicler spent part of his life.[2] By the millennium, there were some thirty monasteries affiliated with Cluny, and this figure was to grow enormously in the ensuing decades.[3] The eleventh century certainly represented a great advance for new religious foundations. There were just over four hundred monasteries founded in France, Belgium, and England in the tenth century and nearly four times that many in the eleventh century.[4]

Nevertheless, we might question whether the millennium marked a real watershed for *female* monasticism. Nearly twice as many nunneries were founded in the area under consideration in the eleventh century as in the tenth century. However, the ratio of new female houses to new male houses was smaller than at any point since the sixth century. Less than 5 percent of all new eleventh-century monastic foundations in Western Europe (including England) were for women. In this context, it is significant that the first Cluniac monastery for women, Marcigny,

---

glish chronology is somewhat different, with one transition in the reign of King Alfred in the late ninth century, another after the Norman invasion in 1066.

2. Rodolfus Glaber, *The Five Books of the Histories*, ed. and trans. John France (Oxford, 1989), 116. Glaber dedicated his history to Abbot Odilo of Cluny.

3. Constance B. Bouchard, "Merovingian, Carolingian, and Cluniac Monasticism: Reform and Renewal in Burgundy," *Journal of Ecclesiastical History* 41 (1990): 365–388 stresses the variety of Cluny's reforms and relations to other monasteries. It is hence very difficult to state the number of houses affiliated to Cluny at any one time, at least until the twelfth century, before which time it is anachronistic, as Bouchard argues, to speak of a "Cluniac Order." Marcel Pacaut, *L'ordre de Cluny (909–1789)* (Paris, 1986), 316, numbers the Cluniac congregation at 33 by the death of Abbot Mayeul in 994. A figure of 27 is given in Barbara H. Rosenwein, *Rhinoceros Bound: Cluny in the Tenth Century* (Philadephia, 1982), xiii–xv.

4. The statistics in this paragraph and the next derive from Schulenburg, "Women's Monastic Communities." Schulenburg's tables on p. 266 indicate a total of 416 monastic foundations in France, Belgium, and England in the tenth century and 1,595 in the eleventh. In the tenth century, 27 of these, or 6.5%, were for women; for the eleventh century, the figure is 68, or 4.3%. Schulenburg's figures for women's foundations differ somewhat from those I give in Chapter 1 because our geographical scopes are not wholly congruent.

was not founded until 145 years after Cluny itself, when the number of male communities associated with the mother house was approaching 100.[5]

If the foundation of Marcigny marked a turning point, it was also the apotheosis of a long tradition. The period circa 890–circa 1080 was one of restoration, an era of recovery from the havoc wrought on female monastic life by invasions and the collapse of public authority. By the late eleventh century, nunneries were relatively uniformly, if thinly, distributed across France and southern England, and there were once again as many monasteries for women as there had been three hundred years earlier. But resettlement is not the only feature that gives this age a perceptible unity. Just as in the early Middle Ages, in the tenth and eleventh centuries, the foundation and endowment of new nunneries were accomplished by the most powerful people in Christendom.

NUNNERIES IN LATE ANGLO-SAXON ENGLAND

David Knowles's four magisterial volumes on the history of English monasticism in the Middle Ages begin, as the subtitle to the first volume announces, in the times of Saint Dunstan.[6] There can be no question of the importance of Dunstan in the remaking of the English church, but it also is important to remember that England was hardly a pagan nation when he was elected to the see at Canterbury in 960, or even when he was made abbot of Glastonbury some two decades earlier. Aside from the legacy of holy Englishwomen from the early Anglo-Saxon period, Archbishop Dunstan and his colleagues built on a vigorous and more immediate heritage of female monastic life that went back some seventy years.

Before the Times of Saint Dunstan

When King Alfred began what his biographer Asser called "his most excellent enterprise," the foundation of the houses of Athelney and

---

5. Pacaut, *L'ordre de Cluny*, 316, counts 73 monasteries at the death of Abbot Odilo in 1048, with Cluny entering its greatest phase of expansion under Saint Hugh (1049–1109). On Marcigny, see the end of this chapter.
6. David Knowles, *The Monastic Order in England: A History of its Development from the Times of St Dunstan to the Fourth Lateran Council, 943–1216* (Cambridge, Eng., 1950), and *The Religious Orders in England*, 3 vols. (Cambridge, Eng., 1960–1961).

Shaftesbury, traditional monastic life in England was perhaps entirely extinct.[7] The Scandinavian invaders, starting with the sack of the episcopal center of Lindisfarne in 793, had devastated the countryside of nearly all of England, making no dispensation for religious people and places. The ancient nunnery of Ely was destroyed, according to a later account, in the year 870: "The company of nuns was sacrificed, like the Innocent Victim . . . and thus the monastery which the true godly Christian Aetheldreda had founded was burnt, along with virgins, ornaments and the relics of saints male and female." The "enemies of the Lord" proceeded to burn down the surrounding town and make off with booty.[8] Many other churches and monasteries were destroyed in the fierce campaigns of the 860s and 870s, battles that nonetheless left intact the kingdom of Wessex under Alfred the Great.[9]

The account of Alfred's monastic foundations given by Asser notes a reluctance on the part of Englishmen to join the monastic life. Before the foundation of Athelney, "for many years past the desire for the monastic life had been totally lacking in that entire race . . . although quite a number of monasteries which had been built in that area still remained, none held to the rule of monastic life in an orderly way." An international, but not particularly harmonious, community was therefore assembled at Athelney. There is no hint of foreign presence or influence in Asser's brief statement that Alfred also founded a nunnery at Shaftesbury, headed by his daughter Aethelgifu, or Algiva. Asser concludes his remarks on the establishment of these houses by noting that the king "lavishly endowed these two monasteries with lands and all sorts of wealth."[10]

There are no other contemporary sources concerning the foundation and early history of Shaftesbury, but later evidence, despite questions of

---

7. Knowles, *The Monastic Order in England*, 33.

8. *Liber Eliensis*, ed. E. O. Blake (London, 1962), 55: "Mactatur, ut victima innocenta, sanctimonialium caterva . . . Sicque monasterio quod vera Dei christicola Aetheldreda construxerat cum virginibus et ornamentis et reliquiis sanctorum sanctarumque combusto, civitate etiam spoliata et cremata, prede ubertate ditati omniaque eiusdem loci adimentes mobilia atque utensilia, inimici Dei redierunt ad propria."

9. For these campaigns and their outcome, see D. J. V. Fisher, *The Anglo-Saxon Age, c. 400–1042* (London, 1973), 215–235.

10. Asser, *Asser's Life of King Alfred*, ed. William H. Stevenson (London, 1904), 79–85, includes the account of both foundations and a plot to kill the first abbot of Athelney. The quotations are from Asser's *Life*, 80–81: "quia per multa retroacta annorum curricula monasticae vitae desiderium ab illa tota gente funditus desierat . . . quamvis perplurima adhuc monasteria in illa regione constructa permaneant, nullo tamen regulam illius vitae ordinabiliter tenente," and 85: "Quae duo monasteria terrarum possessionibus et omnibus divitiis locupletatim ditavit."

authenticity or a lapse of time from the events described, provides a fairly consistent account. A pretended foundation charter has Alfred giving to Shaftesbury one hundred hides of land in several locations and along with this inheritance Aethelgifu, who took the veil on account of bad health.[11] The twelfth-century chronicler William of Malmesbury has two different versions of the foundation. In the *Gesta Regum* he notes that the abbey was founded by Alfred, but tells another story in the *Gesta Pontificum*. Here he attributes the foundation of the city of Shaftesbury to Alfred, but that of the nunnery to Aelfgifu, or Elgiva, the wife of Edmund, king from 939 to 946. (The confusion may well arise from the similarity of the names of Alfred's daughter and Edmund's wife.) Aelfgifu was buried at Shaftesbury in 944 and, according to a late-tenth-century account, was revered as a saint.[12]

At any rate, the available evidence points toward the foundation of Shaftesbury by King Alfred for his daughter—we may safely take Asser's word for it, as he was writing in Alfred's lifetime—and early patronage by the Wessex royal house. The earliest tenth-century charters concerning a nunnery, grants of land by King Aethelstan in 932 and 935, favor Shaftesbury. The community continued to thrive through the tenth century, receiving donations from Kings Eadwig, Edgar, and Aethelred.[13] In 980 Shaftesbury became the resting place of King Edward the Martyr, who had been murdered two years earlier.[14]

Shaftesbury was not the only community for nuns in early-tenth-century England. According to a late medieval legend, King Alfred built a convent at Wilton populated by thirteen women whose numbers were swelled by a group of nuns from another nearby foundation that dated to the early ninth century. Little, if anything, can be believed of this account, which is based on sources dating at the earliest to the late eleventh

11. SASC, no. 357. The Anglo-Saxon text and a translation with commentary are given in *Anglo-Saxon Charters*, ed. A. J. Robertson, 2d ed. (Cambridge, Eng., 1956), 24–25, 284–286. The charter as it stands must date to the 870s, making its authenticity very doubtful. The manuscript in which this and numerous other late Anglo-Saxon charters are contained is a fifteenth-century register of Shaftesbury; for a list of its contents, see SASC no. 54.

12. William of Malmesbury, *Gesta regum Anglorum*, ed. William Stubbs, 2 vols. (London, 1887–1889), 1: 131, and idem, *Gesta pontificum Anglorum*, ed. N. E. S. A. Hamilton (London, 1870), 186–188. See the entry for Shaftesbury Abbey in VCH, Dorset, 2: 73, and the notes to Asser, "Life of King Alfred," in *Alfred the Great*, trans. Simon Keynes and Michael Lapidge (Harmondsworth, Eng. 1983), 273.

13. SASC nos. 419, 429 (Aethelstan, in 932 and 935), 630 (Eadwig, in 956), 744 (Edgar, in 966), 850, 899 (Aethelred, in 983 and 1001).

14. *The Anglo-Saxon Chronicle*, ed. and trans. Dorothy Whitelock et al. (London, 1961), 80 (D [E], year 980).

century, but there were two grants to St. Mary's, Wilton, by King Aethelstan in the 930s.[15] It is again to Alfred, perhaps along with his wife Eahlswith, that the foundation of a community for nuns at Winchester (Nunnaminster) is attributed; the completion of the monastery is said to have been left to their son King Edward the Elder, whose daughter Edburga was abbess.[16]

It is therefore impossible to agree with David Knowles's judgment that there was no organized monastic life in England in the reign of King Aethelstan (924–939). This conclusion has two bases. The first is a series of statements about the monastic life in England that range from the late ninth century to the early eleventh century, and all present difficulties.[17] Observations from the ninth century obviously cannot refer to the situation in the 930s. The remainder, which date from 970 and beyond, are part of a historical and hagiographical tradition that carefully separated the period of reform beginning with the accession of Saint Dunstan to the see of Canterbury in 960 from all that came before. Three of the authorities Knowles cites are *vitae* of the reformers Dunstan, Aethelwold, and Oswald, all from about the year 1000, and none likely to be particularly scrupulous about details of the period preceding their subjects' activities. Such difficulties, along with the complete absence of any relevant statements between circa 895 and 970, do not suffice to *prove* the absence of monastic life in the time of Aethelstan.

Second, Knowles is suspicious of the use of the terms *monasterium, fratres,* and *abbas* in the late ninth and early tenth centuries, because often these terms do not necessarily signal the presence of monastic life in this period. There may have been no English monasteries *stricto sensu* for men in the 930s,[18] but the language of contemporary documents shows that Shaftesbury and Wilton did have a communal existence in the same period. Two grants, one to each house, are in fact unique in their formulations among charters of Aethelstan's reign (924–939). In 932,

15. For the legend, see VCH Wiltshire, 3: 231–233; the (authentic) charters are SASC nos. 424 (933) and 438 (937).
16. For a sketch of the early history of Nunnaminster, see Walter de Gray Birch, *An Ancient Manuscript of the Eighth or Ninth Century* (London, 1889), 3–7. Later legend claimed that the nunnery of Romsey, whose better documented history dates to the 960s, was also founded by Edward the Elder, with his daughter St. Elfleda the first abbess, but this would appear to be a duplicate of the Nunnaminster story, and probably not reliable.
17. Knowles, *The Monastic Order in England,* 36, 695 (app. 1, "The evidence for the disappearance of the monastic life in England before 943").
18. Ibid., 35. It is probably impossible to distinguish, for instance, between a community of canons or priests and one of monks from the available evidence.

Aethelstan gave land "to the most faithful household of nuns who battle for God in a regular life of devout practice in a monastery in the city of Shaftesbury."[19] Aethelstan's grant of 935 is "to the venerable company of Christian women in that famed place called Wilton" and refers to a "monastic army."[20] No other authentic charters of Aethelstan's reign contain such unambiguous reference to monastic life.[21]

The existence of authentic charters for Wilton and Shaftesbury in the 930s shows that there was indeed organized monastic life in England in the days of Aethelstan, although perhaps only for women. It further appears that Shaftesbury, Wilton, and Nunnaminster had continuous histories from the times of Alfred and of his son Edward the Elder. A law code of King Edmund refers to nuns.[22] There is a charter of 947 in which King Eadred granted land to a priest, with reversion of part of it to the nunnery at Winchester.[23] A few years later, shortly before his death in 955, the king wrote a will that included bequests to Nunnaminster of land and money, and of money to Wilton and Shaftesbury.[24] By mid-century, a few more convents come into view. The ancient nunnery of Barking, destroyed in the late ninth century, appears to have been resettled by about 950, when there is a bequest to it in the will of one Aelfgar, the ealdorman of Essex.[25] There was a community of nuns at Romsey by this time, and probably one at Chichester, too.[26]

---

19. CS no. 691 (= SASC no. 419): "fidelissime familie monialium que sub regulari devote exercitationis vita in monasterio civitatis que Schaftesbury vocatur Deo militat."
20. Ibid., no. 714 (= SASC no. 438): "venerabili collegio Christicolarum in illo celebri loco qui dicitur Wiltun . . . vestra veneranda monastice classis, caterva medullata."
21. The charters of Aethelstan's reign are SASC nos. 386–458; most are printed in CS. Nearly all the charters referring to a *monasterium* for men are spurious. A few, as the terms of the charter make clear, refer to an episcopal community, e.g., no. 444 (= CS no. 731).
22. *Councils and Synods with other documents relating to the English Church*, ed. F. M. Powicke et al. (Oxford, 1964–), 1: 63. The code dates to 941–946.
23. SASC no. 526.
24. *English Historical Documents*, vol. 1, *c.500–1042*, ed. Dorothy Whitelock et al., 2d ed. (New York, 1979), 554–556 (no. 107). The charter dates from 951–955. The authors of the essays in David Parsons, ed., *Tenth-Century Studies* (London, 1975) assume the existence of nunneries in pre-950 England without marshalling the evidence; see, e.g., D. H. Farmer, "The Progress of the Monastic Revival," 11; D. A. Bullough, "The Continental Background of the Reform," 34–35; and Martin Biddle, *"Felix Urbs Winthonia:* Winchester in the Age of Monastic Reform," 127–128.
25. Text, translation, and notes of this document, which dates to 946–ca. 951, are in *Anglo-Saxon Wills*, ed. Dorothy Whitelock (Cambridge, Eng. 1930), 6–9 and 103–108.
26. For notes on these two communities, see MRH, 264 (Romsey) and 257 (Chichester). See also the entry in VCH, Hampshire, 2: 126 for Romsey, and note 12 above. Both communities are mentioned by William of Malmesbury, *Gesta pontificum Anglorum*, ed. Hamilton, 174 (Romsey) and 205 (Chichester). The chronicler also states that there existed at

If Englishmen in the first half of the tenth century were still reluctant to join the religious life, as Asser had lamented in the days of Alfred's foundation of Athelney, noble Englishwomen felt no such hesitation. Apparently the three nunneries in southern England did not suffice for the number of devout women. There were a dozen royal grants from the years 939 to 948 for religious women not members of a religious community. The charters sometimes refer to these women as nuns but are often less specific about status, referring to a "servant of Christ dedicated to holy life" or in several cases simply "a religious woman."[27] Like the nuns, these women were of high birth: a charter from the last year of Aethelstan's reign is for his sister Eadburh.[28] The presence of these women, who seem to have been unaffiliated with any monastery and living as anchorites or recluses, testifies further to a vital practice of religious life among Anglo-Saxon women of the early tenth century.

From Dunstan to the Norman Conquest

The appearance of charters granting land to pious women at the end of the reign of Aethelstan (924–939) provides a link to the famed ecclesiastical reforms of the second half of the tenth century. The most important of these reformers was Dunstan, abbot of Glastonbury from circa 940 to 956 and archbishop of Canterbury from 960 until his death in 988. Dunstan, born about 909 of a noble family, was admitted to the community of Glastonbury, however strictly monastic it may have been, as a teenager, but he did not take vows until he joined the *familia* of Bishop Alphege at Winchester about 10 years later. It was during this period, in the late 930s, that he came under the influence of a woman of exactly the kind supported with grants from Aethelstan.[29]

St. Peter's Chichester before the 1070s a community of nuns and it is likely that a charter of 956 in favor of brothers in Chichester (SASC no. 616) concerns a group of nuns as well.

27. SASC nos. 446 (= CS no. 742), 448 (= CS no. 743), 449 (= CS no. 734), 464 (= CS no. 753), 465 (= CS no. 763), 474 (= CS no. 768), 482 (= CS no. 778), 485 (= CS no. 775), 487 (= CS no. 787), 493 (= CS no. 795), 534 (= CS no. 868), 535 (= CS no. 869). This list does not include no. 563 (from 955), which clearly refers to a nun of Wilton. I am grateful to Professor Nicholas P. Brooks for first calling my attention to these charters and for sharing his list of them with me. Grants are most often given "cuidam sancte conversatione dedite Christi ancille" or "cuidam religiose femine."

28. SASC no. 446 (= CS no. 742). This has not apparently been considered to belong with the other charters for holy women, but the language is unambiguous: "venerabili michi amabile christicole spirituali commercio sanctoque velamine Dei nutu devotionis affectu."

29. The literature on Dunstan is considerable. Much of it is synthesized in a recent biography: Douglas Dales, *Dunstan: Saint and Statesman* (Cambridge, Eng., 1988).

The story is told in some detail in the first biography of Dunstan, which dates to only a decade or so after his death and contains the fullest information on his early life.[30] Aethelfleda was a wealthy and noble widow who built herself a cell next to the church at Glastonbury and there lived a life of prayer and contemplation. The young Dunstan spent much time with her, so impressed was he with her way of life. He attended her during the illness that took her life, praying constantly and caring for her as if for his own mother. Aethelfleda shared with Dunstan a heavenly vision, then died after giving him instructions for her burial.[31]

When Dunstan became archbishop some twenty years later, monastic reform was his greatest concern. Joining him in this concern were two monastic prelates, Oswald, bishop of Worcester since 961, and Aethelwold, bishop of Winchester since 963. In or around 970, King Edgar summoned an international council at Winchester to ensure the coherence of the burgeoning cenobitic practice in his lands. The result was the *Regularis Concordia*, the "Monastic Agreement of the Monks and Nuns of the English Nation."[32] The explicit discussion of religious women in the document is a reflection of the importance of religious women in the earlier tenth century, even though there may have been no more than four or five nunneries at the time of the Council of Winchester.

The specific provisions for nuns in the *Regularis Concordia* are few but significant. It is noted that King Edgar had made his queen Aelfthrith the guardian and defender of the communities of nuns, a practice sanctioned by the council. The goal was to obviate scandalous suspicions, but it was clearly a continuation of earlier practice of royal patronage of nunneries.[33] Dunstan himself urged protection of nuns from the interference or depredations of monks or any who have spiritual authority over nuns. As the editor of the *Concordia* notes, from this and other sources concerning monastic revival, it is "quite clear that active participation in the

30. This is the so-called B Life: *Memorials of Saint Dunstan*, ed. William Stubbs (London, 1874), 3–52.

31. Ibid., 17–20. Dales, *Dunstan*, 22–23, gives details and refers to Aethelfleda as Dunstan's spiritual mother, as Alphege was his spiritual father.

32. *Regularis Concordia*, ed. and trans. Thomas Symons (London, 1953). The fuller title mentioning nuns, it should be noted, does not appear in the earliest manuscript. Symons has more recently argued that the date assigned to the Council of Winchester should be moved forward from the usual 970 to 973: Thomas Symons, *"Regularis Concordia:* History and Derivation" in Parsons, *Tenth-Century Studies,* 40–42.

33. *Regularis Concordia*, 2, 10 (proem, chaps. 3 and 10).

work of reform was not confined to the monks."[34] Dunstan's friendship during his youth with the holy woman Aethelfleda may have been one cause for the prominence of women and women's communities in the reforms associated with him as archbishop.[35] But it is equally clear that women's monasticism was hardly dead or moribund by the time of Dunstan's reforms and that there was considerably more continuity of practice between the early and late tenth century in nunneries than in the communities of the monks.

There were a number of new foundations or refoundations in the period of Dunstan's archepiscopate. He and King Edgar were responsible for further restoration of the old abbey of Barking about 965.[36] Romsey was considerably enriched in 968, when Edgar made a gift of land and rededicated the abbey.[37] After the king's death, his widow Aelfthrith oversaw the foundation of two new nunneries, Amesbury and Wherwell.[38] Aelfthrith was an exceedingly powerful figure in the early years of the reign of her young son Aethelred (978–1016) and was rumored to have conspired in the murder of her stepson King Edward the Martyr in 978. Certainly the queen used her special position as defender of nunneries, as prescribed in the *Regularis Concordia*, to consolidate her power during Aethelred's youth. But her motives also were pious, and it would appear that the foundation of Wherwell, with estates close by those of the New Minster at Winchester, suggests the interest, if not the active patronage and assistance, of the churchmen of this reform center.[39]

Most of the nunneries founded in the late Anglo-Saxon age continued to thrive in the eleventh century and beyond. The Warwickshire house of Polesworth appears to have survived the disruptions of new invasions in

34. Ibid., ed.'s intro., xxiii. However, the list of nunneries on this same page is not reliable.

35. On this subject, see Marc Anthony Meyer, "Women and the Tenth Century English Monastic Reform," *Revue bénédictine* 87 (1977): 34–61.

36. MRH, 256.

37. SASC no. 765; MRH, 264.

38. The account that follows is based on the entry for Amesbury in VCH, Wiltshire, 3: 242–259, that for Wherwell in VCH, Hampshire, 2: 131–137, and Meyer, "Women and the Tenth Century English Monastic Reform," esp. 51–61.

39. Meyer, "Women and the Tenth Century English Monastic Reform," 58–60. The early histories of a few other nunneries that existed in the eleventh century and probably date to the late tenth are shrouded in mystery: see MRH, 63 (Leominster) and 263 (Polesworth). The last foundation of the Anglo-Saxon period was Chatteris, in Cambridgeshire, between 1006 and 1016. Its cofounders were Ednoth, the abbot of Ramsey and his sister, the noble widow Aelfwyn, the first abbess of Chatteris. See VCH, Cambridgeshire, 2: 220–222.

1016, when male houses in the area were destroyed.[40] The nunnery of Leominster temporarily survived the abduction of its abbess by Earl Swein recounted in the Anglo-Saxon Chronicle.[41] The Domesday Survey reveals the considerable landed wealth of several monasteries at the time of the Norman Conquest; Wilton and Shaftesbury had incomes over 200 pounds, and Barking and Romsey over 100 pounds.[42] The oldest house, Shaftesbury, held over 300 hides of land by 1086, a substantial increase on the 100 hides Alfred was said to have granted to the nunnery when he founded it.[43] Besides being wealthy, these nunneries were the residences of many of the most noble women of England, and their religious significance was increased by the presence of saints such as King Edward the Martyr at Shaftesbury and Saint Edith at Wilton.

The character of female monasticism in England in the tenth and early eleventh centuries bears considerable resemblance to that of Ottonian Saxony. Karl Leyser has described a lively female monastic culture, exemplified not only by the prominence of Hrothswitha of Gandersheim in tenth-century literature, but also by the large number of nunneries that appeared from 919 to 1024, apparently founded and endowed in preference to those for men. Leyser attributes the presence of these communities to several factors, including the greater life expectancy for women in Germany in this period and the customs of inheritance and landholding relatively favorable to the accumulation of wealth by women. The foundations of many of these communities were owed to "masterful matrons," much like the royal and noble women of contemporary England.[44]

Leyser also notes that these nunneries were the fruits of a recent Christianization, referring to Ottonian Saxony as an "early medieval society." England had a Christian tradition three centuries old when Alfred founded Shaftesbury and Athelney, and the prominence of religious women in late Anglo-Saxon England is reminiscent of the high position accorded to nuns and their communities in early Anglo-Saxon England and in Merovingian and Carolingian Francia, a period that has been called a "Golden Age" of female monasticism.[45] Tenth-century England

40. MRH, 263.
41. *Anglo-Saxon Chronicle*, 109 (C, year 1046).
42. Knowles, *The Monastic Order in England*, 702.
43. For figures, see VCH, Dorset, 2: 73–74.
44. Leyser, *Rule and Conflict*, 49–73, esp. 64–68.
45. See Wemple, *Women in Frankish Society*, 127–188; Hollis, *Anglo-Saxon Women and the Church;* and Schulenburg, "Women's Monastic Communities." Schulenburg speaks of a "Golden Age" (290).

was much different, and women's communities did not outnumber men's (as in Saxony), at least after 950 or so. Nor do we know much at all about recluses, hermits, or anchorites such as Aethelfleda, who, as will be seen, had Continental counterparts, before the tenth century. But in wealth, prominence, and prevalence of patronage and membership by the high nobility, the late Anglo-Saxon nunneries present a profile that might well be thought of as "early medieval." A similar pattern may be observed on the Continent in the same era.

FOUNDATIONS ON THE CONTINENT, CIRCA 930–CIRCA 1080

Many commentators since Rodolf Glaber have identified the beginnings of a new era in Christian history in the early eleventh century, and for good reasons. In the case of female monasticism, the number of nunneries founded or refounded in the Continental area under study more than doubled from the tenth century to the eleventh.[46] However, this quantitative change should not blind us to certain continuities. Just as the activities of religious women and their patrons in the early tenth century broke a trail for foundations in the archepiscopacy of Dunstan, so the old ways of the tenth-century Continent still served in the somewhat more prosperous decades following the millennium.

The Carolingian Twilight

The devastation caused by Norman, Hungarian, and Saracen invasions of the Continent in the ninth and tenth centuries was widespread. Monasteries often were targets of violence for the riches they held, leaving religious communities in constant fear of the approach of bands of marauders. According to legend, the nuns of Saint-Symphorian, near Trier, learned of the fall of the episcopal city to the Normans and of the subsequent destruction of churches and monasteries. Together they prayed for death, and their plea was heard by God, who "released them all at once from this life." They had been delivered from the marauding

---

46. For the figures, see Chapter 1. Penelope D. Johnson's recent study of female monastic life in northern France, *Equal in Monastic Profession: Religious Women in Medieval France* (Chicago, 1991), takes as its parameters the years 1000 and 1300.

Normans.[47] The nuns of Fécamp were not so lucky. After a first incursion of barbarians, the few nuns that chose to remain cut off their noses and lips so their bodies would not be sullied in the event of a second attack. When the Normans came back, they did not rape the nuns, but instead they ripped them apart.[48]

The nature of this period and its effect on regular life are difficult to evaluate, because of the scarcity of sources and the dubious reliability of some accounts of foreign invasions. Certainly, monasticism was never as near extinction on the Continent as in England. Historians traditionally mark the beginning of a new era with the foundation of Cluny in 909. Although the beginnings of Cluniac monasticism had no immediate impact on the religious life for women, a point of departure for female monasticism on the Continent may also be discerned early in the tenth century. It had been nearly fifty years since the last foundation of a new community for nuns on the Continent when Bishop Gauzelin of Toul founded a house near the village of Bouxières in Lorraine.[49] The charters of Bouxières-aux-Dames, as it came to be known, suggest that the early history of this house has much in common with the nunneries of tenth-century England in the highly aristocratic identity of its early supporters and members.[50]

Despite the absence of a genuine foundation charter for this house, much is known about its beginnings.[51] In 930, Bishop Gauzelin gave to a group of women some land around an ancient oratory on a hillside above Bouxières, as well as a path for access to the village below and the tithes of a church there. The community began at once to gather other donations, the very first, sometime before 941, from "a certain noble woman named Hersende." Hersende, donor of numerous parcels of

47. GC 13: 516: "Harum votis Deus obsecrans, omnes uno die ex hoc seculo eripuisse dicitur."
48. GC 11: 201.
49. The last foundation whose history is well attested is Cusset in the diocese of Clermont, founded by the bishop of Nevers in 886. It is said that a house of nuns was founded at Melun at the beginning of the tenth century, but no reliable evidence exists: L.-H. Cottineau, *Répertoire topo-bibliographique des abbayes et prieurés*, 3 vols. (Mâcon, 1935–1970), 1: 936 (Cusset), 2: 1815 (Melun).
50. The charters have been edited in *Les origines de l'abbaye de Bouxières-aux-Dames au diocèse de Toul: Reconstitution du chartrier et édition critique des chartes antérieures à 1200*, ed. Robert-Henri Bautier (Nancy, 1987). Much of the discussion here derives from the analysis in Bautier's introduction (11–50).
51. Bautier argues convincingly (ibid., 11–16) that the so-called foundation charter of 937 is a forgery dating to circa 1100.

land and its laborers, appears to have been related by blood or marriage to the Bosonids, one of whom had married Charles the Bald. The first abbess, Rothildis, also was a cousin of the Carolingians and of the dukes of Burgundy.[52]

Eight more donations dating to 941–965 reflect the patronage of the noble family of which Bishop Gauzelin was a member. As the editor of the charters puts it, the relation of Gauzelin to this clan and the bishop's burial at the convent indicate that the early history of the house was a family matter. At least two women of this family were nuns at Bouxières.[53] Another important donor was Odelricus, later the archbishop of Reims, whose mother was buried there. Odelricus's donation of 959 or 960 refers to a considerable number of nuns at Bouxières.[54]

The death of Gauzelin in 962 marked the close of an era. The new bishop of Toul, Gerard, expanded the patrimony of the house personally, but he did not have the advantage of familial support that has helped his predecessor to expand of the fledgling community at Bouxières. This period was one of tense relations between the West Frankish kings and the emperor to the east, as well as more localized disturbances. Otto I confirmed the possessions of Bouxières twice, in 960 and 965, but a charter of the next decade in favor of the nuns requested a confirmation of the gift from "whichever king God has chosen to rule."[55] However, Bouxières continued to acquire new properties from aristocratic families. The donation of lands by the widow Alda in 978 marked the virtual completion of the patrimony of Bouxières as it is described in a bull of Pope Innocent II nearly two centuries later.[56]

Bouxières-aux-Dames was not the only new nunnery in Lorraine in the tenth century. The proliferation of new communities is especially striking because the region was, compared with other parts of Western Europe, already quite well endowed with convents. Four ancient nunneries in the dioceses of Metz, Toul, and Verdun had survived the Nor-

---

52. Ibid., 70–72 (no. 5) ("quadam nobilis mulier nomine Hersendis"), and 77–80 (nos. 8 and 9); the last of these was probably falsified. See the editor's comments, 19–26.
53. Ibid., 90–95 (nos. 18–24) and 116 (no. 36), gifts known from the confirmations of Otto I in 960 and 965. See 30–37 for analysis. The donor Frambert gives his two daughters Emma and Thiedrada (90–91).
54. Ibid., 87–89 (no. 15). This is an original charter "locello beate Marie genetricis Dei, in villa Buxerias u[bi] non pauca ancillarum ejus multitudo consistit."
55. Ibid., 120 (no. 38): "cujuscumque Deus regno preesse eligerit."
56. Ibid., 41–46, on donations in the time of Bishop Gerard.

man invasions.[57] Still, there were four more new foundations for women in this region, all the work of the ecclesio-political aristocracy of the tenth century.

In the eastern part of the diocese of Metz, Count Sigeric and his wife Bertha built the monastery of Vergaville for Benedictine nuns, endowing it with lands in their county of Sarreburg and placing it under their personal care.[58] This foundation dates to the beginning of the pontificate of Bishop Thierry I of Metz (965–983), who was related by blood and marriage, as his biographer explains, to the leaders of Gaul and Germany.[59] Thierry was a great promoter and protector of the monastic life, and one of his most notable accomplishments was the foundation of the nunnery of Epinal in southern Lorraine. The bishop endowed the house with land, the body of Saint Goeric, and the rights to mint and hold a market to provide for the material and spiritual needs of the nuns. The community was taken under the protection of the emperor Henry II in 1003, and Thierry's successor Aldaberon provided a community of clerics to minister to the nuns and prescribed the Benedictine Rule.[60] Aldaberon also founded a third nunnery in Metz (to house an overflow of nuns from Saint-Pierre) and gave a rural house of canons over to Benedictine women.[61]

A last foundation had origins after the year 1000. Bishop Heimo of Verdun restored an abandoned church just outside the episcopal city and with the help of Abbot Richard of Saint-Vito established the convent of Saint-Maur. Richard chose as abbess one Ava, who still led the community when its possessions were confirmed by a bull of Pope Leo IX. In the early years of Saint-Maur, the patrimony described in the pope's privilege grew rapidly, like that of Bouxières a century before: by 1049 the monastery was the proprietor of numerous estates with the buildings and people on them and about 20 churches or chapels. In addition to holding the body of Saint Maur, the nuns' church was the site of Bishop Heimo's tomb.[62]

57. Two houses in Metz, Saint-Pierre and Sainte-Glossinde, date to the seventh century. In the diocese of Toul, Remiremont is a seventh-century foundation, and Herbitzheim, on the eastern border of the diocese, was founded in the mid-eighth century. On these, see Michel Parisse, "Les religieuses bénédictines de Lorraine au temps de la réforme des XIe et XIIe siècles," *Revue Mabillon* 61 (1987): 257–263.

58. GC 13: 936.

59. Sigebert of Gembloux's remark is in MGH SS 4: 464: "religiosam vero generositatem attollebat cognatorum et affinium eius, primatum scilicet Galliae et Germaniae."

60. Ibid., 469–470 (chap. 12); see also DHGE 15: 605–607.

61. Parisse, "Les religieuses bénédictines de Lorraine," 266.

62. Ibid., 266–267. The bull given by Leo IX in 1049 is printed in GC 13: 559–560.

After southern England and Lorraine, Aquitaine was the third region in which a discernible group of new convents was established in the tenth century, but here information is sketchier than for contemporary England and Lorraine. By the later tenth century there were two houses for women in Poitiers. Monastic life in the ancient house of Sainte-Croix in Poitiers, founded in the sixth century by Saint Radegunde, was apparently not interrupted in the period of invasions; the abbess Hermengarde granted the lordship of some conventual lands to Count Geoffrey Greymantle between 960 and 975.[63]

About this time a new nunnery was founded in the city. As for Bouxières, there is no genuine foundation charter for Sainte-Trinité, but the outlines of its earliest history are clear enough. Adela was the widow of William III of Poitou and the daughter of Rollo, the first duke of Normandy. Her foundation of a new convent in Poitiers appears to date from the period shortly before a charter of 982; she is referred to as "the matron and foundress Adela" and the house as "a monastery recently built in Poitiers, dedicated in the name and honor of the Holy Trinity." Adela is said to have endowed the community with goods necessary for its survival under the Benedictine Rule. By this new charter, King Lothaire also recognized Adela's gift of the church of Saint-Pierre-le-Puellier. As the name suggests, it had once been a community of nuns, but "now the other way around, since fate overturns all" the church was inhabited by thirteen canons. These canons were to minister to the nuns in exchange for prebends, an arrangement that lasted through the Middle Ages. Adela, daughter and wife of tenth-century princes, in her widowhood set a new nunnery on a firm foundation, providing for the material and spiritual needs of the sisters.[64]

---

63. P. de Monsabert, "Documents inédits pour servir à l'histoire de l'abbaye de Sainte-Croix de Poitiers," *Revue Mabillon* 9 (1913–1914), 57–58. The abbess's care to protect the monastic patrimony in a volatile area is notable. Hermengarde ceded some of the abbey's lands in the north of Poitou near Loudun to the count of Anjou, who had invaded that area and become the vassal of the Duke of Aquitaine. At the same time, she demanded in exchange protection of other lands ("pro defensione terrarum nostrarum in sua potestate") from Geoffrey, who came to Poitiers to swear on a relic of the True Cross and in the presence of the nuns and the bishop of Poitiers an oath of agreement. On the political and military history of the region in the tenth century, see Jean Dunbabin, *France in the Making, 843–1180* (Oxford, 1985), 58–63.

64. *Recueil des actes de Lothaire et de Louis V, rois de France (954–987)*, ed. Louis Halphen and Ferdinand Lot (Paris, 1908), 108–110 (no. XLVIII), is the genuine act: "matrona et fondatrix Adela ... cenobio noviter in Pictavica urbe ... constructo et in nomine et honore sancte Trinitatis dicato ... nunc vice versa, quoniam sors omnia versat," with a forgery at 142–145

Thus Poitiers shared with only three other episcopal centers the distinction of having more than one active monastery for women at the end of the tenth century.[65] A few more houses were founded in Aquitaine in this period. Another aristocratic woman, Audearde, the viscountess of Thouars, founded a nunnery near the castle at Thouars, some 60 kilometers northwest of Poitiers, around the time Adela founded Sainte-Trinité. Well to the south, a nunnery at Le Bugue in the Dordogne had its beginnings in the late-tenth-century activities of powerful lords, in particular one Adelaide, later commemorated as the founder of the house.[66]

The origin of a house in Nîmes shows that, just as in the three regions of relatively concentrated nunnery foundation, the impetus for foundation in the Midi lay in the hands of the most powerful secular and ecclesiastical lords in the late tenth century. Frotaire, the first bishop of Nîmes by that name, was a member of the powerful Occitan family later known as the Trencavels. His brother was Bernard-Ato, viscount of Albi and Nîmes. Bernard-Ato's son, also Frotaire, succeeded his uncle as bishop of Nîmes. In 991, Bishop Frotaire I founded in his city the Benedictine abbey of Saint-Sauveur de la Font on the site of an ancient pagan temple.[67]

The World of the Princes

Despite the survival of over forty houses from the early Middle Ages and the new foundations just described, the total number of convents in the early eleventh century was still quite small. Figure 4 shows the thin and uneven distribution of the nunneries in existence around 1000 A.D.[68] Despite the

---

(no. LXI). See the analysis in Denise Caisso-Rivière, "Les origines de l'abbaye de la Trinité de Poitiers," *Bulletin de la société des antiquaires de l'Ouest* 3d ser., 4 (1955): esp. 59–72.

65. On Metz, see above. At Autun, the sixth-century house of Notre-Dame appears to have survived. It was joined in the ninth century by the nuns at Saint-Andoche, restored at episcopal behest. Two early medieval houses in Lyon appear to have been intact in 1000.

66. DHGE 9: 1069–1071 (Bonneval-lès-Thouars); Léon Dessalles, *Histoire du Bugue* (Périgueux, 1857), 7–25. The Benedictine abbey of St-Menoux, in the south of the diocese of Bourges, also appears to have been founded by 1000 A.D., but its history, like that of many other houses founded in the tenth century, is very obscure for the first centuries of its existence. The records of the house were burned in the early modern period. See J.-J. Moret, *Histoire de Saint-Menoux* (Moulins, 1907), 80–81, 94–102.

67. GC 6: 508.

68. The figures in this paragraph, it should be stressed, are approximations. I have tended to assume a house has a continuous history if it reappears without any known refoundation (e.g., the nunnery of St-Sernin in Rodez, about which there is no information at all between

existence of twenty-seven nunneries in episcopal cities, dozens of dioceses and even whole ecclesiastical provinces were entirely without regular religious life for women. There were no nunneries at all in several of the regions most afflicted by Norman and Muslim incursions in the ninth and tenth centuries: the archdioceses of York, Rouen, Tours, Auch, and Aix-en-Provence, that is, northern England, northern and western France, and the extreme southeast and southwest of the area under study. Of the Continental houses in existence at the millennium, two-thirds were in landlocked provinces, less accessible to seafaring invaders.[69] Faster recovery in England made possible foundations close to the English Channel, but there were only four nunneries on the Continent in coastal dioceses: Montreuil-sur-Mer in Picardy, which around the year 1000 became the home for nuns formerly at Pavilly, near Rouen; the ancient house of Saint-Césaire in Arles; Bishop Frotaire's new foundation in Nîmes; and the recently restored Saint-Sauveur in Marseille, the community originally founded by John Cassian.

Figure 5 indicates the distribution of foundations and refoundations from the beginning of the eleventh century to 1080. In general, these new houses were founded in places where convents were few or entirely lacking. Of thirty-six new foundations, twelve were in the archdioceses of Rouen and Tours, where there had been none in 1000. Between the millennium and 1080, nunneries were established in the episcopal cities of Angers, Angoulême, Beauvais, Evreux, Lisieux, Le Mans, Rennes, Rouen, Saintes, Senlis, Tours, and Verdun; the old nunnery of Saint-André-le-Haut in Vienne, destroyed by Saracen invaders, was restored to active life in 1031. By the late eleventh century, the distribution of houses was much more even than around 1000: only the north of England, inland Provence, and Gascony were without convents.[70] By 1080, in France and England there were approximately as many convents as there had been

---

its foundation ca. 880 and the twelfth century). The state of the remaining evidence, written and archeological, is such that there may have been other houses in existence that left no traces.

69. In fact, of 16 nunneries founded in the ninth century that survived to 1000, 12 were in the archdioceses of Sens, Bourges, and Lyon. So in the period of most intense threat of invasion, new foundations were essentially halted in any regions even within easy range of coastline.

70. The history of northern England in the period 1000–1070 is one of continuous strife and violence constituting the last phase of Scandinavian settlement in Western Europe, so it is not surprising that no convents were founded. Provence, Languedoc, and Gascony had weaker traditions of female monasticism from the early Middle Ages than any other parts of the territory considered in this study. There were early medieval convents in Bordeaux, Bazas, and Toulouse, but none lasted to the millennium.

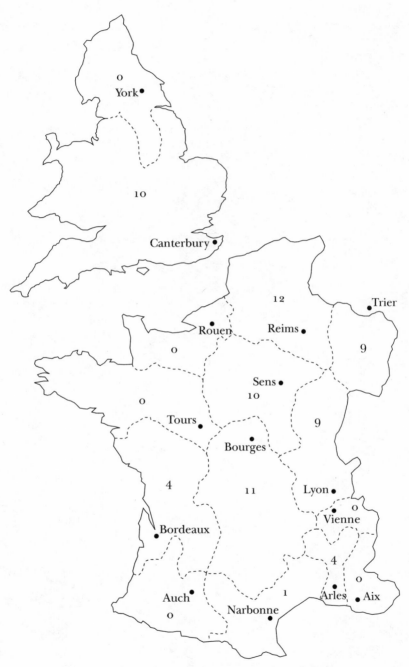

FIGURE 4. Nunneries active in 1000 A.D., by archdiocese

FIGURE 5. Nunneries founded or refounded, 1001–1080, by archdiocese

nearly three centuries before, when Vikings started making their first raids in England and Charlemagne was crowned emperor.[71]

The period from 1000 to 1080, then, was the final phase of restoration after the disorder wrought by invasion and the collapse of Carolingian central authority. As in the tenth century, the founders of new nunneries were the very powerful men and women of Western Europe. The identity of the lay portion of this group had changed somewhat with the progressive weakening of the Carolingian monarchs through the tenth century. After the millennium, the age of French regional principalities was at hand. The sponsors of monastic foundations were very often the leaders of these counties and duchies, men and women commonly related by blood and marriage.[72] Members of this extended family, like Christians of the tenth century, saw to it that the nunneries they built were put on firm economic foundations from their beginnings.[73]

In 1028, the count and countess of Anjou, Fulk Nerra and Hildegarde, founded a nunnery in their city of Angers, which was then the only such monastery in the Loire Valley between Tours and the Bay of Biscay. Fulk and Hildegarde, whose vigor would make it appear that the nunnery was built on her initiative, richly endowed the new foundation, which housed twenty-six sisters when the first abbess was elected.[74] Just about the same time, the duke of Brittany founded a nunnery dedicated

71. My figures are 105 convents in 800 (the majority dating to the seventh century) and 103 in 1080. These are of course approximations, but not just cumulative reckonings; I have taken into account the early disappearance of houses founded before 800 and those which vanished between the millennium and 1080. There were still slightly fewer foundations on the Continent than in 800, because there were 28 convents in England when the Vikings arrived but only 12 late in the reign of William the Conqueror.
72. Dunbabin, *France in the Making*, 162–222, describes the history of the regional principalities in the eleventh century; see also the genealogical tables on 381–392. Dominique Barthélemy, *L'ordre seigneurial XIe–XIIe siècle* (Paris, 1980), regards the fifty years from 980 as marking the final dislocation of the Carolingian monarchy and 1030 as the beginning of "l'âge seigneurial" (9–10).
73. For more detail on the issues sketched below, see Mary Skinner, "Benedictine Life for Women in Central France, 850–1100: A Feminist Revival," in *Medieval Religious Women*, vol. 1, *Distant Echoes*, ed. John A. Nichols and Lillian Thomas Shank (Kalamazoo, Mich., 1984), 87–113, and Jean Verdon, "Les moniales dans la France de l'Ouest aux XIe et XIIe siècles: Etude d'histoire sociale," *Cahiers de civilisation médiévale* 19 (1976): 247–264. See also Johnson, *Equal in Monastic Profession*, for northern French nunneries.
74. *Cartulaire de l'abbaye du Ronceray d'Angers (1028–1184)*, ed. Paul Marchegay and Bertrand de Broussillon (Paris, 1900), 1–9 (nos. 1–5) for the foundation, 16–17 (no. 15) for the election of Leoburga. Bernard S. Bachrach, *Fulk Nerra, the Neo-Roman Consul, 987–1040* (Berkeley, Calif., 1993), 202, points out that Fulk's gifts, not considering Hildegarde's, were far more generous than those to male monasteries or the cathedral of Saint-Maurice in Angers. Bachrach attributes Fulk's largess to recent military successes in the west of his realm.

to Saint George just outside his stronghold of Rennes. Duke Alan built the place for his sister Adela, his "most precious treasure under the sun," whom he dedicated to a life of virginity, service to God, and the practice of monastic learning. In making the initial endowment of lands and goods, Alan was joined by the bishop of Rennes, whose mother and sister entered the new convent, and two local laymen who also gave their daughters to the religious life.[75]

Noble couples sometimes founded houses for both women and men. Fulk Nerra's son Geoffrey Martel married Agnes, widow of William V of Aquitaine and daughter of Count Otto-William of Mâcon, in 1032. Shortly afterward, the couple founded the abbey of La Trinité in Vendôme for Benedictine monks.[76] Fifteen years later, Geoffrey (who had by then succeeded his father as count of Anjou) and Agnes founded a house for women in the new Angevin stronghold of Saintes. The earliest charters from this nunnery reveal the extent of Agnes's activities in assembling a patrimony for the new house. At her request, Geoffrey got the possessor of Corme-Royale, near Saintes, to concede the property to him. Agnes bought half the rights to the mint at Saintes; her husband donated the other half. Most important, Agnes bought Vis, an island on the Sevre River in Poitou, from its lord, William of Parthenay, for the sum of 1,500 solidi. In the foundation charter for Notre-Dame Geoffrey and Agnes gave to the new house all these properties and rights, plus numerous other nearby lands and the restored church of Saint Palladius, in which canons would serve the parish and the nuns. The foundation was witnessed by several dozen secular and ecclesiastical lords, including the duke of Aquitaine, the count of Angoulême, and three archbishops.[77]

Farther north, Viscount Jocelin and his wife Emmeline, lords of Arques, founded two houses in Rouen in the 1030s: Sainte-Catherine for

75. "Cartulaire de l'abbaye de Saint-Georges de Rennes," ed. Paul de la Bigne-Villeneuve, *Bulletin et mémoires de la société archéologique du département d'Ille-et-Vilaine* 9 (1875): 129–311 and 10 (1876): 3–327. The foundation charter is printed at 217–222. The language of this document is richly evocative of the piety and practicality of the founder and his female relatives, who probably participated more actively in the establishment of the house than the form of the charter indicates.

76. Penelope D. Johnson, *Prayer, Patronage, and Power: The Abbey of La Trinité, Vendôme, 1032–1187* (New York, 1981). On the countess, see Johnson, "Agnes of Burgundy: An Eleventh-Century Woman as Monastic Patron," *Journal of Medieval History* 15 (1989): 93–104.

77. *Cartulaire de l'abbaye royale de Notre-Dame de Saintes de l'ordre de Saint Benoît*, ed. Th. Grasilier, vol. 2 of *Cartulaires inédits de la Saintonge* (Niort, 1871), 1–8 (nos. 1 and 2) concerns the foundation proper and its confirmation by churchmen; 55–56 (no. 55) specifies the purpose of Saint Palladius; 70 (no. 77) concerns the mint; 143–145 (no. 225) details the purchase of Vis.

Benedictine monks and Saint-Amand for Benedictine nuns. Both places were richly endowed, and the noble couple eventually retired separately to the houses they had founded.[78] The best known of all paired foundations also are Norman, those of Duke William and Mathilda, the daughter of the count of Flanders. These abbeys originated in a quarrel over the marriage, which the papacy regarded as illegitimate because William and Mathilda were blood relations (Mathilda's mother was a Capetian, as was William's great-grandmother). Instead of dissolving the marriage, it was agreed that the duke and duchess would as penance build two monasteries in Caen, one for men, and one for women. The abbey of Saint-Etienne for men was completed in the early 1060s, and the nunnery of La Trinité was consecrated in June of 1066, just a few months before William crossed the English Channel to seize the English crown. The charter commemorating this event contains a list of the donations by the duke and duchess or other local lords: over 750 acres of land, plus numerous other domains with churches, mills, tithes, and other privileges are named. A pancarte of 1082 lists dozens of properties and privileges belonging to the abbey, and the now-royal couple gave four English manors to La Trinité in the same year.[79]

Mathilda's mother and father, Baldwin and Adela, had also founded a nunnery in their county of Flanders, Messines, in 1057.[80] A few years later, Adela's sister-in-law Anne, the queen of France, founded a house for Benedictine women at Senlis. About the same time, Count Richard II of Evreux, son of Archbishop Robert of Rouen and grandson of Duke Richard of Normandy, founded a house in Evreux, where his daughter Godehilde was a nun. Like the other nobles already mentioned, these mighty people could afford to negotiate the foundation and endowment of a new religious community.[81]

Despite the importance of the founders and their sometimes lavish generosity, the number of nuns in these communities does not appear to have been remarkably large. Twenty-six nuns at Ronceray in Angers elected the first abbess, but when the nuns elected a new leader nearly half a century later, only thirty-three nuns participated, this in spite of

78. Marie-Josèphe Le Cacheux, *Histoire de l'abbaye de Saint-Amand de Rouen des origines à la fin du XVIe siècle* (Caen, 1937), 37–50.

79. *Les actes de Guillaume le Conquérant et de la reine Mathilde pour les abbayes caennaises*, ed. Lucien Musset (Caen, 1967), 52–57 (no. 2), 77–91 (nos. 8 and 9). The largest pieces of land are measured in *acri*. Musset's observations on the early histories of the two houses in his introduction (13–20 and 43–48) are extremely helpful.

80. MB 3: 217–219 discusses the early history of Messines, with bibliography.

81. GC 9: 452 (Senlis); DHGE 16: 184–185 (Evreux).

numerous gifts to the abbey since its foundation.[82] A list of nuns of Mathilda's foundation at Caen who died before 1113, in the first fifty years of the nunnery's existence, contains thirty names, which would suggest that the size of the community was not much larger than that.[83] When Count Baldwin of Flanders and Adela founded Messines, they stipulated that the house was to contain thirty nuns and a dozen canons to serve them. What do these figures from prestigious comital and ducal foundations suggest about the world of religious women in an era of recovery?

RELIGIOUS WOMEN AFTER THE AGE OF INVASION

In the early eleventh century, a monk from Metz named Alpert lived in the diocese of Utrecht. Around 1020 he wrote a short history that he called *De diversitate temporum*. He began it with a story that, although it took place outside the geographical confines of the present study, is a telling illustration of some of the difficulties of religious life for women in this period.[84]

There were in the late tenth century two noble sisters, Adela and Liutgarde, the latter abbess of Elten, founded by their father Wicman in the diocese of Utrecht. A kinsman of theirs, Godizo, had been a member of Adela's household, but he became disgusted by her frivolity and loose living and joined Liutgarde's *clientela*. Soon after, Godizo, tired of the manifold insults to his patron Liutgarde by her sister, as-

---

82. *Cartulaire de l'abbaye du Ronceray,* 17–18 (no. 16). I cannot accept Mary Skinner's identification of 11 early "priories" of Ronceray as a way of accounting for the small growth at the mother house ("Benedictine Life for Women," 93). Careful scrutiny of the language of the charters reveals that in seven of these cases, there is no sign of conventual life, the place in question usually being a parish church. Two churches given to Ronceray in the eleventh century may have been dependent monasteries: that of Saints Cyr and Julitte near Nantes, given by the count of the city in 1038, and Avenières, near Laval, given ca. 1070 *(Cartulaire de l'abbaye du Ronceray,* 257–258 [no. 421] and 220 [no. 360]. There is no hint of any community at Prigny until it is called a *domum conventualem* in a charter of ca. 1175 (274–275 [no. 438]). Prigny is called a *monasterium* on its donation ca. 1080 (75 [no. 99]), but there is no later reference in the cartulary to the site or any community there. These monasteries also may have been little more than cells for two or three monks dependent on the mother house at Angers. On the difficulties of identifying religious communities, see Appendix A.

83. *Les actes de Guillaume le Conquérant,* 47.

84. Alpert of Metz, *De diversitate temporum,* printed in MGH SS, 4: 700–723. The story retold here is in bk. 1, chaps. 2 and 3 (702–703).

sembled a gang to attack and burn Adela's castle. Adela escaped. Alpert proceeded to compare the sisters to Cain and Abel in the difference of their characters. He noted that Adela was "loud, foul-mouthed, over-dressed, and dissolute."[85] Liutgarde, however, was kind, wise, and generous: men came from far and wide to seek her counsel and she gave her entire inheritance to her nunnery. This last fact aroused Adela's special hatred, and she entered on a successful plot to have her sister poisoned. Adela then proceeded to seize all the lands Liutgarde had given to Elten. Forced by the order of the emperor Otto III to give up the lands, Adela proceeded to marry and with her new husband attempted to take Elten by siege, but this plan, too, failed as Otto called a council to guarantee the future safety of the nunnery and its neighborhood.

Elten survived a period of violent upheaval, but its abbess was dead and its lands had been attacked. Even when the threat of foreign invasion had subsided, the problem of internal disorder, especially that resulting from competition for limited resources, remained in the tenth and eleventh centuries. When Agnes of Burgundy bought the island of Vis in 1047 from William of Parthenay to make it part of the patrimony of Notre-Dame of Saintes, she had just such insecurity in mind. According to the terms of sale, in the event of the destruction of the nunnery, the abbess and her veiled nuns would continue to use the income of Vis wherever they fled or were sheltered.[86] Agnes understood well the volatility of her times, and perhaps she also feared familial interference with her donation of the kind that had proved so disruptive at Elten.

From farther south comes evidence of similar difficulties. The first will of Adelaide, the viscountess of Narbonne, was drawn up in 978. In this document Adelaide referred to an unfinished monastery near Narbonne and left the work of its completion to her three sisters and the countess of Carcassonne. She provisionally ceded lands to each sister. At the monastery's completion, these properties were to become the patrimony of the new community, presided over by Adelaide's daughter. But Adelaide carefully specified the destination of these same properties in case

---

85. "Erat clamosa in voce, lasciva in verbis, veste composita, animo dissoluta."
86. *Cartulaire de l'abbaye royale de Notre-Dame de Saintes*, 143–145 (no. 225): "Et si forte, quod absit, locus ille, qui est apud Xanctonas, omnino destrueretur, sic destino anime mee, ut ubicumque aufugeret abbatissa cum monachabus ibi velatis et Deo dicatis, vel deveniret vel hospitaretur, hujus emptionis mee redditionem vel expletum sibi et suis accipiat in vivendi usum."

the nunnery was not completed.[87] So it happened; in a second testament, made twelve years later, Adelaide did not mention the nunnery, and disposed otherwise of the properties that were to have been the endowment of her daughter's house.[88]

Nor was a convent in Languedoc considered permanent once it was founded. The house of Saint-Geniès-des-Mourges, near Montpellier, was founded in 1019. Eight years later, one Rostagnus and his three sons gave over to the care of Saint-Geniès their new foundation for nuns at nearby Gallargues. But the donors stipulated that if the community at Saint-Geniès was dispersed, the daughter house would be free of any obligations, and the nuns who chose to remain there would possess the endowment of Gallargues under the protection of Rostagnus and his successors.[89] Saint-Geniès did survive, but it remained a very small community. The foundation charter indicates that the initial endowment was not more than a church and the lands adjacent to it.[90] A document of 1025 records the election as abbess of Judith, the daughter of the founder of Saint-Geniès. Judith was one of a group of fourteen nuns. When her niece Alimburgis became abbess in 1043, the community appears to have numbered only eleven sisters.[91]

Another persistent habit of the period also limited the number of nunneries. A substantial number of nunneries destroyed in the ninth and tenth centuries were subsequently restored or refounded for monks. Ely in Cambridgeshire is perhaps the best-known example of

---

87. HGL 5: 285–287: "Illud sanctum opus, quod inchoatum habeo subtus Narbonam, in honore omnipotentis Dei sanctique Salvatoris construendi, relinquo sororibus meis et domnae Arsindae comitissae . . . et si ad perfectum perduxerint sancti coenobium, cuncti praefati alodes cum omni integritate illic remaneat et si non perfecerint hunc monasterium . . . et si, permittente Deo, constructum fuerit, rogo ut filia mea sit inde abbatissa."
88. Ibid., 5: 320–324. See Elisabeth Magnou-Nortier, *La société laïque et l'église dans la province ecclésiastique de Narbonne* (Toulouse, 1974), 411. Did Adelaide, too, make final arrangements in fear of interfamilial strife after her death?
89. HGL 5: 384–385: "Et si ipso monasterio suprascripto [sc. Sancto Genesio] ullus homo aut ulla foemina disrumpent, per quem stare non posset ipsa ecclesia suprascripta cum omni superius scripta, fiat liber de eius potestate et illas devotae que ibi voluerint manere, teneant et possideant sine blandimentum de ullumque hominem, et Rostagnus et unus de filiis sui, aut unus de posteris suis . . . teneant ad praevidendum sive defendendum." Elisabeth Magnou-Nortier, citing this text, comments on the fragility of these foundations even in the eyes of the founders themselves in this era: "Formes féminines de vie consacrée dans les pays du Midi jusqu'au début du XIIe siècle," *Cahiers de Fanjeaux* 23 (1988): 212, n. 7.
90. HGL 5: 368–369.
91. Ibid., 378–379 (the election of Judith), and 445–446 (the election of Alimburgis).

this phenomenon. After its destruction in 870 it was restored a century later as a Benedictine house for men and granted a charter by King Edgar.[92] On the Continent, the old nunnery of Fécamp, ruined by the Norman invaders in 876, was restored by the mid-tenth century for Benedictine men.[93] In a few cases, a community of nuns was replaced by one for monks. A nunnery was founded at Vézelay in 867 by the count and countess of Vienne, but the house was soon after handed over to monks. A bull of Pope John VIII explains that, owing to great assaults from outside, the nuns were unable to live regularly there and it was thus better suited to monks.[94] In 949, the nunnery of Homblières in Picardy was transferred to Benedictine monks because, according to a charter describing the events, the nuns did not live honorably or subject themselves to regular life.[95]

How might we account for a pattern of refoundation or transfer that routinely blocked the entrance of women into the regular religious life? It is tempting to discern, especially in the case of Homblières, a thoroughgoing misogyny, a refusal on the part of the society's powerful to accommodate women in monasticism. But this can be only part of the explanation, as a few communities that had housed monks in the early Middle Ages were later restored for women.[96] Very often, the earlier history of a site was simply forgotten, and a restoration was made according to the desires of the new founders. This appears to have been the case with the restoration of the nunnery of Argenteuil, recounted in Helgaud

92. MRH, 64–65.

93. On Fécamp, see GC 11: 201–203. The list of examples is long; there are about ten cases in the tenth century, three times that many in the eleventh. This type of refoundation was primarily, although not exclusively, an English and northern French phenomenon. See Skinner, "Benedictine Life for Women," 90, with important notes.

94. *Monumenta Vizeliacensia: Textes relatifs à l'histoire de l'abbaye de Vézelay*, ed. R. B. C. Huygens (Turnhout, 1976), 261.

95. *The Cartulary and Charters of Notre-Dame of Homblières*, ed. Theodore Evergates and Giles Constable (Cambridge, Mass., 1990), 37–39 (no. 2): "quatenus quibusdam sanctimonialibus inibi non satis honeste viventibus et regulari districtioni subicii nolentibus inde remotis substituerentur monachi qui obedirent regulae et abbati." The editors relate this act to monastic reform led by centers including Cluny (2–3).

96. Skinner, "Benedictine Life for Women," 90, posits that accusations of misconduct occurred when men needed a house, an argument hard to prove or disprove with the kinds of evidence available. Counterexamples included Denain, a house of men and women near Cambrai founded in the eighth century and restored about 1029 as a nunnery by Count Baldwin the Bearded of Flanders (DHGE 14: 218). There appears to have been a male house at Châteaudun in the diocese of Chartres dedicated to St-Avit in the early Middle Ages. A new house with the same patron was erected for nuns in the 1040s (see DHGE 12: 570).

of Fleury's biography of King Robert the Pious. In about 1000, Robert's mother Adelaide established a community for women near Paris and endowed it with numerous lands, including many that had belonged to her husband, Hugh Capet. But neither Helgaud's account nor Robert's charter confirming these donations acknowledges that this was in fact a restoration: the nunnery of Argenteuil was first founded in the seventh century.[97]

Because of the destruction of many ancient nunneries and an apparent reluctance to restore them or found new ones in a time of continuing violence and low priority for monastic women in the distribution of limited resources, in 1050 the number of women's monasteries was still smaller than three centuries earlier. Extant communities were of unequal wealth: the rapid growth of the patrimonies of several Anglo-Saxon houses, as well as those of the new houses in Lorraine, suggests the possibility, at least, of supporting a much larger community than that at Saint-Geniès, and perhaps larger than those of the comital and ducal foundations of the eleventh century. Still, if there was an average of 30 nuns at each house—almost certainly a high estimate—then there were still only about 2,400 nuns in this vast region of Western Europe by 1030, and just over 3,000 in 1080.

The paucity of nunneries did not escape the notice of contemporaries. Shortly after the millennium, a dignitary of the cathedral of Saint Martin at Tours named Hervey assembled a small patrimony for the church of Beaumont, adjacent to the city. He then went to King Robert the Pious, who asked what he intended to do with these properties. Hervey replied that it grieved him that there was nowhere in Touraine a monastery where women might worship and so founded a nunnery at Beaumont.[98] However, the poverty of institutional resources did not necessarily prevent women from leading a religious life. The *religiosae feminae* of early-tenth-century England had Continental counterparts. It is difficult to learn much about these women or their way of living, but scattered hints in the sources point to the existence of a vital culture of

97. Helgaud de Fleury, *Vie de Robert le Pieux*, ed. and trans. Robert-Henri Bautier (Paris, 1965), 82–83. Robert's charter is printed in GC 8, instr., 28–29.
98. PL 141: 953–955 is Robert's charter of 1007: "Cumque eum diligenter fuissemus percontati quid operis de supradictis rebus esset acturus, retulit se tristari admodum non esse in pago Turonico coenobium ubi sanctimoniales feminae Christo possent suae devotionis impendere officium." Robert confirmed the patrimony of the nunnery in 1022, shortly after Hervey's death (966–968).

female religiosity expressed outside the cloister in the tenth and eleventh centuries.

The foundation of a nunnery by Bishop Gauzelin in 930 may well have regularized a religious life already being practiced by women on the hill above Bouxières. A seventeenth-century summary of a lost medieval charter reports that the bishop made his donation "aux religieuses moniales qui faisoient leur residence en sa chapelle" and refers to their "maisonettes." Did a semicenobitic community already exist by 930? The idea is made more plausible by a story in the *vita* of John of Gorze from the late tenth century. A man named Humbert returned to his native Lorraine after a pilgrimage to Rome and became a recluse near Verdun. Two religious women joined him in a nearby cell and absorbed divine knowledge as he taught them from the window of his own cell. Two other women from Verdun, the writer continued, were "set afire" by Humbert's exhortation, and one of them became the mother of the newly founded monastery at Bouxières, the other also joining the community.[99] The story demonstrates the existence of at least two nonconventual holy women who lived near Humbert and suggests that the first nuns at Bouxières at the very least drew inspiration from their example, if they had not in fact been living a similar life before Bishop Gauzelin's "foundation."[100]

Considering that women chose religious lives outside the cloister in Lorraine, an area relatively well endowed with nunneries even in the early tenth century, it is not surprising to find evidence of such activities elsewhere. A charter from early-eleventh-century Brittany signals the existence of a larger nonregular community. Shortly after the foundation of the abbey of Saint-Georges at Rennes circa 1028, a noble woman named Roiantelina went to Abbess Adela with a request. Roiantelina was the leader of a group of religious women in Chavagne, a few kilometers southwest of Rennes. The group had grown to nine women, straining resources. Roiantelina therefore asked Adela that these women be admitted to Saint-Georges, a request that the abbess

99. The question of an earlier eremitic community is raised in *Les origines de l'abbaye de Bouxières-aux-Dames*, 16–18. Bautier strengthens the case that this was so by referring to the *vita* of John of Gorze (MGH SS 4: 351–352). The mother was without question Rothildis, the first abbess of Bouxières.

100. It is probably not just coincidence that the diocese of Verdun lacked a nunnery until Bishop Heimo founded one in the early eleventh century (see above).

granted. There had been no nunnery at all in Brittany before the foundation of Saint-Georges, but this had not prevented at least one group of women from dedicating themselves to "doing battle for God under the yoke of religion."[101] The election of Leoburga as abbess of Ronceray took place in the same year as the foundation of the monastery. The charter concerning this event names twenty-seven nuns of the new community. The early presence of so large a group suggests that before 1028 some Angevin women, like those in Brittany, had lived extramonastic religious lives, possibly in a congregation similar to Roiantelina's in or near Angers.[102]

In a study of religious life for women in the Midi before 1100, Elisabeth Magnou-Nortier considers the response of women in southwestern France to the absence of nunneries and has uncovered what she calls a "slim thread of evidence concerning another form of female life consecrated to God." Pointing to the difficulties of life in regular communities, which needed but did not always find powerful male patrons and protectors, Magnou-Nortier finds that there were alternatives for those who desired to live as *Deo devotae*. Unmarried women and widows, they usually lived in churches, often in the ambit of a bishop or male monastery.[103]

---

101. "Cartulaire de l'abbaye de Saint-Georges de Rennes," *Bulletin et mémoires* 9 (1875): 236–238 (no. 12): "Roiantelina . . . congregationem feminarum sub sanctimoniali jugo Deo militaturam in Cavana plebe aggregare statuit . . . sed cum nonnullas in prefato loco adunasset, senciens eas ibidem regulariter nequaquam subsistere posse oportunitatem loci et indumentum sui, adiit nostram presentiam . . . poscens ut supradictas sorores, numero novem, in nostro collegio reciperemus." This group of nine may have assembled in response to the foundation of Saint-Georges and in hopes of eventual admission to it, but the description of Roiantelina's congregation makes it sound like something that grew over time (the pluperfect *adunasset*) and it is not evident why women who could have joined the newly founded community at Rennes would instead have gathered themselves only a few kilometers distant. Clearly, these women saw the regular religious life as an ultimate goal but had not attained it by the time Roiantelina made her request.
102. *Cartulaire de l'abbaye du Ronceray*, 16–17 (no. 15) concerns the election of Leoburga. In 1028, the closest documented nunnery was the tenth-century foundation of Bonneval-lès-Thouars, over 60 kilometers southeast. It is possible that some of the nuns came from that house, but there is no such indication in the surviving charters.
103. Magnou-Nortier, "Formes féminines de vie consacrée," considers the ecclesiastical provinces of Bourges, Bordeaux, Auch, and Narbonne. She finds only seven nunneries in the ninth through eleventh centuries. My figure is higher, but there is no doubt that nunneries were scarce in this region before 1050. Some women lived a religious life outside monasticism south of the Pyrenees, too. See Montserrat Cabré y Pairet, "'Deodicatae' y 'Deovotae.' La regulación de la religiosidad femenina en los condados catalanes, siglos IX–XI," in *Las mujeres en el cristianismo medieval*, ed. Angela Muñoz Fernández (Madrid, 1989), 169–182.

The practice was not limited to the area south of the Loire, or even to regions with little monastic settlement. In a section of the *Miracles of Saint Benedict* written in the mid-eleventh century, there is a story of a crippled woman who lived in a hut (*tuguriolum*) just outside the gates of Fleury.[104] Even in England, relatively rich in monasteries, women lived semiformal religious lives in the eleventh century. King Aethelred's law code of 1008 distinguishes two types of female religious, nuns (*mynecena*) and others devoted to God (*nunnan*). The Domesday Survey mentions women's communities attached to male houses at Evesham, Bury Saint Edmunds, Ely, and Saint Albans, and there seem to have been more isolated and less permanent arrangements elsewhere. Even in northern England, which lacked formal communities, there appear to have been *nunnan* in the eleventh century.[105] All over northwestern Europe in the eleventh century, women practiced religious lives outside the cenobitic framework in a period of limited access to traditional monasticism.

MARCIGNY AND COMPS: RETROSPECT AND PROSPECT

A salient feature of the pattern of female monastic foundations in the years circa 890–circa 1080 is the usual lack of direct institutional ties to self-conscious reform movements. The most inclusive of these, that of Saint Dunstan, was fairly short-lived and built on a preexisting tradition of religious life for women rather than including women in a wholly original program. The reforming activities of men such as Gerard of Brogne and William of Dijon did not encompass the foundation of nunneries. Most notorious is the case of Cluniac monasticism, the most influential reforming presence in Western Europe in the tenth and eleventh centuries. Cluny included no nunneries in its congregation for a century and a half after its foundation by William the Pious. Thus the consecration in 1055 of Marcigny, the first nunnery to be a member of the *ecclesia Cluniacensis*, was an important departure. But a recent study of Marcigny suggests that origins of the first Cluniac nunnery share much continuity with the past and should be considered in terms of long-

104. *Les miracles de Saint Benoît*, ed. Eugène de Certain (Paris, 1858), 207.
105. Roberta Gilchrist, *Gender and Material Culture: The Archaeology of Religious Women* (London, 1994), 33–36. Gilchrist finds a "diversity of vocations and settlements for religious women" in England which seems very much in accord with the situation on the Continent.

established patterns at least as much as evidence of a new reforming impulse within Cluniac monasticism.[106]

The tale is a familiar one. Marcigny was founded by two brothers on their ancestral lands. Geoffrey, the lord of Semur in Burgundy, provided for the material basis; his brother Hugh saw to the building and consecration of the new community. These two and other members of their family endowed the new nunnery with numerous properties during its early history. From this clan came not only the greatest donations, but also a number of early members of the convent; three of the founders' sisters became nuns there, as did Geoffrey's daughter and daughter-in-law. Geoffrey and his son both entered religious life at Cluny, the latter becoming an official at Marcigny, and three of Geoffrey's granddaughters entered the nunnery, too, all within thirty-five years of its foundation.[107]

It may well have been concern for the safety of their widowed mother and sister Helia that inspired Geoffrey and Hugh to found the nunnery: their father and a third brother had died not long before in plots engineered by Helia's husband, Duke Robert of Burgundy.[108] There was no similar safe haven nearby. The closest attested nunnery was that of Saint-Menoux, some seventy kilometers to the west and north; slightly more distant were convents in the episcopal cities of Autun and Lyon. Like Hervey of Tours, Fulk Nerra and Hildegarde, and many others, Geoffrey

106. Wischermann, *Marcigny-sur-Loire*, is a thorough study, in essence prosopographical but also carefully considering the extant charter evidence concerning the origins of Marcigny, whose foundation charter (along with many other records) has been lost. Noreen Hunt, *Cluny under Saint Hugh, 1049–1109* (London, 1967), 187, stresses the foundation of Marcigny as evidence of a strong reform impulse on the part of Abbot Hugh. She cites two texts, both of which date to the period immediately before Hugh's death, over fifty years after the consecration of Marcigny, and finds in them a harsh criticism of female monasticism in the mid-eleventh century. Hugh wrote that before he founded Marcigny "si qua femina vita saeculari abrenuntiata Deo servire voluit, non sibi opportunum locum ad hoc facile inveniunt"; Hunt calls this "a very sweeping condemnation of the convents of the time." Similarly, Hunt interprets "Licet enim usque ad nostra tempora feminarum congregatio minine haberetur in hujus loci consortio" as the abbot stating "plainly that before the appearance of Marcigny convents were not highly esteemed." The first statement need not necessarily point to anything beyond a lack of a local monastery for women, and the second to a certain insouciance on the part of the Cluniacs. Subtlety was not a hallmark of reformers in this period, and it is difficult to imagine that Hugh would not have made a more direct criticism if he thought it important to do so. It is in any case dangerous to take Hugh's recollections of 1108 or 1109 as an unbiased account of what had happened fifty years earlier.

107. Wischermann, *Marcigny-sur-Loire*, 51–57, 302–303; see the genealogical table of the lords of Semur, 493.

108. Wischermann (ibid., 39–42) persuasively argues this point.

and Hugh were making a place for monastic women, their kin and others, in an area that lacked any such establishment, and like them, they placed the new communities under their protection.[109]

That the Hugh in question here was Abbot (later Saint) Hugh of Cluny is not, of course, unimportant. Aside from his immediate familial interests, Hugh was building on a tradition of concern for women on the part of the abbots that goes back to Cluny's beginnings. Odo, the second abbot of Cluny (926–942), as a novice monk helped a young woman impressed by Odo's vocation to escape from her parents, who had plans to marry her off. Odo first placed her in an oratory near his monastery and later took her to an unnamed nunnery.[110] Abbot Odilo, Hugh's immediate predecessor, participated in 1031 in the restoration of the abbey of Saint-André-le-Haut in Vienne, rebuilt (after its destruction by Saracens) by King Rudolf III and Queen Hermengarde of Burgundy. Odilo also arranged for his mother to take the veil.[111]

Some of the same concerns are apparent in the story of a nunnery founded in another isolated place, Auvergne.[112] A group of hermits around Robert of Turlande established in 1043 the settlement that soon became the abbey of Chaise-Dieu. Robert's disciples included women, but he did not want to found a house for them on the high and isolated plateau of Chaise-Dieu. By 1052, the new monastery received as donation a church and its village, Saint-André de Comps, about a day's journey from Chaise-Dieu and in a milder climate six hundred meters lower. A few years later, the house of Comps had become the first nunnery affiliated with Chaise-Dieu. The community, founded by a lord of nearby Lugeac, might have remained relatively poor and obscure but for a favoring coincidence. Count Raoul of Valois had built up a small principality in northern France through inheritance, conquest, and marriage.

109. Wischermann (ibid., 52–53) points out that Marcigny was bordered by the Loire and the lands of Geoffrey of Semur. She also goes so far as to claim that "Marcigny darf somit als Familienkloster bezeichnet werden" (303). GC 4: 1111 mentions a nunnery near Mâcon in the mid-tenth century, but it does not appear to have survived into the new millennium. Even had it still been an active community in 1055, it was over 50 kilometers across a hilly region from Mâcon to Semur.

110. The story, from John of Salerno's tenth-century biography of Odo, is told in PL 133: 59–60. See Skinner, "Benedictine Life," 101–102. The story is interesting in several ways, not least because the *oratorium* may well be another example of a nonregular religious community for women in the tenth century.

111. Wischermann, *Marcigny-sur-Loire*, 31–33 and notes.

112. For what follows, see Pierre-Roger Gaussin, "Les religieuses de la congrégation de la Chaise-Dieu," in *Les religieuses en France au XIIIe siècle*, ed. Michel Parisse (Nancy, 1985), 107–109 and Gaussin, *L'abbaye de la Chaise-Dieu (1043–1518)* (Paris, 1962), 329–330.

He repudiated his wife to marry the widow of King Henri I, Anne of Kiev, in 1061, and died excommunicate in 1074. Raoul's son and heir Simon was an entirely different type. Pressured by his family to make an advantageous marriage to Judith, daughter of Count Robert of Auvergne, Simon fled to a monastery far from home in the Jura. The principality his father had constructed subsequently dissolved. Judith similarly renounced the world and went to Comps, which was richly endowed by her father. The house now had a substantial patrimony.

In Hugh's founding of Marcigny, we may see the union of two old habits: a fostering of religious women by the abbots of Cluny, and the building of nunneries by powerful lords, often with the interests of their female relatives in mind, in locales distant from other monasteries for women.[113] Still, it would be difficult not to discern the first signs of a new era in the early history of Marcigny. Abbot Hugh was able to offer to Marcigny the reputation and wealth of Cluny, which both protected it and inspired women to join the first Cluniac nunnery. About one hundred women are known to have been nuns at Marcigny in the first forty years of its history; there were this many in the community at once in the time of Peter the Venerable (ca. 1156).[114] It would appear that the congregation at Marcigny was considerably larger than that of many of the other new foundations of the tenth and eleventh centuries, even those whose founders were men and women of greater stature and probably greater wealth than the family of the lords of Semur.

The early history of Comps similarly blends old and new. The place owed its temporal well-being to the generosity of a member of the high aristocracy. Yet its origins are not in religious expressions of the Western European elite. The impulse for foundation came from a group of women, like those to be found elsewhere, living a spiritual life outside the cloister. Also novel is the speed with which these women gained institutional identity in a monastic setting, unlike many of the *religiose femi-*

---

113. We should be careful not to find "reform" motives where they are not apparent and when other explanations are at hand; the foundation of Marcigny is a case in point. If self-conscious reform program had been the attraction, it seems likely that the prestige of Cluny would have attracted a large number of nunneries to the *ecclesia Cluniacensis* in the eleventh and twelfth centuries. In fact, only fifteen nunneries in Western Europe and Italy became affiliated with Cluny before 1200; see the list in Wischermann, *Marcigny-sur-Loire*, 503. Wischermann, nonetheless, insists that Marcigny was part of "reformerisch Absicht" (42) or "Reformbewegung" (303).

114. Wischermann, *Marcigny-sur-Loire*, 309–427, lists all the names to 1150. Peter the Venerable referred to a strain on resources owing to the presence of about a hundred nuns (288).

nae, Deo devotae, and *nunnan* of the tenth and eleventh centuries. Finally, the original donation of Comps came not from the high nobility, but from a modest local lord.

In their rapid early growth, contact with important ecclesiastical figures, and material basis owed to the gifts of an increasingly dynamic lower nobility, Marcigny and Comps were harbingers of the future. The traditions of the tenth and eleventh centuries, which might be viewed as the last phase of the early Middle Ages, were already before the dawn of the twelfth century being transformed in new circumstances—religious, social, economic, and political—that fostered a tremendous multiplication of nunneries starting about 1080. The early histories of Marcigny and Comps presage a new inclusiveness in monastic life that the next two chapters examine.

nunneries in an age of change, circa 1080–circa 1170

Ad hanc [ecclesiam] duae sanctimoniales flatu divinae pietatis inspiratae forte venierunt, altera quarum nominatur Godelindis et altera Heleguidis, quae considerantes opportunitatem loci servitium Deo exhibere inibi elegerunt. Denique laicalis potestas quae antea illam ecclesiam iniuste possiderat, timore Dei percussa, quietam et solutam assensu et concessione heredum suarum ipsam dimisit.

As it happened, two nuns, one named Godelinde, the other Helegunde, inspired by the soul of divine piety, came to this church. Considering the suitableness of the place, they chose to perform service to God there. Eventually the lay power which had previously possessed the church illicitly, stricken by fear of God, without dispute gave it up, with the assent and permission of his heirs.
— Charter of Bishop Gervinus of Amiens, 1095

historians of the Western Church in the central Middle Ages most frequently consider its evolution in terms of self-conscious and programmatic renewal: reform. "Gregorian Reform" is the label given to changes in the secular church, its institutions and people, from the mid-eleventh century, as exemplified by the efforts of Pope Gregory VII (1073–1085). Monasticism, too, has been closely tied to papal reform. The goals of the monks of Cluny and the eleventh-century papacy were consonant, and Cluniac leaders performed many practical services in support of the reforming popes.[1] Equally important is the relation of the Gregorians to the new monasticism of the eleventh and twelfth centuries, which stressed adherence to apostolic ideals through an austerely lived corporate life. Peter Damian, a vigorous propagandist for the reforming pa-

1. H. E. J. Cowdrey, *The Cluniacs and the Gregorian Reform* (Oxford, 1970), 151, calls the goals of monks and popes "basically compatible and complementary." On their collaboration, see 157–187.

pacy, also was committed to this vision of cenobitism, and the popes of the late eleventh and twelfth centuries held the new monasticism, as exemplified by the Cistercians, in high esteem.[2] The influence of the reforming orders of monks and canons on the papacy reached its height in the early and mid-twelfth century. From 1124 to 1159, men of the new orders sat on Saint Peter's throne for twenty-one years, and a Cistercian abbot was pope as Eugenius III from 1145 to 1153. The goals and processes of papal and monastic reform thus overlapped considerably, as mutually inspiriting and supportive projects.

The story of nunneries is another matter, at least according to historians who have considered the place of women in the Church during the Gregorian era. There is a widespread consensus that this age of reform was unfavorable to women, severely limiting their opportunities in the religious sphere. Historians with very different perspectives agree on this point. Some find an inferior quality of monastic life and inferior number of new foundations in the eleventh and twelfth centuries.[3] Another suggests that "one effect of the Gregorian reform was to diminish the possibilities of active female participation in formal religious organizations."[4] Still others concentrate on the subject position of women in the monastic orders of the age, one going so far as to claim that "the early Cistercians were remarkable for their hostility to women."[5] The overwhelming impression to be gained from most writings on the subject is that female

2. For a survey of these developments, see Lester K. Little, *Religious Poverty and the Profit Economy in the Middle Ages* (Ithaca, N.Y., 1978), 61–112.

3. Philibert Schmitz, *Histoire de l'ordre de Saint Benoît*, vol. 7: *Les moniales* (Maredsous, 1956), 76–77, cites the criticism of nunneries by Ivo of Chartres and Bernard of Clairvaux that eventually resulted in the expulsion of the women. Southern, *Western Society and the Church*, 310, states that "in the great period of monastic foundation from the early tenth to the early twelfth century the position of women in the monastic life suffered a sharp decline." Brenda Bolton finds that in the twelfth century nunneries were "exclusive and few in number" and that women of a religious bent were "catered for erratically in the twelfth century" (Bolton, "Mulieres Sanctae," 142, 143).

4. Janet L. Nelson, "Society, Theodicy, and the Origins of Medieval Heresy," *Studies in Church History* 9 (1972): 74. For similar statements, see Jane Tibbets Schulenburg, "Sexism and the Celestial Gynaeceum from 500 to 1200," *Journal of Medieval History* 4 (1978): 124, and David Herlihy, "Did Woman Have a Renaissance?: A Reconsideration," *Medievalia et Humanistica* n.s. 13 (1985): 8.

5. Sally Thompson, *Women Religious: The Founding of English Nunneries after the Norman Conquest* (Oxford, 1991), 94. It seems unlikely that such an unqualified statement will hold up under closer examination of the relationship of the order of Cîteaux to women and their religious communities. For a full study of religious women from the perspective of their participation in new monastic orders, see Fontette, *Les religieuses*. This approach is also used in the article "Women's Religious Orders" by Suzanne Fonay Wemple, *Dictionary of the Middle Ages* 12: 682–689.

monasticism suffered an important setback in the period of reform of the secular and regular church in the eleventh and twelfth centuries.[6]

A survey of women's monastic foundations in northwestern Europe, however, suggests otherwise. In the century that followed the election of Gregory VII, the number of nunneries in this part of Christendom sky-rocketed. There were approximately one hundred nunneries in 1070, but four times that many by 1170.[7] In contrast to the tenth and eleventh centuries, when a new nunnery was founded on average less than once a year, there were at least fifty new foundations in each of four decades from 1121 to 1160. Nor were most of these houses directly affiliated to the new, male-centered monastic orders: only one-quarter of all nunneries active in 1170 had any formal connection to these congregations. The striking expansion of female monasticism from the late eleventh to the late twelfth century was for the most part institutionally independent of the contemporaneous movements with which church historians are usually concerned.[8]

How did these new nunneries get their start? The story recounted by Bishop Gervinus of Amiens illustrates some central themes of this chapter. The foundation of Berteaucourt in an abandoned church in Gervinus's diocese, like that of many other houses, was a process carried out by several people. Godelinde and Helegunde, who began religious life in the church, were in one sense the founders of Berteaucourt. Credit also goes to the unnamed lord who ceded the church to them. The fledgling community owed a great deal to Gervinus, who confirmed the women's

6. Two recent works that eschew such characterizations are Sharon K. Elkins, *Holy Women of Twelfth-Century England* (Chapel Hill, N.C., 1988) and Johnson, *Equal in Monastic Profession*. It is probably not merely coincidental that both Elkins and Johnson devote little attention to juridical issues, instead concentrating on religious women and their lives in a more general and comprehensive fashion.

7. As in Chapter 2, such statistics are not merely cumulative totals, but also reflect the destruction or disappearance of nunneries, of which there were about a dozen cases between 1070 and 1170.

8. See Chapter 1 for detailed statistical breakdowns. To summarize: of the approximately 310 women's monastic communities founded between 1101 and 1175, nearly 140 were autonomous houses following the Benedictine or Augustinian Rules, and another 65 were affiliated with the female-centered orders of Fontevraud or Sempringham. As the new male-centered congregations (e.g., the monastic order of Cîteaux, the canonical orders of Prémontré and Arrouaise) had their beginnings no earlier than the very end of the eleventh century, all of the thirty or so nunneries founded between 1080 and the turn of the twelfth century were autonomous. Thus, nearly 70% of the new houses for women founded between 1080 and 1175 were institutionally independent of the movements that are considered to exemplify the evolution of monasticism in the post-Gregorian period. It is worth reemphasizing that the numbers given are conservative estimates meant not to exaggerate the multiplication of nunneries from the late eleventh century (see Appendix A).

right to the church, prescribed the Benedictine Rule, and took the community under the protection of the see. All of these people were, in significant ways, founders.[9]

It had always been true that the establishment of a monastery often was a cooperative effort, but there are important differences between the foundations in the period of restoration described in Chapter 2 and those which appeared after 1080. As the case of Berteaucourt suggests, more *kinds* of people than before took part in the founding of nunneries from circa 1080 to circa 1170. The participation of the nobility continued, but it was not only, or even often, members of royal or princely families who were the most visible patrons of the nunneries. The initiative of men and women of the lower nobility—to whose ranks the unnamed *laicalis potestas* of Berteaucourt as well as Godelinde and Helegunde probably belonged—were key instigators of the multiplication of nunneries. Without petty nobles and simple local lords, sometimes acting at considerable remove from the influence of the great princes, the growth of female monasticism at such a rate would indeed have been impossible. Gervinus and his fellow bishops, like their predecessors in the tenth and eleventh centuries, were central figures in the early histories of many women's houses. Last, charismatic preachers and hermits, heirs to men such as Robert of Chaise-Dieu, were highly visible from the late eleventh century. These men often were directly responsible for exciting the sort of enthusiasm for spiritual pursuits evident in the story of Godelinde and Helegunde.

Not all of these kinds of Christians participated in the foundation of every nunnery, of course. Different configurations of founders dominate in different regions. And although the number of convents grew everywhere from 1080 to 1170, a notable increase in the number of female monastic institutions was apparent earlier in some places than in others (Figure 6). The five sketches that follow are arranged both chronologically and geographically.[10] The survey begins with western France, for

9. As Sharon Elkins points out, monastic foundations were as much processes as events (Elkins, *Holy Women*, 175, n. 7). The foundation dates I have used throughout this book and in Appendix A necessarily reflect the appearance of evidence, usually a charter, rather than the beginnings of a community, which might be considerably earlier. Mine is more a study of institutions than religious practice. See V. H. Galbraith, "Monastic Foundation Charters of the Eleventh and Twelfth Centuries," *Cambridge Historical Journal* 4 (1934): 205–222, 296–298.

10. I give detailed accounts of the foundation of nunneries in only a few cases, and the footnotes are as a rule brief and on no account to be considered full or definitive. Wherever possible, I have cited sources whose entries include bibliography, such as DHGE or MB.

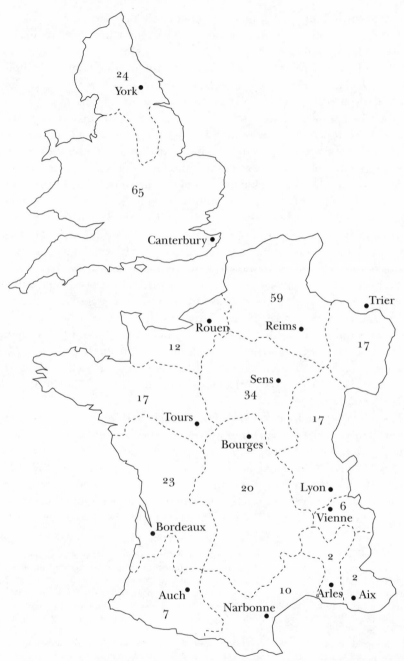

FIGURE 6. Nunneries founded or refounded, 1081–1170, by archdiocese

here the coordinated activities of hermits, petty nobles, and bishops brought about a rapid expansion of monastic life for women that was already discernible at the dawn of the twelfth century.

WESTERN FRANCE

Two new impulses characterized the spirituality of Western Christendom in the late eleventh century. The first was the call to the "desert," the urge to live a poor and simple life in solitude and isolation from a world that from the mid-eleventh century was becoming a more complex and populous place than before. The second was a zeal for preaching the gospel far and wide, both in fields near tiny hamlets and in the stone churches of larger towns. The two aspirations sometimes fused when the faithful sought out hermits, who in turn taught and preached to those who had joined them.

Such charismatic holiness attracted many women, not surprisingly, as the outlets for female religious enthusiasm were still relatively few in France and England around the turn of the twelfth century. Few, if any, of these hermits or preachers intended to found religious houses for their followers, male or female. Some of them had in fact rejected traditional monastic life, hoping to find a more intense religious experience elsewhere. Nonetheless, the roots of about 130 houses for women in France and England are to be found in the religious zeal first inspired by those who sought salvation for themselves and others across the countryside.[11]

The most coherent circle of preaching hermits was active in the great expanse of plain and gently rolling hills defined by the basins of the Loire in the north and the Garonne in the south, from Brittany to Gascony.[12] Many of the hermits of western France were associated with one of the oddest characters of the time. Robert of Arbrissel is best known for his foundation of Fontevraud, one of the largest and wealthiest monasteries for women in Europe. However, it was anything but inevitable that Robert became a monastic founder, for his path to Fontevraud was long and tortuous.

11. On hermits and their activities in general, see Henrietta Leyser, *Hermits and the New Monasticism: A Study of Religious Communities in Western Europe, 1000–1150* (London, 1984), with important bibliography.
12. The classic study of this group of evangelists is Johannes von Walter, *Die ersten Wanderprediger Frankreichs: Studien zur Geschichte des Mönchtums*, 2 vols. (Leipzig, 1903–1906). See also L. Raison and R. Niderst, "Le mouvement érémitique dans l'Ouest de la France (fin XIe–début XIIe siècles)," *Annales de Bretagne* 55 (1948): 1–46.

Robert was born around 1045 in a village thirty-five kilometers from Rennes in southeastern Brittany.[13] His father Damilioch was the aged priest of Arbrissel, his mother probably a peasant.[14] Captivated by the world of letters, as his biographer Baudry of Dol explained, Robert quickly exhausted local sources of education. He wandered restlessly in pursuit of study, eventually leaving his native land "like an exile and fugitive" (*tanquam exsul et fugitivus*) to study in Paris, where he seems to have stayed about ten years. In 1088 or 1089 Bishop Sylvester of Rennes summoned him home to serve the diocese; for four years Robert as archpriest worked to keep peace in the diocese, to free churches from lay control, to guard the sexual mores of clergy and laity, and to stamp out all sorts of sin, especially simony. His reforming efforts did not meet a wholly enthusiastic response, however. On his patron's death, Robert was victim of the hostility of his fellow priests and again left Brittany, this time for Angers. There he studied at the school headed by the poet Marbod, who was soon to succeed Sylvester as bishop of Rennes in 1096.

But by the time Marbod left Angers, Robert was no longer there. While studying, Robert had worn a hairshirt under his robes and eaten sparingly. After two years, he decided to give himself over to the eremitic life. In 1095 he departed Angers with a companion for the forest of Craon near his birthplace, renouncing the world, probably in particular the intrigues of schools and episcopal courts. Battling the weaknesses of

13. Two *vitae* of Robert written around the time of his death are printed in PL 162: 1043–1078. The first of these, by Baudry of Dol (1043–1058), offers the only information available on Robert's early life. The second, that of the monk Andreas (1057–1078), concentrates on Robert's last months. On these and other sources about Robert, see Walter, *Die ersten Wanderprediger Frankreichs* 1: 9–94. On Robert and the origins of Fontevraud, the most important modern work is that of Jean-Marc Bienvenu, "Les premiers temps de l'ordre de Fontevraud (1101–1189). Naissance et évolution d'un ordre religieux" (Thèse de doctorat d'Etat, Paris-Sorbonne, 1980). This monumental study remains unpublished, but Bienvenu has offered many of his conclusions in "Aux origines d'un ordre religieux: Robert d'Arbrissel et la fondation de Fontevraud," *Cahiers d'Histoire* 20 (1975): 227–251 and *L'étonnant fondateur de Fontevraud, Robert d'Arbrissel* (Paris, 1981). Another approach is that of Jacques Dalarun, "Robert d'Arbrissel et les femmes," *Annales* 39 (1984): 1140–1160, and *L'impossible sainteté: La vie retrouvée de Robert d'Arbrissel (v. 1045–1116), fondateur de Fontevraud* (Paris, 1985). In English, see Jacqueline Smith, "Robert of Arbrissel: *Procurator Mulierum*," in *Medieval Women*, ed. Derek Baker (Oxford, 1978), 175–184, and Penny Schine Gold, *The Lady and the Virgin: Image, Attitude, and Experience in Twelfth-Century France* (Chicago, 1985), 93–113. The following outline of Robert's early life derives primarily from Baudry's *vita* (the source of quotations) and its exposition by Bienvenu.

14. Just before he died, Robert noted that "Deus omnipotens ex quodam seniculo et ex quadam paupercula muliere eum nasci fecerit" (PL 162: 1077); see Bienvenu, *L'étonnant fondateur*, 17–19.

body and soul in search of spiritual perfection, Robert gathered around him a crowd of disciples. Although he treated them kindly, he was also tempted to withdraw from them, restrained only by the thought that such a flight might be sinful. Instead, he founded a congregation of regular canons, La Roë. When Pope Urban II was in Angers in 1096, he heard about Robert and summoned him. Robert spoke brilliantly before the pontiff and somewhat reluctantly accepted his pope's charge to preach. He did so, sometimes traveling and sometimes staying at La Roë, until 1098, when, with the permission of the bishop of Angers, he was freed from any obligation and left the canons in order to give himself over to preaching.

Just as Robert the hermit had drawn a crowd, so did Robert the evangelist. Wandering the countryside preaching, Robert acquired a mixed group of male and female followers. As before, he did not dare to push away those in search of God. Eventually he began to look for a place to settle his disciples. Baudry states that Robert wished to avoid the taint of scandal, which he probably had good reason to fear. His old teacher Marbod, now a bishop, wrote a blistering letter to Robert. Marbod thought that the preacher, dressed in skins and a tattered cloak, barefoot, with unkempt hair and beard, made a public spectacle who needed only a club to complete his lunatic's outfit.[15]

Far more worrisome, in the bishop's mind, was the close association with women. Worst of all were Robert's nocturnal arrangements: he slept among women, a fact confirmed a few years later in another critical letter, this one from Abbot Geoffrey of Vendôme.[16] "Syneisaktism" also was an ascetic practice of ancient Mediterranean and Celtic Christians, meant to mortify the flesh by requiring resistance of great temptation to sin.[17] The erudite prelates certainly understood the penitential goal of Robert's behavior, but Marbod nevertheless finished his letter by accusing Robert of having abandoned everything, including his community of

15. Walter, *Die ersten Wanderprediger,* 1: 186: "Quomodo igitur tibi abiecto habitu regulari, opertum ad carnem cilicio cum attrito pertusoque birro, seminudo crure, barba prolixa, capillis ad frontem circumcisis, nudipedem per vulgus incedere, et novum quidem spectaculum praebere videntibus, ut ad ornatum lunatici solam tibi iam clavam deesse loquantur."
16. PL 157: 181–184.
17. On the practice and its condemnation in the early Church, see Dyan Elliott, *Spiritual Marriage: Sexual Abstinence in Medieval Wedlock* (Princeton, 1993), 3, 32–38. Elliott suggests that Robert's actions aroused such a strong reaction because he was testing the very limits of gender division (111), an idea made even more plausible by Robert's desire to choose for the leadership of Fontevraud a Martha, rather than a Mary, who could lead like a man (*viriliter*) (PL 162: 1060). See Chapter 4.

canons, for the sake of these sisters.[18] Clearly Robert's message was particularly powerful for women.

So in 1101, Robert, now over fifty, who had been a student, a reforming diocesan official, a hermit, a leader of a community of canons, and finally an errant preacher, founded the monastery of Fontevraud for women and men. Others aided Robert in this venture. The land on which the house was built was the gift of two lay people who also must be considered founders of Fontevraud. Adelaide Rivière gave the "valley" of Fontevraud for the building of the monastery, with the approval of her lord, Gautier of Montsoreau, a vassal of the count of Anjou, who added his property at Les Loges, across the Loire to the north.[19] The site may well have been suggested by Bishop Peter II of Poitiers, in whose diocese it lay, near a parish personally controlled by the bishop. Certainly, Peter's protection was of critical importance in the early history of Fontevraud, whose possessions he confirmed in 1106, and in a charter of 1109, Robert refers to episcopal assistance in the foundation of the monastery.[20]

Adelaide made her donation "to lord Robert of Arbrissel and the community of religious women which he has gathered for God."[21] Bishop Peter's charter of 1106 states that Robert "gathered many women, whom he made nuns, so that they might live the regular life there."[22] Although there were both men and women at Fontevraud, it seems that women outnumbered men from the beginning. Robert did not wish to supervise the community and never became a monk or a su-

18. On women and ascetic practice, see Dominique Iogna-Prat, "La femme dans la perspective pénitentielle des ermites du Bas-Maine (fin XIe–début XIIe siècle)," *Revue d'histoire de la spiritualité* 53 (1977): 47–64. The interpretations of Jacques Dalarun (see note 13 above) owe a great deal to this article. Iogna-Prat thinks that both Marbod and Geoffrey found this practice to be novel and aberrant, but Marbod does not stress its oddity, focusing instead on the hazards of such cohabitation, to which the crying of babies testifies: "Quod quam periculose sit factum . . . vagitus infantium prodiderunt": Walter, *Die ersten Wanderprediger,* 1: 182.

19. See Bienvenu, *L'étonnant fondateur,* 78–84, and "Aux origines d'un ordre religieux," 238–239. The charters are partially edited in PL 162: 1104 and 1109–1110. On the sponsorship by the house of Anjou and of the Angevin nobility in general of Robert's checkered career, see W. Scott Jessee, "Robert d'Arbrissel: Aristocratic Patronage and the Question of Heresy," *Journal of Medieval History* 20 (1994): 221–235.

20. PL 162: 1089–1091 (Bishop Peter, 1106) and 1085–1087 (Robert, 1109). Robert notes that "tua, Petre pater reverende, cooperante solertia, in vestra diocesi in loco qui Fons Euvrandi vocatur, fundavimus" (1086).

21. Ibid., 1104: "domno Roberto de Arbrissello et conventui mulierum religiosarum quas pro Deo congregavit."

22. Ibid., 1090: "plures congregavit mulieres, quas sanctimoniales constituit, ut ibi regulariter viverent."

perior at Fontevraud. Only a few years after gathering the crowd, Robert returned to the apostolate. He continued his life of errant preaching, making frequent visits to Fontevraud and its daughter communities, until his death. He left two women in charge at Fontevraud. Hersende, the widowed mother-in-law of Gautier of Montsoreau, was assisted by Petronilla of Chemillé, a cousin of Abbot Geoffrey of Vendôme.[23] In 1115, after confirming the monks in their subjection to the sisters, Robert chose Petronilla as the first abbess, the superior of women and men at Fontevraud.

By the time Robert died in 1116, his original community of ascetics living in huts had been utterly transformed. Fontevraud was now a prosperous abbey, the head of a congregation of fifteen monasteries across western France, all of them female-centered religious houses of men and women. Starting about 1106, some properties given to Fontevraud were chosen as sites for new communities; other donations were given with this goal in mind. The mother house appears to have attracted more people than it could shelter, so Robert, as his second biographer Andreas explains, founded new houses that were first settled by experienced nuns and monks from Fontevraud.[24] As before, the efforts of local lords and bishops brought the new houses into being.

The first of these was Les Loges, north of the Loire in the diocese of Angers, on a property Gautier of Montsoreau gave to the fledgling community at Fontevraud.[25] The priory of Orsan, in Berry, was the product of a collaboration between Robert, Archbishop Leger of Bourges, and a local lord, Adelard of Châteaumeillant. Leger, impressed with Robert's personal qualities, wanted a Fontevrist establishment in his diocese. The choice of *villam Ursan* was likely owed in part to the fact that its lord Adelard was the former husband of Agnes, a nun of Fontevraud. Adelard made his donation to Leger in 1107, and several years later Adelard's overlords confirmed it to Robert.[26] Agnes was the first prioress of Orsan, and Robert died there in her presence and that of the archbishop.

---

23. Ibid., 1054; see Bienvenu, *L'étonnant fondateur*, 93–95.
24. PL 162: 1062–1063: "Robertus nonnulla habitacula in diversis provinciis, cooperante Deo, aedificaverat, in quibus sanctimonialium cohortes, divina religione in Fontevraldensi claustro probatas, juxta locorum competentiam includebat." Even if Baudry's figure of 2,000 to 3,000 men and women at Fontevraud during Robert's lifetime (1056) is greatly exaggerated, it is easy to see why new monasteries were needed.
25. Bienvenu, *L'étonnant fondateur*, 108–110.
26. PL 162: 1118, 1103. On the foundation of Orsan, see Dalarun, *L'impossible sainteté*, 164–169; on its history, see F. Deshoulières, "Le prieuré d'Orsan en Berri," *Mémoires de la société des antiquaires du Centre* 25 (1901): 51–138.

The process of founding a priory was not always simple, and in difficult cases the mediation of a bishop could be particularly important. Bishop Peter of Poitiers was the chief episcopal protector of Robert and his monasteries; a charter of Peter's from 1112 illustrates the complexities of one foundation. Robert found a ruined church in a deserted wood called Tusson and wanted to gather some nuns there. The lord of the place, one Fulcaudus Frenicardi, was eager to give it over to Robert and his followers, but Robert demanded the permission of Bishop Peter and his clergy. This granted, Robert ordered building to begin, but it was soon interrupted by a claim from the monks of nearby Nanteuil that the land and ruined church were theirs. Peter asked for documentation of this fact, but the monks could provide none, so he ordered the building to continue. Robert refused and asked for peaceful settlement of the issue. Peter and his retinue went along with Fulcaudus to Nanteuil, where the claim was retracted when Fulcaudus agreed to pay the monks an annual tribute in grain. Peter then proceeded to confirm the possession of Tusson to Robert and the nuns.[27]

Even after Robert's death in 1116, the number of priories continued to grow under the forceful leadership of the first abbess. By the time Petronilla of Chemillé died in 1149, there were nearly fifty daughter houses of Fontevraud. As in Robert's time, the sponsorship of bishops who wanted a Fontevrist house in their diocese was critical, a fact most evident in southwest France.[28] Here, particularly in Gascony, the number of monasteries welcoming women was still very small at the end of the eleventh century.

The most vigorous promoter of Fontevrist implantation was Archbishop William III of Auch (1126–1170). In 1140, the archbishop aided Longuebrune, the widow of Bernard I, count of Astarac, and her son Count Sanche II in the foundation of Boulaur, a few kilometers southeast of Auch. Longuebrune was the first prioress of the new monastery. About the same time William sponsored the foundation of the priory of Vaupillon on the lands of the local lord, Arnaud. The archbishop also participated, along with Count Bernard III of Armagnac and Count Licier of Partiac, in the establishment of the house of Le Brouilh.[29] These three

27. PL 162: 1093–1094.
28. Bienvenu, *L'étonnant fondateur*, 110–111, notes that bishops who wanted a Fontevrist priory often acted determinedly toward that end, citing the activities of the prelates of Orléans, Toulouse, and Lyon, as well as those of Leger of Bourges and Peter of Poitiers, in Robert's lifetime.
29. J. Edouard, *Fontevrault et ses monuments* (Paris, 1873–1874), 2: 253–256 (Boulaur), 276 (Vaupillon), 277 (le Brouilh).

priories of Fontevraud remained the only monastic communities for women in the diocese of Auch until the end of the Middle Ages.

Such was the renown of Fontevraud and its daughter houses that one southern bishop, eager to have a Fontevrist priory in his diocese, resorted to kidnapping. In the time of Bishop Aldebert of Agen, three brothers and their mother ceded to one Forto de Vic a piece of land along the Garonne just west of the city, apparently in the hope of founding a monastery there. Aldebert died in 1128 and was succeeded by a monk, Raymond-Bernard, into whose hands Forto de Vic donated his lands along the Garonne to Fontevraud. To this gift was added in 1130 more land in the same locale, donated by Amalvin of Paravis, his wife, and sons. Raymond-Bernard informed Abbess Petronilla of these donations and began building the monastery of Paravis. He needed only nuns of the order, and an occasion for getting them soon presented itself. Petronilla summoned a group of twenty nuns from the monastery of Bragayrac, in the diocese of Toulouse, to the mother house. While traveling down the Garonne, these women were detained by Bishop Raymond-Bernard, Forto, and Amalvin for their new monastery. The bishop proceeded to write somewhat apologetically to Petronilla, explaining that his actions were the product of his great respect for Fontevrist practice as well as Christian love and piety, and asking that the new monastery be a dependent house of Fontevraud. Unfortunately no reply from the determined abbess has been preserved; however, the monastery of Paravis became a member of the Fontevrist congregation.[30]

The rapid growth of Fontevraud and its daughter houses was the most spectacular development in the expansion of female monasticism in western France. By the late twelfth century, there were nearly seventy houses dependent on Fontevraud, most of them in the Loire and Garonne basins.[31] Still, these were not the only new foundations for nuns in western France. A number of communities for religious women independent of Fontevraud were founded in the late eleventh and twelfth

---

30. Joseph Barrère, *Histoire religieuse et monumentale du diocèse d'Agen* (Agen, 1855–1856), 1: 318–322.

31. Jean-Marc Bienvenu estimates that by 1200 there were about 130 Fontevrist communities in Western Europe, including 3 in Spain and 4 in England (*L'étonnant fondateur*, 109). Bienvenu's thèse d'Etat, "Les premiers temps de Fontevraud," 293–347, lists just over 100 houses, but the evidence for the existence of a number of these is very thin; in a number of cases Bienvenu simply assumes that a property did inevitably become the site of a Fontevrist community. My figure, which excludes the Spanish houses, is 68, with 4 more dating to the early thirteenth century.

centuries, but Robert of Arbrissel's example is evident in the origins of many.[32]

Two charters tell the story of the foundation in 1109 of a house for nuns not far from Craon and La Roë by a disciple of Robert.[33] "So it happened," reads one of them, "that a certain hermit named Salomon . . . prompted by divine inspiration came to Nyoiseau. And through the gift of the lords of that land, he made a place formerly given over to forest beasts and brigands into a glorious abode for the worship of Christ's poor and God's handmaidens in honor of God and the glorious Virgin Mary."[34] The lords were Gautier of Nyoiseau and his family, who donated the deserted land and rights to the Oudon River by which it lay. This action was corroborated three times, first by Bishop Marbod of Rennes, then by Gautier's overlord Fulk, the count of Anjou, and last by Bishop Raginald of Angers, who came and blessed the altar and received further endowment for the new community. Robert of Arbrissel was present when the bishop returned a year later and helped Salomon and Raginald to persuade one of Gautier's relatives to tear down a nearby castle, on the argument that it might cause harm to the new community.[35] Later on, Gautier and his wife entered into religion and then died on the same day at Nyoiseau, which appears to have been, at least in its early stages, a monastery for both men and women.[36] Like Fontevraud, it was ruled by an abbess, and as a bull of Pope Innocent II from 1141 shows, the community followed the Benedictine Rule.[37]

There were no Fontevrist priories in Robert of Arbrissel's native Brittany, but his influence is clear in the origins of the abbey of Saint-Sulpice-

---

32. On Robert's companions in the eremitic phase of his career, see Bienvenu, *L'étonnant fondateur*, 36–41.

33. BN, Collection Touraine et Anjou, vol. 5, folios 116r.–118v. (nos. 1288 and 1288bis). Each document tells of the series of events comprising the origin and early history of the monastery to ca. 1140.

34. Ibid., folio 117v. (no. 1288 bis): "Contigit autem ut quidam heremita nomine Salomon, divina inspiratione promotus . . . veniret Niosellum eumque locum feris sylvestribus et latronibus prius deditum dono illius terrae dominorum fecit in honore Dei et gloriosae virginis Mariae ad opus pauperum Christi et ancillarum Dei habitaculum gloriosum."

35. Ibid., folio 116v. (no. 1288): "videns Salomon magister illius loci quoddam castrum quod fecit Bernardus, in quo stabat Gauterius, fore nocivum ecclesiae, quaesivit per se et per domnum Robertum de Arbresello et per Raginaldum episcopum quomodo castrum illud destrueretur et praecipitaretur . . . quod ipsi [Bernardus et Gauterius] libentissime concesserunt et fecerunt."

36. Paul Marchegay in "L'abbaye de Nyoiseau," *Revue de l'Anjou et de Maine-et-Loire* 1st ser., 1, pt. 2 (1852): 83–84, thinks that the men at Nyoiseau were hermits, the women nuns, but that the male element eventually disappeared.

37. BN, Collection Touraine et Anjou, vol. 5, folios 26r.–27r. (no. 1653).

la-Forêt.[38] A native of a village near the border of Brittany and Maine, Raoul de la Futaye was a monk in Poitou before he joined Robert of Arbrissel in his errant evangelism, then struck out on his own in the dioceses of Le Mans and Rennes.[39] Like Robert, Raoul attracted a multitude of disciples, and he, too, chose to settle them in a monastery for men and women, just northeast of Rennes. Saint-Sulpice, founded about 1112, was, like Fontevraud, ruled by an abbess, and like Robert's foundation, came to be the head of a group of smaller monasteries similarly organized. By mid-century, there were about ten dependent houses of Saint-Sulpice, most of them in Brittany and Maine. The monastery of Locmaria, in Quimper, which dates to the eleventh century, was given by Bishop Robert of Quimper to Saint-Sulpice in 1124. About the same time, a house for women was established at Fontaine-Saint-Martin, southwest of Le Mans, on lands given by Count Fulk V and his wife Eremberge in 1117.[40]

Another hermit of Robert of Arbrissel's circle was Vitalis of Mortain, born in a town about twenty kilometers north of Raoul's native Futaye.[41] Vitalis, a nephew of William the Conqueror, lived for seventeen years in apostolic poverty at Dompierre, where his visitors included Robert. Vitalis is best known for his foundation of the male monastery of Savigny, which later joined the burgeoning Cistercian order, but he also persuaded his brother, Count William of Mortain, to found a house for nuns, Les Blanches, about 1105. Its first abbess was Adeline, sister of Vitalis and William. To the south and east, a hermit of less distinguished family, Alleaume, lived for a number of years in penitential solitude on the lands of Raoul, count of Beaumont-sur-Sarthe. But eventually men and women joined him, and in 1109 Count Raoul gave Alleaume more lands on which to build the Benedictine monastery of Etival-en-Charnie.

38. Pierre Anger, *Histoire de l'abbaye de Saint-Sulpice-la-Forêt* (Paris, 1920), based on his editions of the charters of Saint Sulpice: "Cartulaire de l'abbaye de Saint-Sulpice-la-Forêt," *Bulletin et mémoires de la société archéologique du département d'Ille-et-Vilaine* 34 (1905): 164–262; 35 (1906): 325–388; 37 (1907): 3–160; 38 (1908): 205–280; 39 (1909): 1–207; 40, pt. 1 (1910): 33–192; 40, pt. 2 (1910): 1–89.

39. P. Piolin, "Le moine Raoul et le bienheureux Raoul de la Fustaye," *Revue des questions historiques* 42 (1887): 497–509.

40. Arthur de la Borderie, "Chartes inédites de Locmaria de Quimper (1022–1336)," *Bulletin archéologique du Finistère* 24 (1897): 102–104 (on the donation of Locmaria to Saint-Sulpice and its confirmation in 1152); R. de Linière, "Le prieuré conventuel de la Fontaine-Saint-Martin," *Revue historique et archéologique du Maine* 58 (1905): 6–15.

41. Jaap van Moolenbroek, *Vital l'ermite, prédicateur itinérant, fondateur de l'abbaye normande de Savigny*, trans. Anne-Marie Nambot (Assen, 1990), is a full study of Vitalis and his activities, including the foundation of Les Blanches.

Again, family interest is apparent in the foundation, for Raoul's sister Godealde, formerly a nun at Ronceray in Angers, was the first abbess of Etival.[42]

In short, even though Nyoiseau, Saint-Sulpice, and Etival remained autonomous Benedictine houses, many nunneries founded in northwest France in the late eleventh and twelfth centuries had some connection to hermits.[43] A few southwestern French nunneries founded in the late eleventh and twelfth centuries did remain independent of Fontevraud, and indeed of the eremitic movement. The same Bishop Raymond-Bernard who had abducted Fontevrist nuns for a new priory in his diocese of Auch also founded a monastery for Benedictine nuns, Renaud, just outside the episcopal city. By 1150 the bishop of Comminges and local noble families had built the convent of Fabas, which community some years later founded the abbey of Oraison-Dieu in the diocese of Toulouse.[44] Although the number of new foundations was higher in the north, where hermits were more prominent, the map of female monasticism in the area between the Garonne and the Pyrenees changed most strikingly: where there had been no monastic houses for women at all in 1080, there were ten by 1170.

THE NORTHEAST

Even so, the density of foundations in another part of the Continental regions considered in this study was even higher than in western France. In Flanders, Artois, Picardy, Brabant, Hainault, Vermandois, and Lorraine, dozens of new monasteries for women appeared in the late eleventh and twelfth centuries. There, the growth of foundations comes in two relatively distinct phases. The first, reminiscent of the old pattern of aristocratic foundation described in Chapter 2, lasted from circa 1080 to circa 1120 and occurred primarily in Flanders, Brabant, and the extreme north of France. The second and more important stage, 1120–1150, had

42. DHGE 15: 1285. An edition of the foundation charter (from a vidimus of 1285) is printed in Paul Piolin, *Histoire de l'église du Mans* (Paris, 1851–1863), 3: 677–680.
43. Some such cases may have left insufficient documentation to be evident. The convent of Les Lochereaux in the diocese of Angers was founded about 1120 under unknown circumstances. However, a mid-twelfth-century pancarte containing 19 charters (ADML 251 H 14) records in 15 instances the presence as witness of one "Drogo eremita." Was Drogo a founder of this house?
44. Barrère, *Histoire religieuse et monumentale du diocèse d'Agen*, 1: 324–325 (Renaud); DHGE 16: 301 (Fabas).

more in common with contemporary activities in western France and was geographically more comprehensive.

The first phase began with the foundation of a Benedictine abbey in Artois. Gerard, bishop of Cambrai and Arras, built a community at Etrun, just to the east of Arras, circa 1085.[45] About fifteen years later a very grand establishment appeared further east. Bourbourg was the work of Clementia of Burgundy, the wife of Count Robert of Flanders. About the time Robert returned in triumph from the First Crusade, his countess founded a nunnery that she, Robert, and their successors richly endowed.[46] The widowed Clementia eventually retired to Bourbourg. Shortly before she died there in 1129, she founded another monastery for Benedictine nuns, Avesnes-lès-Baupaume, south of Arras.[47] The countess may also have had a hand in the foundation of Merckem, in southern Flanders. It was founded in the time of Bishop John of Thérouanne (1099–1130), most likely at the beginning of the twelfth century.[48] Shortly afterward, Count Manasses of Guînes founded a nunnery in his comital city, about 25 kilometers west and south of Bourbourg. This community came into being in 1117 with the aid of nuns from Etrun.[49] Well into the twelfth century, then, the pattern of monastic foundation for women in the northeastern part of the region under study remained that of an earlier period.

The beginning of a new era is symbolized by the foundation of a monastery in Vermandois, a community whose prehistory was not wholly unlike that of Fontevraud. The founder of Prémontré was Norbert of Xanten, born about 1080 in a Rhineland town.[50] Destined for the church by his noble parents, Norbert served in the courts of the archbishop of Cologne and Emperor Henry V. He was a member of the expedition to Rome in 1110–1111 that resulted in the temporary imprisonment of Pope Pascal II. In the spring of 1115, Norbert underwent a dramatic conversion after being thrown from his horse by a bolt of lightning. After three years of penitential life in a cell near his birthplace,

45. DHGE 15: 1292; GC 3: 419.
46. DHGE 10: 137–141. Many comital charters, the first of which dates to 1104, are printed in *Un cartulaire de l'abbaye de Notre-Dame de Bourbourg*, ed. Ignace de Coussemaker (Lille, 1891).
47. DHGE 5: 1099–1100.
48. MB 3: 284–285. The bishop's elogium in the annals of Saint-Bertin also mentions the establishment of Bourbourg and Guînes: *Cartulaire de l'abbaye de Saint-Bertin*, ed. Benjamin Guérard (Paris, 1840), 267.
49. DHGE 22: 1099.
50. On Norbert's early life, see François Petit, *Norbert et l'origine des Prémontrés* (Paris, 1981), 19–76.

Norbert was ordained a priest and tried unsuccessfully to reform the worldly existence of the chapter of canons at Xanten. Having met resistance from Rupert of Deutz, among others, for his preaching in the area, Norbert sold his worldly possessions, gave the money to the poor, and set off on a pilgrimage to Saint-Gilles in Languedoc. There, Pope Pascal's successor Gelasius II authorized his activities as an itinerant preacher. In 1119 he traveled in Brabant, Hainault, and northern France, spreading a message of poverty and devotion.

Like Robert of Arbrissel before him, Norbert gathered an entourage. With the advice and support of Pope Calixtus II and Bishop Bartholomew of Laon, Norbert established a religious community at Prémontré in 1120. The new monastery was open to men and women, canons and nuns, as well as lay brothers and sisters, a structure that was repeated as Prémontré quickly became the head of an order of religious communities.[51] The sources of Norbert's concern for the religious life of women are less clear (and were apparently expressed in a less provocative fashion) than those of Robert of Arbrissel. However, Herman of Laon, who knew Norbert personally and wrote the first extant account of him and his order sometime before 1151, stresses Norbert's ministry to women. Although at Cîteaux only men were received, wrote Herman, Norbert decreed that women should be taken into the religious life as well, leading a strictly cloistered existence. "So if lord Norbert had done nothing else (disregarding for the moment the conversion of men) but to attract so many women to divine service by his exhortation, would he not still be worthy of the highest praise?" asked Herman, who claimed that not since the time of the apostles had so many of both sexes become imitators of the perfect life.[52]

The order grew rapidly, especially at first in the region where Norbert had preached at the pope's behest in 1119 and 1120. In the next decades, dozens of Premonstratensian communities were founded in

51. Ibid., 135–139. See also the comments of Chrysogonus Waddell in *Dictionary of the Middle Ages* 10: 84–85. On the women of the order, see Erens, "Les soeurs dans l'ordre de Prémontré."

52. PL 156: 996–997: "Praeterea in Cistellensi coenobio soli viri suscipiuntur, domnus vero Norbertus cum sexu virili etiam femineum ad conversionem suscipi constituit, ita ut etiam arctiorem et districtiorem in ejus monasteriis videamus esse conversationem feminarum quam virorum. . . . Si ergo nihil aliud domnus Norbertus fecisset, sed, omissa conversione virorum, tot feminas servitio divino sua exhortatione attraxisset, nonne maxima laude dignus fuisset? Nunc vero cum utriusque sexus ejus doctrina tot millia Christo famulentur . . . nescio quid alii sentiant, mihi videtur verum esse, quod plurimi asserunt, a tempore apostolorum nullum fuisse qui tam brevi temporis spatio sua institutione tot perfectae vitae imitatores Christo acquisierit."

what are now northern France and Belgium. For the first twenty years of the order, all new houses were for men and women, the latter often outnumbering men.[53] Many of these communities were founded through the generosity of the lower aristocracy, and some of them also had an eremitic prehistory.

In 1117, the lord Walter of Jumigny founded a hermitage on his land near Soissons. In 1122, this community under Luke of Roucy, formerly dean of the cathedral at Laon, joined the new order of Prémontré. Irmengarde of Roucy, widow of Walter of Jumigny and probably Luke's sister, added a female element to the already existing male community and retired there. When she died in 1139 there were 40 nuns at Cuissy.[54] Far to the north, in western Flanders near Ghent, Iwanus, lord of Alost and Waas, founded the Premonstratensian house of Tronchiennes in 1136.[55] Further inland, in Brabant, a Premonstratensian community succeeded where others had failed. About 1110, Walter Berthout, lord of Grimbergen, founded a monastery for Augustinian canons. This community failed, and Walter soon after installed Benedictine monks at Grimbergen at the request of the bishop of Cambrai. The monks, too, disappeared, victims of banditry and poverty. Eventually Walter's heirs appealed to Norbert, who sent canons to restore the religious life there. Women, too, joined the newly configured community, which soon prospered and still exists today, the only surviving house founded by Saint Norbert.[56] On the border of Brabant and the Liegois, Count Arnold III of Looz, with the cooperation of other local lords, founded a monastery at Averbode around 1132.[57]

Despite Norbert's concern for religious women and the inclusion of women in the houses of his new order, the Premonstratensian mission, unlike that of Fontevraud, was not centered on the religious life for women. Here, it was the men who were at the center of the community and who often left the house to preach. The nuns, strictly cloistered, spent much of their time in the making, repair, and washing of clothing,

53. Petit, *Norbert et l'origine des Prémontrés*, 137–139; Norbert Backmund, *Geschichte des Prämonstratenserordens* (Grafenau, 1986), 30.

54. DHGE 13: 1097–1098 and MP 2: 495–496.

55. MB 7: 542.

56. DHGE 22: 269–272; MB 4: 725–726.

57. MB 4: 626–628. The greatest concentration of Premonstratensian communities was in the areas where Norbert preached most, but there also were a number of Premonstratensian settlements in Lorraine, an area already rich in establishments for monastic women, such as Pont-à-Mousson, founded by the duke of Lorraine, a friend of Norbert's (MP 3: 93) and St. Paul in Verdun, a Benedictine house turned over to the Premonstratensians at the request of Bishop Alberon in 1135 (MP 3: 111).

especially that of the lay brothers who worked the lands of the monastery. They also worked in the hostels for the poor, the sick and those traveling, but probably to a much more limited degree.[58] Not long after the death of Norbert (who had been since 1126 the archbishop of Magdeburg) in 1134, the General Chapter began a movement to separate the sisters from the male element in Premonstratensian communities. The importance of this decision will be addressed later; here it is necessary only to consider the fate of the sisters.[59]

In some cases, the order of the General Chapter was ignored for some time. Men and women remained together at Pont-à-Mousson, in Lorraine, until 1181. At Averbode, there appears to have been a plan to relocate the sisters at the end of the twelfth century, but no separation was effected until at least 1225. In other places, however, the transfer of the nuns came quickly. The nuns of Tronchiennes settled around 1138 at Peteghem, on the right bank of the Lys southwest of Ghent. From Peteghem came the first sisters of Serskamp, east of Ghent, who were established with the approval of the bishop of Cambrai in 1148. The generosity of Gerard of Wovertem in 1139 or 1140 made possible the relocation of the sisters of Grimbergen just a few kilometers to the north, in Nieuwenrode.[60] Even more often than the founding of the original Premonstratensian communities for men and women, the relocation of the nuns was primarily the work of the petty aristocracy. Although a large number of houses of Premonstratensian sisters had short histories, in 1150 there were still over forty houses for women in what are now western Belgium and northeastern France.[61]

Traditional nunneries following Benedictine or Augustinian practice continued to be founded, again most often by local lords and bishops between 1120 and 1150. For example, sometime between 1114 and 1130, Bishop Burchard of Cambrai donated a church to a house of Benedictine women, later known as Grand-Bigard, near Brussels. In 1133, Duke Geoffrey I of Brabant confirmed the nuns' possession of a once-deserted

58. Erens, "Les soeurs dans l'ordre de Prémontré," 13–15.

59. In my statistics for this order, I have counted a community of Premonstratensian nuns only once, despite the new foundation implied by separation from the men, so as not to exaggerate the number of new houses for women. For example, the sisters of Prémontré itself were transferred to three different locales in turn, but I have counted this group of nuns only once.

60. MP 3: 93 (Pont-à-Mousson); MB 4: 628 (Averbode); MB 7: 577–582 (Peteghem and Serskamp); MB 4: 851–852 (Nieuwenrode).

61. On the disappearance of these communities and the significance of the separation of women from men, see Chapter 5.

part of ducal property, noted that the house had prospered, and put it under the care of the Benedictine male abbey of Afflighem. The house considered as its founder Saint Wivine, whose life and miracles are told in a *vita* written about 1200.[62]

In France, the counts of Ponthieu founded a Benedictine house for women at Doullens at the beginning of the twelfth century. Here the density of settlement of new monasteries for women is striking: Doullens was less than twenty kilometers from Berteaucourt, whose foundation only a few years earlier was recounted by Bishop Gervinus of Amiens. An episcopal charter of 1138 shows that the nuns of Doullens owned lands and tithes in the area.[63] Ranier, lord of Fonsomme and seneschal of Vermandois, and his wife Elizabeth founded about 1140 the monastery of Fervacques, situated by the source of the Somme. Their daughter Ermengarde was the first superior of the new house.[64] Felicity of Brienne and her husband Simon of Broyes founded a Benedictine house at Andecy, west of Châlons-sur-Marne, shortly before 1131, when Simon fixed the limits of the domain he granted to the nuns.[65] Last, even in Lorraine, which in the late eleventh century already was richer in monastic houses for women than any other region in the purview of this study, new Premonstratensian houses did not satisfy all needs. In the forest of Darney, in the southern reaches of Lorraine a few kilometers from the source of the Saône, the local lord Aubert with his wife and son founded the nunnery of Droiteval about 1128. Other local seigneurs and religious houses joined Aubert and his family in endowing the new community.[66]

CENTRAL FRANCE, NORMANDY TO PROVENCE

Just as in the northeast, the prevailing pattern of monastic foundation elsewhere repeated itself regardless of institutional identifications or membership in monastic orders. There was in the French heartland no religious movement so important for women as the expansion of Fontevraud in the west or Prémontré in the northeast. In the vast tract that stretches from Burgundy toward the northwest across Champagne,

---

62. For details, see DHGE 21: 1083–1084 and MB 4: 221–223.
63. DHGE 14: 744–745 for Doullens; see the beginning of this chapter for Berteaucourt.
64. DHGE 16: 1309–1312. The foundation charter, witnessed by three abbots, is printed in GC 10: 378.
65. DHGE 2: 1556–1557.
66. DHGE 14: 803–805.

the Orléanais, and Ile-de-France to Normandy, and southward to the Mediterranean through the Massif Central and Languedoc in the west, the Dauphiné and Provence in the east, the activities of hermits and preachers had a far less profound impact.

Still, in this region (roughly the Seine basin in the north and the lands to each side of the Saône and Rhône in the south) over one hundred nunneries were founded between 1080 and 1170. The density of new foundations was somewhat greater in the Seine basin than in the Midi, not surprisingly given the more fertile soils and higher population in the north. The bulk of new foundations across this whole region took place slightly later than in the regions already surveyed. Of all foundations between 1080 and 1170, three-quarters appeared in the second half of the period, in both north and south. On the whole, however, the founding activities of bishops and local lords in central France resemble those elsewhere.

Although hermits and preachers were less active in this region than in others, Fontevrist and Premonstratensian foundations were spread thinly across it. Again, some houses that included women had long prehistories. In the tenth century, there appears to have been a Benedictine nunnery at Aubeterre, in the diocese of Clermont, that later came under the aegis of Cluny. But the monastery was in ruins by 1150, when a knight named Gilbert, who had founded a house for Premonstratensian canons a few kilometers distant, placed a new community of sisters there under the leadership of his wife and daughter.[67] In 1140, Hugh IV of Gournay and his wife Melisande founded a house of Fontevraud at Clairruissel, in the diocese of Rouen.[68] At the eastern reaches of Normandy, not far from Beauvais, around 1122 a disciple of Saint Norbert named Ulric established a house of canons and nuns on lands given by Ansculf of Senooz. When the canons relocated in the 1140s, the place became known as Beaumont-les-Nonnains.[69]

Premonstratensian settlement was very light and there were no Fontevrist houses at all in Burgundy and Champagne, the cradle of the most important new monastic congregation of all: the order of Cîteaux.[70] Easily the most successful of the new orders, the Cistercians were distinguished by their austerity and strict adherence to the ancient Benedic-

67. MP 3: 142–143; DHGE 5: 244.
68. Bienvenu, "Les premiers temps de Fontevraud," 340.
69. MP 2: 547, 566.
70. The literature on Cîteaux and the Cistercians is immense. A standard account in English is Louis J. Lekai, *The Cistercians: Ideals and Reality* (Kent, Ohio, 1977).

tine Rule. Their order began with the foundation of Cîteaux in 1098 and grew most significantly in France and England in the years 1120–1160—also the high point of female monastic expansion.[71] The Cistercians were from the beginning a male order, but women's houses started being affiliated to the order around 1125. Although the precise juridical relationship of these nunneries to Cîteaux is not entirely clear, it seems evident enough that some religious women were inspired to follow the customs of the Cistercians, and their houses were regarded as belonging, in some sense, to the order.[72]

Whatever the precise status of these Cistercian nunneries, they were relatively few in Europe before the late twelfth century. About forty-five Cistercian nunneries appeared in France and England before 1170, nearly all of them in the central French regions.[73] Not surprisingly, there were a number in Burgundy and southern Champagne, but Cistercian houses also appeared to the north in Normandy and to the south in Savoy and the Dauphiné, in isolated parts of the Massif Central, and in Languedoc and southeastern Gascony. The first Cistercian house for women was Tart l'Abbaye, located only about thirteen kilometers northeast of Cîteaux. A community of nuns under Elizabeth of Vergy, widow of Thierry III of Mailly, appears to have existed before the donation of a piece of land called Tart between 1120 and 1125. An early pancarte of five donations shows that the foundation of the monastery was a cooperative effort of two successive bishops of Langres, the cathedral chapter, Stephen Harding, second abbot of Cîteaux, Duke Hugh of Burgundy, and the local nobility. It appears that Bishop Josserand of Langres, Abbot

71. For a more detailed comparison of the growth of male and female monasticism, see the Epilogue.

72. For an examination of mostly juridical issues, see Sally Thompson, "The Problem of the Cistercian Nuns in the Twelfth and Early Thirteenth Centuries," in *Medieval Women*, ed. Derek Baker (Oxford, 1978), 227–252. A different approach is made by Constance Berman in two articles, "Fashions in Monastic Patronage: The Popularity of Supporting Cistercian Abbeys for Women in Thirteenth-Century Northern France," *Proceedings of the Annual Meeting of the Western Society for French History* 17 (1990): 36–45, esp. 36–37, and "Men's Houses, Women's Houses: The Relationship between the Sexes in Twelfth-Century Monasticism," *Medieval Studies at Minnesota* 2 (1988): 43–52, with extremely helpful footnotes. Berman argues cogently that most historians of the Cistercians have gone to great lengths to suppress or deny the early recognition of women's houses in the order, but that there is abundant evidence to the contrary. She is at work on a full-length study of Cistercian women. See also the series [Jean de la Croix Bouton, ed.], *Les moniales cisterciennes* (Valence, 1986–), the first volume of which treats the early history of Cistercian nuns.

73. Exact figures are deceptive, as some houses were affiliated to Cîteaux well after their foundation. For example, Vitalis of Savigny's nunnery of Les Blanches joined the order when the small congregation of Savigny joined the Cistercians in 1147.

Stephen, and Elizabeth of Vergy, a great benefactor of Cîteaux, and mother of Elizabeth, the first abbess of Tart, decided to found a Cistercian community for women. Arnoul, the son of the elder Elizabeth, gave with the permission of the chapter of Langres and in the presence of Abbot Stephen, the land at Tart to settle the fledgling community.[74] Aside from the Cistercian connection, then, the beginnings of Tart, with its prehistory of women seeking a religious life and the cooperation of a number of people in the establishment of a regular life, were little different from dozens of other foundations in this period.

The stories of most other foundations for Cistercian nuns are similar. Three have already been mentioned: the houses of Fabas and Oraison-Dieu in Gascony and that of Droiteval in southern Lorraine (not far from the Cistercian heartland). In Normandy, the same Hugh of Gournay who endowed the Fontevrist house of Clairruissel founded the Cistercian house of Bival sometime between 1128 and 1154.[75] Some nuns of Bival settled a new house at Bondeville, near Rouen.[76] There were several foundations for Cistercian nuns in a region that had few other houses for women, Dauphiné. The first of these, Les Ayes, in the diocese of Grenoble, was founded in 1142 by Marguerite of Burgundy, wife of Guy IV of Viennois.[77]

Still, in north and south, autonomous Benedictine communities continued to dominate. The fact is most striking from Burgundy northward. Even in the dioceses surrounding Cîteaux, more than half of all new nunneries founded from 1110 to 1170 remained unaffiliated to it or any other monastic congregation. Rather than detail the origins of Benedictine houses from the Mediterranean to the English Channel, which follow a pattern already familiar, it seems best to call attention to two exceptional developments.

First, a cluster of monasteries founded in Champagne and in the Ile de France had close ties to two very powerful families: the house of Blois and Champagne and the royal Capetians. In 1102, young Count Thibaud[78] gave a chapel near Troyes to a group of religious women. This was the beginning of the house of Foissy, which received donations from local lords and remained under the protection of Thibaud and later of

74. Jean de la Croix Bouton, Benoît Chauvin, and Elisabeth Grosjean, "L'abbaye de Tart et ses filiales au moyen âge," in *Mélanges Anselme Dimier,* ed. Benoît Chauvin (Arbois, 1984), 3: 21–23.
75. DHGE 9: 37.
76. DHGE 9: 824.
77. DHGE 23: 655–656.
78. II of Champagne from 1125, IV of Blois.

Count Henry the Liberal, who added to his father's gifts to the nuns of Foissy.[79] The community of Fontaines-les-Nonnes was established in the 1120s in a chapel given to the bishop of nearby Meaux, with Thibaud's approval, and this community, too, was further endowed by his son Henry, first in 1156 and again thirty years later.[80] Henry himself founded Champbenoît, a Benedictine abbey for women, near Provins, roughly halfway between his father's foundations of Foissy and Fontaines.[81] Shortly after Thibaud's death in 1152, his widow Mathilda purchased lands to build the Benedictine nunnery of La Pommeraie, with the cooperation of Count Henry and his brothers Thibaud and Stephen.[82]

The first of two Capetian foundations for nuns was in 1112. In that year, King Louis VI, in concert with the brothers Amaury and Simon of Montfort, settled on a site some thirty-five kilometers southwest of Paris for a new Fontevrist house. This nunnery was on lands that had been part of the dowry of Amaury and Simon's sister, and Louis's stepmother, Bertrade. Bertrade, whose marriage to Louis's father Philip I had been the subject of scandal and ecclesiastical condemnation, became a nun at Fontevraud after Philip's death in 1108. With Louis's help, conventual buildings were ready by 1113, and shortly thereafter Bertrade herself joined the community at Hautes-Bruyères, where she remained until her death.[83] Twenty years later, Louis VI, with his queen Adela and their son, founded the house of Montmartre and generously endowed it with lands, settlements, and tithes from the area around Paris. Louis VII continued his father's stewardship, which was in turn continued by his son Philip Augustus.[84] The charming abbey church consecrated by Pope Eugenius III in 1147 still stands, now in the shadow of the basilica of the Sacre-Coeur, in the 18th arrondissement of Paris.

79. DHGE 17: 726–729.
80. DHGE 17: 854–858.
81. DHGE 12: 343.
82. The foundation charter is edited in *Cartulaire général de l'Yonne*, ed. Maximilien Quantin (Auxerre, 1854), 1: 493–494. The land was purchased from Heloise, abbess of the Paraclete, and La Pommeraie remained under the supervision of the abbess of the Paraclete. On Heloise, see Chapter 4.
83. On the foundation, see Achille Luchaire, *Louis VI le Gros* (Paris, 1890), 79–80. The uproar over the marriage of Philip, who had repudiated his wife Bertha, a Frisian princess, for Bertrade, the wife of Count Fulk IV of Anjou, is a centerpiece of the discussion of Georges Duby, *The Knight, the Lady, and the Priest: The Making of Modern Marriage in Medieval France*, trans. Barbara Bray (New York, 1983).
84. *Recueil des chartes de l'abbaye royale de Montmartre*, ed. Edouard de Barthélemy (Paris, 1883). The foundation charter of Louis and Adela is at 60–63; for other twelfth-century royal charters, see 63–66, 70–71, 75–76, 78, 85–87, 89–97, 104–105, 109–110 (Louis VII); 113–114, 126–128 (Philip Augustus).

Last, the diocese of Auxerre was the site of a transformation that reversed the usual pattern of the tenth and eleventh centuries. According to legend, a monastery for men called Crisenon was founded by Adela, daughter of King Robert the Pious, in the early eleventh century. There certainly was a community of monks at Crisenon in the early twelfth century after Hugh and Nargoud of Toucy gave to the abbot of Molesme enough lands to build a dependent monastery. In 1134, however, the bishop of Auxerre, the abbot of Molesme, and the count of Nevers met at Crisenon and decided that the site and its appurtenances would henceforth belong to a group of nuns who had come from the nearby convent of Jully and settled at Crisenon and that the abbot of Molesme would provide for the care of souls there. A monastery destined for men was thus turned over to religious women and became a prosperous abbey in the course of the twelfth century.[85]

ENGLAND

The story of female monasticism in England has much in common with that in the Continental realms already surveyed. A glance at the English case thus serves as a summary of the arguments of this chapter. Once again, the primary actors are hermits, preachers, bishops, and the lower nobility, that is those of less than royal or baronial status. Two phases may be discerned. The first, largely confined to southern England, began in the late eleventh century and lasted until late in the reign of Henry I (1100–1135). Hermits and bishops were the prominent figures in this period, one of experimentation and transition from early medieval aristocratic patronage patterns. A new era was at hand with the foundation in Lincolnshire of a shelter for religious women by Gilbert of Sempringham and subsequent foundations under his direction. But these were by no means the only new English women's houses, whose number more than quintupled from 1130 to 1170. A vast majority of new houses were founded by lesser or minor nobles, and most of them remained independent of the Gilbertines and the new Continental orders.[86]

85. For early charters of Crisenon, see *Cartulaire général de l'Yonne* 1: 201–202, 301–302; 2: 54–55. There survives also a cartulary of over 250 twelfth- and thirteenth-century documents, showing how wealthy Crisenon became (BN ms. latin 9885).

86. In this section I rely primarily on three recent studies: Janet E. Burton, *The Yorkshire Nunneries in the Twelfth and Thirteenth Centuries* (York, 1979), Elkins, *Holy Women*, and Thompson, *Women Religious*. Burton and Thompson are particularly good in matters of fact, Elkins in those of interpretation. None of these studies sees the same kind of consonances between English and Continental developments I do; Thompson organizes her material

The Domesday Survey of 1086 listed only eight monasteries for women, all of them southern Anglo-Saxon foundations.[87] Wilton had some renown in the late eleventh century as a center of learning, but the relative poverty of these houses suggests that they were unable to support large congregations: the richest was Wilton, with an income of £246, but only three others had incomes above £100. Chatteris took in only £20, less than one-fortieth the income of Glastonbury, the richest monastery in England at £827.[88] Sometime before 1086, the nuns of Polesworth had been expelled by a layman. A few of them settled at the manor of Oldbury, a property of the abbey, but their income was too small to warrant any notice in the Domesday Survey.[89] Other houses may have been less prosperous than at the time of the Conquest two decades earlier, because they had lost the patronage of Anglo-Saxon royalty and nobility.

The eremitic urge came upon at least one nun from these financially beleaguered (and perhaps also spiritually weakened) convents. Eve, who as a seven-year-old had been received at Wilton, left the abbey and England about 1080 in search of holy solitude. She lived for about twenty years in a cell near Angers, in a neighborhood with other male and female hermits. Around the turn of the twelfth century, she moved again and spent many years in the company of a hermit named Hervey, who had also left his monastery to search for a more perfect life. Eve died shortly before 1125 and was eulogized by the poet Hilary for her rigorous devotion to God.[90]

The paucity of cenobitic outlets for women's spirituality did not escape the notice of bishops, who were the only active founders of nunneries in the early Anglo-Norman era.[91] The first of these was Gundulf, bishop of Rochester, who founded the house of Malling on episcopal

according to Continental monastic orders but does not include a separate section on the native English Gilbertines. Two important books appeared too late for me to use them: Brian Golding, *Gilbert of Sempringham and the Gilbertine Order, c. 1130–c. 1300* (Oxford, 1995), and Roberta Gilchrist, *Contemplation and Action: The Other Monasticism* (London, 1995), which includes a chapter on religious women.

87. The convent at Reading had been destroyed in the early eleventh century, and the nuns of Chichester dispersed shortly after 1066.

88. The figures are cited in Knowles, *The Monastic Order in England,* 702–703. It is noteworthy that the abbey of La Trinité in Caen had an income of £107 in England, and it was not a particularly populous place; see Chapter 2.

89. Elkins, *Holy Women,* 13.

90. This account of Eve derives from Elkins, *Holy Women,* 21–27. See also Therese Latzke, "Robert von Arbrissel, Ermengard und Eva," *Mittellateinisches Jahrbuch* 19 (1984): 116–154.

91. Elkins, *Holy Women,* 13–18; Thompson, *Women Religious,* 191–192, notes that only in this early period were nunneries in fact founded by bishops.

property around 1095. Gundulf, whose mother had earlier become a nun at Caen, endowed the community with buildings and additional income. He personally cared for the spiritual and material needs of the house, not appointing an abbess until 1106, two years before his death.[92] Archbishop Anselm of Canterbury began a house of nuns in the former parish church of Saint Sepulchre in the archepiscopal town. A friend of Anselm, Bishop William Giffard of Winchester (1107–1129), founded the monastery of Ivinghoe in Hertfordshire on episcopal lands.[93] Archbishop Thurstan of York, who had encouraged William the Conqueror's daughter Adela to take the veil at Marcigny, established the house of Clementhorpe in the archepiscopal city between 1125 and 1133, endowing it with episcopal lands in six different locales.[94]

By the early twelfth century, there were more female hermits in England, and the tendency from greater to lesser regularization evident in the story of Eve was being reversed. The most famous of these eremitic women was Christina of Markyate.[95] Christina's experience suggests the kinds of difficulties faced by Englishwomen who wanted to live a religious life but had few options and often saw their aspirations thwarted. As a youth, Christina had been inspired by the atmosphere of Saint Albans abbey and made a pledge of virginity. When Christina was seventeen, Bishop Ranulf Flambard tried first to seduce, then to rape her. She escaped, but the bishop, with the collusion of Christina's parents, forced her into a betrothal. Her parents tried alcohol, love potions, and physical violence to get her to consummate the betrothal. Christina, disguised as a man, fled her parents' home on horseback. She hid for six years and lived as a hermit, first with the anchoress Aelfwyn at Flamstead, then with a hermit named Roger at Markyate. Roger protected her from her bishop, Robert Bloet of Lincoln, who favored Christina's parents. After Roger's death, she came under the protection of Archbishop Thurstan of York, who found her another hiding place where her purity was again severely tested, this time by the lustful advances of the cleric Thurstan had appointed to protect her. After Robert Bloet's death in 1123, Christina was able to return to Markyate, where she lived with other women and developed a close friendship with Abbot Geoffrey of Saint Albans. Christina re-

92. Thompson, *Women Religious*, 192–193; Elkins, *Holy Women*, 15.
93. Elkins, *Holy Women*, 15–16, which also notes the foundation of Stratford at Bow by a bishop of London.
94. Burton, *The Yorkshire Nunneries*, 6.
95. *The Life of Christina of Markyate: A Twelfth-Century Recluse*, ed. and trans. C. H. Talbot, rev. ed. (Oxford, 1987) is the major source for Christina's life. I have used this account and the summaries provided by Elkins and Thompson.

fused to join Marcigny or Fontevraud or to become the head of Archbishop Thurstan's foundation in York. Eventually Abbot Geoffrey helped her to obtain title to Markyate, where a church was consecrated in 1145. Markyate, once a hermitage, had become a Benedictine convent.

A number of other English communities of female hermits were eventually transformed into monastic houses, often with the cooperation of bishops. A hermit named Godwyn was the leader of three women at his settlement of Kilburn in Middlesex; after Godwyn's death around 1130, the place became a convent with the cooperation of the abbot of Westminster.[96] Blithbury and Farewell, two nunneries in Staffordshire, appear to have originated in eremitical communities of men and women. The transformation of Farewell from hermitage to nunnery seems to have been largely the work of Bishop Roger de Clinton (1129–1148), who also may have established the nearby nunnery of Brewood Black Ladies.[97] Flamstead, where Christina had first lived the eremitic life, was by the mid-twelfth century a cloister of women who were probably the successors or disciples of Aelfwyn.[98]

There seem to have been more female hermits in England than on the Continent, yet the most notable development in English monasticism in the twelfth century is reminiscent of the attraction of women to the religious life inspired by men such as Robert of Arbrissel and Norbert of Xanten. Gilbert of Sempringham was born around 1089, the son of lesser nobles in Lincolnshire.[99] He was educated first in England, then on the Continent, returning to be a teacher in his native country. He became a member of the household of Christina of Markyate's adversary Bishop Robert Bloet and remained under Robert's successor Alexander (1123–1148). Alexander ordained Gilbert and offered him an archdiaconate. But Gilbert felt a strong pastoral calling and left the episcopal court to return as priest to Sempringham. He at first wanted to found a monastery for men, but he found no one desirous of submitting to a strict life. Meanwhile, his preaching did inspire some women. In 1131 Gilbert built alongside his parish church an enclosure for seven women who wished to lead a religious life. Gilbert proceeded to augment the community with lay sisters and soon after, lay brothers. About 1139 the

96. Thompson, *Women Religious*, 25–26.
97. Ibid., 195–197.
98. Elkins, *Holy Women*, 73.
99. *The Book of Saint Gilbert*, ed. Raymonde Foreville and Gillian Keir (Oxford, 1987), contains a full edition of the *vita*, miracles, and canonization documents of Gilbert as collected at the beginning of the thirteenth century. The account that follows is based on the *vita* and the introduction to this edition. See now Golding, *Gilbert of Sempringham*.

community was moved to its own compound on lands given by Walter de Gant, lord of Folkingham, and donors and vocations abounded at Sempringham and at nearby Haverholme, founded by Bishop Alexander about the same time. In 1147, Gilbert went to the General Chapter of the Order of Cîteaux to ask that his foundations be attached to that congregation. His request was denied, and Pope Eugenius III, himself a Cistercian, conferred on Gilbert, who was neither monk nor canon, the care of his flock. On returning to England, Gilbert decided to add a fourth element, that of regular canons, for spiritual direction. Thus an order of Benedictine nuns and Augustinian canons was established, much like the mixed communities of Fontevraud.

The order grew rapidly in the last years of the reign of King Stephen. Between 1148 and 1154, seven new Gilbertine houses for nuns and canons were founded, five in Lincolnshire, one in Bedfordshire, and one in East Yorkshire. The founders of these houses were all members of the lower nobility from which Gilbert arose. His brother Roger founded the house of Alvingham. To the north, Eustace fitzJohn founded the Gilbertine house of Watton in atonement for having fought with King David of Scotland at the Battle of the Standard in 1138.[100]

The Gilbertine communities were of considerable size from an early date, and by the late twelfth century each house was assigned a maximum population. The smallest foundation, Catley, was limited to 60 women and 35 men, the largest, Watton, 150 women and 70 men: in all, a total of over 900 women and 500 men.[101] These figures include lay sisters and brothers as well as nuns and canons, but it seems likely that at least several hundred nuns were distributed among ten Gilbertine monasteries by the later twelfth century.[102] It also is evident that, as in the Fontevrist houses, women outnumbered men. Charters of donation give alms to the nuns and the brothers, in that order.[103] Although the Gilbertine canons were not subject to an abbess, as were those of Fontevraud, Gilbert's initial discovery that there was a greater need of new outlets for female spirituality than of monasteries for men was borne out in the development of his order.

---

100. For these houses and others, see *The Book of Saint Gilbert*, xxx–xxxii, as well as Elkins, *Holy Women*, 81–84, and Thompson, *Women Religious*.
101. *The Book of Saint Gilbert*, xxxii–xxxiv. It is not known what proportion of men or women were the religious. But limits may often have been exceeded: there were 200 women at Watton in 1247.
102. Ibid., xxxiii, suggests that these figures are probably smaller than the actual numbers in Gilbertine houses.
103. Ibid., li–lii.

Gilbertine houses were by no means the only new nunneries founded in England in this era, and in fact the pace of foundations generally peaked in the 1140s and 1150s, echoing throughout England the peak of Gilbertine foundations centered in Lincolnshire. Excluding the Gilbertines, there were some seventy new foundations for nuns in England between 1130 and 1170. By the time of Becket's martyrdom, there were approximately one hundred houses for religious women, a fivefold growth in the space of one generation. What follows are a few general observations.[104]

First, the expansion was general across England, with new foundations appearing everywhere except the western reaches of Yorkshire and Cornwall. Multiplication was most impressive in the North, where there had been in the early 1130s only Archbishop Thurstan's foundation at York and the house of Holystone in Northumberland.[105] For the next thirty-five years, a new nunnery was founded north of the Welland River on average more than once a year.[106] But nearly as many new houses were founded south of the Trent, an area already richer in monasteries for women, of Anglo-Saxon or more recent origin. As on the Continent, most of these houses followed the Benedictine or Augustinian rule and remained unaffiliated to any monastic congregation. There were three Premonstratensian and three Fontevrist houses, and nearly a dozen others, most of them in the north, that adhered to Cistercian practice.[107] Still, two-thirds of the new English nunneries were autonomous.

Finally, the lower nobility was the dominant force in foundations. Again, this is even more apparent in the north, where only one house had a baronial founder.[108] A few examples will suffice. Sometime before 1153, Hugh, lord of Hatton and Wroxhall, and his wife Margaret founded the Benedictine house of Wroxhall in Warwickshire, where

104. Sharon Elkins sees a distinctive era between 1130 and 1165. Slight discrepancy in dates notwithstanding, I almost entirely agree with her description of this period in *Holy Women*, 43–101. I differ on only one important point: she finds the aid of male religious more significant than I do. Some of the houses she notes as being founded with the help of monks are really the result of the regularization of an eremitic community often situated on the lands of a layman, as noted above. Thus I would accent even more strongly than Elkins does the importance of lay initiative in this era. For details about individual foundations, see also Thompson, *Women Religious*.
105. On Holystone, see MRH, 280–281.
106. Elkins, *Holy Women*, 76.
107. On houses connected to the Continental orders, see Thompson, *Women Religious*, 94–157. On Cistercians in the North, see Elkins, *Holy Women*, 84–88.
108. Burton, *The Yorkshire Nunneries*, 24; Elkins, *Holy Women*, 77.

Margaret and two of their daughters subsequently became nuns.[109] Wallingwells in Nottinghamshire was founded about 1144 by Ralph de Chevercourt.[110] In northern Yorkshire, Roger de Aske founded the Benedictine house of Marrick in the 1150s, and two of his children took the veil.[111] Most of these houses never attained anything like the size of the Gilbertine communities, and many were designed for the traditional twelve nuns and their superior, as was the case at Flamstead. Even Lillechurch in Kent, a royal foundation for Mary, daughter of King Stephen, was meant to provide for only sixteen nuns.[112] Nonetheless, the kingdom in which nunneries had been so few in 1135 was by the late twelfth century blanketed with them.

NUNNERIES IN THE CHURCH

As the foregoing sketches suggest, the expansion of female monasticism circa 1080–circa 1170 had little to do with the reformist aims or prescriptive policies of contemporary leaders of the Western Church. The role of the papacy is the best example of this dissociation. Even the mostly monastic popes of the first half of the twelfth century took no active part in the foundation of nunneries. Pope Calixtus II did indeed consecrate the Romanesque abbey church of Fontevraud, but not until 1119, three years after the death of Robert of Arbrissel and nearly two decades after Robert settled his community on lands donated by the local faithful. In 1109, fourteen years after the foundation of Berteaucourt by two holy women, a local lord, and Bishop Gervinus of Amiens, Pope Pascal II sent a notice to the nuns. At the request of Gervinus's successor Geoffrey, the pope took the nunnery under his protection, confirmed its properties, and asserted its right to free election of the abbess according to the Benedictine Rule.[113] Materials issued from Rome in the central Middle Ages show that this was the model for papal involvement with the establishment of monasteries for women: supportive but ex post facto.

---

109. Thompson, *Women Religious*, 176–177; Elkins, *Holy Women*, 69–70. According to legend, Hugh was a prisoner in the Holy Land before a vision of St. Leonard told him to build a house for nuns and miraculously transported him back to England.
110. Thompson, *Women Religious*, 230.
111. Ibid., 178.
112. Ibid., 131–132; MRH, 259.
113. BN, Collection Picardie, vol. 93, folios 38r.–40v.

Before the early twelfth century, only a tiny fraction of papal bulls concerned houses of nuns in Western Christendom.[114] The repertory of Philippe Jaffé lists only sixteen bulls addressed to nuns and their houses in the whole tenth century; of over five hundred bulls he sent forth during his thirteen-year pontificate (1073–1086), Gregory VII issued only five concerning female monastics. The proportion of bulls to or concerning nuns began to rise notably only after about 1120.[115] Nearly all of these documents were confirmations of new foundations or a list of properties owned by the nuns, most often issued at the request of an abbess, lay patron, or bishop (such as Geoffrey of Amiens). The amount of business concerning nuns and their communities began to rise only some time after a great number of nunneries were founded in northwestern Europe, appearing to confirm the observation of one historian that "so much papal history now seems more like authority grappling ill-prepared and as best it could with ideas and inspirations fermenting from below."[116] The increased number of papal bulls in the twelfth century reflects new realities—many new nunneries—rather than new (or old) goals.[117]

Nor was there any "episcopal policy" beyond the actions of individual bishops. The support and initiative of these prelates, I have argued, was at the heart of the expansion of female monasticism. But the foundation or regulation of nuns and nunneries was not a central concern of bishops as a group, if the records of episcopal councils are any indication. Ex-

114. This and the following observations are based on the lists of papal bulls from antiquity to the end of the twelfth century in Philippe Jaffé et al., *Regesta pontificum Romanorum ab condita ecclesia ad annum post Christum natum 1198*, 2d ed., 2 vols.(Leipzig, 1885–1888). The incompleteness of this repertory has long been recognized, but it remains the most convenient and accessible handlist. Obviously the figures that follow should be treated with some caution.

115. The percentage began to rise slightly earlier, in the time of the pontificates of Urban II (1088–1099) and Pascal II (1099–1118), when over 2% of all papal bulls concerned nuns. But here the raw data are a bit deceptive, because of the 30 or so bulls, 7 concern Remiremont and another 3 are in favor of Fontevraud.

116. A remark made by H. E. J. Cowdrey, review of *The Papal Monarchy: The Western Church from 1050 to 1250* by Colin Morris, *History: The Journal of the Historical Association* 75 (1990): 473. It is important not to exaggerate this new emphasis in papal business: even in the pontificates of Calixtus II (1119–1124) and his successors, the amount of materials concerning female monasticism hovered around 5%.

117. Marthe Moreau, *L'âge d'or des religieuses: Monastères féminins du Languedoc méditerranéen au Moyen Age* (Montpellier, 1988), 49–50, posits that the preeminence of the diocese of Maguelonne in the number of women's houses among the dioceses of coastal Languedoc was connected to the warm relations of the bishops of Maguelonne with Rome. But no pope ever participated in the foundation of a nunnery in this diocese, so it is difficult to see how the popes were responsible for this "climat favorable à l'éclosion de ces vocations féminines."

tant promulgations of these gatherings contain very little about nuns or nunneries specifically.[118] Most references are to monks and nuns together, as part of a more general statement about the religious.[119] From the 1120s on, there appears to have been some concern among English bishops about nuns wearing habits made of precious cloths and furs, but such prohibitions, like papal bulls, reflect a reactive rather than active role in the furthering of female monastic life.[120] When bishops of the late eleventh or twelfth centuries founded nunneries or aided in their establishment, it appears that they were, like Bishop Gervinus of Amiens, Bishop Peter of Poitiers, and many others, exercising a pastoral (rather than administrative) function by providing a forum for the expression of spiritual aspirations.

Monks were far less visible figures than bishops in the foundation of nunneries. What is most striking about Abbot Geoffrey of Saint Albans's friendship with Christina of Markyate is that his services on her behalf sound like those usually performed by hermits or bishops elsewhere. The reforming orders of monks and canons shied away from making the accommodation of religious women a central concern. The canons of Arrouaise in northern France accepted women into their house and others associated with it in the twelfth century. They did not establish separate houses of nuns, however, and by the end of the period under discussion they were trying to limit severely the number of sisters associated with them.[121] The case of the Premonstratensian sisters, discussed earlier, also indicates reluctance on the part of male religious to take responsibility for nuns. Although there were forty-five or so nunneries in France and England associated with Cistercian practice and organization by circa 1170, the desire for connection with Cîteaux came from the new nunneries rather than from the monks of the order. Abbot Stephen Harding of Cîteaux participated in the foundation of Tart l'Abbaye, but the initiative lay with the widow Elizabeth of Vergy and her fledgling community.

118. *Sacrorum conciliorum nova et amplissima collectio*, ed. J. D. Mansi, 53 vols. (Venice, 1759–1798). Volumes 20 and 21 cover the years 1070–1166, roughly the period considered in this chapter.
119. E.g., ibid., 20: 38, Canon 12 of the Council of Rouen of 1072, which sanctioned the forced return of wandering or expelled religious to the cloister, and 21: 512, Canon 10 of the Council of London of 1138, which forbade anyone to lay (presumably violent) hands on clerics, monks, or nuns.
120. For such prohibitions, see Canon 12 of the Council of London of 1127 (ibid., 21: 358), and Canon 15 of the Council of London of 1138 (21: 513). A tendency toward luxury in dress is also suggested by Canon 7 of the Council of Reims of 1157 (21: 845–846).
121. Thompson, *Women Religious*, 145–150, discusses the women of Arrouaise, with full bibliographic citations.

However, the stories of the foundation of Berteaucourt, of Robert of Arbrissel and the beginnings of Fontevraud, of the establishment of Tart l'Abbaye not far from Cîteaux, and many others do illustrate a theme noted by several monastic historians: the cooperation of lay and religious women and men in varying combinations in founding and organizing new nunneries.[122] Writing to the community of the Paraclete under their abbess Heloise, Peter Abelard doubtless reflected the opinion of many churchmen when he told the nuns that "you are one with us."[123] The path to a religious life for some women might be impeded, even by bishops and clerics, as the case of Christina of Markyate illustrates, but instances of outright hostility to or malicious interference with nuns and their communities are quite rare before the late twelfth century.

If hindsight uncovers a pattern of reluctance on the part of some individuals or monastic congregations to accommodate nuns and nunneries, one may understand better the place of nunneries in the twelfth-century Church by considering a special kind of contemporary document: the mortuary roll. On the death of the superior of a monastic house, a messenger would be dispatched to travel about the countryside, stopping at religious communities to announce the death and to solicit prayers. Members of each house wrote prayers or poems on parchments that were, as they multiplied, stitched together and rolled up. So, as the bearer wandered, the ever-lengthening document carried news and inspiration between houses of monks, canons, and nuns.[124]

One such roll, which circulated after the death in 1113 of Abbess Mathilda of La Trinité, Caen, eventually reached a length of over twenty meters.[125] Before its final return to Caen, the roll grew to include notice of visits to over 250 religious institutions: monasteries, cathedral chapters, and even a few *scolae*, spread across an enormous territory. The messenger(s) traveled extensively in England, going as far north as York. The roll also contains notices from as far east as Champagne and upper Burgundy

122. Penny Schine Gold, "Male/Female Cooperation: The Example of Fontevraud" in *Medieval Religious Women*, vol.1: *Distant Echoes*, ed. John A. Nichols and Lillian Thomas Shank (Kalamazoo, Mich., 1984), 151–168, as well as Gold's *The Lady and the Virgin*; the cooperation of men with women is also a major theme of both Elkins, *Holy Women*, and Johnson, *Equal in Monastic Profession*. Thompson, *Women Religious*, holds a somewhat darker view, seeing female dependence on male support.

123. Cited in Johnson, *Equal in Monastic Profession*, 266.

124. Ibid., 96–98, discusses these *rotuli* in this context generally and refers in particular to that of a thirteenth-century abbess of Saint-Amand of Rouen in particular. The remarks on the roll of Mathilda, the first abbess of her parents' foundation of La Trinité at Caen, are my own.

125. *Rouleaux des morts du IXe au XVe siècle*, ed. Léopold Delisle (Paris, 1866), 177–279.

and as far south as Limoges and Angoulême, and includes a large number of houses from Anjou, Brittany, the Ile de France, and Normandy. Over two dozen nunneries added their prayers and poems. Some of these were ancient urban nunneries, some of more recent origin. Five Anglo-Saxon nunneries were included, as well as the eleventh-century foundations of Beaumont-lès-Tours, Notre-Dame de Saintes, Saint-Georges in Rennes, and Ronceray at Angers. The nuns of Malling solicited prayers from Bishop Gundulf, their founder, who had died only a few years before Abbess Mathilda. A niece of Mathilda at Winchester wrote a poem to the Virgin, praying for mercy for her aunt. Such a document created spiritual links transcending institutional categories and even the distinction of sex.

There were other ways to create bonds, too. When Abbot Suger of Saint-Denis was building a new abbey church, the first in the style that came to be known as Gothic, he received from the abbess of Fontevraud a gift of precious stones with which to ornament the structure.[126] In return, Suger wrote to Pope Eugenius III in 1149, asking the pontiff to take special notice of the sisters of Fontevraud and to shield them from interference from outsiders, in particular the bishop of Poitiers.[127] Mortuary rolls and other evidence of mutual support and affection show that nuns and their houses were considered full members of the larger community of the Church in the first half of the twelfth century.

Of course, the foundation of monastic houses for women was hardly incompatible with the goals of reform-minded popes, bishops, and monks, who sought *inter alia* to draw a firm distinction between those inside and outside the Church. A theme of this chapter has been literal regularization and normalization—imposition of *regulae* and *normae*—of female religious aspiration. This was Bishop Gervinus's goal; Robert of Arbrissel's eremitic community became a traditional monastery, something that Robert probably did not want but also realized he could not prevent.[128] Spiritual seekers of anomalous status, such as Robert of Arbrissel's followers or Christina of Markyate, were encouraged to become nuns, members of a monastery.[129]

---

126. The gift is noted by Suger in chap. 33 of *De rebus in administratione sua gestis*: Suger, *Oeuvres complètes de Suger*, ed. Albert Lecoy de la Marche (Paris, 1867), 195.
127. Ibid., 263–264.
128. Bienvenu, *L'étonnant fondateur*, 125–144, calls the period when Robert made Fontevraud a Benedictine house and appointed Petronilla of Chemillé abbess "l'heure des choix obligés."
129. Magnou-Nortier, "Formes féminines de vie consacrée," 209–211, notes this tendency from 1100 on in the south of France, and finds cases of women who are said to have "monacated themselves" (*se monachare*).

The number of nuns, then, grew enormously in the century from the time of Pope Gregory VII. Although even the grandest comital foundations of the eleventh century rarely accommodated more than a few dozen nuns, it would appear that at least some of the newer foundations were much more considerable. Herman of Laon claimed that there were one thousand sisters at Prémontré and ten thousand in the houses of the order.[130] When Suger asked the pope to have special regard for the nuns of Fontevraud, he remembered that the place had been newly founded when he was a schoolboy and rejoiced that it now included four thousand or five thousand nuns.[131] Medieval statistics are notoriously unreliable, and we should not take these figures at face value, but they certainly convey the impression of a sizable number of nuns. There is surer evidence that some communities were quite large. In 1170, the archbishop of Sens set a limit on the number of nuns at Crisenon: one hundred.[132] The maxima established for Gilbertine houses, that *are* to be taken at face value, also suggest communities much larger than those of the eleventh century. Doubtless, there were many small houses such as those in England on the Continent as well. But it is difficult to escape the impression that the fourfold growth in the number of nunneries in the years 1080–1170 involved an even more remarkable multiplication of the number of nuns.

And still, it appears, this was not enough. According to the twelfth-century *vita* of Saint Hugh of Grenoble, nunneries were too few to receive all the women, such as Hugh's widowed mother, who wanted to enter one.[133] A different sort of indicator is a rare reference to female monastics in the records of an episcopal council, all the more important because it was held at Rome. Canon 26 of the Second Lateran Council of 1139 is titled "That nuns should not live in private homes" (*Ut sanctimoniales in privatis domiciliis non habitent*). The assembled bishops lamented that there were women, who wanted to be called nuns, living together in

130. PL 156: 994, 997.
131. Suger, *Oeuvres complètes*, 264: "utpote tantum tantae religionis locum, quem, cum in partibus illis in scholis essemus, noviter incoeptum esse vidimus, et per Dei voluntatem fere ad quatuor aut quinque millia sanctimonialium jam excrevisse audivimus et gaudemus." This figure could include all the houses dependent on Fontevraud, or be the total of the living and the dead, in the manner of *libri memoriales*, or simply be a guess about the number of women at Fontevraud at the time.
132. *Cartulaire général de l'Yonne* 2: 219.
133. PL 153: 764; the story is noted in David Herlihy, *Medieval Households* (Cambridge, Mass., 1985), 102. The house of nuns nearest Grenoble was that of Saint-André in Vienne. Had she lived a generation later, Hugh's mother could have taken the veil at one of two nunneries in the diocese: Les Ayes and Parmenie.

houses but following no monastic rule: exactly what Godelinde and Helegunde, whom Bishop Gervinus called *sanctimoniales*, had been doing. "So
dishonorable and execrable a disgrace" was prohibited under penalty of
anathema.[134] Apparently Roiantelina of Rennes, whose little band joined
the newly founded nunnery of Saint-Georges in the 1030s, had twelfth-
century successors. The prohibition of 1139 is typical of reform thought
in its desire to keep distinctions of persons clear, but also hints at broadly
experienced yearning for a religious life not satisfied even by the great
multiplication of nunneries. Under what conditions did such a need
arise? And what worldly circumstances made the expansion of female
monasticism possible?

134. *Sacrorum conciliorum* 21: 533: "hoc tam inhonestum detestandumque flagitium ne ul-
terius fiat, omnimodis prohibemus, et sub poena anathematis interdicimus."

social and economic contexts in the eleventh and twelfth centuries

Andegavina filia Arvei Ultrici sanctimonialis effecta dedit Deo et beate Marie et sanctimonialibus Montis Aresii illam terram cum qua maritata fuit, scilicet tres bordarias tam nemus quam terram planam.[1]

Andegavina, daughter of Arveus Ultricus, made a nun, gave to God and the blessed Mary and the nuns of Montazais that land with which she was married, that is three *bordarias*, both forest and field.

—Charter of Montazais (diocese of Poitiers), 1165

at the end of Marie de France's *Eliduc*, the eponymous hero founds two monasteries. First he builds a nunnery on his own territory, alongside an old hermitage, and richly endows the house with land and money. Eliduc's wife becomes the first abbess of a community of thirty nuns. Later on, Eliduc founds a religious house for men nearby and ends his life there as a monk. His second wife also becomes a nun.[1]

Eliduc is fiction, but Marie's account sounds very much like many stories of foundation. Like Adelard of Châteaumeillant, whose wife Agnes became the first superior of Orsan, and the knight Gilbert, whose foundation of Aubeterre circa 1150 was under the leadership of his wife and daughter, Eliduc founds a house for a spouse. Like Gautier of Nyoiseau, who with his wife entered into religion at Gautier's foundation sometime after 1110, and Countess Clementia, who ended her life at Bourbourg in 1129, Eliduc and his wives die in monastic habit. Other details, such as the association of a nunnery with hermits and the size of the new community, confirm the impression of verisimilitude. But Marie's story also provides what is often lacking in our knowledge of the origins of monastic houses for women and men: a prehistory. Luckily, the tale was written

1. Marie de France, *Lais*, ed. Alfred Ewert (Oxford, 1947), 127–157 ("Eliduc"); translation in Marie de France, *The Lais of Marie de France*, trans. Robert Hanning and Joan Ferrante (Durham, N.C., 1978), 196–229.

down in the region, and about the time, of the expansion of female monasticism just described.[2] Thus it is worth considering the whole of *Eliduc* for what it suggests about the circumstances that might lead to the founding of a nunnery (or, for that matter, any monastery) in the twelfth century.

When the story begins, Eliduc is a trusted retainer of the king of Brittany. But envy gives rise to slander against Eliduc, and ultimately he is banished from his lord's court without a hearing. Eliduc flees Brittany, leaving behind his wife Guildeluec, to whom he promises fidelity. Across a sea he arrives in the land of a beleaguered old king who has incited warfare by refusing to marry his daughter and heir to another powerful lord. Eliduc's offer to fight for the old king is accepted, and he wins a great victory for his new lord.

Once again, Eliduc becomes a trusted retainer, but a new difficulty arises. The daughter, Guilliadun, becomes enamored of the valiant knight, who is at first dismayed and thinks of his wife. But Eliduc is flattered by Guilliadun's persistence, which her father encourages. Eliduc, who has failed to tell anyone of his wife overseas, does not reject Guilliadun's affections. Soon, however, Eliduc receives a letter from the king of Brittany, who apologizes for his bad faith and calls his knight home to fight for his liege. Eliduc, mindful of his oath to the king of Brittany and also his wife, departs. Guilliadun wants to elope, but Eliduc puts her off with a promise to return to her on a day she names.

Back home, Eliduc is preoccupied, which his wife notices at once. He tells her that he is sad because he has sworn to return to the service of the king across the water. Eliduc again serves in Brittany with distinction as the day Guilliadun named approaches. Eliduc then departs in secret for the land of the old king, and Guilliadun in her turn leaves her father's house without telling anyone. Eliduc and the princess sail for Brittany together, but a terrible storm comes up. A terrified sailor accuses Eliduc of bringing this upon them by betraying his wife and God's law with Guilliadun and recommends she be thrown overboard. Guilliadun faints in fear and shock: this is the first she has heard of Eliduc's wife.

---

2. Marie's translators cautiously note that Marie wrote down her stories (in French) between 1160 and 1199, but offer strong circumstantial evidence pointing to the first decade or so of that period (*The Lais of Marie de France*, 7–8). Marie's identity remains a mystery, but she was probably a noblewoman, very likely a member of the Anglo-Norman aristocracy, perhaps an abbess. She frequented the court of Henry Plantagenet and Eleanor of Aquitaine.

The ship reaches port, but Guilliadun does not recover consciousness. Her lover thinks her dead and takes her to a hermit's cell in a forest, intending to bury her there and found a monastery on the site. After vowing to become a monk, he leaves Guilliadun for dead on the altar. In secret grief, he visits the forest chapel to mourn his loss. Guildeluec finds out by stealth where he goes, and upon finding the lovely "corpse" in the forest, she realizes that Eliduc is grieving for another love. Guildeluec revives Guilliadun, who tells Eliduc's wife the whole story. Guildeluec is sympathetic. She reveals her identity and promises to take the veil, leaving Eliduc free. Eliduc and his new love are reunited, and he founds the nunnery for Guildeluec, who establishes a rule for the new community. He then marries Guilliadun, and after some years he founds a monastery for himself, fulfilling his earlier vow, and puts his second wife in the abbey in care of the first. All three end their lives in the service of God.

Marie's tale, especially its denouement, reflects in idealized form some social facts revealed in documents such as that recording Andegavina's donation of her dowry lands to the Poitevin nunnery she joined in the mid-twelfth century. For it is possible, albeit difficult, to gather an impression of the circumstances in which female monasticism grew so rapidly in the century or so starting around 1080. The first subjects in this chapter will be the excess of women in the higher reaches of society and the changing circumstances of aristocratic marriage. Of equal importance were the economic and managerial contributions of male and female members of the lesser aristocracy in the endowment and management of the new nunneries. Finally, it appears that the distribution of power in this era, and the often chaotic organization of worldly might in a society of many lords, were actually favorable to the foundation and support of nunneries. Not that religious motivations were insignificant: we might easily read *Eliduc* as a story of redemption made possible by female magnanimity. But in the real world, as in Marie's *lai*, any decision to found a nunnery, to make gifts to a religious community, or even to take the veil, is to be understood against the social, economic, and political background.

FAMILY AND MARRIAGE

Over a century ago, German scholars postulated a late medieval *Frauenfrage*. The "woman question" was a large number of unmarried females in the towns of Flanders and the Rhineland. One solution, historians have long agreed, was the beguinage, a semimonastic urban religious community for women.[3] I will address the issue of beguines and beguinages later on, but I want to argue that the urban *Frauenfrage* of the thirteenth and later centuries had an antecedent in the less densely populated countryside during the eleventh and twelfth centuries. Furthermore, the growth of female monasticism from the late eleventh century forward was at least in part a response to an aristocratic "matrimonial crisis."[4]

Of all the many transformations of the central Middle Ages, no one category of change directly affected more men and women of the European aristocracy than the reconfiguration of family identities, household structures, and marriage patterns. These subjects are still fairly new ones, but there is enough agreement among scholars on the outlines of change to consider the relationship of these changes with the expansion of female monasticism in northwestern Europe in the eleventh and twelfth centuries. On one aspect of change there is general consensus: status, visibility, and opportunity for aristocratic women declined in the period after the millennium. The multiplication of nunneries in the era argues that this generalization should be applied with caution; however, the changing circumstances of women outside the cloister were doubtless of considerable importance for the expansion of female monasticism.[5]

3. The classic statement is Karl Bücher, *Die Frauenfrage im Mittelalter* (Tübingen, 1882). On the connection to beguinages, see Ernest W. McDonnell, *The Beguines and Beghards in Medieval Culture* (New Brunswick, N.J., 1954), esp. 81–100. The concept is reprised in Herlihy, *Medieval Households*, 102, 142.

4. Jacques Dalarun, "Robert d'Arbrissel et les femmes," 1144, refers to "la crise matrimoniale," but one of marital situations rather than an antecedent to the *Frauenfrage*. Only a rarely cited article by Ernst Werner appears to identify something like a *Frauenfrage* around 1100; see "Zur Frauenfrage und zum Frauenkult im Mittelalter: Robert v. Arbrissel und Fontevrault," *Forschungen und Fortschritte* 29 (1955): 269–276.

5. For present purposes, the conclusions of David Herlihy and Georges Duby are especially important. Herlihy's *Medieval Households* contains particularly good material on women. See also his *Opera Muliebria: Women and Work in Medieval Europe* (New York, 1990). Duby has produced no similarly comprehensive work on these subjects, but see (in English) *Medieval Marriage: Two Models from Twelfth-Century France*, trans. Elborg Forster (Baltimore, 1978); *The Knight, the Lady, and the Priest;* and the essays collected in *The Chivalrous Society*, trans. Cynthia Postan (Berkeley, 1977). The clearest statement that the fate of women declined across the Middle Ages is still Jo Ann McNamara and Suzanne Wemple, "Sanctity and Power: The Dual Pursuit of Medieval Women," in *Becoming Visible: Women in European History*, ed. Renate Bridenthal and Claudia Koonz (Boston, 1977), 92–118, an argument reprised in Jo Ann McNamara, "Victims of Progress: Women and the Twelfth Century," in *Female Power in the Middle Ages*, ed. Karen Glente and Lise Winther-Jensen (Copenhagen, 1989), 26–37. On the history of the subject of identities, see T. N. Bisson, "Nobility and Family in Medieval France: A Review Essay," *French Historical Studies* 16 (1990): 597–613, with important bibliography of German, French, English, and American works.

The growth of Western Europe's population from around 1000 A.D. and the contemporaneous decentralization of political power brought with them important changes in the pattern of marriages among the aristocracy. For women, a sea change in Christian ideologies and family strategies radically altered the nature of and possibilities for marriage. Primarily through the influence of churchmen, the principles of monogamy and clerical celibacy were firmly imposed. This meant not only the end of early medieval polygyny and clerical marriage, but also an insistence on the indissolubility of the union once it was consummated by the agreement of both partners to marry.[6] Another ecclesiastical concern coming to the fore in the new millennium was consanguineous marriage. A complex system of prohibitions of marriage between families already linked by blood or marriage meant that many otherwise desirable marriages were impeded, especially between people of similar social station. Men of less than exalted rank could marry up the social scale and might wait to find an heiress.[7]

At the same time, new dynastic identities and ambitions, in particular the desire to maintain an undivided familial patrimony passed down according to male lines of descent, meant that younger sons were often sent off to a wandering knighthood or career in the Church.[8] Furthermore, slim but consistent evidence implies that in the early Middle Ages, eligible men had outnumbered women, but that by the twelfth century, the reverse was coming to be true, further exacerbating the problem of an imbalance between the sexes.[9]

So the number of nubile women was rising in "what one is tempted to call the marriage market."[10] Aristocratic men, especially if they were not eldest sons, had good reasons to postpone matrimony. A second major change, therefore, concerned age at first marriage. The general pattern before the twelfth century appears to have been marriage between part-

6. Duby, *The Knight, the Lady, and the Priest;* Herlihy, *Medieval Households*, 38–39, 49–52, 80–86. On the subject of clerical marriage, see Anne Llewellyn Barstow, *Married Priests and the Reforming Papacy* (New York, 1982), which stresses how widespread the practice was before the mid-eleventh century and how the prohibition met with considerable opposition for at least a century from the accession of Pope Leo IX in 1049. Thus the diminution of numbers of one category of marriageable males, the secular clergy, was a gradual one extending across the eleventh and twelfth centuries.
7. Constance B. Bouchard, "Consanguinity and Noble Marriage in the Tenth and Eleventh Centuries," *Speculum* 56 (1981): 268–287.
8. Georges Duby, "Youth in Aristocratic Society: Northwestern France in the Twelfth Century," in *The Chivalrous Society*, 112–122; see also *The Knight, the Lady, and the Priest*, 267.
9. Herlihy, *Medieval Households*, 102.
10. Duby, *Medieval Marriage*, 11.

ners of relatively equal age, but during the central Middle Ages average age at first marriage of women declined and that of men increased.[11] Thus very young women, frequently just past menarche, were often joined to men considerably their seniors. Since male mortality in a warrior aristocracy was significant, the postponement of marriage by men only diminished the ranks of potential husbands.

The ramifications of this pattern may be glimpsed in a survey made by King Henry II of England in the 1180s. The *Rotuli de dominabus et pueris et puellis* is a list of widows and wards, boys and girls, in twelve counties. The rolls contain the names of some 80 aristocratic widows and note the age of 73 of them. Frequently the figures are not exact; for those over forty especially, the number given is most often a multiple of ten. Nevertheless, this list indicates a great deal about marriage patterns among the aristocracy. Many of these women did indeed marry young and bore children early, like Mathilda, who at age thirty was a widow with eight children, the oldest of whom was sixteen, or the unnamed widow of Simon of Crieuequeor, twenty-four, with four children aged five or younger. The youngest of all, Basilia, was at age eighteen the mother of a son and a daughter, and had been widowed a year when the survey was taken. Basilia's sister-in-law was twenty-five and had lost her husband five years before. Obviously many women were teenage brides and mothers.[12]

The presence of a number of youthful widows suggests that their husbands were older or had a higher mortality rate—not surprising in a culture of warfare—or both. Some women in Henry's survey had been widowed twice, like Ewgenia Picot, who was still only thirty and had a ten-year-old child; Matillis Pecche had eleven children from three marriages, and Maria, forty years old and "born of knights and barons," had lost three husbands as well.[13] The distribution of widows' ages is significant, too: the *Rotuli* name just about as many widows under fifty (37) as there were fifty and over (36).

Taken as a whole, the data point to a large number of widows, young and old, among the English elite in the twelfth century. To be an aristocratic widow was not a particularly advantageous situation: those in Henry II's survey were *de donatione Domini Regis*, indicating that the king

---

11. Herlihy, *Medieval Households*, 103–111. Herlihy states (110–111) that the pattern is clear from about 1200, but much of the evidence he provides, especially concerning the age of marriage of north European women, dates from the eleventh and twelfth centuries.
12. *Rotuli de dominabus et pueris et puellis de XII comitatibus*, ed. J. H. Round (London, 1913), 37, 7, 38.
13. Ibid., 87, 85, 53 ("Ipsa est .xl. annorum et nata de militibus et baronibus").

could exercise his lordly right to control remarriages. Henry could sell the right to marry a widow to the highest bidder, and in some cases a woman could escape unwanted marriage only by paying a fine.[14] European women's property rights were substantially diminished across the eleventh and twelfth centuries, too, both through a system of inheritance that favored male heirs and diminished control of what lands they did have. In particular, a widow might easily lose control of her own marriage portion, especially if she had no children.[15]

There were at least two significant groups of noble women, then, who might be looking for alternatives to marriage: virgins facing poor prospects for marriage, and widows, some still quite young, for whom another union might be difficult or undesirable, especially if imposed by a powerful lord. A third category was that of wives who had abandoned their husbands or been abandoned by them. Marie de France's heroine Guildeluec is a fictional woman who chose to leave a marriage, but there are historical examples of considerably more wretched marital situations. Robert Curthose was married for three months to Mathilda of Laigle before he was captured and imprisoned for life by his enemy, King Henry I of England. Mathilda could not remarry, for her husband was still alive. After years of waiting, she received papal permission and wed Nigel of Aubigny. Out of regard for her noble family, her new husband treated Mathilda well. But after the death of her brother Gilbert, Mathilda's husband repudiated her on the grounds that she was a blood relative and married another woman, the sister of Hugh of Gournay.[16] Nigel's marriages were means of allying himself to powerful Norman families: the lords of Laigle and Gournay. Mathilda was first a victim of strict rules of marital indissolubility, then a pawn in a game of familial alliances, and finally spurned by means of a claim of incest, a ploy often used by aristocrats wanting to end a marriage.

It is not difficult, therefore, to imagine a multitude of situations in which there were, simply put, too few marriageable men for too many nubile women, and others in which marriage, potential or actual, might

---

14. W. L. Warren, *Henry II* (Berkeley, Calif., 1973), 385–386, discusses the powers of feudal lords over the marriage of widows and heiresses and Henry's "obnoxious" abuse of his rights in this matter, following the practice of his grandfather Henry I in the early twelfth century.

15. For a summary of current thinking, see McNamara, "Victims of Progress," 29–33. Duby has argued the case for diminishing rights of property among the aristocratic women of the Mâconnais from the millennium to the twelfth century: "Lineage, Nobility, and Knighthood," in *The Chivalrous Society*, 59–80, esp. 71–73.

16. OV 4: 282–285.

be a less than wholly desirable fate.[17] Baudry of Dol's life of Robert of Arbrissel tells of the many women who followed the errant preacher of western France and settled first in huts at Fontevraud. "The women assembled: poor and noble, widows and virgins, elderly and youthful, whores and those who rejected men."[18] The account of Robert's last hours by Andreas the chaplain tells of the preacher's desire to be buried in the soil of Fontevraud, where reside his priests and clerics, his "holy virgins, widows and continent women, offering prayers to God day and night." Robert's message was evidently attractive to many categories of women, all things to all people, as Baudry put it.[19]

Jacques Dalarun has pointed out that the category of "continents" might include a wide variety of women, from penitent former prostitutes to concubines to those who had left marriage, with or without the consent of their husbands. Aside from the generalized statements of Robert's biographers, we know a good deal about some of the early nuns of Fontevraud. The first prioress was Hersende, who had been widowed twice before joining the new community. Petronilla of Chemillé, who succeeded Hersende as prioress and eventually became the first abbess of Fontevraud, had been a wife and mother, although it is never stated in the sources that she was a widow. Bertrade of Montfort had been condemned for her marriage to King Philip I after abandoning her first husband, Count Fulk IV of Anjou. She became a Fontevrist nun after Philip's death, first at the mother house, then at the priory of Hautes-Bruyères founded by her family. Prioress Agnes of Orsan was the former wife of a generous patron of Fontevraud. Finally, shortly after Robert's death, Philippa, second wife of Duke William IX of Aquitaine, left her husband and his infamous concubine for refuge in Fontevraud.[20]

Robert of Arbrissel's message may have been particularly attractive to mature women who had some experience of life in the world, and extant

---

17. Duby, *The Knight, the Lady, and the Priest*, 87–89, suggests that there might have been a link between new moral standards about marriage, specifically husbandly scruples about simply tossing off unwanted wives, and what he calls the "proliferation of convents for northern France in the eleventh century." As I argue in Chapter 2, the new convents of the eleventh century were more notable for visibility than number, especially when compared to those in the twelfth century. But Duby sees the same connection of marriage patterns and monastic foundations I do, although he views them solely from the male perspective.

18. PL 162: 1053: "conveniebant mulieres, pauperes et nobiles, viduae et virgines, senes et adolescentes, meretrices et masculorum aspernatrices."

19. Ibid., 1073: "ibi etiam sunt sanctae virgines, viduae et continentes, die ac nocte in Dei laudibus perseverantes," and 1053. On Robert's appeal, and the often hostile response, see Elliott, *Spiritual Marriage*, 109–112.

20. See Chapter 3 and Dalarun, "Robert d'Arbrissel et les femmes," 1141–1144.

evidence from other nunneries suggests that virgins rarely constituted an overwhelming majority of professed women. This is most evident from the charters of two eleventh-century foundations: the comital foundation of Ronceray, in Angers, and the Cluniac convent of Marcigny in Burgundy.[21] Seventy charters from circa 1028 to 1184 specify the entry of 78 women into Ronceray. Of these postulants, at most 51 were virgins.[22] Another 27, or about 35 percent, are described as widow, wife, mother, or grandmother. Thus over one-third—and probably more—of those nuns whose entry into Ronceray is recorded in charters had been (or still were) married.[23] Burgundian charters document the entrance of 66 women into the Cluniac life in the late eleventh and early twelfth centuries. Fully one-half of the nuns (34 in all) were identified as wives, widows, or mothers. Abbot Hugh of Cluny had directed that all who took the habit at Marcigny should be at least twenty years old, which indicates that here again, the percentage of virgins could have been even lower than the terms of the charters indicate.[24] Extant eleventh- and twelfth-century charters of the abbeys of Notre-Dame in Saintes, La Trinité in Caen, and Saint-Georges in Rennes also show that at least one-quarter of the inhabitants of those houses had been married before they took the veil.[25]

Evidence from narrative sources, although scanty, confirms what the charters suggest: convents were diverse communities that included virgins, widows, and wives, young and old. The monk Orderic Vitalis wrote his *Ecclesiastical History* in circa 1118 to 1141, charting events in northern

21. Charters concerning entry into Ronceray and Marcigny have been collated in Jean Verdon, "Les moniales dans la France de l'Ouest," 248, 253. The following observations are based on Verdon's analysis, although I have corrected his calculations and added some nuances.

22. In most of these documents, one or more parents gives the entry donation, but the presentation of a daughter (or sister or niece) need not necessarily mean that she had never been married. Petronilla of Chemillé is a case in point: she certainly had been married but came to Fontevraud, according to both *vitae* of Robert of Arbrissel, not from her husband's house but from her father's (see Dalarun, "Robert d'Arbrissel et les femmes," 1143 and notes). Were it not for the fact that she specifies the origins of her entry gift, the Andegavina whose charter is excerpted at the beginning of this chapter would be unidentifiable as widow or wife, and it is not certain to which of these categories she belonged.

23. Verdon, "Les moniales dans la France de l'Ouest," 251, gives a figure of 30.13% married women, which inexplicably omits those identified as mother or grandmother. Nor does Verdon consider the possibility that some women whose marital status is unmentioned might have been married, divorced, or widowed. The 70 documents of consecration to Ronceray cover a long period, but there is no evident variation in the composition of entrants as a group across the first century and a half of the nunnery's history.

24. Ibid., 253–254. Here Verdon's figures do include mothers.

25. Ibid., 251. Of 80 entrants to these three houses, Verdon identifies 19 as widowed or married.

France and England from about 1050 forward.[26] Orderic recounted the entrance of about a dozen women into the monastic life in the course of his chronicle. Only four of these were virgins. Cecilia, daughter of William the Conqueror, was offered as a child to her mother Mathilda's new foundation of La Trinité, Caen, and died as the abbess of that house some sixty years later. Adela, daughter of Richard of Coulance, also entered the nunnery at Caen as a child; at the same time one of her brothers was given to Orderic's own house of Saint-Evroul.[27] Two virgin daughters of Arnold of Echauffour became nuns, Petronilla at Ronceray in Angers, Geva at Caen.[28]

These four young women entered the religious life before 1100; Orderic notes the passage of a number of more mature women into the cloister in the eleventh and early twelfth centuries. Petronilla and Geva's mother was a widow for nearly thirty years before she, too, took the veil.[29] Isabel of Montfort spent the last years of her widowhood at the nunnery of Hautes-Bruyères along with her sister Bertrade. Eremberge of Maule, a patron of local monasticism along with her son, eventually entered religious life. Aubrée, wife of William of Moulins-la-Marche and mother of two sons, was repudiated by her husband on the grounds of consanguinity and afterward became a nun.[30]

Near the end of his history, Orderic recounts the stories of three noble wives who eventually became nuns in the twelfth century. A natural daughter of King Henry I of England named Juliana joined her husband in rebellion against her father; she eventually reconciled with Henry and "some years later abandoned the self-indulgent life she had led for the religious life and, becoming a nun, served the Lord God in the new abbey of Fontevraud." Mathilda, daughter of Count Fulk V of Anjou, was married at age twelve to King Henry's son and heir William, who soon afterward died in the White Ship disaster of 1120. Ten years later, on the advice of Bishop Geoffrey of Chartres, she joined by then thriving Fontevraud. Last, Adela, who as countess of Blois had ruled her husband's lands when he went on crusade, also renounced the world in her widowhood and spent her last fifteen years at Marcigny.[31]

26. See the remarks of Orderic's modern editor, Marjorie Chibnall, on the chronology of composition: OV 1: 45–48.
27. Ibid., 3: 8–11 and notes (Cecilia), 230–231 (Adela).
28. Ibid., 2: 128–131.
29. Ibid., 2: 124–127.
30. Ibid., 3: 128–129 (Isabel), 190–193 (Eremberge), 132–133 (Aubrée).
31. Ibid., 6: 278–279 (Juliana); 5: 228–229 and notes, and 6: 330–331 (Mathilda); 6: 42–45 (Adela, the daughter of William the Conqueror and mother of King Stephen of England).

Orderic described the veilings of Isabel of Montfort and Juliana in particular as conversions from a wicked life to one of reformed piety. The story of Aubrée, however, reveals that the monastic habit and life might be a welcome relief from unfortunate marital experiences. Guibert of Nogent's account of his mother's history provides another case in point. "From her youth she was full of God's fire in Zion," and her beauty and nobility also made her attractive to suitors. Still very young she was given in marriage by her father to Evrard, a vassal of the lords of Clermont, near Beauvais. According to rumor, the young bride's stepmother had wanted one of her nieces to marry Evrard and used magic to prevent the consummation of the marriage. In any case, Guibert's mother remained a virgin in secret for three years. When Evrard made the difficulty known, his kin tried to persuade him to divorce and become a monk. His wife was hounded by the family, who threatened to annul the marriage, give her to another husband, or send her far away, and "certain rich men," apparently titillated by the situation, tried to seduce her. Finally the spell was broken and the couple produced a number of children, of which the future abbot, whose birth nearly killed his mother, was the youngest.

Guibert's father died only a few months after his last child was born, leaving his widow to be plotted against by Evrard's relatives, who wanted to seize her property. One of Evrard's nephews, greedy for wealth, proposed remarriage, but Guibert's mother refused to marry any but one of higher nobility than her dead husband. She was left alone to raise her children while leading a life of charity and penitence, covering a hairshirt with the fine clothes suitable to her station. When Guibert was twelve, his mother placed him in the care of Bishop Guy of Beauvais. She began to live in a hut near the male monastery of Fly, emulating the severity of life of an older female companion. This process of "divorcing herself from the world" continued many years. Finally, in her old age, she took the veil, as she had been instructed to do by the Blessed Virgin in a vision.[32]

Most of the women whose stories are told in narrative accounts entered wealthy and prestigious houses such as Ronceray, La Trinité in Caen, or Fontevraud. But a diverse community of nuns was not confined

---

32. Guibert of Nogent, *Autobiographie [De vita sua, sive monodiae]*, ed. and trans. Edmond-René Labande (Paris, 1981), 16–20, 74–86, 98–106, 242–246, contains Guibert's account of his mother, of which the preceding is a summary. An English translation is *Self and Society in Medieval France: The Memoirs of Abbot Guibert of Nogent (1064?–c. 1125)*, ed. John F. Benton (New York, 1970), 41–42, 63–68, 72–76, 132–134. The story is also told in Johnson, *Equal in Monastic Profession*, 32–33, with different details and emphasis. Guibert's English translator suggests that Guibert's mother may have been of higher social rank than his father, likely in northern France in the mid-eleventh century: Benton, ed., *Self and Society*, 236.

to abbeys founded by the high nobility. The surviving documents for a more modest twelfth-century foundation demonstrate that the same pattern held in a smaller and less elite monastery. The Fontevrist house of Montazais in southern Poitou was founded around 1119 on lands donated by a local lord, Aimeric of Bernard, whose widow was its first superior. Over two hundred twelfth-century documents from this monastery have survived.[33]

Thirty-eight charters record the entrance of forty-two women into the religious life from circa 1140 to circa 1205. Most of the charters are framed simply as donations to Montazais. Some are quite explicitly tied to the entrance of a postulant, as shown by the formula *pro matre sua Beatrice quando se consortio sanctimonialium Montis Aresii coniunxit* ("for his mother Beatrice when she joined the religious community of nuns at Montazais"),[34] but in other cases the situation is referred to only in shorthand, by noting that a gift was given along with a female relative.[35] At least fifteen of these women (over one-third) had been married, and here, too, the documents might simply have neglected to mention the marital status of a woman entering a convent. So in a modest house in Poitou, as in grander monasteries elsewhere, a considerable number of mature women became nuns.

The most striking feature of these documents from Montazais is the variety of situations they evoke. What is usually considered the standard

33. In 1854, M. Faye edited a small cartulary of Montazais ("Notice sur le monastère de Montazai, de l'ordre de Fontevrauld" *Mémoires de la société des antiquaires de l'Ouest* 20 [1853], 120–128) consisting of 26 charters before 1150. There are also 206 documents in a manuscript of the late fifteenth or early sixteenth century (ADML 186 H 3, 28 parchment quarto folios, unpublished), 12 of which duplicate material from the smaller cartulary. This larger cartulary, apparently incomplete, breaks off in the middle of a document at the bottom of folio 28 and is not organized chronologically or geographically. Only 49 charters are dated; the earliest is from 1162, the latest, 1196. The date or approximate date of 27 other documents can be derived from the names of currently reigning lay or ecclesiastical lords. This leaves 130 of the 206 charters undated. Luckily, all the documents, whether dated or not, contain the names of individuals who initiated, confirmed, allowed, or witnessed business with the priory—over 1,000 people in all. Because many individuals appear in a number of documents, analyzing names, groups of names, and the dates at which they appear makes it possible to estimate dates for many undated charters and to divide most of them into two broad categories. Including the dated charters of the larger cartulary, and the documents Faye found in pre-1150 copies, the totals are: 65 charters from the founding of the priory to ca. 1165 and 127 charters from ca. 1165 to ca. 1205. My observations here and in Chapter 5 are based on these 192 charters.

34. ADML 186 H 3, folio 4v.(#40).

35. E.g., ADML 186 H 3, folio 20r.(#146), "pro filia sua," and folio 8r.(unnumbered), "cum filia sua."

scenario by which a woman became a nun, oblation by one or both of her parents, occurred fourteen times, or in only one-third of the cases known from the Montazais charters. Eight women, three widows, two wives, and three others of unknown marital status made entry donations for themselves. On eight occasions, the brother or brothers of the postulant made a donation, and another ten women entered into religion at the same time their child or children made a gift to the house. Two men sponsored the entry of their nieces, and one married couple made a donations in favor of the wife's sister. These documents thus point to the diversity of circumstances in which aristocratic women lived with their kin in the twelfth century, but also raise some central questions about vocation and choice. Were massive numbers of women being thrust willy-nilly into the cloister by (usually) male relatives eager to rid themselves of the responsibility of caring for them and in some cases to come into control of the women's property?

Doubtless, some women who had no inclination to a monastic life were indeed given over to religion, consigned to what is called "enforced monachation." But in an age of arranged marriages in which the personal suitability of potential partners was not necessarily an important criterion, "enforced marriage" must have been equally (if not more) common. As Penelope D. Johnson has cogently argued, we must understand the question of choice in contemporary terms, as a matter of familial consideration and strategy, rather than as decisions made by wholly autonomous individuals. "Since the heavy hand of family authority touched everyone, it would be misleading to think that medieval nuns generally felt more dragooned into the cloister than their male counterparts."[36] Certainly, it is hard to find a story more heart-rending than Orderic Vitalis's autobiographical account, which draws parallels between the course of his early life and the fates of the heroes of Genesis. Orderic's father Odelerius was a Norman priest in England, his mother an Englishwoman.

> And so, O glorious God, who didst command Abraham to depart from his country and from his kindred and from his father's house, thou didst inspire my father Odelerius to renounce me utterly, and submit in all things to thy governance. So, weeping, he gave me, a weeping child, into the care of the monk Reginald, and sent me away into exile for love of thee

---

36. Johnson, *Equal in Monastic Profession,* 13–34, treats the relationship of nuns to their families in Northern France in the eleventh, twelfth, and thirteenth centuries and offers ample evidence from charters and other sources; quot., 18.

and never saw me again. . . . And so, as a boy of ten, I crossed the English Channel and came into Normandy as an exile, unknown to all, knowing no one. Like Joseph in Egypt, I heard a language which I did not understand. . . . I was received as an oblate monk in the abbey of Saint-Evroult by the venerable Abbot Mainer in the eleventh year of my age, and was tonsured as a clerk on Sunday, 21 September. In place of my English name, which sounded harsh to the Normans, the name Vitalis was given me. . . . I have lived as a monk in that abbey by thy favor for 56 years.[37]

This is not to claim that women were not sometimes made members of a nunnery very much against their will. But there were probably also many cases when a woman's sincere vocation was delayed or even permanently impeded. The large number of wives and widows taking the veil, some of whom, like Andegavina of Montazais, did so without any apparent support from relatives, suggests the possibility of some long-postponed decisions to become a nun.[38] Guibert of Nogent's account of his mother, colored by a son's admiration as it is, must have some basis in fact; here was a woman who married young, survived a widowhood and its attendant difficulties, and after her children were provided for, embarked on a path of her own choosing. Guibert's mother was able to choose a religious vocation, a life of simple and lofty aims, no doubt in part as a conscious rejection of her life in the world. Christina of Markyate's parents determinedly opposed her religious vocation, which the young woman was able to pursue only through deception and the aid of those outside the family. Most telling of all, Robert of Arbrissel is said to have refused "disobediently and to the death" to send wives back to the husbands they had fled, either when the men asked or when ordered to do so by the bishop of Angers.[39]

37. OV 6: 552–555.
38. Andegavina's donation to Montazais appears to have been made counter to the wishes of family members, who took no part in her cloistering and on two separate occasions tried to claim the property as their own (ADML 186 H 3 folios 8r.–v.). This suggests something more than the standard attempt by a monastery to obtain *laudatio parentum* and to make alliances with the family of a nun. Johnson, *Equal in Monastic Profession*, 14–15, points out that individual choice might be difficult to discern from the surviving evidence when it did occur and cites the entrance of widows as a particularly likely context for it.
39. François Picavet, *Roscelin: Philosophe et théologien* (Paris, 1911), 132: "Vide enim dominum Robertum feminas a viris suis fugientes, viris ipsis reclamantibus, recepisse, et episcopo Andegaviensi ut eos redderet praecipiente, inobedienter usque ad mortem obstinanter tenuisse." The remark comes in the famous nominalist's letter to Peter Abelard. Roscelin had no known connection to Fontevraud, but it seems unlikely that he would have invented such a story not long after Robert's death in a letter to someone from western France, and what he says accords with the rest of what we know about Robert's mission and character. See also Werner, "Zur Frauenfrage und zum Frauenkult im Mittelalter."

The monastic life of the eleventh and twelfth centuries, what Orderic Vitalis called "the security of obedience and poverty,"[40] had broad appeal and included women of varied experiences and aspirations. How did economic and political circumstances make it possible to create so many new places in religion for women in the eleventh and twelfth centuries?

WORLDLY GOODS

Around the year 1000, Western Christendom began to show marked signs of internal expansion, and a century later change and growth were rapid.[41] Population, which in the tenth century had probably reached its lowest point since the fall of Rome, was increasing by the eleventh century, a phenomenon that would intensify in the mid-twelfth century before stasis was reached shortly before 1300. Much of this later expansion took place in cities, but in 1100, more than 90 percent of all Europeans lived in small rural settlements.[42] Rising population in the countryside brought about increased demand for food and other goods essential to even a subsistence-level agricultural life. Cropland, and therefore food supply, was increased through reclamation of waste land as well as the manufacture of wholly new arable through forest clearance and marsh drainage. These phenomena were particularly notable in northern France and Flanders; growth in the south appears to have begun earlier but been less marked.[43] English expansion, on the other hand, had been quite considerable by the time of the Domesday Survey

40. OV 6: 550–551.
41. Norman J. G. Pounds, *An Historical Geography of Europe, 450 B.C.–A.D. 1330* (Cambridge, Eng., 1973), 227. Pounds's is one version of the now-standard account of postmillennial growth. Georges Duby, *Rural Economy and Country Life in the Medieval West,* trans. Cynthia Postan (Columbia, S.C., 1968), is a detailed synthesis of much older scholarship; Philippe Contamine et al., *L'économie médiévale* (Paris, 1993), 136–209, is a briefer survey of developments in the period 930–1180, based largely on work since the mid-1970s.
42. Pounds, *An Historical Geography,* 253, 275.
43. For summaries, see ibid., 275–281; Contamine et al., *L'économie médiévale,* 166–168. A series of regional studies, some in an older tradition of agricultural history (e.g., Jacques Boussard on Anjou, Charles Higounnet on the Parisian basin, Adriaan Verhulst on Flanders), others on the model of Georges Duby's study of the Mâconnais (e.g., George Beech on the Poitevan Gâtine, Michel Bur on Champagne, André Chédeville on Chartrain, André Debord on Charente, Guy Devailly on Berry, Robert Fossier on Picardy, Jean-Pierre Poly on Provence, Roland Sanfaçon on Haut-Poitou) outline more specific patterns of expansion. See the Bibliography for full citations.

in the 1080s.[44] Despite regional variations of chronology and intensity, it is clear that expansion of the agricultural economy and population was general across northwestern Europe in the decades around 1100.

Often this growth was directed by religious institutions, but even when the Church could not expand the profitability of its own lands, lay people gave pious donations toward the increase of ecclesiastical patrimony. Such donations were crucial to new monasteries for women, whose modest beginnings were often the result of foundation by a petty lord. But from such an impulse could come great wealth, a fact most striking in the case of the early growth of Fontevraud, which started in 1101 as a group of huts on land provided by Adelaide Rivière and her overlord Gautier of Montsoreau but half a century later was a wealthy abbey, the head of a federation of dozens of French monasteries. The survival of a large number of early charters of Fontevraud affords the best opportunity to examine the relationship of the expanding rural economy and society to the flowering of female monasticism.[45] Table 3 describes the transactions

44. For details, with local variation, e.g., the slower pace of expansion and settlement in the north, see H. E. Hallam, *Rural England, 1066–1348* (Sussex, 1981), 17–23. See also Edward Miller and John Hatcher, *Medieval England: Rural Society and Economic Change, 1086–1348* (London, 1978), 28–41.

45. The cartulary of the abbey of Fontevraud, the so-called Grand Cartulaire, is a precious source for the history of female monasticism. It contains scores of charters from the first half of the twelfth century, many of them from the period before the death of Robert of Arbrissel, the founder of the community, in 1116. But the history of the manuscript is a confusing one and its present state is fragmentary: more than half of it has been lost. Because there exist other copies or printed editions of many charters, a nearly complete reconstruction of the Grand Cartulaire remains possible. Jean-Marc Bienvenu is engaged in this difficult task, which requires the collation of copies in manuscripts and published works dating from the early twelfth century to the late eighteenth.

The larger fragment of the Grand Cartulaire (BN, ms.nouv.acq.lat. 2414) has been analyzed by R. I. Moore, "The Reconstruction of the Cartulary of Fontevrault," *Bulletin of the Institute of Historical Studies* 41 (1968): 87–95. This fragment of the cartulary was redacted in several stages; in many places the hand appears to date to the early twelfth century, yet there are later additions with dates as late as 1222. After examining the contents of the charters and the signature numbers just described, Moore argues that the contents of quires i and ii, part of iii (nos. 658–717), and vii through xv (nos. 790–915) were compiled as a unit. Some of these charters have dates; many more charters can be span-dated from the notation of reigning secular and ecclesiastical lords, and most are from the lifetime of Robert of Arbrissel, often noted as a recipient of charity along with God, Mary, and the nuns. While dozens of charters do not contain any aid to dating, there is no reason why any of those for which there is some guide *must* postdate Robert's death by more than a year or two. Thus, Moore posits, all these 199 charters are a collection compiled soon after the death of the founder in 1116 at the behest of Petronilla of Chemillé, the first abbess of Fontevraud (1115–1149). I cannot accept Moore's entire reconstruction. The codicological evidence is somewhat more complex than he indicates, including apparent changes in quire numeration and different colors of ink, and the existence of a quire (xix) that clearly

recorded in these documents.[46]

This collection of records is remarkable for several reasons. The first is its sheer bulk, especially compared with figures from other new monasteries. Constance Bouchard has examined all extant charters of Burgundian Cistercian houses in the twelfth century. Sixteen Cistercian monasteries generated a total of approximately 200 recorded transactions between 1098 and 1140: less than the number that are known from

belongs with the group Moore describes, but is not consecutively numbered. Still, my own examination of the manuscript leads me to the conclusion that a vast portion of this fragment was indeed copied soon after Robert of Arbrissel's death in 1116 (even if such a conclusion does not solve all the problems related to this manuscript). Furthermore, I am quite confident that the 24 charters in quire xix, folios 9–14, date to the same time, as all internal evidence points to redaction no later than 1118. This means that there are a total of 223 charters from the first two decades of the history of Fontevraud in contemporary copies.

J.-P. Migne published a number of early Fontevraud charters in the *Patrologia Latina*, most of them in truncated versions. Of these, 39 are among the 223 Grand Cartulaire copies just discussed, and another 11 concern people and places known in these early Fontevraud charters. Migne took a number of his texts from the 190 charters printed by J. de la Maineferme in the late seventeenth century. Since the Grand Cartulaire was still nearly complete around 1650, we may assume that Maineferme made his editions directly from it and included no longer extant early copies. Migne's excerpts are accurate partial transcriptions of the charters for which early manuscripts remain, so I have also made use of an additional 23 printed charters for which there appears to be no surviving early manuscript authority. (Jean-Marc Bienvenu, master of early Fontevraud documentation, uses these editions of the charters.)

My discussion of the early history of Fontevraud's property therefore rests on analysis of 246 charters, 90% of which still exist in early twelfth-century copies. The number of charters is not exactly the same as the number of transactions discussed; some documents were copied twice in the early twelfth century, and a few others contain descriptions of two (and in one case three) discrete events. Given their sheer number, it is hard to imagine that these do not constitute the bulk of the charters of Fontevraud's earliest period. Even if they do not, there is no reason to assume that what remains is anything other than a random sample preserved through the accidents of history, and that the description here presents a roughly accurate portrayal of the means by which Robert of Arbrissel's little eremitic community rapidly became a populous and wealthy abbey.

46. The figures for subcategories must be regarded as approximate, because in some cases gifts and sales were mixed in the same transaction and/or included more than one type of property or right: I have chosen whichever category seems most appropriate. Constance B. Bouchard, *Holy Entrepreneurs: Cistercians, Knights, and Economic Exchange in Twelfth-Century Burgundy* (Ithaca, N.Y., 1991), 61–64, 67–68, 92–93, argues that documents in which the actor gives or concedes in return for money or goods are actually gift and countergift, continuations of older social and economic practices explicated by Georges Duby. However, to declare that such transactions belong to one of two distinct categories is extremely difficult for the early Fontevraud charters. Some "countergifts" (usually "ex karitate ecclesie") were considerably larger than what are clearly sale prices: there is, for example, a sale for only 3 ½ solidi, but also one "countergift" of 6 pounds, another of 10. A few transactions are fairly obviously those of gift and countergift—like those involving land or a mill given by a layman and a saddle or horse or pig given by the nuns in return—yet the language of sale is used in at least 30 cases of the 53 listed. For present purposes, I have put all such transactions in one category because in every case, the nuns returned something to the lay person involved.

Table 3. Number of transactions made at Fontevraud, circa 1101–circa 1118, by type

Donations	
Land	97
Buildings	18
Customs and tolls	9
Rights in pasture, forest, waterways	7
Annual income	6
Other or unknown	4
	141
Purchases of land/gifts of land with countergifts	
Return of <50 solidi	10
Return of 50 solidi or more	17
Goods	6
Unstated	20
	53

Confirmations, concessions, and quitclaims

	Property discussed in other charters	Property otherwise unknown	Total
Land	18	7	25
Buildings	12	3	15
Rights	2	0	2
Other	2	2	4
			46
Other			5
Total			**245**

Fontevraud alone in a period only half as long.[47] The composition of the transactions is equally striking. Well over one-half were outright gifts of property to Fontevraud; if to these are added a handful of confirmations of donations unknown in other charters, then over 150 transactions are evidence of gifts to the monastery. Again, comparison to Burgundian Cistercian houses is suggestive: sixteen monasteries gathered a total of

47. Bouchard, *Holy Entrepreneurs*, 24, provides a bar graph describing numbers of transactions by decade. There is no precise tabulation of figures, but it would appear that the total number from the foundation of Cîteaux to 1140 was just under 200. It should be noted that a vast majority of these date to 1120–1140; still, there were fewer in that age of Cistercian expansion than in the first two decades of Fontevraud's existence. Of the sixteen monasteries, eight were founded before 1122.

about 180 transactions of donation by 1140.[48] Most Fontevraud property was land: usually arable, sometimes pasture, forest, or waste. The other major category of acquisition was buildings, in nearly all cases mills, which account for almost 15 percent of early donations. All in all, the charters contain an average of nearly ten donations per year to Fontevraud. As most surviving charters date to the period after 1108, the figure is higher for the years circa 1108–circa 1118.[49]

Such data show that Fontevraud had gathered up a considerable patrimony at an early date. This impression is confirmed by the amount of cash involved in Fontevraud's transactions only a few years after its foundation. Two documents that date to 1106–1108 have the nuns paying a total of 18 pounds, in one case a sale price of 8 pounds, the other 10 pounds paid to an overlord for agreeing to a donation of land on his fief to Fontevraud.[50] Other transactions in or before 1108 include returns to lay people of four horses, two sets of saddle and reins, a cow, a chicken, a tunic, and a total of over 70 solidi.[51]

A religious institution that could draw on such resources less than a decade after its foundation was not only fortunate, but also a ready participant in the complexities of the local and regional economy.[52] Not content merely to own lands for cultivation and pasturage, the nuns were especially careful to gather up rights to mills, the focus of concern in about three dozen documents. In one case, a married couple donated a mill and one adjacent *opera* of land (a unit that could be plowed in one day), in order to build a homestead at the site. Another lord was owed an annual tribute on the mill, but he chose to donate this right to Fontevraud, which now had full control of the mill, nearby lands, and all economic rights concerning the property.[53] The nuns had to act vigorously to defend their rights to a second mill. A man and his wife donated it, in the presence of Robert of Arbrissel and Bishop Peter of Poitiers,

---

48. Ibid., 67.
49. Of 245 transactions, only about 50 must date to 1108 or before, a fact usually signaled by the notice that the charter was drawn up in the reign of King Philip of France. Very few of the early Fontevraud charters have precise dates, however.
50. BN, ms.nouv.acq.lat. 2414 folios 8or.(#795), 100r.–v.(#846).
51. Ibid., folios 10v.–11r.(#591), 12v.(#600), 37v.–38r.(#681), 43v.(#697), 8or.–v.(#796), 115v.(#867), 131r.–v.(#906).
52. For the expansion of arable and economic activity in the regions around Fontevraud, see George T. Beech, *A Rural Society in Medieval France: The Gâtine of Poitou in the Eleventh and Twelfth Centuries* (Baltimore, 1964), 25–26; Roland Sanfaçon, *Défrichements, peuplement et institutions seigneuriales en Haut-Poitou du Xe au XIIIe siècle* (Quebec, 1967), 31–62; and Jacques Boussard, "La vie en Anjou au XIe et XIIe siècles," *Le Moyen Age* 56 (1950): esp. 49–67.
53. BN, ms.nouv.acq.lat. 2414 folios 126r.–127v.(#894–895).

upon the "reception of our daughter into the church of the new congregation of nuns at Fontevraud." This donation was recognized by the overlords of the property, but was subject to two challenges within a few years. Some relatives of the donors seized grain from the mill, and returned it only when Hersende, the mother-in-law of Gautier of Montsoreau and Fontevraud's first prioress, took the case to court in Loudun. Another man, claiming (as the charter puts it) that he had taken bad advice, came to Fontevraud to give up his own claim to the mill, receiving in return a horse.[54]

Still more complicated was the acquisition and oversight of property around what is now the hamlet of Raslay, not far from Fontevraud on the Petite Maine, a Loire tributary. Here, too, Fontevraud began to gather property very early. Starting about 1108, the nuns collected rights to land and the mill of Raslay in at least five different transactions. One lord donated his rights to the mill's watercourse, tilled land, forest, and tithes in the area. Two families ceded their rights to allodial lands at Raslay, each garnering 30 solidi from Hersende. Shortly afterward, an overlord confirmed a donation (no other record of which appears to have survived) by two of his vassals in the same locale. Another man sold the nuns arable and fishing rights at Raslay as well as neighboring meadowland, and some tithes, for 74 solidi. Three separate claims were afterward made on the land. A neighbor of the lord who had donated the waterway made a claim against the nuns, which he withdrew when Hersende offered him 40 solidi. Another man, his niece, and her husband claimed rights to the mill itself; they were persuaded to yield, apparently at no cost to the nuns. Finally, a second claim to the waterway was settled very much to the nuns' advantage, for the claimant gave up the suit and proceeded to donate two pieces of land to Fontevraud, receiving in return a countergift (*de karitate*) of 15 solidi for herself, 12 deniers for her son, and 6 deniers for her daughter.[55]

Because nearly all charters contain the names of a number of lay men and women who acted as donors and vendors or who consented to, confirmed, or witnessed a transaction, hundreds of people had some significant contact with the new community in its early years. Only a few of these individuals were members of the upper nobility. Count Fulk V of

---

54. Ibid., folio 125v.(#892, "pro Dei amore et filiae nostrae in ecclesia novae congregationis monacharum Fontis Evraudi susceptione"), 128v.(#899), 121v.–122r.(#885), 126r.(#893, "Ego Radulphus . . . diu malo consilio abusus").
55. Ibid., folios 111r.–v.(#859), 12r.(#600), 124v.(#890), 133v.–134r.(#911), 81r.(#798), 30r.(#659), 129v.(#902), 30v.(#660).

Anjou and his wife Eremberge of Maine were protectors of Fontevraud and gave a number of properties to Robert of Arbrissel's community, but their influence was felt only from about 1108, when Fulk's mother Bertrade of Montfort became a nun.[56] The only other titled patron who appears in the early charters is Aimeric, viscount of Châtellerault, who gave land to Fontevraud and served as witness to several other transactions.[57] Somewhat below these men on the social scale were castellans such as Gautier of Montsoreau, one of the first supporters of the new community, and Gilbert of Loudun, who protected the nuns' rights in his sphere of influence, to the south of Fontevraud. Although these men were important patrons, their names do not often appear in the charters (in only about twenty-five cases) up to circa 1118.

The vast majority of the lay people involved in the early transactions of Fontevraud, then, were of relatively modest station, probably in most cases landed petty lords and knights who also were the chief supporters of the new male houses proliferating in twelfth-century France. Many of Fontevraud's patrons and guardians were obscure men and women who left to posterity no traces of their activities beyond their participation in the building of a monastic patrimony. It is possible to assume two things about them, however. First, the people who participated in transactions concerning Fontevraud were, in at least some general fashion, tolerant of religious women as neighbors and allies.[58] It was important for Fontevraud's future to have the support of the local powerful: hence the eventual appearance of the count of Anjou in the charters. But the cooperation of other, less elite members of the landed aristocracy was prob-

56. BN, ms.nouv.acq.lat. 2414, folios 45r.–v.(#701–702), 92r.–97v.(#839–844, which begins with the rubric "Incipiunt cartae comitis Fulconis"), 103v.–104r.(#850), 107v.–110r. (#853–855) are charters of Fulk and Eremberge, most of them printed or excerpted in PL 162: 1097–1102. On the delayed participation of the counts of Anjou, see Bienvenu, *L'étonnant fondateur*, 113–116.

57. E.g., ibid., folios 117v.–118r.(#873, a donation of land by Aimeric, partially edited in PL 162:1108), 10v.–11r.(#591), 31v.–32r.(#664), 32v.–33r.(#667), 118v.–119r.(#877), 135v.–136r.(#914). Viscount Aimeric also founded the house of l'Encloître-en-Gironde, about 18 kilometers west of Châtellerault. He is probably best known as a cuckold; his overlord William IX of Aquitaine took Aimeric's wife when he tired of his own, the Toulousin princess Philippa. Philippa subsequently founded a Fontevrist house near Toulouse. The viscount's daughter Aenor married William X, the son and heir of Aimeric's rival. William and Aenor were the parents of Eleanor of Aquitaine, who in her turn became a patroness of Fontevraud late in the twelfth century.

58. That transactions recorded in charters created bonds between a religious house and the surrounding lay community in the twelfth century is a theme of Bouchard, *Holy Entrepreneurs*, esp. 170–184, an analysis drawing considerable inspiration from studies by Barbara H. Rosenwein and Stephen D. White.

ably even more crucial, especially when they went by names such as Jerorius Fat Lips, Ogerius Sword-Rattler, Peter Booty-Seizer, Geoffrey Bad Monk, Hugh Briton-Chewer, and Raginald Who Folds Up Peasants.[59]

Jerorius, Geoffrey, and others, including the brothers Arraudus and Andrew Livid as well as Honey-Sated John, were early patrons of Fontevraud.[60] Many men and women from the nonelite aristocracy had gained sufficient wealth from the expansion of the agricultural economy in the fertile Loire region to be able to use some of their possessions for the good of their souls.[61] Thus Fontevraud was the beneficiary of the pious generosity of a wide spectrum of society, from the counts of Anjou to dozens of otherwise unknown knights and their families. Once again, the pattern conforms to that of Cistercian Burgundy, where support by titled nobles and churchmen was combined with far more frequent contact with castellans, lords, and knights. Something like half, and perhaps more, of Cistercian transactions were between the monks and their knightly neighbors.[62] At Fontevraud, too, the nuns were able to ensure the cooperation, and frequently the pious generosity, of different strata of the local and regional aristocracy.

No other twelfth-century French monastic community for women is as well-documented as Fontevraud, but there is every indication that a similar pattern held for other new houses of the late eleventh and twelfth centuries: a rapid aggregation of landed patrimony and wealth, offered for the most part by the local petty aristocracy. In the northern part of the Continental region, too, nunneries drew their wealth from the local rural economy. Etrun, a nunnery in Artois founded about 1085 by the local bishop, received a confirmation of its possessions in 1119 from Pope Calixtus II. In thirty-five years, the nuns had gathered up properties

59. BN, ms.nouv.acq.lat. 2414 folios 31v.(#663, "Jerorius crassa labra"), 82v.(#803, "Ogerius verberans ferrum"), 12r.–v.(#598, "Petro trahente predam"), 8v.(#587, "Gaufridus malus monachus"), 11r.(#593, "Hugonis manducantis britonem"), 135r.–v.(#913, "Raginaldus plicat vilanum").
60. Ibid., folios 31v.–32r.(#664, "Arraudus Lividus"), 83r.(#804, "Johannes saturatus melle").
61. I do not mean to suggest that donors considered their gifts a kind of "luxury," for their piety was sincere (see below). But it is impossible to imagine the expansions of Fontevraud's patrimony, or that of hundreds of other religious houses, without some basis in economic expansion.
62. Bouchard offers the following breakdown of the men and women in twelfth-century Burgundian Cistercian transactions: 8% upper (titled) aristocracy, 7% churchmen, 22% "castellans and powerful lords," and 26% knights. Bouchard suggests that most of the 37% who are of unknown social status were likely knights, meaning that something like half of the principals in Cistercian transactions belonged to the lowest rank of the aristocracy; *Holy Entrepreneurs*, 165, 170.

in nearly fifty locations, some nearby, others more distant. Although Etrun was only a few kilometers from the episcopal city of Arras, nearly all the nuns' wealth was connected to the rural economy. Most of the patrimony was made up of arable land with *curtilia*, in this case most probably fenced-in dwellings. The nuns had patronage of four parish churches and owned three mills. They were also in the brewing business: they had seven malthouses in nearby Arras. Of the thirty or so male and female patrons of Etrun who are mentioned in the bull, only one is of high status: Countess Clementia of Flanders, who founded two other nunneries in the region.[63] By the 1120s, Etrun itself was populous enough to start a colony in Hainault: the nunnery of Ghislinghien, which in its turn was generously endowed by members of the local aristocracy in the twelfth century.[64]

Far to the south, a new Fontevrist house managed to attract a number of donations in its early years. The house of Jourcey was founded circa 1130 in the rough landscape of Forez, a mountainous region to the west of Lyon. Documents concerning the house drawn up around 1150 show that, even in a region far less fertile and populous than the lower Loire Valley, Artois, or Hainault, it was possible to support the religious life on lands donated by the faithful. Besides the land right around the monastery, sited on the right bank of the upper Loire, the nuns acquired a number of possessions, including vineyards, on both sides of the river.[65] The records of Jourcey show that agricultural exploitation was already considerably advanced in the region by 1150 and that the estate was assembled with the donations of obscure local men and women. Here, as elsewhere, donations of land at entry made up a significant portion of the new monastic patrimony. The fourteen initial transactions contain

63. Ulysse Robert, *Etude sur les actes du pape Calixte II* (Paris, 1874), xxxviii–xl, is an edition of the bull. On the founding of Etrun, see Chapter 3. "Curtilis" (or, as here, "curtile") can have a number of meanings, but this seems the most likely because it is always listed separately from lands (e.g., "ex dono Hermowere, septem curtilia et terram arabilem" [xxxix]. See J. F. Niermeyer, *Mediae latinitatis lexicon minus* (Leiden, 1984), 294. The nuns owned at least 50 of these homesteads, the total of those listed is 40, and there are 5 instances in which a donation included an unspecified number of "curtilia."

64. DHGE 20: 1182–1183. About half the property that Ghislinghien controlled in the early modern period was assembled by the end of the twelfth century. See Daniel Van Overstraeten, *Inventaire des archives de l'abbaye de Ghislinghien* (Brussels, 1976), 203–218.

65. Edouard Perroy, "Les plus anciennes chartes du prieuré de Jourcey," *Bulletin de la Diana* 28 (1943): 172–185. I am using the materials Perroy assembled for slightly different purposes than the author's. Perroy finds the chief importance of these documents as filling a void in monastic archives in the region, which are otherwise very slim for the period 1130–1175, and uses the records primarily to consider the state of agriculture and the relatively favorable position of peasant tenants around 1150.

provision for nine women entering Jourcey: four sisters, three daughters, and two wives of donors.[66] As at Montazais in Poitou, entry donations were considerable importance in assembling a patrimony.

For southwestern France, Languedoc and Gascony, the information about nuns and their properties is very scanty, a reflection in part of a density of new nunneries far lower than that of any other part of the region under consideration except the northern and western reaches of the English archdioceses. But once again, the evidence points to rapid growth of rural wealth through the generosity of the lower aristocracy. The Benedictine nunnery of Gigean, founded near the Mediterranean coast around the turn of the twelfth century, had gathered sufficient property to request a bull from Pope Alexander III in 1162.[67] Fabas, founded before 1150 with the support of the bishop of Comminges on the lands of the lords of Benque, was set in the fertile valley of a Garonne tributary at the foot of a forest. Local nobles, in particular the counts of Montesquieu and Comminges, donated property to the nuns at Fabas in the convent's early years. (Although these men were styled "count," they were considerably less grand than their northern counterparts: there were far more petty but titled aristocrats in the south.) Most telling is the foundation from Fabas of another nunnery, Oraison-Dieu in the diocese of Toulouse, around 1167.[68] Several other southern houses founded in the twelfth century also appeared to have prospered from a relatively early date, sometimes in concert with nearby male monasteries.[69]

There is relatively little evidence concerning the dozens of English nunneries founded in the twelfth century.[70] However, a very rich collection of Lincolnshire records has survived, including 115 original twelfth-century charters concerning the property of Bullington, a Gilbertine house founded in the last years of the reign of King Stephen by Simon of Kyme, a local lord. Some 70 documents concern donations to Bullington in the first half-century of its history. The pattern observed on the Continent held in the English countryside as well: the nuns (and canons) gathered a

---

66. Ibid., 182–184. The "tableau analytique" shows the 14 different donations, summarized in a parchment roll redacted about 1150.
67. Marthe Moreau, "Les moniales du diocèse de Maguelonne au XIIIe siècle," *Cahiers de Fanjeaux* 23 (1988), 248–249.
68. DHGE 16: 301.
69. Constance Berman has suggested that the success of some male Cistercian houses was owed at least in part to their connection with nearby nunneries, citing the monasteries of Silvanes, Grandselve, and Valmagne and their relations with the female houses of Nonenque, l'Espinasse, and Le Vignogoul (Berman, "Men's Houses, Women's Houses").
70. On this paucity of original charters and cartularies, see Thompson, *Women Religious,* 7–8, 11–15.

primarily agricultural patrimony from the local gentry, who had wealth but
were not of England's baronial class. Over 50 transactions are concerned
primarily with land, and about two-thirds of these give a figure concerning
the size of the donation. The nuns amassed over three hundred acres of
arable and over twenty-six bovates, plus numerous other gifts described in
different measures; the total may have approached one thousand acres.
There were two important differences between the patrimony of Bullington and that of most Continental houses: the Gilbertines had a number of
urban and suburban properties (in and around Lincoln), and they were in
the wool business, owning pasture for a total of 1,100 sheep. Still, agricultural wealth was the mainstay of the Lincolnshire nuns.[71]

Surviving evidence for other English houses points to the same kinds
of wealth as that gathered in Bullington and deriving from the same social milieu, if usually on a smaller scale. Shortly after the foundation of
the Lincolnshire house of Greenfield, the nuns requested that Archbishop Theobald of Canterbury confirm their first gifts. Theobald's
charter lists six donors, local lords, whose gifts amount to 114 acres of
arable, two *culturae*, one whole forest and parts of two others, and other
territories of unspecified size.[72] A charter of the bishop of Lincoln confirms the first properties, located in northern Leicestershire, of Langley.
Its founder, William Pantulf, gave the nuns his forest and arable around
Langley, two parish churches, one of which included six bovates of land,
and four more bovates of land nearby. The initial endowment of the
house, then, was substantial.[73]

Even at a long-established English nunnery, the lower aristocracy were
the chief patrons in the post-Conquest period. Eighteen donations at

71. *Documents Illustrative of the Social and Economic History of the Danelaw*, ed. F. M. Stenton
(London, 1920), 1–74. Fifty-six charters are simple donations; 15 acquisitions otherwise
unknown are revealed in 12 confirmations and 3 quitclaims. The calculation assumes 20
acres per bovate (see xxviii). There are also donations with measures in carrucates, selions,
perticatae, and *andennae* and over a dozen documents that give no figure at all. A number of
these donations specify the inclusion of one or more tofts on the land. Elkins, *Holy Women*,
92–93, gives different figures.
72. *Documents Illustrative*, 72 (#117).
73. *English Episcopal Acta I, Lincoln, 1067–1185*, ed. David M. Smith (London, 1980),
88–89. William Pantulf's original grant includes the information that the church of Little
Dalby included 6 bovates of land (*Documents Illustrative*, 308). *English Episcopal Acta I*,
127–129, are confirmations of early grants to the Lincolnshire monastery of Nun Cotham.
Not every foundation had such modest beginnings: the nunnery of Godstow in Oxford-
shire received a confirmation of its possessions in 1139, not long after its foundation by a
noble widow who became its first abbess. Godstow had received donations from King
Stephen and his queen, Archbishop Theobald, three other bishops, two abbots, and a large
number of laymen, including the count and countess of Leicester (20–22).

entry to Shaftesbury circa 1086–circa 1121 document postulants and patrons. This Anglo-Saxon house, just barely nudged out by Wilton for the
title of richest nunnery in Domesday England, was supported in large
part by local landholding families, Norman and English. Just as elsewhere, these donors, whose kin went into the religious life in the late
eleventh and early twelfth centuries, were not of the high aristocracy:
none of them was among the wealthiest barons in post-Conquest England. Even the tenants-in-chief who made donations to Shaftesbury
were of the very lowest economic rank of their class.[74]

Holy Stewardship

The lower aristocracy of the eleventh and twelfth centuries also made
contributions of another kind to the growth of female monasticism:
their mothers, wives, sisters, and daughters. Although the nuns of this
period were nearly all of high birth, the social composition of the nunneries was somewhat more diverse in the twelfth century than previously. At Ronceray in Angers, for example, entry donations from 1028
to 1184 show that the largest number of entrants of the highest status
came by 1100, and the records of Queen Mathilda's foundation at Caen
show a less socially prominent group in the early twelfth century than
earlier. Very noble women certainly continued to enter monastic life in
the twelfth century, but entry donations such as those at Montazais show
that a large number of nuns came from the lower reaches of the landed
elite.[75]

It is not simply sentimental to regard these women as gifts, for that is
the way they are described in the language of the charters. The usual
formula for donations at entry, repeated in scores of twelfth-century
documents, announces a gift of real property *cum filia, matre,* or *sorore,*
"along with" a daughter, mother, sister, or other female relative. A donation to Notre-Dame in Saintes from 1148 has a local couple "offering
their daughter" (*offerentes filiam suam*) along with a number of lands and

---

74. Kathleen Cooke, "Donors and Daughters: Shaftesbury Abbey's Benefactors, Endowment and Nuns, c.1086–1130," *Anglo-Norman Studies* 12 (1990): 29–45.
75. Verdon, "Les moniales dans la France de l'Ouest," 247–249. Verdon does not note
change across time, but cites 11 women of high birth who entered Ronceray. Of these, 7
had entered by ca. 1100, and an eighth was the abbess elected in 1122, styled "clara styrpe
progenita," an imprecise description. Recruitment at La Trinité, Caen, appears to have
been at a less exalted level after the death of Abbess Mathilda in 1113 (250).

tithes.[76] Furthermore, these donations are often said to be to God and the saints as well as to the community: "to God, to Mary, and to the church of Fontevraud" is a standard formula in Fontevrist charters.[77] These expressions reflect the piety of men and women who gave their goods, their kin, and sometimes, as in the case of Andegavina at Montazais and others, even themselves, to facilitate a life of prayer for the salvation not only of the donors and their families, but also of Christendom in general.

It is an old generalization that it was cheaper to place a daughter in a religious house than to provide a dowry.[78] The evidence on the point from the great era of female monastic growth is far too scanty to allow such a generalization, especially as a significant population in religious houses in this era was not made up of unmarried daughters. Still, it is worth considering whether the striking prevalence of members of northwestern Europe's lower aristocracy in the foundation and support of nunneries might reflect at least some measure of economic calculation concerning provision for daughters. Given the case of women such as Christina of Markyate, resisting her parents' desire to see her married, it is hard to think that this particular consideration was always paramount. Some families might have desired to ensure the safety and security of their female members by sparing them the perils of marriage and childbirth and even in some cases decided that an entry gift, or even the foundation of a nunnery with relatives in mind, was a "good investment."[79]

76. *Cartulaire de l'abbaye royale de Notre-Dame de Saintes*, 126 (no. 202).
77. "Deo et sancte Marie et ecclesie Fonte Evraudi"; BN, ms.nouv.acq.lat. 2414, folios 11r.–12r.(#593–597), 39v.–41v.(#686–693), etc.
78. Cooke, "Donors and Daughters," 37–39, 44, takes on the problem and finds that in the case of Shaftesbury, the members of the lower aristocracy who made entry donations for their daughters were making an economic choice, finding a way of providing for female family members that was cheaper than providing a dowry. As Cooke admits, the evidence for this point is thin and support for the generalization very hard to find in eleventh- and twelfth-century records.
79. Alternatively, of course, a family could hope to gain status through an advantageous marriage, however expensive in the short term. Any monocausal explanation of monastic expansion, especially one based on the assumption that medieval people's decision making was, as modern economists would put it, entirely rational, will not serve here. On the subject of marital and monastic portions see Johnson, *Equal in Monastic Profession*, 23–24, where the data, admittedly based on meager and difficult evidence, suggest that a lump-sum payment for a marriage portion might be less than the total of annual monastic dowry payments if the woman remained in the monastery more than seven years. If this is true, the large number of monastic widows, who had shorter life expectancies than child or adolescent oblates, may reflect economic realities as well as marital patterns. That is, a widow and her family might gamble that retirement on a pension to monastic life was ultimately less expensive than remarriage. But generalizations are at the moment impossible; a series of detailed studies of the problem in specific periods and regions would illuminate the matter.

The women, once veiled, often made contributions beyond those of prayer for their kin. Charters show that some twelfth-century monastic superiors were remarkably adept managers of properties and people. Robert of Arbrissel never advocated utter rejection of the world and indeed chose Hersende of Montsoreau and Petronilla of Chemillé to lead Fontevraud in his absence because he knew the first to be a woman of faith and insight, the second an expert landlord: a "wise, hard-working, and very cautious" team.[80] Some of Hersende's activities in pursuit of the mundane needs of the community have already been noted. Hersende died by 1112, and according to Robert's second *vita*, written shortly after his death by the chaplain Andreas, the aged errant preacher wanted to appoint an abbess to lead the nuns and monks of Fontevraud. "But how," Robert asked, "can any claustral virgin, who knows only how to sing psalms, suitably manage our external affairs? Tell me: one always accustomed to being occupied with spiritual things, did she ever direct mundane matters reasonably?" Robert wanted a Martha, he explained, not a Mary.[81]

Not surprisingly, Robert's choice was Petronilla. "Indeed it seems to me fitting that one who bore along with me the labor of traveling and poverty also should bear any burden of support and good fortune. Although she is once-married, it seems to me that by virtue of necessity, no-one is more suitable for this prelacy."[82] Petronilla, a member of the lower aristocracy of the region, became the first abbess of Fontevraud in 1115, and for over 30 years supervised and encouraged the growth of the congregation of Fontevraud. The vigor with which Petronilla pursued Robert's charge, even long after his death, is evident from numerous charters of her abbacy. The patrimony of Fontevraud continued to grow. And like Hersende before her, Petronilla was a careful

---

80. PL 162: 1054: "Vivebat autem Hersendis et magnae religionis et magni pariter consilii. Huic autem Hersendi conjunxit et Petronillam procurationis mansionariae gnaram. . . . Has itaque duas feminas quoniam cognoverat prudentes et industrias et magnae cautelae personas, aliis, ut dictum est, praefecerat sororibus."

81. PL 162: 1060: "Sed quomodo poterit quaelibet claustrensis virgo exteriora nostra convenienter dispensare, quae non novit nisi psalmos cantare? Quid enim rationabiliter cantavit terrestria, quae semper consuevit operari spiritualia? Liceat Mariae coelestibus continuo inhiare, et eligatur Martha, quae sciat exteriora sollicite ministrare."

82. Ibid., 1061: "Dignum quippe mihi videtur, ut quae portavit mecum laborem peregrinationis et paupertatis, portet enim pondus qualecunque consolationis nostrae et prosperitatis. Licet enim monogama fuerit, cogente tamen necessitate, nulla mihi convenientior videtur huic prelationi." These linked statements allow for the possibility that Petronilla joined Robert's wandering troupe in flight from her husband, like other women of Fontevraud. Otherwise why not style Petronilla *vidua* rather than *monogama*?

steward of the properties of Fontevraud and brooked no interference with them:

> I, Petronilla, who then by the grace of God held the primacy of Fontevraud, have taken care to commend to the memory of the living and of posterity that one day, when I had stopped briefly to refresh my-self at La Pignonnière, Helignandus of Longchamp and Elisabeth, wife of the oft-mentioned Achardus, came up together for the sake of visit-ing me. And when we had said quite a lot, among other things I re-minded Elisabeth that her son Buccardus should concede to lord Robert and the nuns subject to him this land, which his father Achardus and she herself had conceded to them in perpetual ownership. She replied to me in words to this effect: the land had been bought and ac-quired by her [or "them"] so that they could leave it and give it to whomever they pleased, freely and peacefully. Then I, Petronilla, not wishing to acquiesce to her statement, with the advice of our friends and with her assent, on this account went to the place called Escharbot with some brothers and laymen.[83]

At these proceedings, the right of the nuns was recognized, and another lay patron gave Buccardus a small money tribute to recognize that he had, in fact, given the land to Fontevraud. Petronilla's insistence to Elis-abeth was both understandable and necessary, for the nuns had paid 10,000 solidi for the land, which had subsequently been subject to two claims, the first by the grandson of the vendor, who was declared to be underage and his suit dismissed. The second claim was by Achardus Es-charbot and Elisabeth, who had indeed been given 300 solidi and a horse to concede La Pignonnière to Fontevraud shortly before the action

---

83. BN, ms.nouv.acq.lat. 2414, folio 103r.–v. (#849): "Memoriae tam presentium quam posterorum commendare curavi quod ego Petronilla quae tunc Dei gratia Fontis Ebraudi prioratum tenebam, dum uno die apud Pignorariam paululum me recreassem, Helignandus de Longo Campo et Elisabet uxor sepedicti Achardi, me visitandi gratia, pariter ad me venerunt. Cumque satis plura dixissemus, haec inter cetera ipsi [sic] Elis-abet reduxi memorie ut filius suus Buccardus domno R[oberto] et feminis sibi subposi-tis concederet terram quam pater eius Achardus et ipsa perpetuo eis tenendam concesserat. Quae meis itaque verbis huiusce modi verba respondit: quia predicta terra de emptione sua et adquisitione fuerat et cui ipsi voluissent eam libere vel quiete dare ut dimittere potuissent. Tunc ego Petronilla nolens suis adquiescere dictis, consilio am-icorum nostrorum et suo assensu, ad locum qui vulgo Escarbot appellatur de fratribus et saecularibus hominibus huius rei gratia transmisi." These events date to the earliest period of Petronilla's abbacy, or possibly even before it, as Robert of Arbrissel was ap-parently still alive.

described in the quoted document.[84] One guesses that the abbess would have been a match for Peter Booty-Seizer or Ogerius Sword-Rattler had the opportunity arisen.

Such determined action was not unusual for Petronilla, who saw no conflict between spiritual aims and temporal necessities and was more explicit than her male contemporaries about what she regarded as coherent parts of a larger whole.[85] "Often putting aside the glory of reading and prayers, we turn to management of temporal goods for the advantage of our successors, which indeed we do for this reason: that when we are sleeping in our tombs, we may be helped by their prayers before God." Shortly after becoming abbess, Petronilla appealed to Count Fulk for the restoration of properties claimed by a foreigner, as the document has it, acting at the devil's inspiration. Some years later two brothers seized mills belonging to Fontevraud. The abbess, called "a very wise woman," arranged matters in such a way that the claimants "not only humbly made amends for the wickedness they had committed, begging for mercy, but also confirmed the gift of their brother [who gave the mills], confessing to have done evil against the family of God."[86]

Like her male contemporaries, Petronilla knew the importance of a written record. "The goods of the church of the holy mother of God at Fontevraud are committed to writing, lest on account of the swiftness of fleeting life they be given over to oblivion by our successors. Therefore Lady Petronilla, first religious abbess, ordered that gifts to the above-

---

84. Ibid., folios 97v.–100r.(#845 and 845bis), 101r.–102v.(#848).

85. The Cistercians, once thought the prime example of those who fled the world and its business, are now recognized to have been active and even innovative participants in the economy of the twelfth century; see in particular Berman, *Medieval Agriculture, the Southern French Countryside, and the Early Cistercians* (Philadelphia, 1986), and Bouchard, *Holy Entrepreneurs*, esp. 185–198, which shows that scholarly focus on "legislative" provisions has obscured Cistercian involvement with the economy from the earliest days of the order. But most monks of the early twelfth century, especially those of the "reforming" orders, were less blunt than Robert and Petronilla.

86. BN, ms.nouv.acq.lat. 2414, folio 71v.(#768, dated 1119): "Sepe postpositis lectionis oracionumque floribus, ad disponenda temporalia propter successorum utilitatem nos inclinamus, quod nimirum idcirco facimus ut cum in sepulchris dormierimus, earum precibus apud Deum adiuvari valeamus"; folio 105v.(#852): "denuntiamus quamdam iniuriose calumpnationis iniuriam quam quidam vir advena, Gireus nomine . . . diabolico instinctu nobis fecit"; folio 64r.(#746): "Abbatissa itaque tunc temporis de Chimilliaco Petronilla, mulier sapientissima, adeo ut eos contigit non tantum quod male fecerant misericordiam eius implorantes suppliciter emendarent, verum eciam donum fratris sui se contra Dei familiam male fecisse confitentes, confirmaverunt."

mentioned place made in her time be written down."[87] It was probably at Petronilla's behest that the first cartulary of Fontevraud, containing the charters discussed above, was redacted, shortly after the death of Robert of Arbrissel.[88]

The size of the Order of Fontevraud, as it came to be known, grew steadily through the first half of the twelfth century. Starting with Pascal II in 1106, every twelfth-century pope except the short-lived Celestine II confirmed to Fontevraud and its dependent houses privileges and properties, strengthening ties between the abbey and Rome. In 1119, Calixtus II dedicated the Romanesque abbey church at Fontevraud.[89] Abbess Petronilla's energies remained undiminished in the 1140s, when she took advantage of papal connections during a protracted wrangle with Ulger, the bishop of Angers. The immediate cause of the quarrel was the maltreatment of one of Petronilla's secular allies, a man known to us only as Basset, whose houses were wrecked and possessions stolen by agents of Bishop Ulger. The matter became a cause célèbre. Bernard of Clairvaux sent an outraged letter to the bishop, lamenting the *scandalum*, as he called it. "It is more fitting to weep," began the venerable abbot, "than to write a letter."[90] Basset went to Rome to appeal in person to Pope Innocent II.[91] However, the difficulty was not simply maltreatment of Petronilla's ally. Basset held lands adjacent to those of the bishop along the Loire. The violence against him was thus connected to a larger and more important issue: Fontevraud's rights on the Ponts-de-Cé near Angers, at that time the only passage over the Loire in Anjou and hence an extremely lucrative property. In 1144, Pope Lucius, writing to Petronilla about the ongoing troubles between her and Ulger, appointed a commission of five bishops to settle the case. Arbitration over rights on the Ponts-de-Cé was completed by the following year, and Fontevraud's rights

---

87. Ibid., folio 58r.–v.(#734): "Bona ecclesie sancte Dei genetrici Marie Fontis Evraudi in scriptis mittuntur, ne a posteriis nostris, propter velocitatem transeuntis vitae, oblivioni tradantur. Ideoque domna Petronilla prima religiosa abbatissa illius loci dona supradicti suo tempore facta scribere iussit."

88. The suggestion that Petronilla had the first cartulary made is R. I. Moore's; see note 45. It is interesting to note Petronilla's statements and activities in the context of recent studies on orality and literacy in the central Middle Ages, e.g., M. T. Clanchy, *From Memory to Written Record: England, 1066–1307*, 2d ed. (Cambridge, Mass., 1993).

89. PL 163: 1121. The church and several other twelfth-century structures, including a fascinating octagonal kitchen, have survived.

90. [Bernard of Clairvaux], *Sancti Bernardi Opera*, ed. J. Leclercq, C. H. Talbot and H. Rochais (Rome, 1957–), 8: 57 [Letter 200]: "Lacrimas magis dare quam litteras libet."

91. PL 179: 635–636.

confirmed, but not until the early spring of 1149 was restitution to Basset settled at 1,000 Angevin solidi.[92]

The abbess died a few weeks later. As she was already married when she joined Robert of Arbrissel's religious community at the dawn of the twelfth century, Petronilla was an old woman by 1149. The necrology of Fontevraud refers to her as "our incomparable and irrecoverable mother."[93] Owing in large part to Petronilla and Hersende before her, there were by the mid-twelfth century over fifty monasteries in the order. All of them were, like Fontevraud, mixed communities headed by a female superior, distributed across the region bounded by northern Champagne, Lyonnais, and Aragon. The number of daughter houses grew some in the decades that followed, but until the French Revolution the Order of Fontevraud remained very much what it had become under the guidance of Hersende and Petronilla: the largest and wealthiest federation of monasteries for women in Catholic Europe.

There is similar evidence of managerial skill on the part of another *quondam* wife turned nun, who also is possibly the most famous woman of the twelfth century. Heloise's parentage is unknown; she was probably of a lineage similar to Petronilla's. She grew up in the nunnery of Argenteuil in Paris.[94] As a teenager, in the care of her uncle Fulbert, a canon of the cathedral of Notre-Dame, she became the student of the fiery intellectual Peter Abelard. The story is well known. The two became lovers; Heloise had a child; she and Abelard married but soon after parted. At her husband's insistence, Heloise returned to Argenteuil in a nun's habit. Fulbert proceeded to take violent revenge on the man he suspected of spurning his niece: Abelard was castrated. Abelard became a monk and retired to Champagne, living in a hermitage called the Paraclete, located six or seven kilometers from Nogent-sur-Seine, northwest of Troyes. Called to be abbot of a monastery in his native Brittany in 1126, he remembered that his isolated oratory was deserted when he heard that the nuns of Argenteuil, now led by Heloise, had been expelled by Abbot Suger of Saint-Denis, who laid claim to the property. In

92. Jean-Marc Bienvenu, "Le conflit entre Ulger, évêque d'Angers, et Pétronille de Chemillé, abbesse de Fontevrault (vers 1140–1149)," *Revue Mabillon* 58, no. 248 (1972): 113–132. The document concerning the final settlement, which is known only through a seventeenth-century edition, is printed at the bottom of the columns in PL 179: 923–926.
93. ADML 101 H 225 bis, p. 242: "incomparabilis et irrecuperabilis mater nostra."
94. See Charlotte Charrier, *Héloïse dans l'histoire et dans la légende* (Paris, 1933), 50–52; Enid McLeod, *Héloïse: A Biography* (London, 1971), 8–12; and Robert-Henri Bautier, "Paris au temps d'Abélard," in *Abélard en son temps* (Paris, 1981), 75–77, for speculations on Heloise's parentage.

1129, some of Heloise's community went to the Paraclete, where Abelard came to install them and to pay a rare visit to Heloise.

Heloise is best known through her correspondence with Abelard. Most of the letters concern personal and theological matters, but Heloise also asked Abelard to write a rule for the Paraclete, pointing out that the Rule of Saint Benedict was inadequate for women.[95] Most of Abelard's erudite and lengthy reply concerned matters of internal organization and practice, but he did make some telling remarks about the choice of a superior. He scorned the "pernicious practice" of electing virgins instead of those who have known men, and younger women over older ones, echoing the sentiments of Robert of Arbrissel (whom he did not mention). Abelard also cautioned against the choice of powerful noblewomen as abbesses, for they might became proud to the disadvantage of the convent, especially if they were local people whose families might interfere with monastic life.[96] Heloise, neither a virgin nor of local origin, proved a remarkable leader. Peter the Venerable, abbot of Cluny, admired Heloise's community, wished that she were a nun at Marcigny, and praised her as a philosopher for having exchanged logic for the Gospel, Plato for Christ, school for the cloister.[97]

Less famed are Heloise's skills in management of temporal matters, but these were quite exceptional. The Paraclete was a poor foundation at the beginning; Abelard notes that the nuns' life there "was full of hardship at first and for a while they suffered the greatest deprivation."[98] But this period of want was over by 1147, when Pope Eugenius III issued a bull confirming the possessions of Heloise and her nuns.[99] Eugenius named over fifty donors; these include Count Thibaud of Champagne (mentioned twice) and his countess, a viscountess, the bishop of Troyes,

---

95. [Abelard and Heloise], "The Letter of Heloise on Religious Life and Abelard's First Reply," ed. J. T. Muckle, in *Mediaeval Studies* 17 (1955): 241–253, esp. 242–244. Translation in *The Letters of Abelard and Heloise*, trans. Betty Radice (Harmondsworth, Eng., 1974), 159–179.

96. [Abelard], "Abelard's Rule for Religious Women," ed. T. P. McLaughlin in *Mediaeval Studies* 18 (1956): 252–254; *Letters of Abelard and Heloise*, 200, 202.

97. Peter the Venerable, *The Letters of Peter the Venerable*, ed. Giles Constable, 2 vols. (Cambridge, Mass., 1967), 1: 303–308; *Letters of Abelard and Heloise*, 277–284. The abbot wrote to Heloise in 1144.

98. Abelard, *Historia calamitatum*, ed. Jacques Monfrin, 100; *Letters of Abelard and Heloise*, 97.

99. *Cartulaire de l'abbaye du Paraclet*, ed. Charles Lalore, Vol. 2 of *Collection des principaux cartulaires du diocèse de Troyes* (Paris, 1878), 6–14. On the early properties of the Paraclete, see the remarks in McLeod, *Héloïse*, 210–215, and Charrier, *Héloïse dans l'histoire*, 261–273. The observations that follow will be superseded by Mary Martin McLaughlin's forthcoming study of Heloise and the Paraclete.

and the archbishop of Sens. But the rest of the Paraclete's patrons were of lesser rank, a few identified as *miles*, most obscure landed men and women. Less than twenty years after the refugees arrived there, the Paraclete had properties or rights in over eighty places. Most of the patrimony was land, the rest mills and annual tributes. Unlike Fontevraud, which only a few years after its foundation had possessions spread across a large part of western France, the Paraclete's holdings were compact. With a lone exception, all of the Paraclete's properties in 1147 were within fifty kilometers of the mother house. A vast majority were within fifteen kilometers, in a region reaching north across the Seine and south and east toward Troyes. There were also properties somewhat farther south, along a smaller river, and a number near Provins, a town twenty-three kilometers northwest of the Paraclete. Because most of the original charters of the Paraclete have disappeared, it is difficult to know much about the process by which this patrimony was assembled. But the surviving evidence hints that the model of Fontevraud holds in this case: a skilled manager's careful handling of goods acquired primarily through donation by pious local people.

A charter of 1133 outlines the donation of some properties in and around Provins, including forty solidi in tithes at Provins and nearby Lesines, with the proviso that if some or all of the sum cannot be obtained there, the donor is obliged to make up the difference from another holding. It is then repeated that the tithes at Lesines are granted by the donors, one of whom entered the Paraclete; this woman noted that her brother Robert also had granted them.[100] Heloise apparently realized two things about this donation: first, that a gift of tithes involved some risk, and would constitute a reliable source of income only if carefully acquired. Second, more than one or two people often considered themselves to have title to a property or right in the early twelfth century, and it was necessary to specify who they were. This is clear from a document written three years later, in which the archbishop of Sens, acting at Heloise's request, gave to the Paraclete the tithe of Lesines, which he noted that the same Robert and another man had previously conveyed to him personally.[101] Such complexities notwithstanding, Heloise multiplied the Paraclete's properties to the extent that by 1146 the nuns could afford to pay 120 pounds for lands and tithes near the monastery.[102]

100. *Cartulaire du Paraclet*, 62–63.
101. Ibid., 64.
102. Ibid., 70–71.

Abelard observed that once he left Heloise and the nuns, "their worldly goods were multiplied more in a single year than mine would have been in a hundred, had I remained there, for as much as women are weaker, so much the more pitiable is their poverty, which easily rouses human sympathy, and the more pleasing is their virtue to God and to men."[103] Despite Abelard's insistence on female frailty, it is very doubtful that Heloise and her community were simply passive recipients of pious donations. The relative compactness of the Paraclete's possessions suggests that Heloise gathered wealth quite deliberately, perhaps frequently exchanging or buying lands nearby as she did in 1146. Furthermore, the same pattern is visible in the patrimony of a daughter house of the Paraclete. La Pommeraie was founded in 1151 on lands of Mathilda, dowager countess of Champagne, not far from the Yonne River north of Sens.[104] A papal bull of 1157 lists the properties of this new house, which were mostly along the banks of the lower Yonne and near the confluence of Yonne and Seine.[105] One of Heloise's modern biographers refers in this context to "a strong practical sense which might almost be called business ability."[106] No such qualification is necessary, for Heloise was obviously a very successful businesswoman whose legacy as abbess was not only her reputation for learning and piety but also landed wealth, ensuring that by the late twelfth century, sixty nuns could worship in the Paraclete.[107]

For abbesses and their deputies to be in charge of property and other business was, at least at Fontevraud and the Paraclete, a matter of course. When he appointed Petronilla as abbess, Robert of Arbrissel also drew up a set of rules for Fontevraud. Stipulations about the conditions under which the abbess, prioress, and other nuns might be allowed to leave the cloister show that travel for the purposes of doing business was normal.[108] The *maior priorissa* was to be received in all Fontevraud's churches and cells and was to be second only to the

103. Abelard, *Historia calamitatum*, 100–101; *Letters of Abelard and Heloise*, 97.
104. For the foundation, see *Cartulaire général de l'Yonne*, 1: 493–494.
105. *Cartulaire du Paraclet*, 18–20.
106. McLeod, *Héloïse*, 211.
107. *Cartulaire du Paraclet*, 33–34, is a papal letter of 1196, enjoining that the number of nuns not exceed 60. Such a request suggests that the community was or had been larger; see Chapter 5.
108. The history of the rules is very complex; see Walter, *Die ersten Wanderprediger Frankreichs*, 1: 65–82, 189–195, and Gold, *The Lady and the Virgin*, 98–101. Although none of the three remaining fragments seems to be Robert's original rule, all date to the first half of the twelfth century, and the portion I cite comes from a redaction of about 1117 which excerpts part of the first text.

abbess in executing the business of the community.[109] The Paraclete statutes known as *Institutiones nostrae*, which date to Heloise's time, contain regulations anticipating this same need for mobility in order to conduct business. As a modern commentary on the *Institutiones* puts it, the rules are "quite liberal: nuns and lay-sisters are authorized to handle business which might otherwise have been delegated to bailiffs and other officials charged with monastery affairs."[110] So the superior's job included the distribution of tasks to other nuns. In the twelfth century, management of *temporalia* by women such as Hersende, Petronilla, and Heloise was, in theory and in fact, a central and legitimate responsibility of abbesses.

Unfortunately, we can find out even less about most other superiors of new nunneries than about the precise nature of their place in local social and economic structure. Surely, these women were significant figures, women whose experience in the world, like that of Eliduc's first wife Guildeluec, could be a useful attribute in a position of monastic leadership. A telling hint is provided by the earliest surviving charter from a nunnery near Carcassonne. An 1162 donation is addressed to "God and the church of the Blessed Mary of Rieunette and to you, humble Raina, business manager [*praesidenti negotiis*] of the monastery of this church."[111] As the document was drawn up in the convent, this language makes it clear that both the nuns and their patrons regarded the temporal aspect of the superior's duties as considerable. Sadly, lists of twelfth-century abbesses and prioresses are often incomplete, and it is quite usual to know nothing more than the names of these women. But their very obscurity argues that, like the men and women who founded and endowed the houses over which they presided, most female monastic superiors of this era were of less than exalted lineage. And like Hersende, Petronilla, Heloise, and Raina, they were charged with overseeing possessions as well as prayer.

Expert property management by women of the lower aristocracy was not the stuff of sanctity in the central Middle Ages. There were always more male than female saints in medieval Europe, just as there were al-

---

109. Walter, *Die ersten Wanderprediger Frankreichs* 1: 191 on leaving the monastery, 1: 193 on the duties of the *maior priorissa* ("habeatque potestatem post abbatissam de negotiis ecclesiae agendis"). The rules of Fontevraud are edited differently in PL 162: 1079–1086.
110. *The Paraclete Statutes: Institutiones Nostrae*, ed. Chrysogonus Waddell (Trappist, Ky., 1987), 116.
111. *Cartulaire et archives des communes de l'ancien diocèse et de l'arrondissement administratif de Carcassonne*, ed. Alphonse Mahul (Paris, 1857–1882), 5: 22: "damus Deo et Ecclesie B. Mariae de Rivo nitido, et tibi humili Rainae praesidenti negotiis domus istius ecclesiae."

ways more monasteries for men.[112] In the early medieval era, up to the tenth century, royal and noble women who founded monasteries were the most usual kind of female saint. But in the new millennium, the number of female saints dropped to its lowest level in the entire Middle Ages. The customary explanation is a perceived decline of female monasticism in a time of male insouciance (at best). It has also been seen as part of a general deterioration of women's position within the family and over resources: simply put, princesses and nobles no longer had the access to wealth that would allow them to found monasteries and become holy abbesses.[113] But the findings of this study regarding female monasticism and the women who supported and participated in it make these suggestions untenable.

A better answer, I think, draws on the work of Dyan Elliott, who sees the impact of Gregorian reform ideals in a new light. The institutional reforms of the eleventh and twelfth centuries sought, above all, to separate the world and the spirit, kingship and priesthood, clergy and laity. Celibacy was, Elliott finds, the most visible line of demarcation; she goes on to posit a bifurcation of spirituality along gender lines: in this age, men firmly divided the mundane and the supernal and fled the former while women blurred the boundaries. Robert of Arbrissel, who evoked and sponsored female spirituality, was criticized precisely because he had showed little interest in adhering to the newly sanctioned boundaries, in theory or in fact.[114]

Women who retired to the monastery in widowhood, Heloise, who dared to write that she preferred to be Abelard's whore, and Petronilla, forceful advocate and supervisor of both property and prayer—these women neither were of sufficient social status nor made spectacular enough conversions to warrant attention to their particular kind of holiness in a time of what R. W. Southern ironically called ecclesiastical rightmindedness.[115] But the appearance of a vast array of nunneries rests very

---

112. See Schulenburg, "Sexism and the Celestial Gynaceum," and Herlihy, "Did Women Have a Renaissance?" Each scholar uses a different list of saints for comparing male and female sanctity across time in the Middle Ages, so their figures are rather different. But they agree that the eleventh and twelfth centuries represent a low point for female sanctity. Herlihy finds that male saints outnumber female 12 to 1 in the period 1000–1150.

113. Schulenberg, "Sexism and the Celestial Gynaceum," 122–124; Herlihy, "Did Women Have a Renaissance?" 7–8.

114. Elliott, *Spiritual Marriage*, 94–95, 109–112. That scholarly opinion about the early Cistercians and business is so slow to move away from the old "fleeing the world" paradigm is a testament to the power of the contemporary rhetoric dividing the world and the spirit.

115. Southern, *Western Society and the Church*, 310.

largely on the accomplishments of women whose vocations united spiritual search and practical acumen without conflict.

WORLDLY AND UNWORLDLY POWER

Without "causing" it in any mechanistic way, the changing familial and economic circumstances of Western Europe's elite were essential contexts for the fourfold multiplication of nunneries in France and England from 1080 to 1170. One other basic social fact seems relevant: the fragmentation of power in this time and place, a Europe not of government but of often violent and coercive lordship. In the old Carolingian lands, royal power disintegrated in the years around the millennium, to be replaced in the eleventh century by regional and local lordships. In England the break came a little later, with the Norman Conquest of 1066–1070. It has long been assumed that from the late eleventh century on, centralized power made a slow but steady resurgence, resulting eventually in the emergence of the bureaucratic state and national monarchies in full flower by the thirteenth century.[116] The turning point, according to the old understanding, came in England with William the Conqueror and his immediate successors, especially Henry I (1100–1135), and in France with King Louis VI (1108–1137), the reign of whose father, Philip I (1060–1108), is universally agreed to have been the nadir of the Capetian monarchy. This conception, which posits an essentially linear "process" toward the "natural conclusion" of strong centralized monarchies,[117] is now challenged by Thomas N. Bisson, who sees instead the invention of accountancy and bureaucracy as a response to a widespread and severe crisis of power, solutions to the excesses of unregulated lordship on grand and petty scales.[118]

The solutions—bureaucratic institutions and a notion of accountability that to us are familiar aspects of a national state—are less important than the chronology and nature of the crisis that brought them about.

116. The classic statement is Joseph Strayer, *On the Medieval Origins of the Modern State* (Princeton, N.J., 1970), esp. 15–56.
117. Ibid., 31.
118. For a sketch of the argument, to be made at length in a forthcoming book, see Bisson, "The 'Feudal Revolution,'" esp. 28–39. Against a tradition that sees the decline of exploitative petty lordship from the eleventh century forward, Bisson finds that "bad lordship came of age in the twelfth century" (33). For one instance of crisis and response, see idem, "The Crisis of the Catalonian Franchises (1150–1200)," *Estudi General* 5–6 (1985–1986): 153–172.

Bisson points to the chaos that ensued in Flanders upon the murder of Count Charles the Good in a church in 1127 and the lengthy civil war in England during the reign of King Stephen (1135–1154) as evidence that the emergence of government as we know it in the West was by no means inevitable, and that lasting centralization should not be imagined to have begun before the later twelfth century. The last books of Orderic Vitalis's *Ecclesiastical History* relate the story of Normandy between circa 1090 and 1140. The chronicler provides a catalogue of violence, disorder, and dislocation of power in a Continental principality (which is nonetheless said by 1100 to have been notable for its "integrity" and precocious evolution into a territorial principality).[119] As Orderic would have been quick to point out, his chronicle reads much less like 2 Samuel, which recounts David's reign over a united kingdom, than 2 Kings, the story of the disintegration of Israel and Judah.

Whereas the changes in familial and economic structures outlined here came about very slowly and at different rates in different places the chronology of the crisis of power is somewhat more precise. By the times of King Henry II of England (1154–1189), who also controlled a vast Continental domain, and his rival Philip Augustus of France (1180–1223), the worst period of disorder was ending. But so was the great era of nunnery foundations. It appears that decentralization of power, even in a time of seigneurial violence, produced a climate at the very least not unconducive to the foundation of religious houses for women (and men), and perhaps positively favorable to it.

The most striking case is the English one. Of one hundred nunneries founded in the century after the Conquest, half appeared in the twenty-year reign of King Stephen, a time of disorder.[120] The pattern was especially pronounced in the north, where thirty nunneries were founded between 1135 and 1154. In Lincolnshire, this was the period of the birth and expansion of the Gilbertine order, England's most original contribution to medieval monasticism. Sharon Elkins has profiled the founders of English houses from 1130 to 1165 in some detail. Nearly all new houses in the north were founded by lay people, and in only two cases were founders feudal magnates. Neither founders nor their overlords represented one side in either of two great political cleavages of the post-Conquest era, first pro- and anti-Norman, then adherence to Stephen or his rival the Empress Mathilda. In the south, when lay people became the

119. Dunbabin, *France in the Making*, 199.
120. The pattern holds for male monasteries. See the Epilogue for details and statistics.

dominant founders of nunneries from the 1130s forward, the same held true. Members of both sides in the civil war founded and endowed women's houses; here "support of female monasticism did not correspond to party lines" and was not restricted to any one social group.[121] Lack of royal direction provided opportunity for patronage of religious houses, some in newly improvised forms, on the part of England's landed elite, echoing the arguments of other feminist and feminist-inspired historians who have found that women in traditional European societies have generally fared better in times of decentralization.[122]

So it happened on the Continent as well. The foundation of Fontevraud occurred at a time of decline in Angevin comital power; by 1100 or so, Fulk IV was enfeebled, a count in name only. The site of the new monastery was in an oasis of relative security, in the region controlled by one of Fulk's few remaining loyal vassals, Gautier of Montsoreau.[123] But it was also notable for its marginality: it lay at the intersection of the lordships of Anjou, Poitou, and Touraine, within the see of Poitiers but only a few kilometers from the boundaries of the dioceses of Tours and Angers. Thus Fontevraud represented security in a time of disorder and was located in a place far from the seats of power, however strong or weak.

When lay people founded or endowed a monastery in the central Middle Ages, their actions reflected a certain degree of independence and in some cases perhaps served as announcements of aspiration to greater importance.[124] To establish a religious institution invested a family with a certain prestige, and it appears that the foundation of nunneries often coincided with an ascendancy of power. If power was indeed still fragmented and control highly localized through most of the twelfth century, then the prominence of petty lords as founders and patrons of the monastic life seems logical: these were the men and women of real local

121. Elkins, *Holy Women*, 94–97, 61–62.
122. Ibid., 61, 97. See also Wemple, *Women in Frankish Society*, 189–197, which considers early medieval France as well as other premodern European societies. It should be noted that Wemple refers to secular and ecclesiastical decentralization of power. I fully agree with regard to "state" power (as Wemple somewhat anachronistically calls it), but the findings of the present study make the matter more complex as regards ecclesiastical power and might, which is traditionally said to have been ascending from the times of Pope Gregory VII and the First Crusade in the late eleventh century. For the argument that a prominent male house provided security in times of disorder, see Rosenwein, *Rhinocerous Bound*.
123. Bienvenu, *L'étonnant fondateur*, 52–55, 82–83.
124. Johnson, *Prayer, Patronage, and Power*, 13–14, makes this argument concerning the founders and patrons of one (male) house; I suspect the observation applies generally to monastic patronage in the eleventh and twelfth centuries.

importance, whose promotion of the religious life was a prerogative of power, just as it had been for the titled aristocrats in the tenth and eleventh centuries.

The independence of most of these petty seigneurial families was short-lived, but some lordships grew strong and remained so. Against the odds, the county of Champagne became a coherent principality whose formation was one of the most striking political developments of twelfth-century France, standing in some contrast to the forces of disorder so prevalent elsewhere. From 1100 to 1181, Champagne emerged from relative fragmentation and backwardness to become much the stronger half in the familial partnership of Blois and Champagne.[125] Orderic Vitalis noted that Count Thibaud (1125–1152) "had many powerful vassals, who were violently hostile to their fellow countrymen and neighbors."[126] But Thibaud and his son Henry the Liberal (1152–1181) prevailed in Champagne. As a youth, Thibaud founded the nunnery of Foissy, near Troyes, which he and his son generously endowed. Thibaud also founded Fontaine-les-Nonnes, his widow La Pommeraie, and his son Champbenoît.[127] It is probably no mere accident that all four houses were in Champagne, increasingly wealthy and politically integrated, rather than Blois, which came more and more under the sway of the Capetian kings in the twelfth century. The newly strong county remained independent of the crown for a hundred years afterward, much longer than most other twelfth-century lordships and principalities.[128] In this territorial lordship, as in many others of lesser size and duration, leaders made gestures of legitimacy by patronizing religious communities.

This is not to say that the men and women who founded convents did not do so for spiritual reasons. Despite the efforts of self-conscious reformers, most medieval Christians, nuns such as Petronilla of Chemillé and lay people, did not make a sharp division between "religious motivation" and "worldly motivation." We must not mistake them either for holy fools or for cynics who manipulated religious institutions and traditions solely for their own selfish ends. To found or endow a monastery involved the expectation of reward, to be sure, but the benefits could be of

---

125. Dunbabin, *France in the Making*, 310–318.
126. OV 6: 160–161.
127. See Chapter 3.
128. Philip II and his grandson Louis IX (1226–1270) gathered up vast stretches of territory, including all the Angevin lands except Gascony, and Toulouse. Champagne, the last territory to be annexed before the Hundred Years War, came to the crown only by the marriage of Philip IV (1285–1312) to Joanna, heiress of a principality left without a male successor to her father.

various description. A foundation in Brabant is a case in point. Leaving for crusade in 1096, the knight Gilbert of Alost gave to the monks of Af-flighem land on which they were to build a nunnery for his mother and sister.[129] Obviously Gilbert wanted to provide for his female relatives, not a purely "religious" motivation, but he did it by means of a pious gift before leaving to fight for the Christian God in the East, a perilous enterprise. A Burgundian crusader, Robert Damas, made a donation to Marcigny in 1106 on the condition that if he died his wife and daughter could join the community if they so desired.[130]

In many other instances discussed in this chapter and the last, people acted for the benefit of their kin: to found nunneries for them, to facilitate their entrance into the religious life, or to benefit relatives who had already taken the veil. But such acts must be understood as having been performed in the context of religious conviction, especially as in so many cases there is *no* other apparent motivation.[131] The foundation charter of Jully-les-Nonnains (circa 1115) is notable for its explicit statement of intention. Count Milo of Bar-sur-Seine installed religious women in a castle on the border of Champagne and Burgundy whose former possessors had "preferred to suit the place to demons rather than to God" and pillaged the surrounding countryside. As Milo modestly put it, "by my agency God committed the ravaged place to the possession of the faithful."[132] The

129. MB 4: 189–190. Here, as elsewhere, the house is called "Forest."
130. *Le cartulaire de Marcigny-sur-Loire (1045–1144): Essai de reconstitution d'un manuscrit disparu*, ed. Jean Richard (Dijon, 1957), 79–80. In addition, the house of Brageac in the Auvergne is said to have been restored ca. 1100 by two brother knights who had just returned from the East, perhaps as fulfillment of a vow made in the heat of battle (DHGE 10: 370.) I wonder if the expansion of female monasticism starting in the late eleventh century might be another manifestation of the same impulse that caused so many to take up the cross, refocused for aristocratic women who did not (excepting Eleanor of Aquitaine!) go on crusade. For connections between English nunneries and the crusaders, see Thompson, *Women Religious*, 176–177. On the motivations of crusaders and lay religious culture of this era, see Marcus Bull, *Knightly Piety and Lay Response to the First Crusade: The Limousin and Gascony, c. 970–c. 1130* (Oxford, 1993).
131. For a vigorous dismantling of the notion that monastic patronage is to be understood in terms of secular motivations, especially attempts to gain wealth or power, see Constance B. Bouchard, *Sword, Miter, and Cloister: Nobility and the Church in Burgundy, 980–1198* (Ithaca, N.Y., 1987), 224–246. Elkins, *Holy Women*, 95–97, posits that the patrons of female monasticism in northern England in the twelfth century acted with no political or economic gains in mind, in contrast to those who supported Cistercian houses for men.
132. "Ego Milo, comes Barri . . . manifestare cupio . . . donum quod feci de Juliaco . . . quo memorati castri, scilicet Juliaci, quondam habitatores, quia hunc eumdem demoniis quam Deo aptare maluerunt, depopulationi submissi probantur; ac denuo, ut ita dicam, post positione excoctum longissima per me hunc Dominus possessioni fidelium deputat" ("Cartulaire du prieuré de Jully-les-Nonnains," ed. Ernest Petit in *Bulletin de la société des sciences historiques et naturelles de l'Yonne* 3d ser., 2 [1880]: 256). Some of the first nuns of Jully came from

count then makes use of the standard formula about how he does this for the salvation of his family, living and dead, which has more meaning in this case than ordinarily, as it is likely that some of his forbears were those brigands in the castle at Jully.

To make a gift to religious people, women or men, was a *normal and accustomed* act among the elite in this era.[133] As Marc Bloch asked, "Who can fail to recognize in the fear of hell one of the great social forces of the age?"—or hope of heaven, it should be added.[134] And if "crisis" was a normal social state for much of the twelfth century, then religious communities can be said to have benefited in some fashion from crisis. Certainly, Western Europe in the late eleventh and twelfth centuries was a society in the midst of rapid change, the last stage in what R. W. Southern called the making of the Middle Ages. But the distinctive Western Christian society that emerged after 1200 was not inevitable, and the direction of evolution in social, economic, and political matters could not have been clear to the men and women who lived before that time. The difficulties historians have in describing the distribution and management of power and landed wealth in the eleventh and twelfth centuries are suggestive: how can the relationships between people be described, and how far can we generalize about them?[135] The confusion, but also the creative possibilities, of the period are well represented by the story of Eliduc, who has two lords for whom he fights, as well as two loves. One of his loves helps to unravel part of the knight's

---

Molesme, where from its origins ca. 1075, as elsewhere in the eleventh century (see Chapter 2), a community of religious women existed alongside that for men. On that early community and on Jully and her eight daughter houses, see *Cartulaires de l'abbaye de Molesme, ancien diocèse de Langres, 916–1250*, ed. Jacques Laurent (Paris, 1907–1911), 1: 253–266.

133. Bouchard, *Sword, Miter, and Cloister*, 238–240, posits that families whose fortune was evidently waning or waxing were motivated by their situation to make pious donations. Probably most families were aware that status changed frequently within the kin groups of the aristocracy: perhaps this consciousness might have contributed to patronage of male *and* female monastic prayer and security so prevalent in France and England in the eleventh and twelfth centuries?

134. Marc Bloch, *Feudal Society*, trans. L. A. Manyon, 2 vols. (Chicago, 1961), 1: 87.

135. For an excellent summary of and commentary on twentieth-century historians' redefinitions of the aristocracy and social organization in old West Frankland, see Theodore Evergates, *Feudal Society in the Bailliage of Troyes under the Counts of Champagne, 1152–1284* (Baltimore, 1975), 144–153. See also T. N. Bisson, "Nobility and Family in Medieval France," esp. 611–613. On definitions of nobility, Bisson remarks that "it is contemporaries' sense of the matter we are learning to take seriously." Could it not have been the case that many twelfth-century people had somewhat vague and contradictory senses of the meaning of "nobility" and their place in the power structure (to use a convenient, if anachronistic, expression)?

tangle by leaving the world for the nunnery, but Eliduc ultimately solves the problems of loyalty and lordship only by committing his property, and in the end himself, to one undisputable and unwavering Lord.

Women's monastic communities in France and England multiplied at an unprecedented rate from 1080 to 1170 in a period of fluidity and growth. Social and institutional change with strong centripetal tendencies fostered originality and experimentation in many spheres, including the religious life. Such novelty was acceptable to, although often not directed by, the leaders of the ecclesiastical hierarchy in a period of creativity and initiative so multifaceted that any measure of control over it seemed impossible. But in this configuration lay the seeds of another, and in the last third of the twelfth century the atmosphere was changing radically. One component of this transformation was a pronounced check on the foundation of nunneries.

the end of an era,
circa 1170–circa 1215

Quoniam instant tempora periculosa et Ecclesia supra modum gravatur, communi consilio capituli statuimus ut amodo nullam sororem recipiamus.

Because dangerous times are at hand and the Church is burdened beyond measure, by common agreement of the chapter we have decreed that from now on we shall receive no sisters.

—Statutes of the General Chapter of Prémontré, late twelfth century

*A*lthough the preceding two chapters have focused on the circumstances favorable to the expansion of female monasticism in the century or so from the time of Pope Gregory VII, it would be a mistake to characterize even so remarkable a period of growth as a "golden age." An early-twelfth-century conflict involving the nuns of Ronceray in Angers illustrates some of the difficulties an established and prestigious community could encounter.[1] On the night of All Saints, 1110, a parishioner of the nuns' church of Notre-Dame was ambushed and mortally wounded on his way to services. The dying man first declared that he wished to be buried in the nuns' cemetery, but the abbot of Saint-Serge, a Benedictine house across the Maine from Ronceray, heard the man's confession and persuaded him to be buried at Saint-Serge. The monks claimed the body and put a shroud on it. A brawl broke out between partisans of each monastery, and the nuns and their *familia* were attacked with cudgels and candelabra. Ronceray's supporters seized the corpse, and although the archdeacon of Angers forbade diocesan clergy to officiate at a burial, the nuns persuaded an out-of-town priest (*peregrinum presbiterum*) to inter the man. Despite threats from Bishop Raginald, the nuns held firm until the body was exhumed

1. The charter narrating the events is in *Cartulaire de l'abbaye du Ronceray*, 49–53 (no. 58). Paul Marchegay provided a close reading of the text in "Un enterrement au douzième siècle," *Revue de l'Anjou et de Maine-et-Loire*, 1st ser., 1, pt. 2 (1852): 177–186.

one night and taken to Saint-Serge. The nuns wished to bring a formal complaint, but even those clergy and laity who recognized the justice of their cause discouraged them from beginning an action, which Raginald forbade anyway. To placate the now-hostile bishop, the abbess went before him and agreed to make whatever amends he deemed necessary for the crime of seizing the body. Raginald ordered the nuns to surrender the shroud; they refused. The angry prelate replied that he would never again enter the nuns' church and that the nuns should expect no favor from him concerning their persons or properties (*nec se valiturum eis vel earum rebus in bonum*). The nuns, as the charter explains it, feared the use of a piece of cloth as pretense for further evil against them by strong men and wily clerks, some of whom were not very spiritual and desired to expand their power in the name of the saints.[2] When further negotiation proved fruitless, it was decided that the anger of the bishop was too much to endure, and in April of 1111, the nuns returned the *pallium* to him.

The nuns of Ronceray found themselves caught in a web of difficulties and rivalries and were fearful of the consequences of making powerful enemies. Bishop, cathedral clergy, other monastics—all had an interest in a matter that mingled concerns about pastoral duties, legal jurisdictions, and even material welfare, which the bishop's thinly veiled threat seemed to compromise. To maintain a community and a patrimony was no simple matter in this era. Similar pressures are visible already at the origins of two nunneries in the late twelfth century.

In September 1188, a family assembled in the court of Bishop William of Gap, a town in the foothills of the French Alps.[3] Adelaide, wife of Arnold, lord of nearby Roche-des-Arnauds, along with her four sons and in the presence of a number of clerics, gave the territory of Bertaud to the nuns of Prébayon, a house near Orange.[4] The gift was confirmed before relatives, other lay people, and a local priest, in the castle of Roche. The territory was not entirely Adelaide's to give, however. The community of Prébayon, acting probably through a priest and two *fratres* present at the ceremony, redeemed Bertaud (*hunc territorium redemerunt*) from the canons of Gap for 1,150 solidi, and then paid Adelaide and her sons 350 solidi. Precise details about the building of a cloister are lacking, but

2. Marchegay, "Un enterrement," 185.

3. *Chartes de Notre-Dame de Bertaud*, ed. Paul Guillaume (Paris, 1888). The editor presents an outline of the early history of the house, xi–xvi, and then the charters of 1188, 1–4.

4. On the history of this convent, see Marc Dubois, "Chartreuse de Prébayon et de Saint-André-de-Ramières (611–1340)," *Revue Mabillon* 26 (1936): 43–62.

it appears that before the end of the century, there was an active community of nuns at Bertaud.[5]

The process of establishing nuns at Bertaud bears some resemblance to the cooperative efforts of earlier twelfth-century foundations. However, there are important differences. Neither the gift of Adelaide nor the participation of the episcopal *familia* was wholly disinterested, for the family of Roche and the canons of Gap stood to gain from a carefully orchestrated transaction. Furthermore, the nuns of Prébayon chose to start a community at Bertaud, rather than to try to supervise a property nearly one hundred and fifty kilometers distant, through rough country, from their home in the Rhône Valley.[6] Apparently, then, the most important impetus for the foundation of Bertaud came directly from Prébayon, which was able to establish a colony only by paying a substantial sum of cash for its initial patrimony. Bishop William, a Benedictine monk who might have been a key founder or patron of an early-twelfth-century nunnery, contributed his official presence and position rather than be a prime mover in the actual foundation.

A nunnery founded in the Rhône Valley a few years later also had its origins in the desires of an already established monastery to start a daughter house. In 1200, William, prior of Bollène, "at the urging, assent and will" of several of his monks, gave the church of Notre-Dame-du-Plan and its appurtenances to God and the Blessed Virgin as a house for women. The new community, however, came into being under some carefully specified conditions. The nuns were to choose a superior and expand their patrimony only in consultation with the monks of Bollène, whose rule they were to adopt and on whom they were to rely for pastoral care. Most important, the number of nuns was not to exceed thirteen, unless the property of the place had been augmented sufficiently (*nisi tanta augmentatio bonorum dicti loci*) that the prior of Bollène and the nuns agreed that expansion was feasible.[7]

The beginnings of Bertaud and Notre-Dame-du-Plan bespeak new constraints on monastic foundations. To found Bertaud required the nuns of Prébayon, operating through intermediaries, to pay a substantial amount of cash to ensure the cooperation of several parties. The original endowment of Notre-Dame was a portion of another monastery's property so small as to require careful monitoring of its future gains before

---

5. *Chartes de Notre-Dame de Bertaud*, xvi.
6. In fact, the surviving charters suggest that ties between the two monasteries slackened considerably not long into the thirteenth century (ibid., xviii).
7. The charter of foundation is printed in GC 1, instr. 136.

any thought could be given to expanding the community. These foundation charters are very different from those of the earlier era of growth, which had been for the most part outright gifts of land by local people, with little reference to larger economic and institutional complexities. In the late twelfth and early thirteenth centuries, however, nunneries arose in a less compatible economic, organizational, and cultural atmosphere than previously.[8]

FOUNDATIONS

Expansion Slowed

Figure 7 shows the distribution of new foundations between 1171 and 1215. In only two archdioceses, Narbonne and Arles, did the pace of new foundations increase.[9] Some new nunneries appeared in areas where few, or none, are known to have been founded in the previous 150 years. Three houses were founded in the extreme northwest of England: Armathwaite and Seton in Cumberland and Lambley in the western reaches of Northumberland. Ten new nunneries were founded in the rough terrain of the Massif Central, most near tributaries of the upper Dordogne, and another two appeared in mountainous Haute-Provence. Whereas these houses appeared in isolated areas, a few other clusters of nunneries were in places less distant but nonetheless lacking in women's monastic institutions. A handful of convents arose in the central Loire basin, in Vendômois and Orléanais, and another ten or so appeared in the central Rhône Valley and near the Languedocian coast of the Mediterranean. Although the pattern was not quite so simple a matter as "filling in gaps," there were fewer new foundations in regions that had already a number of houses for religious women, like central England and the lower Loire and Garonne Valleys. The extreme southwest, including much of Gascony, as well as peninsular Brittany, remained without a single documented nunnery well into the thirteenth century.

8. For accounts of decline after the middle of the twelfth century, see Elkins, *Holy Women*, 105–160, and Johnson, *Equal in Monastic Profession*, 248–265. The following account borrows from these studies, but my formulation, based on new foundations, the individuals involved, and economic and social contexts, is different.
9. That is, in these two the number of new foundations in this 45-year period was more than half that between 1081 and 1170. The figure is exactly one-half in the provinces of Rouen, Vienne, and Aix-en-Provence. In the other 10 archdioceses, there were fewer than half as many new foundations.

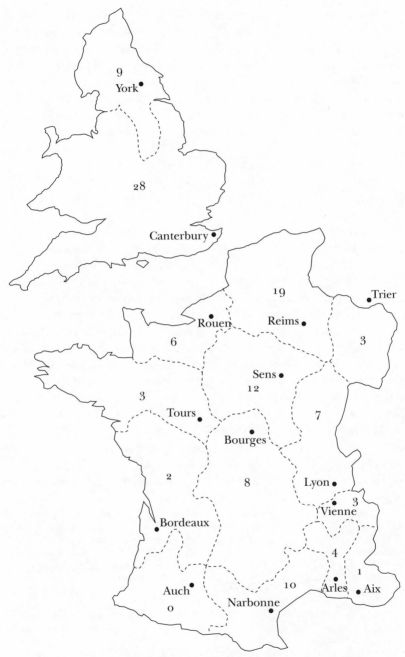

FIGURE 7. Nunneries founded or refounded, 1171–1215, by archdiocese

Marked decline began just after 1150 on the Continent, in the late 1160s in England. The decline in number of new nunneries was, if not precipitous, very pronounced. The pace of foundation remained higher than in the eleventh century, but the number of new convents that appeared in the years 1170–1215 was approximately the same as the figure for 1140–1160 alone (about 115 houses in each period). Put another way, in the half century before 1170, growth averaged just over five houses per year, but for the next fifty years, the figure dropped to well under three. Never again in the Middle Ages would the number of new nunneries rise so quickly as it had in the years around 1150.[10]

Founders

The decreasing number of new nunneries corresponds to a change in the identities of the people who founded women's houses in the late twelfth and early thirteenth centuries.[11] The configuration of errant country evangelists, pastorally minded bishops, and petty aristocrats as the primary actors in foundations broke down after the middle of the twelfth century. In France and England, the great age of rural itinerant evangelists had passed, and no new generation of individuals with the inspirational powers of Robert of Arbrissel, Norbert of Xanten, or Gilbert of Sempringham replaced them. The lone heir to these men in the late twelfth century was Fulk of Neuilly, who is best remembered for his fervent preaching of the Fourth Crusade at the behest of Innocent III.[12] But before he became a spokesman for holy war, Fulk was an errant reforming preacher in northern France whose activities are detailed in Jacques de Vitry's *Historia Occidentalis* (ca. 1220). Like Robert of Arbrissel a century earlier, Fulk drew large and diverse crowds, including prostitutes who wished to repent. Most of them married, but Fulk persuaded others

10. The decline is probably even more significant than the figures suggest. I have no doubt that the expansion from the late eleventh century forward was real and does not simply reflect surviving evidence. However, accidents of preservation may exaggerate somewhat the suddenness of growth about 1080, hence the attention to qualitative as well as quantitative change in Chapters 2 and 3. But because documentation for the history of Western Europe increases rapidly in the twelfth century, the reduction in numbers starting about 1170 is all the more striking, as it is less likely that foundations in this period left no mark in the historical record.

11. The origins of approximately two-thirds (about 90) of the convents founded between 1170 and 1215 are well documented. The following remarks are based on a survey of the founders of these houses.

12. Milton R. Gutsch, "A Twelfth-Century Preacher: Fulk of Neuilly," in *The Crusades and Other Historical Essays*, ed. L. J. Paetow (New York, 1928), 183–206.

to join the monastic life, and in about 1198 he founded the nunnery of Saint-Antoine-des-Champs outside Paris to receive some of these women. Saint-Antoine prospered, but Fulk died in 1202, and no other preacher-founders of his type succeeded him.[13]

The role of bishops in female monastic foundation was considerably less from the mid-twelfth century. In England there was only one instance of episcopal foundation between 1170 and 1215.[14] Foundations through episcopal initiative were almost equally rare on the Continent, totaling perhaps no more than half-a-dozen in fifty years.[15] Some prelates still took part in cooperative efforts of foundation. Bishop William III of Valence worked along with local lords and an abbot in founding Le Bouchet in the late twelfth century.[16] Far to the north, William's colleague Desiderius of Thérouanne lent his support to the lords of Aire in the establishment of Blandecques, near St-Omer.[17] But for the most part, the participation of bishops, when it occurred, appears to have been supplementary and more official than pastoral.

The greatest continuity from the earlier period of growth was the prominence of the lower aristocracy in nunnery foundations. On the Continent and in England, untitled lords and knights continued to be partially or wholly responsible for establishing the majority of new women's houses.[18] However, from mid-century on, the participation of the most powerful families of the landed elite became more pronounced than it had been for over a century. In England, the founders of Bungay, Castle Hedingham, and Shouldham were of high rank; Shouldham, the

13. Jacques de Vitry, *Historia Occidentalis*, 99–100, with bibliography at 273–274 (Fulk of Neuilly), 290 (Saint-Antoine-des-Champs).

14. Archbishop Richard of Canterbury founded Ramstede in Sussex between 1174 and 1184. Ironically enough, Ramstede was disbanded by Richard's successor Hubert shortly after 1200; Elkins, *Holy Women*, 121–122.

15. Bishop Roger of Cambrai established a house of canonesses in his diocese about 1185 (GC 3: 166); the bishop and chapter of Marseille were responsible for the establishment of a nunnery in nearby Aubagne in 1205 (DHGE 20: 331). Bishop Manasses of Orléans saw to the foundation of Voisins in 1213 (GC 8: 1588–1591), and Gérard of Cahors was responsible for the establishment of Grâce-Dieu or Leyme in his diocese a year later (DHGE 21: 1013). These are the only authentic instances of episcopal initiative I have found, and although bishops may have been the instigators of other houses whose origins are very obscure, it seems unlikely that the participation of bishops would have gone unnoted in more than a few cases.

16. DHGE 9: 1049.

17. Ibid., 117. The foundation took place in 1182.

18. The lower aristocracy participated in a little over half of the well-documented foundations in 1170–1215 (see note 11). Because this group is less likely to have left records than the secular and ecclesiastical elite, laymen and laywomen of lesser status probably were also behind many obscure foundations.

last Gilbertine double house, was established by Geoffrey fitz Peter, earl of Essex and chief justiciar of England.[19] Another English baron, Robert of Leicester, founded a house for nuns in Normandy. The house of Saint-Agil owed its establishment in 1190 to the viscount of nearby Châteaudun.[20] A few years afterward and forty kilometers south, the young count Thibaud VI of Blois continued family practice when he founded a nunnery near Château-Renault, in northern Touraine.[21] The comital family of Forez was responsible for two new nunneries in their domains: the first begun by Countess Wilmette in 1199, the second by her husband Guy III and his brother Renald, the archbishop of Lyon, seven years later. The duke and duchess of Lower Lorraine built a community in Brabant, and the comital family of Flanders was responsible for the establishment of two houses in Ghent in the early thirteenth century.[22] A few members of the greatest houses of Western Europe founded nunneries as well. Empress Mathilda, mother of King Henry II of England, was the primary patron if not the founder of the house of Saint-Saens in Normandy, and her great-grand niece, too, founded a house in northern France.[23] King Philip Augustus of France founded a nunnery in the church of Saint-Corentin at Mantes, where in 1201 his wife Agnes was buried.[24]

To account for this pattern—the reduction in number of new communities, their geographical distribution, and the changing identity of the founders—is difficult. The two previous chapters argue that the great expansion of female monasticism from 1080 to 1170 came out of a complex of aspirations and opportunities. It was, in effect, accidental; nobody, least of all Robert of Arbrissel, set out to found great monastic federations for women. By the same token, there is little reason to suspect that before or after 1170, individuals or groups often made a con-

---

19. Thompson, *Women Religious*, 175–176 (Bungay), 180–181 (Castle Hedingham), 75 (Shouldham).

20. DHGE 17: 835–836 (Fontaine-Guérard, not far from Rouen); GC 8: 1290 (St-Agil).

21. DHGE 10: 58 (Le Boulay). In the early thirteenth century, the chaplain of Thibaud's nephew and successor, also Thibaud, founded a nunnery in the diocese of Soissons on land given to him earlier by the count; DHGE 6: 902. On the foundations of the house of Blois-Champagne, see Chapter 4.

22. DHGE 9: 1004 (Bonlieu and St-Thomas-les-Nonnains); DHGE 11: 565 (La Cambre, in Brussels); DHGE 8: 1491 (Byloque); MB 7: 293 (Nieuwenbosch).

23. Saint-Saens, in the diocese of Rouen, was founded shortly before the Empress's death (GC 11: 324). Mathilda of Brunswick, sister of the Emperor Otto IV, founded Les Clairets in her husband's domain of Perche, 40 years later (GC 8: 1324–1325).

24. GC 8: 1300–1302. A church already existed at the site, perhaps a dependency of the nearby convent of Saint-Cyr. According to legend, the new nunnery was to accommodate 120 religious.

scious choice *not* to found houses for nuns. But the concerns of the Premonstratensian General Chapter about dangers and burdens, unspecific as they are, provide a way into understanding the confluence of changes in the period 1170–1215. Dangers and burdens, actual and perceived, are the focus of enquiry in the remainder of this chapter, which uses information about old and new houses to situate the slowing of monastic foundations for women.

TOWN AND COUNTRY, LAND AND MONEY

A fundamental reality for Europeans in the new millennium was demographic and economic growth. Both continued in the late twelfth century and beyond, but expansion was thereafter centered in a new venue. From the end of antiquity to the eleventh century, the cities of Western Europe, many of them old Roman *civitates*, had served primarily as seats of the lords of the Church and the world. Thereafter, these cities grew, and other towns multiplied, in their capacity as commercial centers. In the last decades of the twelfth century, "urban vitality came definitely to prevail over that of the countryside everywhere . . . hereafter rural areas would always lag behind in economic development." This transformation, most visible in England and the old Frankish lands, was the result of long, slow growth in a time of increased circulation of money and trading activities.[25]

The "commercial revolution"[26] rested firmly on agricultural expansion and surplus in the countryside, an agrarian evolution that was also one mundane context for the great expansion of women's monasticism

25. Georges Duby, *The Early Growth of the European Economy*, trans. Howard B. Clark (Ithaca, N.Y., 1974), 263–270; quot., 263. Twice Duby specifically identifies the 1180s as the time when this change became apparent. Duby's older account is particularly sensitive to the relationship of the economy to other social structures and trends. Newer surveys have different emphases, but roughly the same scheme of periodization. Robert Fossier, *Enfance de l'Europe, Xe–XIIe siècle: Aspects économiques et sociaux*, 2 vols., 2d ed. (Paris, 1989), also sees a break around 1180, the end of Europe's social and economic "childhood." See esp. 1: 595–601 and 2: 1064 on the chronology, 2: 729–799 on the development of the market economy. Contamine et al., *L'économie médiévale*, uses an eightfold periodization scheme, of which the fourth phase ends around 1180; see esp. 179–195. Gérard Sivéry's "long thirteenth century" begins around 1180 (*L'économie du royaume de France au siècle de Saint Louis [vers 1180–vers 1315]* [Lille, 1984], 11–29). The break is not so evident in England, but on new towns and trade in the twelfth and thirteenth centuries, see Miller and Hatcher, *Medieval England*, 70–83.

26. A classic formulation is Robert S. Lopez, *The Commercial Revolution of the Middle Ages, 950–1350* (Englewood Cliffs, N.J., 1971).

starting in the late eleventh century. But even as the economic center of gravity was shifting to the towns, most new nunneries continued to be founded away from population centers.[27] Some of the new foundations were in or near cities, like the Fontevrist house of La Rochelle, begun around 1180 by no less a figure than Eleanor of Aquitaine.[28] At least a few houses were founded by townsmen. About 1175, a local citizen called Jean Homdedeu founded a nunnery a few kilometers west of Perpignan. Another Jean, this one a wealthy merchant of Narbonne, established a monastery for women near his city. Last, a man known as William, son of William the Goldsmith, founded the nunnery of Saint Helens in London about 1214.[29] These three foundations mark the first use of urban merchant and artisan resources in the establishment of traditional female monastic communities.[30]

But these are exceptional cases, as the relative isolation of new nunneries from cities persisted into the early thirteenth century. In 1080, nearly one-half of the hundred or so nunneries in France and England were in or within a few kilometers of an episcopal or other urban center.[31] Table 4 shows the distribution of foundations according to distance from the nearest city in 1081–1170 and 1171–1215.

The distribution changed very little from period of greatest growth to that of the marked check from 1171 to 1215. Urban areas, sites of many eleventh-century foundations, were not favored places for new nunneries in the twelfth century. In the period 1080–1215 over 70 percent of all new foundations were more than 15 kilometers from the nearest city and only 10 percent were in or adjacent to one—hence the emphasis on local petty lordship and the rural agricultural economy in Chapter 4. Houses continued to be founded primarily in the countryside to 1200 and beyond, even as economic vitality moved into the city.[32] The effect on the

27. It should be noted that this urban trading economy was based primarily on exchange of agricultural products, such as foodstuffs or wool for weaving, in relatively localized or regionalized patterns of exchange (Pounds, *Historical Geography*, 297). Hence the agricultural basis of the monastic patrimonies even in more urbanized settings, as described below.

28. Paul Marchegay, "Chartes de Fontevraud concernant l'Aunis et la Rochelle," *Bibliothèque de l'Ecole des Chartes* 19 [4th series, vol. 4] (1858): 133–134.

29. DHGE 15: 1386 (Eule); HGL 4: 686 (Les Ollieux); Thompson, *Women Religious*, 225 (London).

30. Three houses, or 2% of all foundations in this period, is not much of a dossier; these are the first documented cases of foundation by townsmen in France and England.

31. The figures here and in the Epilogue derive from a roster of cities listed and described in Appendix B. The total number of cities is 165, of which about 80% are episcopal seats.

32. There is a certain logic to founding houses in the countryside if they already existed in cities. But many cities, even episcopal towns, remained without a nunnery through the twelfth century.

Table 4. Number of nunneries founded, 1081–1215, by distance from urban center

Distance from a city	1081–1170	1171–1215
5 kilometers or less	33 (10.5%)	10 (8.8%)
6–15 kilometers	56 (17.8%)	25 (21.9%)
16–25 kilometers	61 (19.4%)	26 (22.8%)
26–35 kilometers	61 (19.4%)	26 (22.8%)
36–45 kilometers	55 (17.5%)	15 (13.2%)
46 kilometers or more	48 (15.3%)	12 (10.5%)
	314 (100%)	114 (100%)

economic situation of rural monasteries is evident in the charters of Montazais, a Fontevrist monastery in southern Poitou.[33]

The property on which this house was built had been given to Fontevraud about 1119, and an active community was there from shortly afterward. The nuns of Montazais left valuable relics of their first decades, over two hundred charters documenting the history of their properties in the twelfth century. These documents, most of them unedited, are especially precious for historians as large collections of charters from women's houses spanning the twelfth century are relatively rare.[34] The charters of Montazais may be conveniently divided into two groups, those from the period up to about 1165, and those from circa 1165 to the early thirteenth century. Table 5 summarizes the transactions described by these charters.[35] These sets of figures are of consider-

33. On these charters, see Chapter 4, note 33.
34. This remark applies primarily to new foundations. There survive dozens of twelfth-century documents from some older houses such as Notre-Dame in Saintes, Ronceray in Angers, and Marcigny. But for houses that appeared in the late eleventh century and beyond, the story is much different. The largest printed collection of this kind is Ignace de Coussemaker's edition of the charters of Bourbourg, which includes 92 charters from 1104 to 1198. A number of early charters have survived from such prestigious twelfth-century foundations as Montmartre and the Paraclete. The charters of Fontevraud, the vast majority of which survive for the first twenty or so years of its history, are far less complete after about 1118. There are about 65 documents from 1134–1200 in the late-thirteenth-century cartulary of Yerres, a modest Benedictine monastery south of Paris (Paris, Archives Nationales, LL 1599B.) The charters of Montazais are, however, the largest collection I have found for what might be considered a "typical" twelfth-century nunnery, founded in the countryside by local lords, never the site of patronage by the ecclesiastical or secular elite, and never particularly large or prominent.
35. The number of transactions does not match exactly the number of charters, as some documents describe more than one action and a few repeat the contents of others more or less verbatim.

Table 5. Number of transactions made at Montazais, circa 1135–circa 1205, by type

	ca. 1135– ca. 1165	ca. 1165– ca. 1205
Donations		
Land	39	35
Buildings	11	6
Annual tribute in money	8	36
Annual tribute in kind	5	20
Rights on lands and waters	3	–
Other	4	4
	70	101
Leases	5	15
Purchases	3	2
Quitclaims	3	4
Other	5	4
Total	**86**	**126**

able interest when compared among themselves and also with those from early twelfth-century Fontevraud described in Chapter 4.[36] Four-fifths of the Montazais transactions record donations to the community. But the profile of donations was from the outset somewhat different from that at Fontevraud, and the character of new Montazais patrimony changed considerably across the century.

An outstanding characteristic of the early Fontevraud charters was the predominance of records documenting outright gifts of arable, forest, mills, and other buildings, which account for over 80 percent of all donations. At Montazais, lands and buildings, accounted for over 70 percent of donations (50 out of 70) before about 1165, but only 40 percent (41 out of 101) in the later period. The number of mills donated

36. See Table 3 in Chapter 4. The comparison of the records of the two houses cannot be extremely precise, as each set of documents has come down to us in rather different form. The Fontevraud documents are from contemporary copies and are probably a nearly complete set (see Chapter 4, note 45). But most of the Montazais documents are from a cartulary drawn up centuries later, and it is not surprising that the kinds of records deemed worthy of copying at that time were of a somewhat different stamp. In particular, the near absence of confirmations and quitclaims in the later Montazais cartulary stands in contrast to the large number of such records in the Fontevraud collection. Perhaps more existed at one time, and it may well be the case that the Montazais copyists found no reason to preserve such records if the monastery's title to a particular piece of property was documented well enough by a charter of donation.

dropped too: ten in the first era, five in the second. The difference was made up, after 1165, by a different category of gift: annual tributes, either in cash or in goods, in the latter case almost always a measure of grain. Montazais in this period received more donations of annual income than any other kind, and after 1165, tributes in money or kind made up 55 percent (56 of 101) of all donations. Across the century, pious donors changed the emphasis of giving from grants of land to the products of that land, direct and indirect.

A phenomenon understood to be at the root of the commercial revolution—the circulation of money—is quite visible in the Montazais charters. But what the nuns were able to do with their ready money is different from the activities described by the early Fontevraud charters. Fontevraud was able to use its wealth to obtain title to more lands, often paying out substantial sums for new real estate. In sharp contrast, only five or six documents of sale are to be found among over two hundred Montazais charters of the twelfth century. The nuns neither bought more land nor made other kinds of investment—mills, furnaces, rights to toll—that were part of the Fontevraud patrimony. Some of the difference is made up by leases, which are not found among the early Fontevraud charters. By these instruments, apparently meant to describe permanent arrangements, lay people granted to Montazais land (or, in a few cases, other kinds of property) in exchange for an annual tribute, almost always in cash. The documents often are quite detailed, sometimes specifying partial payments two or more times in the year or simply stating that the money was to be handed over at harvest time.

The impression given by these documents, particularly by their changing profile across the twelfth century, is of a decreasing rate of growth of the agrarian economy in the area around Montazais, a decrease common to much of Haut-Poitou in the later twelfth century.[37] Simply put, it became increasingly more difficult for the nuns of Montazais to expand their landed patrimony. To augment their income, they had to rely on other arrangements, that were less secure than simple title to land. It was probably easier to enforce ownership of a field than to make sure that an annual tribute was paid regularly and in full. A hint of the difficulties of

37. The whole region around Montazais, in which most of its patrimony lay, showed signs of strain, and there is evidence that some cleared land was too marginal to be profitably cultivated: Sanfaçon, *Défrichements, peuplement et institutions seigneuriales*, 46–47, and, for other parts of Haut-Poitou, 31–62. Land clearance continued into the thirteenth century, but the bulk of such activity took place in the eleventh and twelfth centuries. See also Beech, *A Rural Society in Medieval France*, 25–26, 125–127.

making such arrangements firm may be found in the charters themselves. In many cases, donations of an annual tribute specify the territory from which the offering is to be made and the names of the tenant or tenants. The donors wished to shift responsibility for ensuring payment away from themselves.[38] Bad times could be disastrous for the tenants and the religious community. Peasant farmers would be very unlikely to have other sources of income to draw upon in a year of poor crops or other kinds of disruption, and the specificity of language in the charters suggests that the donors would not be inclined to make up the difference from other properties. The same kind of problem might occur in reverse for lands leased by Montazais: would not the lessor expect payment from the nuns regardless of the income provided by the specified property?[39]

Georges Duby's observation of the "first symptoms of landhunger" in the late twelfth century seems to accord with the situation in the countryside seen in the Montazais charters.[40] Such an evolution suggests a partial explanation for the marked decrease in the numbers of nunnery foundations in more rural regions. Furthermore, it looks as if new convents were often founded in marginal areas, or with insufficient resources to guarantee economic health, or both. In many parts of northwestern Europe, the increase in arable land was slowing notably well before 1200.[41] In Charente, for instance, reclamation of land began before 1000, and, although it continued into the thirteenth century, appears to have reached its apogee by about 1100.[42] The archdiocese of Bordeaux, of which Charente and Poitou are a large part, had very few new foundations after the mid-twelfth century. In interior Flanders, the great land clearing efforts that had been part of comital policy since the

38. E.g., ADML 186 H 3 folios 4v.(#38), 9r.(#70), 11r.–v.(#82, #83), 14r.(#102, #103), 17r.(#123), 20r.(#145), 22r.–v.(#158, #160, #161).

39. On Cistercian monks and leases in twelfth-century Burgundy, see Bouchard, *Holy Entrepreneurs*, 43–52. Bouchard understands such instruments to be advantageous to the monks, obviating the need for lump-sum payments to get control of property. Leasing was a significant economic tool for these Burgundian monks from the origins of their order in 1098, but I have found very little of it in documents of early twelfth-century nunneries. Hence my suspicion that leases, in combination with the lessening of outright gifts of real property, are less a sign of entrepreneurial innovation than of straitened resources on the part of the nuns of Montazais and their lay neighbors and patrons. Bouchard does find that too many obligations from leases burdened Cîteaux in the late 1170s (52), and it would appear that the monks of the order shied away from such transactions in the last 20 years of the twelfth century (see bar graphs 24, 44).

40. Duby, *Early Growth*, 270.

41. For a summary, see Contamine et al., *L'économie médiévale*, 166–168.

42. André Debord, *La société laïque dans les pays de la Charente, Xe–XIIe s.* (Paris, 1984), 324–326.

early eleventh century came to a halt under Count Philip of Alsace
(1168–1191).[43] This pause corresponds to the pattern of nunnery foundations in the diocese of Cambrai, which covered much of eastern Flanders: there are eleven known foundations in 1081–1170, but only three
more in 1171–1215. One of those, Herlaimont, was disbanded in the
late thirteenth century; the most successful was La Cambre in Brussels,
founded by the duke and duchess of Lower Lorraine.[44] Picardy had, by
the last quarter of the twelfth century, undergone the economic developments that made it the premier agricultural region of the French kingdom.[45] By then the dioceses of Arras and Amiens were home to eight
nunneries, seven founded since 1080; however, the figure grew by only
another four between 1175 and 1215. Two of those experienced difficulties later on. In 1208, Pope Innocent III declared that the community
at Beaurepaire, founded about thirty-five years earlier, was too large for
its meager resources and therefore its number was to be reduced by attrition to twelve. The nuns of Brayelle-lès-Annay were forced to relocate
because of poverty around 1250.[46] In Provence, the nuns of Bertaud
were less than fifteen kilometers from the episcopal city of Gap, but in an
isolated valley inaccessible to this day except on foot.[47]

Extension of arable land was not *the* decisive factor in the distribution
of new nunneries, before or after 1170, but there is a significant correlation between the apogee of rural land clearance and monastic growth. In
addition, it is important not to exaggerate the contrast of town and country in this age; in the late twelfth century, even wealthy townsmen were
"still more than halfway to being peasants."[48] By the same token, nearly
all monasteries for women and men, even in the most densely populated
and urbanized parts of Western Europe, were more than halfway to
being agrarian and rural, at least in terms of their economic base, into
the thirteenth century. The nunnery of Clerkenwell was founded about

43. Adriaan Verhulst, *Histoire du paysage rural en Flandre de l'époque romaine au XVIIIe siècle*
(Brussels, 1966), 100–105.

44. MP 2: 378–379 (Herlaimont); MB 4: 441–445 (La Cambre).

45. Robert Fossier, *La terre et les hommes en Picardie jusqu'à la fin du XIIIe siècle*, 2 vols. (Paris,
1968), 1: 299.

46. *Cartulaire de l'abbaye de Cysoing et de ses dépendances*, ed. Ignace de Coussemaker (Lille,
1886), 89–90 (Beaurepaire); DHGE 10: 471–472 (Brayelle-lès-Annay). The nuns of
Brayelle fared better in their new home, gaining the patronage of aristocratic women such
as Marguerite of Constantinople.

47. *Chartes de Notre-Dame de Bertaud*, viii–x, describes the locale. There is still no road to it.
A few kilometers to the northeast are the lifts of a modern ski resort, suggesting what harsh
conditions the nuns must have endured in the winter.

48. Duby, *Early Growth*, 254.

1144, just outside London (*iuxta Lond'* in many charters), a fast-growing center of trade and administration. King Richard's confirmation of the properties of this house shows that the expansion of its patrimony across a half-century had something in common with that of isolated Montazais.[49] The royal charter lists, besides the land on which the monastery was built, fifty-seven different donations, mostly by lay people. Over half of these (thirty) were grants of land, and another seven, grants of churches and their appurtenances, but fully one-quarter of donations, fifteen in all, were of annual income. Most of these gifts were from the country: only thirteen donations concerned property in the city of London.[50] Most of the rest of the Clerkenwell holdings were in counties along the Thames, but the nuns also had rights in more distant Hampshire, Cambridgeshire, Suffolk, Norfolk, Lincolnshire, and Cheshire. Like those at Montazais, the nuns of Clerkenwell assembled a patchwork patrimony of various description, and a substantial part of their income was derived from donations of annual tributes.[51]

Even in an urbanized and economically vital setting, then, monastic women continued to rely largely for their material support on old-fashioned agrarian holdings. For new monasteries, this continuity was not wholly advantageous. Even where growth of the agricultural economy appears to have continued more rapidly than in Poitou, the holdings of fledgling communities did not grow as quickly as they had in the century or so before 1170. The scarcity of surviving charters documenting the early history of the patrimonies of nunneries founded in the late twelfth and early thirteenth century is a telling indicator, and those which have come down to us do not show the kind of vast expansion indicated in the fuller collections of the earlier era. Early charters of the nunnery of Ravensberg, in the fertile and relatively well-populated region where Artois and Flanders meet, illustrate one case of slow expansion.[52]

---

49. The charter is printed in *Cartulary of St. Mary Clerkenwell*, ed. William O. Hassall (London, 1949), 5–8 (no. 6). On Clerkenwell and its properties in the twelfth century, see Elkins, *Holy Women*, 65–69.

50. These were eight grants of land and the buildings on them, four annual incomes, and one church. The breakdown, then, is roughly the same as for rural properties, except that it is usually specified that there are houses on urban properties.

51. Not until after 1200 did Clerkenwell begin to take in more London properties than rural ones; see *Cartulary of St. Mary Clerkenwell*, xix–xx, for a breakdown of charters by chronology and location.

52. The extant charters of this house are inventoried and summarized in Edmond de Coussemaker, "Notice sur l'abbaye de Ravensberg," *Annales du comité flamand de France* 6 (1862): 249–282. This list is collated from a number of collections, but because one of them was a late-thirteenth-century cartulary, it probably includes a majority of the early Ravensberg charters.

Ravensberg was founded circa 1191 by the local *domina*, Christina. She donated a house and the land it was on for the nuns, as well as a number of allods, a mill, an annual tribute in cash, another in butter, some marshland for digging peat, and 100 solidi to pay a chaplain.[53] Her son and heir, two bishops, Pope Celestine III, and Count Baldwin of Flanders issued charters confirming these same grants in the next several years, but the next new gift (of two rams per annum) dates to 1202. An exemption from toll and one-third of a mill are the only further gifts until Christina, perhaps aware of the slow expansion of her foundation's wealth, gave more land, another mill, and a measure of grain for the use of the nuns' priest. The only other donations from the first twenty years of Ravensberg's history are a tithe and a cash gift of 300 pounds, payable over three years. This last is the only major gift besides those by Christina and shows that as for the nuns of rural Montazais and suburban Clerkenwell, cash payment was a significant kind of wealth.[54]

For old convents and new ones, in both more and less densely populated and commercialized sectors, some measure of strain often becomes apparent after 1170. The difficulties of expansion were felt acutely in the late twelfth century by the nuns of the old suburban nunnery of Saint-Paul, a few kilometers west of Beauvais. This house, rebuilt in the early eleventh century, established colonies of nuns as a means of managing distant properties and also, perhaps, to relieve overcrowding in the mother house. The first of these was Ezanville, south of Beauvais near Paris, established about 1080. Fifty years later, the nuns added another outpost northwest of Beauvais, not too far from the coast of the English Channel. By the mid-twelfth century, under the enterprising abbesses Thecia (1122–1155) and Marsilia (1155–1176), Saint-Paul had a large patrimony.

But the establishment of a third dependent house in the 1180s shows that a century and a half of steady expansion was at an end. In 1183, the nuns had Roger of Mortimer confirm the donation of his grandfather

53. This foundation charter is printed in GC 3, instr., 123. Johnson, *Equal in Monastic Profession*, 186–191, 225–226, discusses the "sacramental disability" of nuns, who needed to retain the services of a priest for several purposes, to say mass in particular. The relations between nuns and the clergy who served them were often tense, and the inconvenience and expense were probably all the more burdensome in times of economic strain. Mixed houses such as those founded by Robert of Arbrissel and Gilbert of Sempringham had a ready solution at hand, but the major period of growth of the Fontevrist and Gilbertine congregations was over by the later twelfth century.

54. For the charters discussed in this paragraph, see Coussemaker, "Notice sur l'abbaye de Ravensberg," 249–255. Of twenty documents up to 1212, only seven are charters of donation, and the bulk of gifts were owed to the founder.

Radulphus, who had long ago granted the church and appurtenances of Sainte-Beuve-aux-Champs when Radulphus's sister entered the religious life. There the nuns of Saint-Paul set up a new community. The significance of starting a third dependency on an old property rather than a new one is evident from another document of 1183. Bishop Philip of Beauvais issued a proclamation offering the faithful indulgences for various offenses if they would lend aid to the nuns for the alleviation of their poverty (*ad levamen egestatis earum*): even the considerable resources already gathered up were no longer sufficient. It looks as if the foundation of Sainte-Beuve was part of an attempt to reduce the size of the community at Saint-Paul in a time of economic difficulties, an impression strengthened by Bishop Philip's decree that there should be no more than fifty nuns at the mother house. In any case, a long-established nunnery found itself in difficulty in the late twelfth century.[55]

New nunneries had troubles, too. In the 1180s, Countess Eleanor of Saint-Quentin restored an old house of regular canons in the diocese of Soissons, replacing it with a community of Fontevrist nuns and monks. Eleanor built a new church and granted the community of Longpré lands, mills, fishing and pasturage rights, and a number of tributes in money and kind. A few years later, a local lord donated money and land as an entry donation for his daughter.[56] But despite these generous gifts (and there were probably others that have left no trace), Longpré was already under economic stress only a decade or so after its foundation. In 1196, Pope Celestine III issued a bull to the community Eleanor had founded and endowed, expressing concern "lest the anxiety of material things either restrain them from their purpose or, God forbid, diminish the vigor of sacred religious life." With the assent of the abbess of Fontevraud, the pope enjoined that the number of nuns at Longpré not exceed sixty.[57]

The story of Longpré illustrates that even houses established by very wealthy and generous patrons found themselves in difficulty and that it was not easy to match enthusiasm for religious life with sufficient material resources. Small wonder, then, that more men and women of extremely high station were increasingly often the prime movers in

55. E. Deladreue, "Histoire de l'abbaye de Saint-Paul-lès-Beauvais," *Mémoires de la société académique de l'Oise* 6 (1865–1866): 36–218, 411–504, surveys the history of the house to the eighteenth century. For the charters cited, see 57–70 (summaries) and 472–474 (edited texts).

56. Claude Carlier, *Histoire du duché du Valois*, 3 vols. (Paris, 1764), 1: 543–544.

57. *Epistolae pontificum Romanorum ineditae*, ed. Samuel Loewenfeld (Leipzig, 1885), 257–258: "ne rerum inquietatio mundanarum aut eos a proposito vel robur, quod absit, sacre religionis infringat . . . ne sexagesimum numerum moniales in eo servientes excedant."

foundations from the late twelfth century forward: only the very rich could easily endow a new monastery with sufficient worldly goods. Of course, sixty was a large community by medieval standards, so the papal injunction is not a reflection of dire need so much as of concern that resources could all too easily be tested and found wanting.

The problem *could* become dire, however, for new houses founded by those of lesser status than the countess of Saint-Quentin. Around 1181, Thibaud of Saint-Loup founded on his lands a monastery for his daughter Lucy, who was the first superior of the house of Vauxbons. But Thibaud, a petty Burgundian lord like dozens of others who founded religious houses in the twelfth century, was apparently not able to endow his foundation very richly or to encourage others to do so. In 1216, Bishop William of Langres issued a charter that declared that Vauxbons, "crippled with the burden of poverty, had nearly arrived at extreme want, such that there was no help of revival" and was thereafter to be in the charge of the dean and chapter of Langres. The goods of the house were put into receivership. The nuns were deprived of the right to alienate anything belonging to them, and the size of the community was to be reduced through attrition to twelve nuns, an abbess, and a priest and not to exceed that number thereafter. Vauxbons survived as an independent nunnery to the end of the fourteenth century, but there is no indication that it ever grew beyond the limits prescribed in 1216.[58]

So there are numerous signs, direct and indirect, of new pressures on material resources for the institutions whose spectacular success in the century or so before 1170 had been closely tied to the expansion of the rural agricultural economy. We know about these problems of the late twelfth and early thirteenth century in part because of actions designed to remedy them, and the agency of that aid is important. In each of the cases just discussed, it was male ecclesiastics who dictated the solution. In the late twelfth and early thirteenth century, instead of participating in new foundations, a number of bishops took on the roles of protectors and directors of women's houses, responsibilities that were as much administrative as pastoral. Some houses enjoyed increased security while submitting to a certain degree of external regulation. The contemporaneous impetus from lay lords and churchmen alike toward increased control and imposition of order over the people and institutions of Christendom did not encourage

58. GC 4: 656 and instr. 201. The episcopal charter begins "Ego Willermus divina miseratione Lingon. episcopus notum facio omnibus praesentibus et futuris, quod monasterium de Valbeon onere paupertatis deprehensum fere ad extremam devenisset inanitionem, ita quod nullam spem resurgendi haberet."

creativity. Spiritual impulses, even those as idiosyncratic as Robert of Arbrissel's, or the desire of petty aristocrats to found and endow monasteries as an expression of identity were fulfilled without difficulty for much of the twelfth century. But more strongly assertive hierarchies of authority began, in late twelfth century, to regulate more—and foster less.[59]

THE FORCES OF ORGANIZATION

The New Monarchy

The devolution of power that had characterized much of Western Europe in the eleventh and early twelfth centuries was first stopped, then reversed by men whose activities eventually led to the emergence of strong national monarchies in England and France in the thirteenth century. Just as petty lords and nobles, castellans and knights, had founded monasteries in the eleventh and early twelfth centuries—pious acts which were also proclamations of legitimacy—so now did kings assert dominance through their actions regarding religious houses.

Perhaps the most innovative of these men was Henry Plantagenet, at age twenty-one lord through inheritance and marriage over a vast constellation of territories including the kingdom of England, the duchies of Normandy and Aquitaine, and the county of Anjou. But even before he came into power, Henry (1133–1189) had already begun to exhibit his benevolence toward women's houses. One of the first extant charters of the young prince, called "son of the duke of Normandy and count of Anjou," is a confirmation to the nuns of the Norman abbey of Almenèches of their rights in his forest land (*mea foresta de Goffer*) nearby.[60]

---

59. Elkins, *Holy Women*, calls the section of her study about the period 1165–1215 "Regulation." After a great period of foundation, need for new houses decreased, and as momentum lessened, "a counterforce for stabilization became stronger. The wisdom of the novel arrangements that had proliferated in the period of experimentation was challenged. A desire to preserve and standardize the forms that had evolved became more pronounced" (105). I am not convinced that the multiplication of nunneries in northwestern Europe was in fact sufficient to satisfy all female religious aspirations, and I place more emphasis on the social and economic changes in England and on the Continent. However, much of the next section draws on Elkins's model about the new concerns for order and stability and applies them in a wider geographical area.

60. *Recueil des actes de Henri II, roi d'Angleterre et duc de Normandie concernant les provinces françaises et les affaires de France*, ed. Léopold Delisle and Elie Berger, 3 vols. (Paris, 1916–1927), 1: 11–12 (no. vii). The editors date the charter to 1146–1150, before the investiture of Henry as duke of Normandy in late 1149 or early 1150.

After he accumulated the lands and titles that made him one of the most powerful people in Europe, Henry continued to guard the interests of communities of religious women in his domains on both sides of the English Channel.

Between the late 1140s and the 1180s, Henry issued charters to two dozen Continental nunneries.[61] His favorite object of charity was Fontevraud. Shortly after the death of his father Geoffrey in 1151 and his accession to the lordship of Anjou, the new count confirmed to Fontevraud seventeen houses in Saumur, not far from the monastery.[62] Henry issued another two dozen charters to Fontevraud in the course of his lifetime. Most of these simply confirmed Fontevraud's ownership of rights or properties or noted the settlement of disputes concerning them, but some were also donations of land by Henry himself. The largest single gift was in Henry's last testament of 1182, in which he granted to Fontevraud and its dependent houses 2,000 marks of silver. (By comparison, he ceded to all other religious houses in Anjou only 1,000 marks, to be divided and distributed by the bishops of Angers and Le Mans.)[63] Eleanor of Aquitaine also was a patron of Fontevraud. In 1152, shortly after her divorce from King Louis VII of France and subsequent marriage to Henry, Eleanor went to Fontevraud and in the nuns' chapter confirmed all gifts of her forbears to Fontevraud in addition to a gift she and her then-husband, the king of France, had made.[64] Over thirty years later, Henry confirmed Eleanor's gift of 2,000 solidi to be paid annually from Poitevin grain and grape crops.[65] Henry's body was taken to Fontevraud after he died at his castle of Chinon in 1189; Eleanor, too, was buried there fifteen years later.

As his most distinguished modern biographer notes, "It is not easy to assess Henry II's attitude to religion."[66] There is no reason to dismiss the possibility of genuine piety in his activities, but they were certainly

---

61. The *Recueil des actes de Henri II* includes nearly 70 documents referring to 23 different Continental houses, plus several in England. Some of these are simply charters confirming arrangements concerning properties; others are donations to communities. He also issued general confirmations of the various properties of La Trinité at Caen, the work of his great-grandmother (2: 199–203 [no. 601]) and the recently founded Norman house of Bondeville (2: 387–390 [no. 747]).
62. Ibid., 1: 37–38 (no. 30).
63. Ibid., 2: 219–221 (no. 612). The only larger gift to one house and its dependencies was 3,000 marks to Grandmont. Henry also gave 100 marks each to four nunneries in his Continental domains.
64. Ibid., 1: 31–32 (no. 24).
65. Ibid., 2: 270–271 (no. 655).
66. Warren, *Henry II*, 211.

not entirely disinterested. In his first charter to Fontevraud, confirming the abbey's possessions in Saumur, Henry asserted his position for the present and future in two ways: the phrase *de meo dominio* is used twice in a short charter, and the young count retained whatever seigneurial rights and customs his ancestors had over these properties.[67] So Henry made himself eternally present at Fontevraud, an action strengthened by the issuing of charters to the house at regular intervals and having his son John educated at Fontevraud for five years.[68] Henry's notion of his role is expressed in a charter from the middle period of his reign. Addressing his officials and *fideles* in Anjou, Maine, and Touraine, Henry declared that all the possessions of the nuns of Fontevraud "are in my hand and care and protection."[69] A measure of dependency was the price of security.

The proem of another charter implies the same thing and also seems to define a role for kings with regard to religious communities. In 1172, Henry awarded privileges to the nuns of Locmaria, in peninsular Brittany, explaining first the context of his grant: "Word has gone out to the whole world concerning the disaster and misery with which Brittany was long afflicted and oppressed by tyrants, which [land] at long last merciful and pitying God most kindly visited in the times of pious Henry, king of the English, through his aid and counsel and dominion alike. This man, among the other goods he conferred on the Britannic race. . . ."[70] The return of God to Brittany, then, coincided with Henry's control of the province, which he ruled as regent starting in 1166.[71] Tyrants, Henry implies, are bad for the practice of religion, but a pious king is beneficial to a people and its institutions. The charter was witnessed by two papal legates and three bishops from Brittany, who apparently acquiesced with Henry on the subject of benevolent (albeit forceful) lay rulership.

---

67. *Recueil des actes de Henri II*, 1: 37–38 (no. 30).

68. Bienvenu, "Les premiers temps de Fontevraud," 575–583, discusses Henry's relationship with the abbey, noting that it lay at the center of a region of strategic importance and that strong ties to Henry counterbalanced the ties of Fontevraud to the papacy.

69. *Recueil des actes de Henri II*, 1: 554–555 (no. 424): "Sciatis quod omnes res et possessiones monialium de Fonte Ebraudi . . . sunt in mea manu et custodia et protectione." The document is dated by the editors to 1165–1172/73.

70. Ibid., 1: 581 (no. 446): "Calamitatis et miserie qua Britannia per tyrannos diu fuit afflicta et oppressa in omnem terram sonus exivit, q[u]am tamdem misericors et miserator Dominus temporibus Henrici piissimi regis Anglorum per ejusdem auxilium et consilium pariterque dominium clementissime visitavit. Iste, inter cetera bona que genti Britannice contulit. . . ."

71. Dunbabin, *France in the Making*, 332.

Henry was a patron of female monasticism in England as well,[72] but the most famous instance of his involvement shows his will to control as much as his piety. In 1177, the king expelled the nuns from the Anglo-Saxon house of Amesbury and replaced them with twenty-four sisters from Fontevraud. The act was supposedly part of his penance for his role in the murder of Archbishop Thomas Becket in 1170. Henry's charter confirming the goods of the newly constituted house states that the removal of the old community was owed to the disgraceful life of the nuns and the public infamy of their behavior, but Sharon Elkins has convincingly reconstructed a very different version of events by considering the prehistory of the expulsion.[73] About 1160, the abbess of Amesbury forcibly ejected a parish priest nominated by King Henry and Archbishop Theobald, apparently because she thought the advowson was hers. Henry did not forget this affront to his dignity. In 1176, Pope Alexander III informed the abbess of Fontevraud of the king's intention to increase the endowment of Amesbury and make it a Fontevrist house. This background is omitted from the charter account, which simply notes that early in 1177, Henry sent two bishops to investigate troubles at Amesbury. The bishops returned with tales of debauchery justifying the dispersal of the community and the pensioning off of the abbess, alleged to be the mother of three children. The abbess was given her freedom and a pension of ten marks of silver a year.

As Elkins notes, it is unlikely that Henry would have been so generous to a genuinely wicked abbess, making the whole story highly suspect. It is more likely that Henry had simply decided to transfer Amesbury to the charge of Fontevraud and met with resistance from the abbess, rising like so many other superiors of her day to fierce defense of the rights of her community. So in order to ensure the replacement of this stubborn woman with a nun of Fontevraud, over which Henry exercised considerable influence, the king "broadcast the sensational scandal to discredit the abbess and gain sympathy for his plan to introduce congenial nuns from Fontevrault."[74] Whatever his methods and motivations, Henry proceeded to spend 880 pounds on the restoration of the convent over the next decade. Thus he cemented the relationship between the royal house and Amesbury, now headed

72. Elkins, *Holy Women*, 68, 120–121, 148, 150; Thompson, *Women Religious*, 65–66, 69, 71, 122–124, 140, 156, 174, 176, 182–183.
73. Elkins, *Holy Women*, 146–147, is the basis for what follows. Henry's charter is published in *Recueil des actes de Henri II*, 2: 113–116 (no. 539).
74. Elkins, *Holy Women*, 147.

by a former subprioress of Fontevraud, which persisted for over a century.[75]

For Henry Plantagenet, generosity and control were inextricably linked. His archenemies, the Capetian kings, also worked to strengthen their ties to communities of religious women, with motives perhaps equally ambiguous. There survive about 800 charters of King Louis VII, who ruled from 1137 to 1180, over sixty of them concerning nuns.[76] Among women's houses, by far the most frequent recipient of the king's favor was Montmartre, the Benedictine house founded by his parents, but Louis had dealings with another twenty houses, from Saint-Paul-lès-Beauvais in the north to Cusset, near Clermont, in the south. The king made his own personal proximity to some nunneries a benefit by conferring on them a particular kind of donation, a portion of the revenue raised for the royal entourage while he stayed at a specified place nearby. For example, in 1161 or 1162 Louis granted to the nuns of La Pommeraie, a daughter house of the Paraclete, a tenth of the wine consumed whenever he was at Sens, and a few years later granted the Fontevrist priory in Orléans a tenth of both food and bread during his sojourns in that city.[77]

Louis's generosity to and protection of some nunneries, then, was closely linked to the progress of his entourage. Late in his reign, however, the king began to supplement this kind of intermittent influence with more direct dominion. In the last years of his life, Louis limited the size of four women's communities: there were to be no more than eighty nuns at Notre-Dame de Soissons, sixty at Montmartre, forty at Saint-Jean-aux-Bois, and one hundred at Faremoutiers.[78] The charters for the first three of these houses were issued on the same day, indicating that Louis had embarked on a new policy concerning women's houses in his realm. Montmartre and Saint-Jean-aux-Bois, by virtue of their foundation by Louis's forbears, were royal monasteries, that is, houses over which the king had virtual control of abbatial elections and the right to take in hand monastic temporalities during a vacancy.[79] A few years earlier Louis

75. VCH, Wiltshire, iii, 244–248.

76. Achille Luchaire, *Etudes sur les actes de Louis VII* (Paris, 1885), 97–346, is a chronological catalogue of royal charters.

77. Ibid., 243–244 (no. 447, for Pommeraie), 262 (no. 513, for La Madeleine-lès-Orléans). Similar gifts are indicated in 134 (no. 108), 211 (no. 347), 221 and 406 (no. 378), 234–235 and 414–415 (no. 421), 253 (no. 478), 268 and 427 (no. 530), 330 (no. 738).

78. Ibid., 315 (nos. 685 and 686), 316 (no. 690), 319–320 (no. 702).

79. On royal monasteries and bishoprics, see Robert Fawtier, *The Capetian Kings of France: Monarchy and Nation (987–1328)*, trans. Lionel Butler and R. J. Adam (New York, 1960), 71–73; William Mendel Newman, *Le domaine royal sous les premiers capétiens (987–1180)*

had also gained control of the ancient abbey of Faremoutiers, removing it from the authority of the bishops of Meaux.[80] The nature of the king's rights at Notre-Dame de Soissons is less clear, but there, too, he felt able to exercise overlordship.

The charters limiting the number of nuns mention poverty as the primary cause of concern, and given other signs of material strain in the late twelfth century, it is likely that Louis's concern for the welfare of the nuns was sincere. Nonetheless, an evolution is clear: first the king ingratiated himself with donations or protection, then proceeded to exercise a considerable measure of authority. Louis's son Philip, who succeeded to the throne in 1180, continued his father's policies of increasing control through making his own presence beneficial and restricting the number of nuns in some houses. Shortly after his accession, Philip issued charters reasserting his father's limitations of the number of nuns at Soissons, Montmartre, and Saint-Jean-aux-Bois.[81] Later on, Philip restricted the size of two more nunneries: in 1193 he declared that owing to an insufficiency of resources, the ancient monastery of Chelles was to house no more than eighty nuns, and fourteen years later, he made the same rule for the nuns of Yerres, a seigneurial foundation dating to the 1130s.[82]

While continuing his father's practice of forceful interference, Philip was on the whole less generous to religious women than Louis had been. Although Philip issued over twice as many charters as his father, a smaller number of them concerned nuns.[83] The vast majority of Philip's charters are simply confirmations of arrangements between nuns and other patrons. One document from early in his reign suggests that Philip was not above manipulating religious women for political ends. His father had strengthened royal authority in his own demesne, but had also acquired rights in other parts of France that Philip and others used to expand their realm.[84] One of these regions was Auvergne. Louis VII had issued a

(Paris, 1937), 67–85, 202–224; and Marcel Pacaut, *Louis VII et les élections épiscopales dans le royaume de France* (Paris, 1957), esp. 59–82.

80. Luchaire, *Etudes sur les actes de Louis VII*, 267 (no. 528).

81. *Recueil des actes de Philippe Auguste*, ed. H.-F. Delaborde, Charles Petit-Dutaillis et al., 4 vols. (Paris, 1916–1979), 1: 7–8 (no. 6), 89–90 (no. 69), 101–102 (no. 79).

82. Ibid., 1: 529–530 (no. 442); 3: 21–22 (no. 976).

83. The four volumes of the *Recueil des actes de Philippe Auguste* contain over 1,800 charters, fewer than 60 of them concerning nuns and their houses. His interest also appears to have faded across the course of his 43-year reign; nearly half of all his charters to nuns were issued between 1180 and 1195.

84. Dunbabin, *France in the Making*, 299.

charter confirming the possessions of the nunnery of Cusset, founded in the ninth century in the diocese of Clermont. The king promised that the abbey, under royal protection, would never leave the king's care.[85] Philip, pressing his father's advantage, made a somewhat more intrusive arrangement. In return for royal favor, the nuns of Cusset pledged to the king half of many of their revenues, including proceeds of justice, tolls on animals and merchandise passing through Cusset, and profits from fairs.[86] This looks very much like a means for Philip to increase his prerogatives in the region through a demand for protection money from a wealthy old monastery.[87] The Capetians were perhaps somewhat less high-handed than Henry Plantagenet, but they, too, firmly asserted dominance over monasteries in their realm and even, in the case of Cusset, used an already existing house to increase their authority, just as in the early twelfth century, local lords had founded nunneries for the same purpose.

The New Church

Henry, Louis, and Philip succeeded in installing in their realms practices recognizable as early versions of modern bureaucratic government.[88] They also gained more control than their predecessors over the persons and institutions of the Church in their kingdoms. Henry managed to emerge from the Becket affair with increased powers to limit the activities of the clergy in England, and Louis VII was a subtle and careful manipulator of episcopal elections.[89] Two of Louis's brothers and two of his nephews were elected bishop; the house of Champagne and Blois, with which the Capetians intermarried, provided many of the bishops for the province of Reims.[90] In the reign of Louis VII, half the elected archbishops whose social origins are known were relatives or close allies of the king.[91] Rulers' in-

---

85. Luchaire, *Etudes sur les actes de Louis VII*, 289–290 (no. 601).
86. *Recueil des actes de Philippe Auguste*, 1: 145–146 (no. 119).
87. On Philip in the Auvergne, see John W. Baldwin, *The Government of Philip Augustus* (Berkeley, Calif., 1986), 199–200. Philip succeeded in conquering the region in the early thirteenth century, on the pretext of protecting churches from the depredations of local lords.
88. See Warren, *Henry II*, esp. 301–396; Yves Sassier, *Louis VII* (Paris, 1991), 401–421; and Baldwin, *The Government of Philip Augustus*.
89. Warren, *Henry II*, 518–555; Pacaut, *Louis VII et les élections épiscopales*.
90. Bernard Guillemain, "Les origines des évêques en France au XIe et XIIe siècles," in *Le istituzioni ecclesiastiche della 'societas christiana' dei secoli XI–XII*. Miscellanea del Centro di Studi Medioevali 7 (Milan, 1974): 380–381.
91. Pacaut, *Louis VII et les élections épiscopales*, 143–145.

terests were well served by the bishops, often protégés of politically innovative and increasingly powerful princes.

The friends and relations of royal and princely rulers had long been put in high ecclesiastical office, but there was a significant shift in the identity of French bishops in the time of Louis VII. Bernard Guillemain has investigated the careers of bishops in nine French ecclesiastical provinces from 996 to 1200. For most of that period, the episcopate was almost evenly split between those of monastic background and the secular clergy. But from the 1130s forward, the seculars, nearly always former members of the cathedral chapter, came to dominate. From the accession of Louis VII in 1137 to the end of the century, only 32 percent of 214 elected bishops whose origins are documented came from the ranks of the religious.[92] Here, then, was another series of changes unlikely to favor the monastic life. There were by the late twelfth century fewer bishops of the kind that had so often fostered religious women and participated in the foundation of monasteries for them in the eleventh and early twelfth centuries. The bishops of the late twelfth century were administrators, regulators who may well have regarded as troubling the ancient organizational anomaly of west European monasticism, in particular its inclusion of women.[93]

The prestigious Cistercian Order came to bureaucratic solutions concerning the problem of women.[94] The status of Cistercian nuns had been ambiguous from the start. The foundation of Tart l'Abbaye with the cooperation of Abbot Stephen Harding made it clear that from the 1120s, some major figures of the order were willing to tolerate the existence of female communities associated in some manner with the Cistercians. At the same time, the all-male General Chapter as a whole did not appar-

92. Guillemain, "Les origines des évêques," 385–387, 397.
93. Constance B. Bouchard, *Spirituality and Administration: The Role of the Bishop in Twelfth-Century Auxerre* (Cambridge, Mass., 1979), 142–143, concludes that spirituality decreased in importance among qualities desired in a bishop, and that strong monastic vocation was an impediment to the increasing administrative demands of the prelacy in the twelfth century. On the increased number of episcopal councils in the late twelfth century, after a long period with few such assemblies, see Raymonde Foreville, "Royaumes, métropolitains et conciles provinciaux," in *Le istituzioni ecclesiastiche della 'societas christiana' dei secoli XI–XII.* Miscellanea del Centro di Studi Medioevali 7 (Milan, 1974): 272–313.
94. There is still much to be said about Cistercian nuns in the central Middle Ages. Aside from the studies cited in Chapter 3, see Lekai, *The Cistercians: Ideals and Reality,* 347–363, and Thompson, "The Problem of Cistercian Nuns." Thompson's observations should be treated with caution, for she assumes that the Cistercians were hostile to women from the start and only accepted Cistercian nunneries under pressure later on. For a different interpretation, see below.

ently take any specific responsibilities for the nuns in these communities. For most of the twelfth century, membership in the Cistercian congregation was probably understood as either foundation or direction of a community of nuns by a Cistercian abbot or the adoption of Cistercian practices of dress, liturgy, and internal organization.[95] Toward the end of the century, steps toward a more formal integration were visible, probably because some nuns and their patrons had taken matters into their own hands. In Spain, the royal foundation of Las Huelgas was the site of a chapter of Cistercian nunneries first held in 1189 in the presence of bishops and some Cistercian abbots.[96] By the late twelfth century, the abbot of Cîteaux, recognizing that Tart *propria est filia Cisterciensis*, authorized an annual Michaelmas meeting of eighteen abbesses from other French houses at Tart to be attended by the abbot of Cîteaux or a deputy.[97]

But even these steps toward regularization proved insufficient, perhaps because the number of nunneries, Cistercian by one definition or another, had grown so rapidly since the 1160s. By 1215, there were over one hundred Cistercian female houses in France and England, including some of the new foundations discussed earlier in this chapter. Apparently the Cistercian General Chapter had, sometime between 1190 and 1213, made provision for full and formal incorporation of nunneries into the Cistercian Order. The more ad hoc arrangements of personal supervision or the ambiguities involved in having relatively autonomous communities of nuns in white habits had given way to the organizing impulse first visible in the authorization of a chapter of nuns at Tart and finally resulting in the promulgation of specific regulations regarding nuns of the Order. Rather than bowing to pressure and reversing an earlier "policy," the Cistercians evolved stricter definitions of and controls over membership in their order.[98]

95. See J.-B. Van Damme, "Les pouvoirs de l'abbé de Cîteaux aux XIIe et XIIIe siècle," *Analecta Cisterciensia* 24 (1968): 74. Van Damme's observations match the line of reasoning of Constance Berman, "Men's Houses, Women's Houses," 43–45, with which I strongly agree: the records of the Cistercian General Chapter do not necessarily constitute the only, or even the best, means of understanding the relationship of the order to monastic women.
96. Lekai, *The Cistercians*, 348; Thompson, "The Problem of the Cistercian Nuns," 229, 237–238.
97. A charter to this effect is edited in GC 4, instr. 157. See Lekai, *The Cistercians*, 347–348. This sort of recognition implies something other than what Lekai calls "a policy of aloofness" and "negative attitude" of the General Chapter of Cistercians in the twelfth century.
98. For the standard paradigm, see Southern, *Western Society and the Church*, 314 ("the inability of even the Cistercian Order to keep women out"); Lekai, *The Cistercians*, 349 ("the gates of the Order had been forced open for the admission of nuns . . . this seemingly unex-

Interestingly, the first mention of incorporation was not a procedural dictate by the General Chapter. The declaration of 1213 concerning Cistercian nuns was meant, instead, to regulate: it specified that nuns already incorporated into the Order should stay strictly cloistered and that no new house should be admitted unless it was a strictly cloistered community. This appears to recognize a kind of de facto integration of earlier times. But for the future, the price of admission to the Order was a strict discipline, especially the oft-repeated injunction that no Cistercian nun should leave her house without permission from the abbot in whose care the community had been placed.[99] Statutes passed after 1213 included rulings that the supervising abbot could limit the number of nuns in a house, that the nuns could receive no visitors without permission, and that their confessor had to be appointed by their superior abbot.[100] When a community of nuns wanted to be admitted to the Order, it had to be inspected by two abbots who were to confirm a suitable location, the acceptance of claustration, and, significantly, a sufficient endowment of worldly goods.[101] For religious women, the security of membership in the most prestigious monastic congregation in Europe was counterbalanced by strict supervision by that "most authoritarian of all governing bodies,"[102] the Cistercian General Chapter.

"Authoritarian" might also serve to describe the attitude of the popes of the late twelfth and early thirteenth centuries. The papacy, long dominated by monks, became from the election of Alexander III (1159–1181) the seat of lawyers in a time of vastly increased business in the papal court. Across the period addressed in this chapter, the percentage of business concerned with nuns and their communities dropped. In the first year of his reign, Innocent III (1198–1216) issued over five hundred bulls, only four of them addressed to nunneries.[103]

---

pected about-face"); and Thompson, *Women Religious*, 94 ("The pressures proved too great, and the Cistercians, who at first seemed to have thought a Cistercian nun was a contradiction in terms, eventually sheltered and organized a large number of nunneries").

99. *Statuta capitulorum generalium ordinis Cisterciensis*, vol. 1, *Ab anno 1116 ad annum 1220*, ed. Josèphe-Marie Canivez (Louvain, 1933), an. 1213, c. 3 (the first mention of incorporation), an. 1213, c. 59, an. 1219, c. 53, an. 1220, c. 54 (on claustration).

100. Southern, *Western Society and the Church*, 316, calls the process a "long struggle to discipline the women." This is a better description of the whole evolution of Cistercian policy from the late twelfth century forward than that the General Chapter was forced to accept nuns into the order (314.)

101. Fontette, *Les religieuses*, 32.

102. Southern, *Western Society and the Church*, 316.

103. Jaffé et al., *Regesta pontificum Romanorum*; Auguste Potthast, *Regesta pontificum Romanorum inde ab a. post Christum natum 1198 ad a. 1304*, 2 vols. (Berlin, 1874–1875).

The character of papal contact with nuns changed, too. Whereas most bulls of the monastic popes had confirmed the rights, privileges, and goods of nuns, exhorting them to a holy life, those of the lawyer-popes were more likely to intervene. Alexander III ordered the nuns of Etrun and Bourbourg to stop quarreling with their neighbors and directed the archbishop of Reims to restore order among nuns who had ejected their abbess.[104] This pontiff also directed the abbess of an ancient French nunnery, Jouarre, to grant a prebend to an unemployed priest whose personal qualities he praised. Celestine III (1191–1198) enjoined the nuns of Saint-Césaire in Arles to obey their archbishop and limited the number of nuns at the Paraclete to sixty. Celestine also told the community of Notre-Dame at Soissons that they could admit "some outstanding nuns," apparently overruling the limitation on numbers imposed by King Louis VII and repeated by his son Philip Augustus.[105] Whether the pope intended to undermine royal authority is unclear, but in any case the nuns of Soissons had another authority imposed on them.

Because Innocent III is often said to represent the zenith of the medieval papacy, by then a far more powerful institution than in the days of Gregory VII, it is worth considering briefly this pope's contribution to the monastic life for women. Like the Cistercians, this pope appeared more interested in regulating nuns than in encouraging them. From a canon lawyer, the impulse was perhaps natural. But it is worth noting that canon law was especially unfavorable to women regarding liturgical functions and ecclesiastical governance.[106] Given his background and training, Pope Innocent's response to what he learned in 1210 about the Cistercian nuns of Spain is unsurprising. Upon hearing that some abbesses blessed their own nuns, heard confessions, and even preached publicly, the pope ordered two bishops and a Cistercian abbot to put an end to what he regarded as "incongruous and absurd" as the Lord commended the keys to the kingdom of heaven not to the Virgin Mary, but to the apostles.[107] Innocent simply found such activities utterly inappropriate for nuns.

---

104. Jaffé et al., *Regesta pontificum Romanorum*, nos. 10675, 10869, 12062.
105. Ibid., no. 13715 (Jouarre); no. 17099 (Arles); no. 17442 (Paraclete); no. 17449 (Soissons; see also PL 206: 1203).
106. The classic article on the subject is René Metz, "Le statut de la femme en droit canonique médiéval," *Recueils de la Société Jean Bodin* 12 (1962): 59–113.
107. PL 216: 356: "Cum igitur id absonum sit pariter et absurdum, nec a nobis aliquatenus sustinendum, discretioni vestrae per apostolica scripta mandamus quatenus ne id de cetero fiat auctoritate curetis apostolica firmiter inhibere, quia licet beatissima virgo Maria dignior et excellentior fuerit apostolis universis, non tamen illi, sed istis, Dominus claves regni coelorum commisit."

Innocent's goals as a reformer were exemplified by his leadership of the Fourth Lateran Council, held at Rome in November 1215. Although the council was attended by over 400 bishops and twice many monastic superiors, it was completed in less than a month, suggesting that the pope and his councilors had formulated in advance most of the canons to be published.[108] The primary concerns of the council were the recovery of Jerusalem, the reform of the church, and the extirpation of heresy.[109] Of seventy canons promulgated by the Fourth Lateran Council, only Canon 64 addressed female monasticism directly. "Because the disgrace of simony has infected so many nuns so much that they scarcely receive any sisters without payment, wishing to conceal a crime of this kind under the pretext of poverty, we prohibit this being done any more."[110] As a modern historian of simony points out, this emphasis on women as transgressors is wholly new, despite widespread concern about the propriety of all monastic entry gifts which had grown since the mid-twelfth century. To specify female transgression shows that nuns found their economic situation to be dire, less a pretext than a reality, if the evidence of charters is admitted, perhaps more so than that of men, who were not subject to the kind of strict claustration envisioned in Cistercian legislation.[111] The new shift toward criticizing the nuns might also reflect an increased concern with their regulation and limitation by male clergy, what Innocent thought necessary for the nuns in Spain.

An Age of Anxiety?

The attack on simoniacal entry into nunneries unites two themes: growing economic strain on female monasticism and growing desire to regulate and control religious women. In the later twelfth century, other signs of male discomfort with religious women emerged, as expressed in both fiction and action. At Fontevraud, there was after 1150 what one scholar calls "proximity anxiety," expressed both in the latest versions of the

---

108. Joseph H. Lynch, *Simoniacal Entry into the Religious Life from 1000 to 1260* (Columbus, Ohio, 1976), 193.

109. Colin Morris, *The Papal Monarchy: The Western Church from 1050 to 1250* (Oxford, 1989), 449–450.

110. *Sacrorum conciliorum*, 22: 1051–1054: "Quoniam simoniaca labes adeo plerasque moniales infecit, ut vix aliquas sine pretio recipiant in sorores, paupertatis praetextu volentes huiusmodi vitium palliare, ne id de cetero fiat." Only at the end does the text contain a note that this prohibition applied to monks and other regulars too.

111. Lynch, *Simoniacal Entry*, 194.

statutes and the division of space in the abbey church that was still under construction for some time after Robert of Arbrissel's death in 1116. By the late twelfth century, the nave was the space for nuns, the choir for the monks, the two groups probably separated by a barrier.[112] An even greater level of separation between men and women was attained at a site in the Limousin, where, unlike Fontevraud, women were not the center of a mixed congregation. Stephen of Obazine, yet another preacher who attracted men and women to religious life, founded the convent of Coyroux, not far from the male community, in 1142. Stephen placed the sisters in a narrow gorge, where a monastic compound was squeezed into a small space, a notable contrast with the abbey of Obazine, on a sunny hilltop nearby. The sisters themselves may have chosen this isolated spot, but maybe the monks also were hoping that the convent, which represented a burden to them, would eventually disappear. Certainly, the choice of site precluded great growth.[113]

The proximity anxiety of the Premonstratensian Order resulted in the greatest setback for monastic women in the central Middle Ages. The Premonstratensians began separating male and female members of their congregation around 1140, usually accomplishing the division by sending the sisters to a new location, sometimes nearby, sometimes at a considerable remove.[114] Several papal documents of the period reminded the canons of their continuing obligations to the sisters, both material and spiritual. But these duties were apparently still too much for the Premonstratensians, who, according to a bull of Innocent III in 1198, had sometime before declared that sisters would no longer be received into the order.[115]

There were over fifty settlements of Premonstratensian women in France and England in the middle of the twelfth century, almost all of

112. Loraine N. Simmons, "The Abbey Church at Fontevraud in the Later Twelfth Century: Anxiety, Authority, and Architecture in the Female Spiritual Life," *Gesta* 31 (1992): 99–107.
113. Bernadette Barrière, "The Cistercian Convent of Coyroux in the Twelfth and Thirteenth Centuries," *Gesta* 31 (1992): 76–82.
114. For example, the sisters of Prémontré went first, in 1141, to a site 4 kilometers away, then shortly after to another, equidistant from the mother house, then in 1148 to the final site, Bonneuil, 33 kilometers from Prémontré (MP 2: 484). The house of Flabemont, northeast of Langres, remained double until about 1180, when the women moved to a nearby spot (MP 3: 71, 74). The sisters of Cuissy, however, were sent first to a site 45 kilometers away, then to Rouez, 70 kilometers from that first colony (MP 2: 496, 505, 530).
115. For general accounts of women in the Premonstratensian Order, see Erens, "Les soeurs dans l'ordre de Prémontré," 8–11; Fontette, *Les religieuses*, 18–19, 24–25; Thompson, *Women Religious*, 134–139.

them the segregated portion of an earlier community of religious men and women.[116] The women's houses of the order faded away in the late twelfth and thirteenth centuries, mostly by attrition. Some Premonstratensian houses for women must have stopped accepting new members shortly after the separations of the 1140s, as about fifteen of them leave no trace in the record after 1200. The bulk of the disappearances came somewhat later, following on the prohibition of new sisters in the order at the end of the twelfth century. Another thirty or so houses disappeared within the next half century, probably when the last inhabitants died. There were two sisters left at Nieuwenrode, near Brussels, in 1270, but most other houses were already gone by then.[117] By 1300, only eight houses of Premonstratensian sisters survived in the area under consideration, three in England, five on the Continent.

Perhaps in part because they were so much more numerous than before, nuns seemed to present a kind of threat to some clerical observers. In a late-twelfth-century update of the principles espoused in Ovid's erotic poetry, a tongue-in-cheek how-to book addressed to a young protégé, Andreas Capellanus specifically tackles the question of loving nuns. He commands his student that nuns are to be assiduously avoided because divine and human authority punish transgressions of this type severely. "So I would have you utterly unacquainted with the addresses suitable to importuning nuns." But Andreas cannot stop himself. "There was once an occasion when the chance of making advances to a nun came my way. I was not ignorant of the theory of soliciting nuns." The teacher claims that he caught himself before he sinned, but "only with difficulty could I avoid [love's] baneful snares and withdraw without contamination of the flesh." In the right place for wanton sport (*lascivis ludis locum . . . aptum*), a nun "will not hesitate to grant you what you desire."[118]

Inclination to wantonness, one element of the Western misogynist tradition, was imputed to nuns by other clerical satirists of the era.[119] An early example of the debate poems concerning the relative merits of cler-

---

116. The figures in this paragraph derive from the sketches in MP. Because these ephemeral communities often left few (if any) traces in the record, a detailed study of the disappearance of the female Premonstratensian communities is impossible.

117. On Nieuwenrode, see MP 2: 286, 312.

118. Andreas Capellanus, *Andreas Capellanus on Love*, ed. and trans. P. G. Walsh (London, 1982), 210–213.

119. On this tradition, see R. Howard Bloch, *Medieval Misogyny and the Invention of Western Romantic Love* (Chicago, 1991). Bloch thinks that the ideal of courtly love which developed in the course of the twelfth century was not a rejection of the misogynist tradition but a powerful new tool for the "possession and repossession of women."

ics and knights as lovers is the so-called "Council of Remiremont," a Latin satire of circa 1160. In the course of 235 verses, an abbess and several nuns conclude that it is clerics who are the best men for this purpose and issue an excommunication of all who love knights.[120] The poem is neither very original nor very accomplished, but its interest is considerable nonetheless. The author places this debate in a real convent, an ancient Benedictine house in the diocese of Toul. Furthermore, some of the names of the interlocutors in the debate are the same as those mentioned in the *Liber memorialis* of Remiremont for the mid-twelfth century.[121] So the satirist placed arguments about who make the better lovers into the mouths of actual religious women of Remiremont. Along with Andreas's advice manual to a young lover, this poem shows nuns to be willing (and experienced) sexual partners. Writings such as these might be considered backlash, an expression of fear of the female power and independence that found its greatest expression in the cloister. That power was easily summarized for satirical purposes in aggressive female sexuality, a stock-in-trade of the Western literary tradition.

A series of events in northern England shows how one incident could evolve into a major (and fairly hostile) examination of the lives of nuns with strong overtones of sexual panic. In about 1166, Aelred of Rievaulx wrote of a miracle that had saved the nuns of the Gilbertine house of Watton from scandal.[122] The context of the miracle, however, is a story of shocking violence. A nun of Watton was impregnated by her lover and chained in a cell by her fellow nuns. The man was captured by some of the monastery's brothers, who handed him over to a group of nuns. They restrained him and forced the pregnant nun to castrate him; another nun "grabbing the parts of which he had just been relieved, fouled with blood as they were, thrust them in the mouth of the sinful woman." (Aelred remarks that it is impossible to condone the deed, but zeal

---

120. The poem is edited and translated into French in Charles Oulmont, *Les débats du clerc et du chevalier* (Paris, 1911), 93–107.

121. Michel Parisse, "Le concile de Remiremont: Poème satirique du XIIe siècle," *Le Pays de Remiremont* 4 (1981), 10–11. By the thirteenth century, Remiremont had become a house of secular canonesses, but as Parisse points out, there is no reason to suspect earlier secularization, as in the twelfth century, the same abbess directed Remiremont and what remained a Benedictine nunnery, Saint-Pierre in Metz.

122. PL 195: 789–796; partially translated by John Boswell in *The Kindness of Strangers: The Abandonment of Children in Western Europe from Late Antiquity to the Renaissance* (New York, 1988), 452–458. A careful and sympathetic account is Giles Constable, "Aelred of Rievaulx and the Nun of Watton: An Episode in the Early History of the Gilbertine Order," in Derek Baker, ed. *Medieval Women* (Oxford, 1978), 205–226. Boswell's translation uses Constable's corrections to the PL text from the lone surviving manuscript.

against evil is commendable.) The wretched nun subsequently approached the time of birth, still confined to a cell. In a dream an archbishop came to her, and two women accompanying him carried away a baby. When she awoke, she was no longer pregnant. Her guards first accused her of murdering her own baby, but found no corpse, nor any sign on her body of childbirth or even pregnancy. Later, the chains and fetters binding her fell off, which satisfied Gilbert of Sempringham and Aelred that God had performed miracles in order to obviate scandal.

Shortly afterward, the entire Gilbertine Order came under the scrutiny of Pope Alexander III, in order to correct a "certain great scandal."[123] Five letters to the pope in defense of Gilbert have survived: one from King Henry II, three from bishops, and one from a monk. All five letters assume that sexual license was the scandal, although subsequent hearing by the archbishops of Canterbury and York focused on the dissatisfaction of the lay brothers, who were governed very strictly in the Gilbertine houses. Still, the only legislative result of the enquiry was increased segregation of nuns and canons in Gilbertine houses. The final settlement of the whole issue did not come until 1178.[124] Gilbertines were found to be innocent of wrongdoing, but "the damage of years of suspicion could not be erased . . . growth and experimentation came to a halt."[125] By the 1190s, Gerald of Wales was telling a story of one of Gilbert's nuns who was so lascivious that she lusted after her aged master.[126]

What emerges from architecture, statute, satire, and incident are mistrust and suspicion of nuns, specifically of their sexuality. The last was perceived as antithetical to religious ideals, a dangerous threat to the women themselves, and, as the story from Watton shows, the men around them: a danger and a burden. Suspicion may have been intensified because so many twelfth-century nuns, including well-known and powerful abbesses such as Petronilla of Chemillé and Heloise, were not virgins. But as Penelope Johnson demonstrates, monks and nuns in mid-

123. This paragraph is a much-reduced version of the account given by Sharon Elkins, *Holy Women*, 111–117, which differs considerably in its emphasis from the classic account of David Knowles, "The Revolt of the Lay Brothers of Sempringham," *English Historical Review* 50 (1935): 465–487.
124. *The Book of Saint Gilbert*, lx–lxii. Elkins and Knowles found the crisis to have been settled by 1170.
125. Elkins, *Holy Women*, 117. Elkins notes (111) that there is no explicit connection in surviving documentation of the trouble at Watton and the investigation of the order, but whether cause or symptom, the incident marked the beginning of a period of crisis and reevaluation of the relationship between the sexes in the Gilbertine houses.
126. Gerald of Wales, *Gemma Ecclesiastica*, ed. John S. Brewer, vol. 2 of *Giraldi Cambrensis Opera*, ed. John S. Brewer (London, 1862), 247–248.

thirteenth-century Normandy were censured for unchastity in approximately equal proportion in the visitation records of Archbishop Eudes Rigaud. Furthermore, there was in Eudes's time a significant correlation between communal poverty and sexual misconduct, for monks and especially for nuns.[127] A perception of connection between want and wickedness is hinted at in a charter from the last years of the twelfth century. About 1192, a few years after the canons of Cysoing in Artois established a house for sisters at Beaurepaire, the abbot gave the nuns some land. He did so, he explained, so that they would be able to persist in the religious life, having put aside the cares of Martha, lest on the advice of the devil they "turn back their eyes" (like Lot's wife?) toward material necessity.[128] Poverty and waywardness, then, were connected in the minds of contemporaries. Very likely, the change in attitude in a period of material strain is not simple coincidence, and both guardians and satirists of monastic women in the years around 1200 feared a breakdown of discipline in convents under economic duress. This would account for the efforts by kings and bishops to limit the numbers in some houses.

Amidst economic troubles, authoritarian tendencies, and a failure of nerve in the relations of men and religious women and without the catalysts of wandering preachers, pastor-bishops, and a dynamic lower aristocracy, it is perhaps not very surprising that the expansion of women's monasticism was checked in the years 1170–1215. During the last years of Innocent III's pontificate, the rate of nunnery foundation in northwestern Europe dropped to its lowest point in a century. Two charters of the late twelfth century summarize the findings of this chapter. The first is a bull of Alexander III, who wrote to the archdeacon and chapter of Brindisi concerning a certain married woman. She had been received into a monastery with her husband's permission, but he had no inclination to take up a religious life and in his wife's absence sinned by sleeping with a servant and her daughter. He begged the pope for the right to

127. Johnson, *Equal in Monastic Profession,* 112–130. I would posit further that in an atmosphere of suspicion of female sexuality, nuns were more likely to be accused and reprimanded for misbehavior than monks, meaning that monastic women in the aggregate may in fact have been *more* chaste than men.

128. *Cartulaire de l'abbaye de Cysoing et de ses dépendances,* ed. Ignace de Coussemaker (Lille, 1886), 69: "attendans etiam devotionem mulierum devotarum in domo de Belrepaire religiose viventium, que, postpositis Marthe tumultuosis negotiis, optimam sibi partem Marie elegerunt que non auferetur ab eis, paterna sollicitudine earum tranquillitati et paci prospiciens, ne antiqui suggestione deceptoris ad corporales necessitudines, occasionem habeant oculum retorquendi, ad relevandas necessitates . . . terram . . . concedo." The nuns were in serious financial trouble two decades later (see above, note 46).

remove his wife from the convent to prevent further crime on his part. The canons were to make sure that the woman returned to do her conjugal duty. The decision might seem "abominable" to some, Alexander conceded, but it was more tolerable than if the man were to keep up his adulterous habits.[129] The pope, in short, was ordering exactly what Robert of Arbrissel had successfully refused: the surrender of an unwilling wife back to the husband she had abandoned.

The example of Robert is also important for evaluating the second charter. Shortly after the foundation of Fontevraud, Robert chose Hersende of Montsoreau and Petronilla of Chemillé, with their combined qualities of faith, wisdom, and skill in property management, to lead his community. The dedication in 1186 of a new abbey church for the nuns of Avenay in Champagne was occasion to praise the ideal qualities of Abbess Helisende, *dignitate excellentissima, honestate morum valde perspicua, temporalium rerum satis opulentissima*: most excellent in worthiness, quite outstanding in the honor of her ways, and really quite rich.[130] It was Helisende, a viscount's daughter, who had paid for the restoration of the church, whose beauties are described in some detail. Piety and acumen, the qualities Robert prized, had been replaced, eighty years later, by a less specifically religious respectability and wealth.

Ironically, even this kind of prestige was not sufficient to guarantee the well-being of the ancient house of Avenay. Fifteen years after the dedication of the new church, Archbishop William of Reims, citing the importunities of neighboring magnates and of creditors, declared that the number of nuns at Avenay was to be reduced to forty.[131] So the women there, harassed by debt on one hand and impositions by the local powerful (some of whom may have been trying to place female relatives in the house without the entry gift now held in such suspicion) on the other, were forced to scale back their community under the aegis of their bishop. Poverty, powerlessness, and subordination: such was the lot of the nuns of Avenay and many others in France and England at the turn of the thirteenth century. A great creative episode in the history of medieval Christianity had come to an end.

---

129. PL 204: 807–808, note 24: "licet nonnullis abominabile videatur ut mulier de claustro ad nuptias saeculares debeat revocari. . . . Tolerabilius enim est ut vir antefatus uxorem hujusmodi habeat, quam per adulteria multa discurrat."

130. Louis Paris, *Histoire de l'abbaye d'Avenay*, 2 vols. (Paris, 1879), 2: 85. *Dignitas* can mean several things, including high rank and worldly fortune; all these meanings are implied here.

131. Ibid., 2: 94.

epilogue

NEW NUNNERIES IN A NEW EUROPE

The foundation of nunneries in France and England did not end after the Fourth Lateran Council. In fact, the number of new monasteries for women rose again after 1215, and by 1260 almost one hundred fifty more convents had appeared. But these foundations were very different from those that preceded them. In their geographical distribution and the profile of their patrons, foundations of the post-1215 period are rather more like those of the eleventh century than of the twelfth: the very powerful established convents in or near their seats of power. Furthermore, there were by now more options, tolerated if not actually sanctioned, for women with religious aspirations. Female monasticism itself was no longer characterized by the creativity and variety of the twelfth century, especially its first half.

Figure 8 shows the distribution of new foundations in the years 1216 to 1260. The most striking feature of the pattern is its unevenness. Over half the new houses were in the archdioceses of Reims and Sens alone, and when Bourges, Narbonne, and Arles are added, the figure rises to above 70 percent. By far the densest settlement was in the regions of Flanders, Brabant, Hainault, Champagne, and the Ile de France, with significant new activity in the lower Rhône Valley and along the Languedocian littoral: Western Europe's most populous and urbanized commercial sector. Where the economy grew significantly, so did the number of nunneries.[1]

1. Sivéry, *L'économie du royaume de France au siècle de Saint Louis,* map 2, shows the regions in

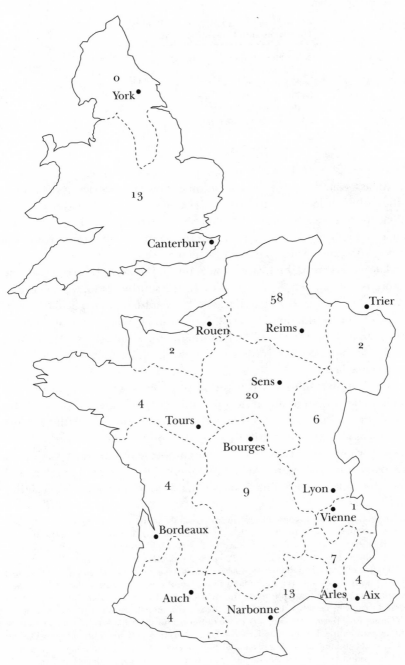

FIGURE 8. Nunneries founded or refounded, 1216–1260, by archdiocese

Table 6. Number of nunneries founded, 1216–1260, by distance from urban center

5 kilometers or less	47 (32.2%)
6–15 kilometers	25 (17.1%)
16–25 kilometers	26 (17.8%)
26–35 kilometers	26 (17.8%)
36–45 kilometers	15 (10.3%)
46 kilometers or more	7 (4.8%)
	146 (100%)

An associated change is the location of new monasteries in relation to cities: whereas in the period 1080–1215 only 10 percent had been in or adjacent to cities, the figure tripled after 1216 (see Table 6). Also notable is the drop in number of nunneries in the distant countryside. Between 1080 and 1170, 30 percent of all new foundations were more than 35 kilometers from the nearest town, but in the period 1216–1260, the figure is only 15 percent. Expansion in the southern tier, which continued at a pace much like that in the twelfth century, was particularly characterized by foundation in towns. New nunneries appeared in Béziers, Bordeaux, Cahors, Cavaillon, Montauban, Montpellier, Narbonne, Nîmes, Périgueux, and Toulouse, and two each in the cities of Avignon and Marseille.

The founders of these thirteenth-century houses were, on average, of higher status than at any time since the early and middle years of the eleventh century, when the comital and ducal families of the French provinces were the most visible patrons of women's monasticism. Of thirteen new nunneries founded in the archdiocese of Canterbury between 1216 and 1260, five were owed to members of very eminent families, and Eva, the daughter of William Marshall, is said to have founded a sixth.[2]

which economic growth—agricultural, industrial, and commercial—occurred from the late twelfth century onward. It is primarily in these vital sectors that female monasticism continued to grow. On expansion of the arable in a few regions in the first half of the thirteenth century, see Guy Devailly, *Le Berry du Xe au milieu du XIIIe siècle* (Paris, 1973), 553–558, and Charles Higounet, *Défrichements et villeneuves du bassin parisien (XIe–XIVe siècles)* (Paris, 1990), 91–203. Berry and upland Champagne are the most important areas of new female monastic foundation outside the urbanized zones; these are the places in which agrarian growth, largely eclipsed by the urban commercial revolution, was still rapid.
2. Thompson, *Women Religious*, 50–52 (Aconbury, a hospital that was transformed into a nunnery under the direction of Margaret de Lacy), 169–170 (Lacock, founded by Ela, the countess of Salisbury and widow of a bastard son of Henry II), 171 (Marham, founded by Isabel, the widow of the earl of Arundel), 172 (Cornworthy, perhaps founded by Eva, daughter of William Marshall), 228 (Rothwell, founded by the Clare family); MRH, 267 (Usk, in

On the Continent, too, the high nobility once again led the foundation of women's monasteries. The French royal family founded five new houses. King Louis IX (later Saint Louis, 1226–1270) founded in the course of his reign one convent in Orléans and another at Vernon, in the diocese of Evreux. Louis's sister Isabel founded the house of Long-champs, just outside Paris. Blanche of Castille, mother of Louis and Isabel, founded the Cistercian house of Maubuisson in 1241 and joined her son the king in another Cistercian foundation, Le Lys, in the diocese of Sens, a few years later.[3]

The still mighty house of Blois-Champagne continued to sponsor new houses for women. The widowed countess Blanche, along with her son Count Thibaud the Great, founded the Cistercian nunnery of Argen-solles, which was to house 90 nuns, 10 *conversae*, and 20 laymen and clerics. Thibaud himself founded two more houses in Champagne and arranged for a hospital in Bar-sur-Aube to be made into a nunnery following the Augustinian Rule.[4] Farther west, Countess Blanche of Brittany founded the Cistercian nunnery of Joie-Notre-Dame in the diocese of Vannes.[5] The count of Chartres founded a house in Chartres and was joined by Countess Isabel in establishing a nunnery just outside Arras; the widowed Isabel later founded a convent in the diocese of Orléans.[6] Another powerful comital family not only founded nunneries but also served as protector of numerous others. Count Ferrand of Flanders and Countess Jeanne founded the house of Marquette; Jeanne also founded two other nunneries. Her sister and successor as countess, Marguerite, founded two more convents. Countess Jeanne was the patron of another fifteen nunneries: urban houses such as Spermalie in Bruges and rural ones such as Lady Christina's house at Ravensberg.[7]

Probably the patrons of nunneries in the thirteenth century had many of the same motives as the petty nobles who founded houses in

---

Monmouthshire, the project of Richard de Clare and his son Gilbert). King Henry III is the first known patron of a house of sisters in Worcester (MRH, 288).

3. GC 8: 1570–1571 (Orléans); GC 11: 662 (Vernon); GC 7: 943–944 (Longchamps); GC 7: 927–928 (Maubuisson); GC 12: 247 (le Lys).

4. DHGE 4: 16–19 (Argensolles); GC 9: 973–974 (Vitry-en-Perthois); GC 12: 255 (Mont-Ste-Catherine); DHGE 6: 550 (Bar-sur-Aube).

5. GC 14: 968.

6. GC 8: 1326 (Chartres); GC 3: 185 (le Verger); GC 8: 1592–1593 (le Lieu-Notre-Dame).

7. McDonnell, *The Beguines and Beghards*, 111–112. In 1226 Countess Jeanne issued a charter declaring herself patron of Ravensberg. She and her husband also made donations to the house, whose grateful inhabitants provided for a chaplain to celebrate Mass for Jeanne and Ferrand. Coussemaker, "Notice sur l'abbaye de Ravensberg," 258–260.

the twelfth century: they, too, had asserted legitimacy for the benefit, broadly conceived, of their kin. But in an age of resurgent monarchies and a complex commercial economy, only the most wealthy and powerful found it easy to afford sponsoring female monasticism. Blanche of Castille's foundation of Maubuisson is a case in point. The queen specified that the new convent included a church, dormitory, refectory, cellar, other necessary buildings, the surrounding walls, and the land on which they stand: "all of which we had acquired by means of our own wealth."[8] Blanche's pride is understandable, for she had gone to considerable trouble to buy up property from several parties, at a cost of hundreds of Parisian pounds, for the nuns' estate. Shortly after the house was established, the queen paid another 400 pounds to a local lord for two houses and more land.[9] In 1244, her son Louis IX exempted the abbey from secular taxes and placed it in royal custody.[10] Blanche visited the convent frequently (she had a small house within the walls) and died at Maubuisson in 1252.[11] Her son and his descendants continued to be the chief patrons of the house. Their generosity was necessary because very few others made donations to Maubuisson.[12]

It would appear that the social status of the nuns, too, was on average higher than in the days when Robert of Arbrissel welcomed all sorts and conditions of women at Fontevraud. Just outside the area under consideration here, the ancient house of Andenne, near Namur, declared in 1207 that women to be consecrated there had to be daughters of two noble parents.[13] Such a standard suggests that nunneries were becoming a preserve of the aristocracy, and that houses needed the income an entry gift from a noblewoman could provide. Even after the prohibition

---

8. *Cartulaire de l'abbaye de Maubuisson (Notre-Dame-la-Royale)*, ed. A. Dutilleux and J. Depoin (Pontoise, 1890–1913), 2: "Donavimus etiam imperpetuum et concessimus abbatie memorate ac personis ibidem Deo servientibus et in posterum servituris locum ipsum cum fundo in quo sita sint: monasterium, dormitorium, refectorium, celerium et omnia ac singula edificia infra ambitum murorum contenta cum eisdem edificiis et muris . . . quae omnia acquisieramus de nostris propriis bonis."
9. Ibid., 90–91.
10. Ibid., 6–7.
11. T. N. Kinder, "Blanche of Castille and the Cistercians: An Architectural Re-evaluation of Maubuisson Abbey," *Cîteaux: Commentarii Cistercienses* 27 (1976), 167–168 and n. 32.
12. *Cartulaire de l'abbaye de Maubuisson*, 92–169, shows that to obtain rights in various locales, the nuns usually paid cash to their neighbors.
13. Michel Parisse, *Noblesse et chevalerie en Lorraine médiévale: Les familles nobles du XIe au XIIIe siècle* (Nancy, 1982), 265. For other comments on the increasingly high nobility of female monastic communities in thirteenth-century Lorraine, see ibid., 266–270.

of the Fourth Lateran Council, "the entry gift stayed a pragmatic—if not an official—requirement."[14] The threat of material want was changing the identity of the founders of nunneries and of the women who joined them. At Blanche of Castille's Maubuisson, it was deemed necessary in 1267 to place an upper limit of 140 on the number of nuns at the house, only five years after a bull from Urban IV allowed the nuns to refuse entry to economically burdensome pensioners. Less than a year after the first limitation came another; this time Pope Clement IV charged the community to reduce itself by attrition to 120, only 100 of them nuns, unless its patrimony increased enough to warrant growth. In 1285, Honorius IV charged a canon of Saint-Quentin with the job of restoring to the abbey properties that had slipped out of its control. Even one the richest and most populous nunneries in France found its resources strained.[15]

Besides location and the status of founders, the third major departure of the thirteenth century was in the institutional affiliations of new houses. In sharp contrast to earlier times, nearly two-thirds of all new convents founded between 1216 and 1260 *were* associated with a male-centered religious congregation. The majority of these seventy-five or so nunneries were Cistercian. The order first tried to prohibit further affiliation of nunneries in 1220, only seven years after the General Chapter made it clear that women's houses could join, subject to various disciplinary regulations. Nonetheless, incorporations of Cistercian nunneries, mostly in the northern reaches of the Continental region under scrutiny, continued until the mid-thirteenth century.[16]

The other major category of nunneries was that affiliated with the mendicant orders: the so-called second-order Franciscans and Dominican nuns. By 1260, there were about twenty-five Franciscan nunneries in France, most of them in towns in Provence and Languedoc. The life of the friars, their evangelism and poverty, was the greatest novelty in orthodox religious life in the thirteenth century, but neither Franciscan

---

14. Johnson, *Equal in Monastic Profession*, 25, and for other examples of post-1215 female monastic dowries, 25–26. Johnson finds that the frequent assertions by thirteenth-century donors that they made such gifts to alleviate the poverty of the house are rhetoric designed to disguise simony, but I suspect that the strain on resources was often very real.

15. *Cartulaire de l'abbaye de Maubuisson*, 22, 23–25, 29.

16. Simone Roisin, "L'efflorescence cistercienne et le courant féminin de piété au XIIIe siècle," *Revue d'histoire ecclésiastique* 39 (1943): 342–378, is the classic study and contains much detail on the incorporation of new Cistercian nunneries. See also Lekai, *The Cistercians*, 349–352, and Roger de Ganck, "The Integration of Nuns in the Cistercian Order, Particularly in Belgium," *Cîteaux: Commentarii Cistercienses* 35 (1984): 241–243.

nor Dominican nunneries resembled very closely the communities of their male counterparts.[17] When his disciple Clare took vows from Francis of Assisi, she was sent off to one Benedictine nunnery and transferred to another before becoming the leader of her own community of San Damiano. The first set of statutes for Clare and others who had been attracted to the ideals of Saint Francis, issued by Pope Honorius III in 1219, was essentially an adaptation of the ancient Rule of Saint Benedict. It did not mention poverty and enforced a strict claustration that prohibited the sisters from ministering to the poor, a passion of Clare's. The first Rule for Franciscan sisters, decreed by the papacy while Francis was absent from Italy, contained nothing specifically Franciscan.[18] Although Clare did manage, shortly before her death, to get a new Rule that forbade ownership of property and tied the sisters closely to the friars, it applied only to San Damiano and other houses that chose to adopt it.[19] The French houses of Franciscan nuns were very little different from those that had no formal ties to any religious congregation, and except for Longchamps, founded by Princess Isabel, none of them was very large or wealthy.

Because there were only a handful of Dominican nunneries in the area considered here, it is ironic that Saint Dominic's first foundation was for southern French women.[20] Sent to preach against heresy in Languedoc, Dominic offered women an alternative to heterodox religious life by founding in 1207 the monastery of Prouille. Alone of all the "mendicant" nunneries in southern France, Prouille became a large and wealthy community by the late thirteenth century. Still, the life there was much different from that Dominic prescribed for his fellow preachers; the nuns of Prouille were enjoined to hold property like other monasteries and were strictly cloistered. After the death of Saint Dominic in 1221, women at Prouille and elsewhere who wished to be members of the Dominican Order waged a long and ultimately largely

---

17. Herbert Grundmann, *Religiöse Bewegungen im Mittelalter*, 2d ed. (Hildesheim, 1961), 199–318, is a thorough study of the religious and institutional relationship of the mendicant friars and religious women.

18. John Moorman, *A History of the Franciscan Order from Its Origins to the Year 1517* (Oxford, 1968), 32–39.

19. Ibid., 209, 211–213. On the Rule, and for recent bibliography on the Poor Clares, see Elizabeth Alvilda Petroff, *Body and Soul: Essays on Medieval Women and Mysticism* (New York, 1994), 66–79.

20. On Dominic and Prouille, see M.-H. Vicaire, "L'action de saint Dominique sur la vie régulière des femmes en Languedoc," *Cahiers de Fanjeaux* 23 (1988): 217–240, on which this paragraph is based.

unsuccessful battle to maintain close contact with the friars.[21] Like the Franciscans, the Dominicans remained rather distant from the sisters who in any case led religious lives far less novel than those of their male counterparts.

Behind the tendencies of the period 1216–1260—the founding of new houses by wealthy people in populous and economically vital regions and locales, the association of so many of them with the by now prestigious and respected Cistercian Order, the "normalizing" of the lives of religious women in Franciscan and Dominican nunneries—lurks a measure of insecurity. To some, nuns seemed more dangerous than ever; the combination of spiritual and psychological unease with the ever-present threat of poverty sometimes gave rise to outright hostility toward monastic women. When, shortly after 1270, the Premonstratensians divested themselves of the remaining communities of women attached to their order, one abbot issued a furious justification. Conrad of Marchthal raged that because familiarity with women was a worse ill than the poisons of asps and dragons, "we have decreed with common consent and by common counsel that for the salvation not only of our souls and bodies, but even of our property . . . we should under no conditions receive, to the increase of our perdition, any more sisters, but avoid their reception as if they were poisonous animals."[22] By the late thirteenth century, harsh language expressed the twin concerns of spiritual damage and economic strain, already clear in the much milder Premonstratensian statute of nearly a century earlier (cited at the beginning of Chapter 5).[23] With such dangers, real and perceived, surrounding nuns, it is little wonder that from 1260 to the arrival of plague in 1348, only about sixty new nunneries were founded in northwestern Europe—fewer than had been founded in the 1150s alone.

Yet when creativity yielded to constraint in regular monastic life, it resurfaced in a completely new forum for religious expression. The beguines, urban religious women who lived singly or in communities, first appeared in and around Liège shortly after 1200; their practices soon

---

21. For the details, see Fontette, *Les religieuses*, 115–127.
22. Cited in Erens, "Les soeurs de l'ordre de Prémontré," 10–11 (n. 20): "quodque venena aspidum et draconum sanabiliora sunt homini et mitiora quam familiaritas mulierum, decrevimus pari consensu et communi consilio, saluti tam animarum quam corporum, et etiam rerum, in posterum providere volentes, ut aliquas de cetero sorores, ad augmentum nostrae perditionis, nullatenus recipiamus, sed ea[s] quasi venenata animalia recipere devitemus."
23. Conrad's outburst is quoted in Southern, *Western Society and the Church*, 314, as if it is contemporary with the late twelfth-century statute.

spread across western and northern Europe.[24] Beguines took no vows, had no constitutions or Rule, and were not answerable to any ecclesiastical authority. They dedicated their lives to God through acts of charity, meditation, and prayer, and some of them produced remarkable visionary and devotional writings. The appearance of the beguines has long been tied to the *Frauenfrage*, an excess of women in the cities of northern Europe. As I have argued in Chapter 4, this urban and primarily middle-class *Frauenfrage* had an antecedent in the situation of rural aristocratic women of a century or so before. But as nunneries became more exclusive, and city populations grew rapidly, the number of women seeking fulfillment in a religious life expanded among new social groups and moved inward to population centers.[25]

Thus, the most original feminine religious movement of the thirteenth century came about in a new setting and purposefully avoided the strictures of monasticism as women by then experienced it.[26] A different kind of non regular female religious movement arose in England, with its paucity of large population centers (compared to the nearby Continent) that offered haven for beguines. Instead, more and more Englishwomen turned to the anchoritic life, whose adherents had inspired Saint Dunstan in the tenth century. There were male recluses, too, but in thirteenth-century England anchoritism was an increasingly female phenomenon. The movement produced a famed vernacular guide for anchoresses, the *Ancrene Riwle*, and, like the beguine movement on the Continent, it was far more socially diverse than contemporary female monasticism.[27] In the

24. Scholarly literature on the beguines is copious and growing. The most influential treatments are Grundmann, *Religiöse Bewegungen*, 319–354, and McDonnell, *The Beguines and Beghards*. Southern, *Western Society and the Church*, 319–331, offers an excellent short account. For recent bibliography, see Carol Neel, "The Origins of the Beguines," *Signs* 14 (1989): 321–341 and especially Walter Simons, "The Beguine Movement in the Southern Low Countries: A Reassessment," *Bulletin de l'Institut Historique Belge de Rome* 59 (1989): 63–105. The information in this paragraph is derived from these studies.

25. Simons, "The Beguine Movement," 68–76, finds that perhaps half of all beguines were of rural, not urban, origins; the geographical area of recruitment thus overlapped with that of traditional nunneries, which were becoming more exclusive. These conclusions dovetail nicely with mine, in particular because I suspect that the *Frauenfrage* so evident in thirteenth-century towns had earlier roots in the countryside. Simons cites studies that find female majorities a general characteristic of urban migration.

26. Southern, *Western Society and the Church*, 319, calls the emergence of the beguines "a series of reactions to the conditions of urban life and commercial wealth, combined with disillusionment about elaborate structures of government and systems of theoretical perfection."

27. Ann K. Warren, *Anchorites and Their Patrons in Medieval England* (Berkeley, Calif. 1985), 19–26.

thirteenth century, then, female monasticism was eclipsed by two alternatives: the life of the beguine—the product of wholly new social, economic,
institutional, and ideological environments—and the life of the recluse,
a withdrawal from society that, nine centuries earlier in the deserts of
Egypt, had been the antecedent of the monastic life. The very old and the
very new now offered the most varied opportunities for the broadest spectrum of women who desired to lead a religious life.[28]

WOMEN'S HOUSES AND MEN'S HOUSES IN THE CENTRAL MIDDLE AGES

Although this book has examined monastic foundations for women, I
want to suggest, by way of conclusion, that a number of its findings
might apply to monasticism in general. Figure 9 illustrates the pace of
monastic foundations for both sexes in England and Wales from the
time of William the Conqueror to 1300.[29] Both similarities and differences are evident. There were numerous new houses for men soon
after the Conquest, but those for women did not multiply significantly
until well into the twelfth century. Both male and female communities
were expanding most rapidly in the mid-twelfth century. The numbers
fell for both sexes in the later twelfth century. The number of foundations for men remained relatively stable from the 1220s to the 1280s;
numbers for women rose slightly in the mid-thirteenth century but re-

---

28. Elliott, *Spiritual Marriage*, 109, notes "begrudging acceptance" for a religious life pursued in the world by the thirteenth century. The description is a good one, but I would
stress that social and economic conditions had changed radically since Gregory VII tried to
draw boundaries between the Church and the world. The acceptance may have amounted
to little more than a kind of admission of the impossibility of enforcing on women *or* men
old ideals in new contexts. Elliott's remark applies best to extramonastic religious people,
such as the beguines or the chastely married; monastic women's claustration, for instance,
was a matter of great concern for churchmen. See Johnson, *Equal in Monastic Profession*,
150–163.
29. Source for men's houses: MRH. The numbers cited are my own tabulations from the
lists in this repertory and do not correspond exactly to the somewhat confusing figures assembled by the compilers on pp. 489–495. I have counted the eleven Gilbertine priories
for women and men as women's communities and omitted houses of Knights Templars,
Knights Hospitallers, and hospitals from the calculations because their purposes were so
different from those of traditional monasteries. Because it is difficult to know exact foundation dates in some cases, for houses of men as well as of women, there is some guesswork
involved in assigning houses to periods as short as decades. But the uncertainty factor is
small enough to permit confidence in general and limited conclusions derived from these
calculations.

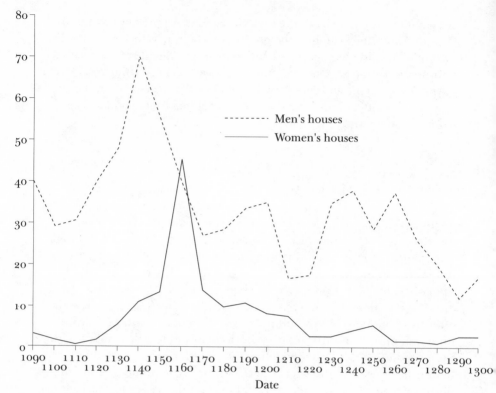

FIGURE 9. Monasteries founded or refounded in England and Wales, 1081–1300 (by decade)

mained very small. In England and Wales, then, the forces fostering monastic foundation appear to have acted in a relatively similar fashion in the period circa 1120–circa 1220, with more differences before and after.[30]

Some periods proved more conducive to the foundation of nunneries than others. Most remarkable are the decades 1141–1170, during which over 35 percent of all new monastic foundations were for women. Some of these communities were quite large (a few of the Gilbertine houses were intended to accommodate over one hundred religious women), whereas men's foundations were often cells or small priories composed

30. That is to say, the shape of the curves is quite similar. The displacement of the curve describing women's houses is probably owed in large part to the caution I have exercised in estimating foundation dates, as explained in Chapter 1 and Appendix A, and the lack of reliable information about the founding date of many English nunneries. The slight difference in chronology suggested by this graph is more apparent than real.

of only three or four monks.[31] Thus it would appear that for a time in the mid-twelfth century, approximately as many new places in the regular religious life were being created for women as for men. This pattern did not endure, however, and after 1210, new foundations for women were never more than one-fifth of the total.

It is impossible, unfortunately, to make similar comparisons between the number of male and female monasteries founded on the Continent, as there is not yet a reliable comprehensive repertory of male houses for the central Middle Ages.[32] However, what we know about the establishment of new male monasteries in Western Europe, circa 1000–circa 1300, points toward the existence of a pattern not unlike that found across the Channel. The following observations, albeit impressionistic, can help to place the expansion of female monasticism within the larger context of monastic growth in the central Middle Ages.

Over one hundred new monasteries for men appeared in Lorraine between 1001 and 1300 (see Table 7). Nearly 70 percent of them were founded in only seventy-five years, during the last quarter of the eleventh century and the first half of the twelfth. After 1150, the number of new foundations dropped considerably, rising again somewhat in the early thirteenth century, then maintaining a fairly steady level, albeit much lower than that for 1076–1150, until about 1275.

Everything indicates that such a pattern of expansion is typical of Western Europe in this period. As John Van Engen persuasively argues, traditional Benedictine monasticism, long considered to have suffered a "crisis" between 1050 and 1150, in fact remained vigorous until the late twelfth century. Benedictine communities continued to multiply and thrive, meaning that the twelfth century, especially its first half, marked

31. MRH, 488–495, provides estimated counts of numbers of communities and numbers of religious. The population of female houses appears to have been on average only slightly higher than that for men in 1154: 19.7 religious per women's community, 17.7 per men's. But at this time 116 lesser priories, cells, and alien priories for men were supporting fewer than 600 monks, whereas 74 convents housed over 1,450 nuns and canonesses. The average size of male and female communities was rather more different by 1216: 22.6 religious for each convent, 15.8 for each male monastery.

32. On the difficulties of assembling a list of convents alone, see Appendix A. To make a similar repertory for male houses for the central Middle Ages would entail many years of work. Jane Tibbetts Schulenburg estimates the number of male communities founded in England, France, and Belgium between 500 and 1100 at nearly 3,000; the number of new foundations in the twelfth and thirteenth centuries would be many times more. See Schulenburg, "Women's Monastic Communities," 266.

Table 7. Number of male monasteries founded in Lorraine, 1001–1300

Period	Number of houses*
1001–1025	2
1026–1050	7
1051–1075	3
1076–1100	28
1101–1125	11
1126–1150	38
1151–1175	3
1176–1200	2
1201–1225	6
1226–1250	4
1251–1275	7
1276–1300	1
	112

Source: Michel Parisse, *La Lorraine monastique au Moyen Age* (Nancy, 1981), 129–141, which includes an inventory of monasteries and convents.

*These numbers are estimates. Usually a community can be attributed confidently to a given quarter-century, but Parisse assigns some communities simply to the twelfth century. These houses have been distributed here according to the ratio of communities known to have been founded in each quarter of the twelfth century, so as not to change the *relative* prominence of any 25-year period. As for England, the figures do not include military or hospital orders.

the apex of Benedictine expansion.[33] Therefore, the new forms of cenobitic life which appeared in the late eleventh and early twelfth centuries should be regarded as an addition to, rather than a replacement of, Benedictine vitality. The foundation of Cistercian communities for men also slowed markedly in the late twelfth century. By 1200, there were over 250 Cistercian male monasteries in the area considered in this study. Three-quarters of the total were founded 1121–1160, exactly the peak period of foundation in for all women's houses.[34] So the continuing expansion of traditional Benedictine monasticism was concurrent with the appearance of numerous houses affiliated with Cîteaux. These facts

33. Van Engen, "The 'Crisis of Cenobitism' Reconsidered."
34. The source for these figures is Marcel Pacaut, *Les moines blancs: Histoire de l'ordre de Cîteaux* (Paris, 1993), 367–382, a list of male houses of the order. Because Pacaut has identified location only by modern political boundaries, I have used Cottineau, *Répertoire topobibliographique des abbayes et prieurés* to ensure that the count includes only the regions under scrutiny here.

account for a pattern like that found in Lorraine, which experienced its most rapid multiplication of monasteries in the three-quarters of a century before 1150, followed by a sharp decline in new foundations soon afterward.

Mendicant communities accounted for eleven of the eighteen new male monastic communities in thirteenth-century Lorraine, an area that was in fact more thinly settled by the friars than many other parts of France. All over northwestern Europe, mendicant houses appeared in considerable number. The significance of the mendicants lies not only in the number of new communities, but also in their location. The distribution of monastic settlement between 900 and 1200 had been heavily weighted toward the countryside. The mendicants, by contrast, settled in towns and cities. The most important era of foundation of mendicant houses was the 1250s and 1260s, producing a total of well over 400 friaries in France by 1275. This was a short-lived peak: the number of new communities fell after 1275.[35] Once again, novelty should not blind us to the continuing appearance of new monastic communities of a more traditional stamp, especially those in the countryside. But in Lorraine, the influx of the mendicants meant that the number of new monastic communities, on the decline since the late twelfth century, rose again. In the parts of France where mendicant settlement was denser, this increase was probably even more marked.

As in England, then, significant multiplication of new male houses on the Continent began in the late eleventh century. Here, too, the number of new male monasteries fell considerably during the late twelfth century, rising again after 1200 until the last quarter of the thirteenth century. In England and on the Continent, the number of both women's and men's communities in the first half of the twelfth century appears to have increased at the same time, and for both groups the second half of the twelfth century was less favorable to new foundations. Women's houses in France shared much more in the new boom of monastic foundation in the thirteenth century than they did in England, although the number of new foundations for women dropped again earlier than that of male monasteries. Equally important, the friaries of the thirteenth century were predominantly urban, just as for the first time since the

---

35. Richard W. Emery, *The Friars in Medieval France: A Catalogue of French Mendicant Convents, 1200–1550* (New York, 1962), 3 (statistics), 17 (friars in Lorraine). The observation that the period 1250–1270 was the most important is my own, based on a chronological ordering of the communities, which Emery catalogued according to location.

mid-eleventh century new women's monasteries began to appear largely in urban or suburban settings.

The relationship of the growth of female monasticism to the development of male monasticism in the central Middle Ages is complex, but the rates of expansion of men's and women's communities, at least, had much in common. Although the role of women in the expansion of Benedictine, especially Cluniac, monasticism in the tenth and eleventh centuries was very small, available evidence suggests that from the late eleventh century until the mid-thirteenth, convents multiplied in a pattern that mirrors the growth of male monasticism. At only a few junctures, and in a few areas, did the number of new places in monastic life for women equal those for men, but for a period of nearly two centuries, the forces encouraging and discouraging the foundation of monastic communities for both men and women appear to have had similar effects, producing tremendous growth from the late eleventh century until 1150 or so, a check in the later twelfth century, and another important, if less spectacular, increase in the number of new houses for several decades in the thirteenth century.

The similarity in patterns of rise and fall for male and female foundations in the twelfth century argues that it is no longer suitable to consider female monasticism to have been outside the mainstream, especially in the twelfth century. Such a conclusion suggests in turn a need to reconsider our vision of medieval monastic history, to try to describe its evolution in close conjunction with our increasingly nuanced understanding of social, economic, and cultural change. If "reform" is not a full or adequate description, explanation, or analysis of the growth of female monasticism, is it adequate for male monasticism either? Giles Constable has described monastic life in the twelfth century in terms not of reform but of diversity and pluralism, a paradigm wholly appropriate to the development of women's monasticism in the great age of growth, circa 1080–circa 1170.[36] Creativity and experimentation were features of all spheres of life in the twelfth century, and even as the religious fled the world, they were helping to make a new one.

Descriptions tied to more mundane kinds of social change can also be just as relevant to men's monasticism as to women's: many of the developments I have found to be important in the growth of female monasti-

36. Giles Constable, "The Diversity of Religious Life and the Acceptance of Social Pluralism in the Twelfth Century," in *History, Society, and the Churches*, ed. Derek Beales and Geoffrey Best (Cambridge, Eng., 1985), 29–47. Constable deals only in passing with women's monasticism, but his comments accord well with the findings of this study.

cism could apply to male monasticism as well. Monks, too, were the beneficiaries of an expanding agricultural economy. New reproductive and patrimonial strategies affected men as well as women. Might not the life of the cloister have been appealing to some younger sons, who, deprived of an inheritance in an age of primogeniture, did not relish the prospect of landless knighthood? And it surely was no less a gesture of legitimacy and concern for kin to found a house for monks than one for nuns. I also strongly suspect that the decline in the number of new male monasteries in the later twelfth century reflects something more than spiritual decadence and the absence of inspiration between the death of Bernard of Clairvaux and the appearance of Francis of Assisi. It no longer seems adequate to describe and explain the patterns of monastic expansion in the central Middle Ages solely in terms of supernal ideals and inspirational figures.

There is precedent for describing the eleventh- and twelfth-century Church in terms other than those of spiritual aspiration. Around 1220, Jacques de Vitry completed his *Historia Occidentalis*, which addressed the renewal of the Christian West after a period of sinful disorder. Jacques described innovation in this way: "Every day the state of the Western Church was reformed for the better." But at the same time he used other metaphors, describing in the language of Isaiah the natural growth of the times: "The valleys overflowed with grain, the fields of the Lord were filled with richness, vines blossomed . . . in the lairs where dragons had lived arose the greenness of reed and rush. Herds grazed in the ways, and their pastures were in all the plains. . . . Firs arose where there had been thorns, and myrtles grew up in place of nettles."[37] As Jacques realized, the tremendous creative accomplishments of the period were the by-product of both tangible organic growth and invisible idealism.

The history of any religious institution is more than the story of its properties and social milieu. But things material and mundane are the most basic context for any human life, religious or otherwise. The foundation of a monastery is an attempt to reconcile the demands of spirit and flesh and thus to join together things divine and mortal. Grounding the experience of monastic women and men in their environment involves, among other things, careful scrutiny of the documents monks

---

37. Jacques de Vitry, *Historia Occidentalis*, 107: "Singulis autem diebus status occidentalis ecclesie reformabatur in melius . . . valles abundabant frumento et campi domini replebantur ubertate, vinee florebat. . . . In cubilibus, in quibus dracones habitaverunt, oriebatur viror calami et iunci. Super vias pascebatur et in omnibus planis erant pascua eorum. . . . Pro saliunca ascendebat abies et pro urtica crescebat myrtus."

and nuns produced and received. This is an exciting prospect. As a great scholar-archivist noted 150 years ago, it is in the charters of the Middle Ages that we may find "the true countenance, the interests, the passions, the laws, and the beliefs of this epoch."[38] In such materials, especially those from the twelfth century, men and women, laity and clergy, reveal their hopes, joys, fears, and frustrations in sometimes surprisingly intimate ways. We should listen to these obscure individuals sensitively and sympathetically, for it is mostly those about whom we know very little (or nothing) who entered Europe's monasteries, who chose to seek perfection in what they knew was an imperfect world. These women and men understood what Robert of Arbrissel preached, that virtue is to be found amid vice.[39] We owe them no less than to acknowledge the ever-present dialectic of ideals and realities in their lives.

38. Paul Marchegay, "Recherches sur les cartulaires d'Anjou," *Archives d'Anjou: Recueil de documents et mémoires inédits sur cette province,* 3 vols. (Angers, 1848–1850), 1: 186.

39. J. de Petigny, "Lettre inédite de Robert d'Arbrissel à la comtesse Ermengarde," *Bibliothèque de l'Ecole des Chartres* 3d ser., 5 (1854), 225: "Virtus enim medium vitiorum est."

Repertory of monastic foundations and Refoundations

a complete list of women's religious communities in medieval Europe is a major desideratum for the study of monasticism and women in the Middle Ages. Fortunately the arduous task of establishing such a roster has been undertaken by a cadre of scholars.[1] Because this ambitious project is still under way, I have completed a considerably more limited machine-readable database of women's monastic, that is, regular, communities in fifteen European archdioceses founded from the fifth century to the Black Death. Each nunnery is represented by one computer record containing the name, location, monastic order or rule of the house, the date of foundation and dates of any subsequent destruction, restoration, or refoundation.

Statistics from my database are cited throughout this book, but it seems important to include here a handlist of nunneries founded during the period of most significant expansion, from the tenth century to the thirteenth, in the area under consideration. My boundaries are diocesan, because, unlike political and even linguistic boundaries, diocesan structure in northwestern Europe was remarkably stable from the early Middle Ages to the fourteenth century. The geographical scope of inquiry includes the two English archdioceses of Canterbury and York. The Continental area encompasses eleven entire archdioceses as they existed in the central Middle Ages: Aix-en-Provence, Arles, Auch, Bordeaux, Bourges, Lyon, Narbonne, Reims, Rouen, Sens, and Tours. Also included are the non-Alpine dioceses of the archdiocese of Vienne (Die, Grenoble, Valence, Vienne, and Viviers), as well as the three suffragan dioceses of Metz, Toul, and Verdun, but not their metropolitan see of Trier, which by the twelfth century extended eastward to the Rhine and beyond. Outside this area, the pattern of women's monastic foundation is considerably different from what is described in this study, as noted in Chapter 1. My book describes patterns of expansion and decline common, in broad outline, to a large region, but that did not occur uniformly across Christian Europe, or even what we think of as Western Europe. In other words, part of my argument is that the trends I describe are *not* universal.

As David Knowles noted in introducing a monastic repertory for England and Wales, "no catalogue of this kind can hope as yet to be complete or final. . . . [I]t would be vain to hope that notice has been taken of all the possible sources of information already existing. Moreover, many of the dates are only approximate."[2] This, of course, is all the more true for a list that covers a considerably larger area. The central problem in compiling a list of medieval nunneries is that records for many communities are scant or altogether lacking, and it is important to consider the degree to which the state of evidence affects our picture of the past. Frequently, a nunnery appears ex nihilo, all information concerning the date and circumstances of its establishment absent. For this reason, many of the dates given are *terminus ante quem* only; a significant number of convents were probably founded some time before they come into view. In all cases, including those when the foundation date is known to be sometime during a period of years, I have used the latest date in statistical calculations.

A linguistic problem also arises in compiling a list of monastic communities. Smaller monastic communities, whether dependent or independent of a mother abbey, were denoted in the Middle Ages by a number of words, but the Latin form of *priory*, the term we most often use for such establishments, was a relatively late development. Not until the end of the eleventh century did *prioratus* ever mean "priory," and this usage only gradually became widespread.[3] But *prioratus* did not always signal a full-fledged community and was used in the twelfth century and beyond as a synonym for *obedientia*, which could be either a monastic community or simply a domain.[4] By the thirteenth century, a distinction was made between conventual and nonconventual (or simple) priories.[5] Clearly, *prioratus* sometimes means "priory" as we understand the word, but it can also mean, roughly, "property" and refer simply to part of a monastery's landed wealth. Often it is hard to know which sense is intended, for instance, if a *prioratus* listed in an episcopal or papal confirmation of a convent's possessions is in fact a smaller, dependent community of nuns.[6] By the same token, it is sometimes difficult to tell whether an *ecclesia* is a parish church or a monastic community.

Given these difficulties, I have constructed the database so as not to exaggerate the central finding of this study: the establishment of a large number of nunneries in a relatively short period. I have been inclined to assume that a community survived the age of Norman and Muslim incursions, even when there is no evidence across a long period, unless there is a subsequent *re*foundation or no later documentation at all. Thus the description of the increase in numbers of nunneries in Chapter 1 is conservative: if the number of houses existing in the year 1000 was indeed smaller than the estimated seventy, the rise was even greater. That is, the curve describing the total number of nunneries would rise more steeply.

The method of counting houses founded after 1000 is designed so as not to inflate the figures for female monastic communities, requiring reliable, and preferably contemporary, evidence for the existence of a community. For example, the abbey of Notre-Dame de la Règle in Limoges, founded in the Carolingian era, owned many parcels of land across the Midi and remained a leading convent in the region through the Middle Ages. Some of its properties eventually became the sites of monasteries, but because there is no evidence that this happened as a general rule or in a regular pattern, I have assumed that "simple" priories did not become conventual priories unless and until there is evidence otherwise.[7]

Documentation for the Church, like documentation for almost all aspects of medieval society, becomes much richer in the thirteenth century than previously; episcopal visitations and registers are important sources of information for the thirteenth century and beyond. We are more likely, then, to know at least of the existence of a community, one like a priory of La Règle or an autonomous convent, after 1200, and especially after 1250, when episcopal visitation records become common. If such houses did in fact come into being earlier, it would increase the total figures for the twelfth and early thirteenth centuries, making that period stand out still more. The number of convents coming into view, then, cannot simply be a reflection of the state of the evidence; if this were so, the count of new nunneries would increase rather than decrease in the period 1200–1350.

In short, this is an exclusive rather than inclusive list. The estimate of total numbers of female monastic institutions is, if anything, low. The thorough search of archives to be accomplished by scholars in the future should modify and slightly augment the list presented here. In any case,

in this book, the importance and significance of the era during which
the most nunneries were founded are under- rather than overestimated.

Each entry in the following alphabetically arranged list includes a reference to a source. Most of these houses are listed in L.–H. Cottineau's
Répertoire topo-bibliographique des abbayes et prieurés, but these massively ambitious volumes are, unfortunately, not terribly reliable, and entries in
them have often been superseded. Whenever possible, I have referred to
a modern repertory or encyclopedia, such as the superb *Monasticon Praemonstratense* or *Dictionnaire d'histoire et de géographie ecclésiastiques*. Sometimes more precise or fuller information is found in monographs or
earlier reference works such as the eighteenth- and nineteenth-century
volumes of the *Gallia christiana*. In no case, however, am I simply repro-
ducing a lone reference; every item in the list has been checked against
other sources and verified by documentary evidence whenever possible.

I have located each nunnery in its archdiocese, as keyed in the list. Because of their peculiar history (see Chapters 3 and 5), it is difficult to inventory the houses of Premonstratensian nuns. At the risk of confusion,
I have used the name of the place where the women last resided, but if
the community had its origin in a monastery of men and women, I give
the date of that first foundation. This method ensures that no group of
Premonstratensian sisters is counted more than once.

NUNNERIES FOUNDED AND REFOUNDED, 900–1300

Dates

c.   century
ca.   circa
–   in or before this year. Hence "–1145" describes a house that first appears
        in the historical record in 1145 but may have been founded earlier.
x   an unspecifiable year between two dates, inclusive. Thus, "1125x1138" de-
        scribes a house whose foundation is datable to the years 1125 to 1138.[8]

Provincial codes

1. Archdiocese of York
2. Archdiocese of Canterbury
3. Archdiocese of Reims
4. Dioceses of Metz, Toul, and Verdun

5. Archdiocese of Rouen
6. Archdiocese of Sens
7. Archdiocese of Tours
8. Archdiocese of Lyon
9. Archdiocese of Bordeaux
10. Archdiocese of Bourges
11. Dioceses of Die, Grenoble, Valence, Vienne, and Viviers
12. Archdiocese of Auch
13. Archdiocese of Narbonne
14. Archdiocese of Arles
15. Archdiocese of Aix

References
For full citations see the Bibliography

Agathange	P. Agathange de Paris, "L'origine et la fondation des monastères de clarisses en Aquitaine au XIIIe siècle"
AP	J.-M. Besse et al., *Abbayes et prieurés de l'ancienne France*
Bienvenu	J.-M. Bienvenu, *L'étonnant fondateur de Fontevraud, Robert d'Arbrissel*
Cottineau	L.-H. Cottineau, *Répertoire topo-bibliographique des abbayes et prieurés*
DHGE	*Dictionnaire d'histoire et de géographie ecclésiastiques*
GC	*Gallia christiana*
HGL	Claude Devic and Joseph Vaissete, *Histoire générale de Languedoc*
MB	*Monasticon Belge*
MP	Norbert Backmund, *Monasticon Praemonstratense*
MRH	David Knowles and R. Neville Hadcock, *Medieval Religious Houses,* 2d ed.
WR	Sally Thompson, *Women Religious*

Database

Name	Date	Archdiocese	Reference
Abbaye-aux-Bois	1202	3	AP 18: 166
Aconbury	1216	2	WR, 217
Albaron	1238	14	GC 1: 870–871
Alès	13th c.	13	Cottineau, 47
Alix	–1285	8	DHGE 2: 464
les Allois	1140x1158	10	DHGE 2: 620–621
Almenèches	1066[9]	5	DHGE 2: 651
Alost (= Forest)	1096	3	MB 4: 193
Alvingham	1148x1154	2	WR, 218
Amesbury	ca. 979	2	MRH, 104

Name	Date	Archdiocese	Reference
Amilly	ca. 1240	6	AP 6: 18
l'Amour-Dieu	1232	3	DHGE 2: 1337[10]
Andecy	ca. 1131	4	DHGE 2: 1556
Angers (la Ronceray)	1028	7	AP 8: 99–100
Angoulême (St-Ausone)	ca. 1028[11]	9	GC 2: 1039
Anguillers	–1170	7	AP 8: 221[12]
Anizy-le-Chatêau	10th c.	3	AP 17: 134
Ankerwyke	–1163	2	WR, 218
Antwerp (Ter Nonnen)	1279	3	MB 8: 632–633
Apt	1299	15	DHGE 3: 1081
Arboras	ca. 1215	13	DHGE 3: 1470
Arden	ca. 1147x1169	1	WR, 218
Argensolles	1222	3	DHGE 4: 16
Argenteuil	ca. 1000	6	GC 8, instr. 28–29
l'Argentière	ca. 1273	8	DHGE 4: 39–40
Armathwaite	–ca. 1201	1	WR, 218
l'Arpajonie	1297	10	DHGE 4: 664–665
Arthington	ca. 1150	1	WR, 218
Asnières	1124	7	DHGE 4: 1055
Ath (= le Refuge)	–1234	3	MB 1: 359
Aubagne	1205	14	DHGE 20: 231
Aubenas	–1296	11	AP 9: 157[13]
Aubepierre	–1272	10	AP 5: 245[14]
Aubeterre	ca. 970/ca. 1150[15]	10	MP 3: 142
Aumont	–1140	3	MP 2: 547
Auterives	1256	13	Agathange, 21
Averbode	ca. 1132	3	MB 4: 626
Avesnes-lès-Baupaume	1128	3	AP 14: 318
Avignon (St-Laurent)	–950	14	AP 2: 138–139
Avignon (St-Véran)	1140	14	AP 2: 139
Avignon (Ste-Catherine)	1254	14	AP 2: 140
Avignon (Ste-Claire)	1250	14	AP 2: 132
Avigny	ca. 1145	3	MP 2: 477–478
les Ayes (= Hayes)	1142	11	DHGE 23: 655–656
Bar-sur-Aube	1238[16]	8	DHGE 6: 550–551
Barking	ca. 950	2	MRH, 256
la Barre	1235[17]	3	AP 17: 45
Barrow Gurney	–ca. 1201	2	WR, 218
Basse-Fontaine	1143	6	MP 2: 479
Bayonne	–1283	12	Agathange, 21–22
Baysdale	ca. 1139xca. 1159	1	WR, 218
Beaufays	ca. 1126	8	DHGE 7: 123
Beaulieu	ca. 1140[18]	6	MP 2: 481
Beaulieu	1298	13	DHGE 7: 162
Beaulieu (St-Antoine)	–1259	10	DHGE 7: 146
Beaulieu-en-Roannais	–1121	8	DHGE 7: 159
Beaulieu-lès-Sin-le-Noble	ca. 1224	3	GC 3: 449, instr. 90–91
Beaumont-les-Autels	ca. 1130	6	DHGE 7: 192
Beaumont-les-Nonnains	ca. 1122	5	MP 2: 547
Beaumont-lès-Tours	ca. 1002	7	DHGE 7: 199
Beaupré	1228	3	MB 7: 310

Name	Date	Archdiocese	Reference
Beaupré-sur-la-Lys	1204	3	DHGE 7: 236
Beaurepaire	–1182	3	[19]
Beauvoir	1234	10	DHGE 7: 317
le Béchet	–1170	6	AP 6: 159[20]
Belhomer	–1132	6	DHGE 7: 761–762
Belian	1243x1245	3	DHGE 7: 764
Belleau	–1242	6	GC 12: 534
Bellecombe	ca. 1148	10	DHGE 7: 837
Belle Tanche	ca. 1140	4	MP 3: 56–57, 104–105
Belmont-aux-Nonnains	–1140	8	DHGE 7: 945
Benoîtvaux	13th c.	4	DHGE 8: 275
Bertaud	1188	15	DHGE 8: 922
Berteaucourt	1095	3	AP 16: 113
Bertricourt	1124[21]	3	MP 2: 544, 547
Béthanie (= Veurnes)	1252	3	MP 2: 428
Beyries	1256x1261	12	Agathange, 23
Béziers	–1259	13	Agathange, 25–26
Béziers	ca. 1300	13	AP 4: 160
Biaches	1235	3	AP 16: 157
Bival	1128x1154	5	DHGE 9: 37
Blackborough	1200[22]	2	WR, 218
les Blanches	ca. 1105	5	DHGE 9: 104
Blandecques	1182	3	AP 14: 423
Blessac	1049	10	AP 5: 216–217
Bleurville	–1100	4	GC 13: 1068[23]
Bliez	1136	8	AP 10: 138–139
Blijdenberg	–1253	3	MB 8: 542
Blithbury	1120x1147	2	WR, 218
Bois-Goyer	–1140	9	AP 3: 193[24]
Bois-les-Dames	–1130[25]	3	MP 3: 57–58, 61
Bondeville	ca. 1150	5	DHGE 9: 824–825
Bonham	1223x1224	3	AP 14: 427
Bonlieu	ca. 1140[26]	8	MP 3: 63, 108
Bonlieu	1171	11	DHGE 9: 1007
Bonlieu	1199	8	DHGE 9: 1004
Bonlieu	1219	7	DHGE 9: 1005
Bonnecombe	ca. 1150	11	GC 16: 213
Bonnesaigne	ca. 1059	10	DHGE 9: 1049
Bonneuil	ca. 1122[27]	3	MP 2: 484, 521
Bonneval-lès-Thouars	969x975	9	DHGE 9: 1069
Bordeaux	–1239	9	Agathange, 27
Boubon	1106	10	AP 5: 217
le Bouchet	late 12th c.	11	DHGE 9: 1466
Boulancourt	ca. 1150	6	DHGE 10: 54
Boulaur	1140	12	AP 3: 16
le Boulay	1191x1197	7	DHGE 10: 58
Bourbon l'Archimbault	ca. 1172	10	DHGE 10: 135
Bourbourg	1103	3	DHGE 10: 137
Bourges (St-Hippolyte)	–1145	10	GC 2: 124
Bouxières-aux-Dames	930	4	DHGE 10: 280; see Chapter 2

Name	Date	Archdiocese	Reference
Bragayrac	1122	13	DHGE 2: 1185
Brageac	ca. 1100[28]	10	DHGE 10: 370
la Brayelle-lès-Annay	1196	3	AP 14: 428
Brewood Black Ladies	−ca. 1150	2	WR, 219
Brewood White Ladies	−1186	2	WR, 219
Bricot-en-Brie	ca. 1150	6	DHGE 10: 682
Brienne	1259	8	AP 10: 94–95
Bristol	−1173	2	WR, 219
Brive-la-Gaillard	−1296	10	Agathange, 22
Broadholme	1148x1154	1	WR, 219
Broomhall	−1157x1158	2	WR, 219
le Brouilh	1145	12	AP 3: 16
Bruges	ca. 1260	3	GC 5: 302
Brussels (Ste-Catharine)	1270	3	MP 2: 326–327
Bruyères	1130[29]	3	MP 2: 484–485, 487
Bucilly	950	3	MP 2: 365
Buckland	ca. 1186	2	WR, 219
le Bugue	late 10th c.	9	DHGE 10: 1096
Buix-lès-Aurillac	−1162	10	DHGE 10: 1097; DHGE 11: 213
Bullington	1148x1154	2	WR, 219
Bungay	1183	2	WR, 219
Burnham	1266	2	WR, 219
Bussières	−1160	10	DHGE 10: 1428
Byloque	1215	3	MB 7: 336–337
Caen (La Trinité)	1066	5	AP 7: 135–136
Cahors	ca. 1210	10	DHGE 11: 212
Cahors	1230x1234	10	Agathange, 29
la Cambre	1201	3	MB 4: 445
Cambridge	ca. 1147x1154	2	WR, 219
Campsey Ash	−1195	2	WR, 219
Cannington	ca. 1129xca. 1153	2	WR, 219
Canonsleigh	1284[30]	2	WR, 220
Canterbury	−1087	2	WR, 220
Carcassonne	−1290	13	Agathange, 22
Carrow	ca. 1136	2	WR, 226
Cassaniouze	1276	10	AP 5: 277[31]
Castle Hedingham	−1191	2	WR, 220
Catesby	ca. 1150x1176	2	WR, 220
Catley	1148x1154	2	WR, 220
Caumont	1130[32]	3	MP 2: 367, 400
Cavaillon	−1252[33]	14	AP 2: 154; GC 1: 963
Cella Dominarum (= Ste-Marie-au-Bois)	−1140	4	MP 3: 93, 103
la Celle	−1160	15	AP 2: 9
la Celle-Roubaud	−1260[34]	13	AP 2: 43
Cerisiers	−1131	9	[35]
Chaise-Dieu-du-Theil	1146	5	AP 7: 182[36]
Champbenoît	1138	6	DHGE 12: 343
la Chana	ca. 984	8	AP 10: 136
la Chapelle d'Oze	1145	6	AP 12: 419

Name	Date	Archdiocese	Reference
Chapelle-aux-Planches	−1137	8	MP 2: 490
Charité-les-Lézinnes	1184	6	DHGE 12: 418
la Charme	1098	3	AP 17: 205
Chartres (l'Eau)	1226	6	DHGE 12: 571
Chartreuve	ca. 1130	3	MP 2: 493, 495
Châteaudun	1045	6	AP 1:242
Chatteris	1006x1016	2	MRH, 257[37]
Chaumontois	−1163	6	
Chaussy-lès-Thoury	−1153	6	AP 1: 371[38]
Chebret	−1220	3	MP 2: 495
Cheshunt	−1165x1166	2	WR, 220
Chester	ca. 1141x1153	2	WR, 220
Chézeaux	−1150	8	AP 12: 406
Chichester	−956	2	MRH, 257
Chicksands	1147x1153	2	WR, 220
les Clairets	1204	5	AP 1: 246
Clairmarais	ca. 1222	3	DHGE 12: 1045
Clairruissel	1140	5	AP 7: 76
Clavas	−1223	10	DHGE 12: 1080
Clementhorpe	ca. 1125x1133	1	WR, 231
Clerkenwell	ca. 1141x1144	2	WR, 225
Clermont	−1280	10	DHGE 12: 1452
Collinances	−1135	3	AP 18: 188
Compiègne	−1240	3	AP 18: 70
Comps	ca. 1052	10	AP 5: 275
Condom	−1269	9	Agathange, 22
Cook Hill	−1155x1156	2	WR, 220
Cordillon-aux-Nonnains	−1200	5	DHGE 13: 835
Cormoranche	−1174	8	AP 10: 139
Cornworthy	−1238	2	WR, 220
Cortenberg	−1105	3	MB 2: 253–254
Costejean	−1220	10	DHGE 13: 935
les Couëts	1149	7	AP 8: 253[39]
Coulanges	ca. 1140	8	DHGE 13: 944
Cour-Notre-Dame-lès-Gouvernay	−1225	6	DHGE 13: 948
la Couronne	1116	9	Cottineau, 899
Courpière	−1260	10	GC 2, instr. 90
Coyroux	1142	10	DHGE 13: 1003
Crabhouse	ca. 1181	2	WR, 220
Crécy	ca. 1137	3	MP 3: 64
Crépy-en-Valois	1184	3	AP 18: 142
Crisenon	1134[40]	6	DHGE 5: 954
Cubas	−1171	9	AP 3: 205[41]
Davington	1150x1161	2	WR, 220
Dax	−1283	12	Agathange, 23
Denain	ca. 1029	3	DHGE 14: 218
Derby	−1154x1159	2	WR, 221
Derses	−1218	10	DHGE 14: 330–331[42]
Dionne	1124[43]	3	MP 2: 501, 509
Doornzele	−1226x1227	3	MB 7: 293
Dorengt	ca. 1126[44]	3	MP 2: 370, 501

Name	Date	Archdiocese	Reference
Dorisel	–1231	3	DHGE 14: 673[45]
Dormans	1134[46]	3	MP 2: 502, 533
Douai	–1216	3	DHGE 14: 726
Douë	ca. 1138	10	MP 3: 149
Dougillard	ca. 1125	7	AP 8: 264[47]
Doullens	ca. 1100	3	AP 16: 129
Droiteval	ca. 1128	4	DHGE 14: 803
la Drouilhe-Blanche	–1212	10	AP 5: 217[48]
Easebourne	–1248	2	WR, 221
Eewen	ca. 1130[49]	3	MP 2: 283, 330
Ellerton	ca. 1189x1204	1	WR, 221
Elstow	1076x1086	2	WR, 221
l'Encloître-en-Chaufournois	–1108	7	DHGE 15: 454[50]
l'Encloître-en-Gironde	ca. 1109	9	DHGE 15: 455
Epagne	1178	3	AP 16: 158
Epargnemaille	ca. 1137	3	AP 17: 173[51]
Epinal	ca. 983	4	DHGE 15: 605
Epinlieu	1216	3	DHGE 15: 609
Epluques	1234	3	AP 18: 163[52]
l'Esclache	ca. 1160	10	DHGE 15: 858
Esholt	–1184	1	WR, 221
Espagnac	ca. 1211	10	DHGE 15: 891–892
l'Espinasse	1114	13	AP 4: 288
Esteil	1151	10	DHGE 15: 1052
l'Etanche	–1157	4	MP 3: 65
l'Etanche-sur-Saulx	1148	4	DHGE 15: 1107
Etival	ca. 1140	4	MP 3: 67–71
Etival-en-Charnie	1109	7	DHGE 15: 1285
Etrun	ca. 1085	3	DHGE 15: 1292
Eule	ca. 1175	13	DHGE 15: 1386–1387
Evreux (St-Sauveur)	ca. 1060[53]	5	DHGE 16: 184
Exeter	ca. 968	2	MRH, 473
Ezanville	ca. 1080	3	[54]
Fabas	–1150	13	DHGE 16: 302
Farewell	ca. 1139x1147	2	WR, 221
la Fermeté-sur-l'Izeure	ca. 1145	6	DHGE 16: 1083
Fervacques	ca. 1140	3	AP 17: 190
Feuchère	1129x1135[55]	3	MP 2: 373, 398
Fieux	–1297	10	DHGE 16: 1453
Flamstead	–1157x1162	2	WR, 221
Flines	1233x1234	3	DHGE 17: 492
Flixton	1258x1259	2	WR, 221
Foissy	ca. 1102	6	DHGE 17: 725–726
Fongrave	1130	9	DHGE 17: 796
la Font-St-Martin	–1162	9	DHGE 17: 990
Fontaine-Guérard	ca. 1198	5	DHGE 17: 835
la Fontaine-St-Martin	ca. 1117	7	DHGE 17: 848
Fontaines	ca. 1120	9	DHGE 17: 851
Fontaines-les-Nonnes	1120x1130	6	DHGE 17: 854
Fontenay-sur-Conie	–1186	6	DHGE 17: 907
les Fontenelles	1216	3	DHGE 17: 954

Name	Date	Archdiocese	Reference
Fontevraud	1101	9	DHGE 17: 961
Fontgauffier	1095	9	DHGE 17: 977
Fonts-lès-Ales	1200x1225	13	DHGE 17: 990–991
Fosse	−1184	2	WR, 221
Fossemore	ca. 1132[56]	6	MP 2: 499, 502
Fougereuse	−1117	9	DHGE 17: 1267
Foukeholme	−1203x1204	1	WR, 221
les Fours	1238	13	DHGE 17: 1341
Franchevaux	1159	6	DHGE 18: 574
Freistroff	−1200	4	MP 3: 74–75
Fresnaye	−1179	7	[57]
Fronsac	−1100	9	DHGE 19: 179[58]
Gaillac	−1268	10	HGL 4: 670–671
Gallargues	1027	13	HGL 4: 826
la Gasconnière	1108x1115	9	DHGE 19: 1347[59]
Gemenos	1205	14	DHGE 20: 331
Gercy	1269	6	DHGE 20: 851
Ghent	1286	3	DHGE 19: 1052
Ghislinghien	1126	3	DHGE 20: 1182–1183
Ghistelles	early 12th c.	3	MB 3: 247
Gif	−1180	6	DHGE 20: 1273
Gigean	ca. 1104	13	DHGE 20: 1285
Glatigny	−1150	10	DHGE 21: 171
Godstow	−1133	2	WR, 221
Gokewell	1147x1175	2	WR, 221
Gomerfontaine	ca. 1207	3	AP 18: 176
Goring	−1135	2	WR, 222
Goujon	1135x1148	13	DHGE 21: 938
la Grâce	1223	6	DHGE 21: 1004
Grace Dieu	−1236x1242	2	WR, 222
Grâce-Dieu	−1249	13	DHGE 21: 1017
Grand-Bigard	1114x1130	3	DHGE 21: 1083
le Grand-St-Bibien	ca. 1130	9	DHGE 21: 1150
Grangia Dominarum	1132x1138	4	MP 3: 71, 74
Greenfield	1148x1166	2	WR, 222
Grelonges	1112	8	DHGE 22: 117
Grimsby	−1171x1180	2	WR, 222
Groeningen	−1236	3	DHGE 22: 319
Guesnes	1106x1109	9	AP 3: 253
la Guiche	1273	6	DHGE 22: 781
Guînes	1117	3	DHGE 22: 1099–1100
Guyzance	−1152x1167	1	WR, 222
Haliwell	−1162	2	WR, 225
Hamewiller	ca. 1130[60]	4	MP 3: 75, 81
Hampole	−1156	1	WR, 222
Handale	−1133	1	WR, 222
Harchies	ca. 1132[61]	3	MP 2: 412, 433
Harrold	ca. 1136xca. 1138	2	WR, 222
Hautes-Bruyères	1112	6	DHGE 23: 581–582
Haverholme	1139	2	WR, 222
Hemelsdale	1237	3	DHGE 23: 974

Name	Date	Archdiocese	Reference
Henwood	1149x1157	2	WR, 222
Herlaimont	–1181	3	MP 2: 378
Hesse	ca. 1010	4	DHGE 24: 281–282
Heynings	ca. 1147x1152	2	WR, 222
Hinchinbrooke	1186x1190[62]	2	WR, 223
Hof ten Vrouwen	ca. 1135[63]	3	MP 2: 413, 429–430
Holystone	–1124	1	WR, 223
Hombeek	–1233	3	MP 2: 299
Horsely	–ca. 1201	2	WR, 223
Hyères (Lamanarre)	1220	15	AP 2: 124–125
Ickleton	–1158	2	WR, 223
Ilchester	–1281[64]	2	MRH, 288
les Iles	1219	6	DHGE 25: 828[65]
Ivinghoe	1107x1129	2	WR, 223
le Jardin	–1229	6	AP 6: 149
Jarsay	ca. 1110	10	AP 5: 46
Javages	1124x1126[66]	3	MP 2: 508, 537
la Joie	1230	6	AP 6: 43
la Joie-Notre-Dame	1252	7	AP 8: 328–329
la Joie-Sainte-Claire	1240	3	AP 18: 178
Jourcey	ca. 1130	8	AP 10: 140–141
Jully-les-Nonnains	ca. 1115	8	AP 12: 417–418
Keldholme	1154x1166	1	WR, 223
Kilburn	–1128x1134	2	WR, 223
Kington	–1142x1156	2	WR, 224
Kirklees	–1190	1	WR, 224
Lacock	1232	2	WR, 224
Lambley	–1187x1188	1	WR, 224
Lancharre	–1236	8	GC 4: 979
Landais	1115	10	AP 5: 36[67]
Lande-en-Beauchêne	–1115	9	Bienvenu, 110
Langley	1148x1166	2	WR, 224
Laon	1220	3	AP 17: 195
Larrey	ca. 1078	8	[68]
Laval-aux-Nonnains	1163	6	AP 1: 144
Laval-Bénite	–1164	11	AP 9: 33[69]
Lavassin	ca. 1195	10	AP 5: 112
Laveine	ca. 1131	8	[70]
Legbourne	–1148x1166	2	WR, 224
Leigneux	ca. 1050	8	AP 10: 142
Leominster	–1046	2	MRH, 69, 476[71]
Leyme (la Grâce-Dieu)	1214	10	DHGE 21: 1012–1013
Libaud	ca. 1137	9	AP 3: 185[72]
le Lieu-Dieu	ca. 1150	8	GC 4: 504
le Lieu-Notre-Dame	1250	6	AP 1: 364
Lieu-Restauré	1138	3	MP 2: 513
Ligueux	–1115	9	AP 3: 204
Lillechurch	ca. 1150x1152	2	WR, 223
Limebrook	–1221	2	WR, 224
Lisieux	ca. 1050	5	AP 7: 202
Lissac	1286	10	AP 4: 37

Name	Date	Archdiocese	Reference
Littlemore	−1156	2	WR, 224
Llanlugan	−1236	2	MRH, 274
Llanlyr	ca. 1180	2	MRH, 272
Llansaintfraed	−1174	2	MRH, 274
les Lochereaux	ca. 1120	7	AP 8: 107[73]
Locmaria	ca. 1050	7	AP 8: 275
les Loges	ca. 1106	7	Bienvenu, 108–110
Londieu	1281	10	AP 4: 34
London	1293	2	MRH, 286
London St Helens	−1214	2	WR, 225
Longchamps	1260	6	AP 1: 96
Longefont	ca. 1116	10	AP 5: 46
Longpré	ca. 1185	3	AP 17: 206–207
Longueau	−1140	3	[74]
Lourcine-lès-St-Marcel	ca. 1270	6	GC 7: 950–951
Lunéville	1034	4	GC 13: 1365
Lyminster	−ca. 1201	2	WR, 225
le Lys	1244	6	AP 6: 43–44
Maagdendale	−1231	3	MB 7: 362–363
Macquincourt	ca. 1130[75]	3	MP 2: 417
la Madeleine-lès-Orléans	1113	6	AP 1: 368
Malling	ca. 1095	2	WR, 225
Malnoüe	−1129	6	GC 7: 586
le Mans (St-Julien)	ca. 1050	7	AP 8: 159
Marcigny	1055	8	GC 4: 486; see Chapter 2
Marcilly	1239	8	GC 4: 502
Marenz	−1168	13	GC 13, instr. 23–24
Marey	1150x1178	4	[76]
Marham	1249	2	WR, 225
Markyate	1145	2	WR, 225
Marlow	−1194x1195	2	WR, 224
Marquette	1226	3	GC 3: 313
Marrick	1154x1158	1	WR, 225
Marseille (St-Sauveur)	ca. 1000[77]	14	AP 2: 106–107
Marseille (Mont-Sion)	1242	14	AP 2: 107–108
Marseille (Nazareth)	1254	14	AP 2: 95
Maubuisson	1241	6	AP 1: 91
les Mazures	−1274	3	GC 9: 179
Megemont	−1274	10	GC 2: 409
Merckem	ca. 1100	3	GC 5: 325
Mercoire	−1207	10	GC 1: 112
Messines	1057	3	MB 3: 217
Metz (Ste-Marie)	ca. 985	4	GC 13: 832
Metz ("Clairvaux")	1133	4	GC 13: 835
Metz	ca. 1133[78]	4	MP 3: 84, 88
Meung-sur-Loire	−1178	6	[79]
Millau	1291	10	Agathange, 29–30
Minster in Sheppey	ca. 1130	2	WR, 201–202, 226
Molèze	−1189	8	GC 4: 1035
Mollèges	1208	14	GC 1: 625–626
Moncé	1212	7	GC 14: 335

Name	Date	Archdiocese	Reference
Monchy-le-Perreux	1238	3	AP 18: 180
Mont-de-Marsan	1275	12	Agathange, 34
Mont-Notre-Dames-lès-Provins	1236	6	AP 6: 44
Mont-D'Or	ca. 1214	3	MB 3: 484
Mont-Ste-Catherine	ca. 1230	3	GC 12: 255
Montauban	1258	13	Agathange, 32
Montazais	ca. 1119	9	AP 3: 253
Montgousson	ca. 1184	6	[80]
Monthodon	1133[81]	3	MP 2: 518, 535
Montivilliers	1030[82]	5	AP 7: 63–64
Montmartre	1134	6	AP 1: 72
Montpellier	1250	13	Agathange, 38–39
Montreuil-les-Dames	1136	3	AP 17: 199
Montreuil-sur-Mer	ca. 1000	3	AP 14: 357
Montseau	–1129	13	HGL 4: 827–828
Moreaucourt	–1146	3	AP 16: 174
Moutons	–1135	5	AP 7: 109
Moxby	–1158	1	WR, 226
Mureau	ca. 1147[83]	4	MP 3: 89, 92
Nantelle	1141x1142	4	MP 3: 78, 92
Narbonne	–1246	13	Agathange, 42
Nazareth	ca. 1225	3	MB 8: 109
Neasham	–1157	1	WR, 226
Netlieu	1195	13	AP 4: 136
Neufchâteau	1280	4	Cottineau, 2056
Neumunster	ca. 1000	4	GC 13: 832
Neuville-les-Dames	–1184	8	AP 10: 143
Newcastle	1143x1149	1	WR, 226
Nieuwenbosch	ca. 1210	3	MB 7: 293
Nieuwenrode	1128[84]	3	MP 2: 286, 312
Nîmes (St-Sauveur)	991	13	AP 4: 215
Nîmes	ca. 1240	13	HGL 4: 839
Noëfort	1127	6	AP 1: 324
Nogent l'Artaud	ca. 1299	3	GC 9: 504
Nonenque	1146	10	AP 4: 109
Nonnenbossche	–1113	3	MB 3: 273
Northampton	ca. 1145x1153	2	WR, 226
Notre-Dame-aux-Bois	1215	3	MB 7: 393
Notre-Dame-des-Fonts	–1229	13	DHGE 1: 1322
Notre-Dame-des-Prés	–1231	6	GC 12: 612
Notre-Dame-du-Plan	1200	14	AP 2: 114
Nun Appleton	ca. 1148x1154	1	WR, 226
Nun Cotham	1148x1153	2	WR, 226
Nun Monkton	1151x1153	1	WR, 227
Nunburnholme	–1199	1	WR, 226
Nuneaton	ca. 1147x1155	2	WR, 227
Nunkeeling	1143x1154	1	WR, 227
Nyoiseau	1109	7	AP 8: 101–102
Odeghem	ca. 1110[85]	3	GC 5: 281
l'Olive	–1233	3	MB 1: 373
les Ollieux	ca. 1200	13	AP 4: 125

Name	Date	Archdiocese	Reference
Oost-Eeclo	–1228	3	MB 7: 439
Oraison-Dieu	–1167	13	DHGE 16: 301
Orange	ca. 1110	14	GC 1: 789
Orford	1153xca. 1156	2	WR, 227
Orimont	–1152	8	AP 12: 420
Orléans (St-Loup)	–1235	6	GC 8: 1570
Ormont	1234	3	AP 1: 319
Ormsby	1148x1154	2	WR, 226
Orsan	ca. 1107	10	AP 5: 46–47
Pamel	1137[86]	3	MP 2: 314, 317
le Paraclet	1129	6	AP 6: 148
le Paraclet-des-Champs	1219	3	AP 16: 165
le Paravis	1130	9	AP 3: 144
le Parc-aux-Dames	1205	6	AP 18: 185
Paris (St-Antoine-des-Champs)	1198	6	AP 1: 85
Parmenie	1157	11	AP 9: 87
Penthémont	1217	3	AP 18: 186
Périgueux	1251	9	Agathange, 42
Perpignan	1263x1270	13	Agathange, 47–48
Perray-aux-Nonnains	1247[87]	7	AP 8: 101
Peteghem	1136[88]	3	MP 2: 409, 420
Petit-Bigard	1235	3	MB 4: 306–307
Peyreux	–1254	13	GC 6: 140
Piété-Dieu	1229	6	GC 12: 609–610
Pinley	–1125x1150	1	WR, 227
Plainemont	1143[89]	4	MP 3: 75–76, 92
Poitiers (Ste-Trinité)	ca. 965	9	AP 3: 244–245
Polesworth	ca. 980		
	ca. 1138x1144	2	WR, 227[90]
Polsloe	–1160	2	WR, 227
Pomarède	–1165	10	AP 4: 39
la Pommeraie	1151	6	AP 6: 41–42[91]
Pommereux	1128	3	AP 18: 163
Pont-à-Mousson	ca. 1125	4	MP 3: 93
le Pont-aux-Dames	1226	6	AP 1: 319
Pont-de-Gennes	1092	7	AP 8: 183
Pontratier	–1208	10	[92]
Pontrouard	ca. 1235	3	GC 5: 359
Port-Royal-des-Champs	1204	6	GC 7: 910
Pouilly-les-Nonnains	–1202	8	AP 10: 144[93]
Poussay	ca. 1050	4	GC 13: 1097
Pralon	ca. 1140	8	AP 12: 590
les Préaux	1040	5	AP 7: 203
Prémol	1232	11	AP 9: 86
Prémy	ca. 1185	3	GC 3: 166
Prés Porchins	1230	3	MB 1: 470–471
Presle-en-Porcien	1212	3	[94]
Prouille	1207	13	AP 4: 339
Provins	1248	6	AP 6: 21
Puits d'Orbe	1112x1125	8	AP 12: 400–401
la Puye	–1106	9	AP 3: 253

Name	Date	Archdiocese	Reference
Quesnoy	ca. 1233	3	GC 3: 167
la Rame	ca. 1130	12	AP 3: 40
Ramières	–963[95]	14	AP 2: 157
Ramstede	1174x1184	2	WR, 227
Ravensberg	ca. 1191	3	GC 3, instr. 123
Reading	ca. 980	2	MRH, 74, 480
le Réconfort	1244	6	GC 4: 505
Redlingfield	1120	2	WR, 228
la Regrippière	ca. 1115	7	AP 8: 251
Reims	1220	3	GC 9: 330–331
Relay	ca. 1108	7	Bienvenu, 110
Renaud	1144	9	AP 3: 116
Rengeval	1153	4	MP 3: 96–97, 99
Rennes (St-Georges)	ca. 1032	7	AP 8: 211–212
Rieunette	–1162	13	AP 4: 173
Rieval	ca. 1124	4	MP 3: 99, 101
Rives	ca. 1116	9	AP 3: 253[96]
Rivreulle	1125x1126[97]	3	MP 2: 361, 394
la Rochelle	ca. 1180	9	AP 3: 157; see Chapter 5
Romsey	ca. 907	2	MRH, 264
la Ronze	–1279	10	DHGE 2: 621
Roosendael	–1227	3	MB 8: 141
la Roquette	ca. 1255	14	AP 2: 80
Rosedale	ca. 1130xca. 1160	1	WR, 228
les Rosiers	–1241	3	GC 9: 179
Rothwell	–1249	2	WR, 228
Rouen (St-Amand)	1030	5	AP 7: 62
Rouez	1122[98]	3	MP 2: 495–496, 504, 530
Rougemont	–1105	8	AP 12: 398
Rousillon (Ste-Croix)	1234	15	DHGE 3: 1081
Rowney	ca. 1146xca. 1160	2	WR, 228
Rozoy-le-Jeune	ca. 1106	6	GC 12: 188–189
Rupt-aux-Nonnains	–1136	4	GC 13: 1068
Rusper	–1174	2	WR, 228
St-Agil	1190	6	GC 8: 1290
St-André-au-Bois	1130	3	MP 2: 562
St-Aubin	1200	5	AP 7: 75
Ste-Beuve-aux-Champs	1183	5	[99]
St-Bernard-lès-Bayonne	ca. 1260[100]	12	AP 3: 57; GC 1: 1068
St-Corentin-lès-Mantes	–1201	6	AP 1: 243
Ste-Croix de Volvestre	ca. 1145	12	[101]
St-Cyr-au-Val-de-Gallie	–1156	6	AP 1: 243
St-Dizier	1227	8	GC 9: 973
Ste-Gemme	1148	6	AP 1: 289
St-Genès-les-Monges	–1067	10	AP 5: 119–120[102]
St-Geniès-des-Mourges	1019	13	HGL 4: 826
St-Georges-de-Grehaigne	–1146	7	AP 8: 233[103]
Ste-Hoïlde	ca. 1229	4	GC 13: 1121
St-Jean-aux-Bois	ca. 1150	3	AP 18: 157
St-Julien-la-Geneste	–1184	10	AP 5: 120[104]
St-Just-en-Chausée	–1107	3	MP 2: 564

Name	Date	Archdiocese	Reference
St-Laurent	1151	12	AP 3: 47
St-Loup-sur-Loire	−945	7	GC 14: 189
St Mary de Pré	1194	2	WR, 228
St-Menoux	−1000	10	AP 5: 43
St-Michel-du-Bois	ca. 1150	5	AP 7: 160
St-Orens	ca. 1095	13	HGL 4: 600
St-Paul-lès-Beauvais	ca. 1035[105]	3	GC 9: 812
St-Remy-des-Landes	1160	6	AP 1: 245
St-Saens	ca. 1167	5	AP 7: 67–68
St-Silvane	ca. 1020	9	GC 2: 1490[106]
St-Sulpice-la-Forêt	ca. 1112	7	AP 8: 212–213
St-Thomas-les-Nonnains	1206	8	AP 10: 144–145
St-Zacharie	−1267	14	AP 2: 108[107]
Saintes (Notre-Dame)	1047	9	AP 3: 292–293
Salettes	1299	8	AP 9: 18
la Salvetat de Montdragon	−1260[108]	10	HGL 4: 762–764
le Saulchoir	1234	3	MB 1: 378–379
la Saussaye	−1191	6	GC 7: 635
le Sauvoir sous Laon	ca. 1228	3	GC 9: 640
Seauve-Bénite	−1228	10	GC 2: 777
Seche-Fontaine	ca. 1173	6	AP 12: 424
Sempringham	1131	2	WR, 228
Senlis (St-Remy)	ca. 1050	6	AP 18: 164
Seton	−1210	1	WR, 228
Severac-le-Château	1103	10	AP 4: 102
Sewardsley	1148x1166	2	WR, 228
Shouldham	ca. 1197x1198	2	WR, 228
Sinningthwaite	−1155	1	WR, 228
Sisteron	ca. 1285	15	GC 1: 513–514
Sixhills	1148x1154	2	WR, 229
Soissons (St-Paul)	1228	3	AP 17: 115
Sopwell	ca. 1140	2	WR, 229
Sorps	1255	15	AP 2: 60
Sourribes	−1160	15	AP 2: 50
Soyons	−1179	11	GC 16: 351
Spermalie	−1200	3	MB 3: 455
Spinney	1148xca. 1154	2	WR, 229
Stainfield	−1168	2	WR, 229
Stamford	1135x1154	2	WR, 229
Stixwold	1139x1142	2	WR, 229
Stratford-at-Bow	−1122	2	WR, 229
Studley	−1175x1189	2	WR, 229
Swaffham Bulbeck	−1199	2	WR, 229
Swine	ca. 1143x1153	2	WR, 229
Tarrent	−1169x1176	2	WR, 229
Tart l'Abbaye	ca. 1125	8	GC 4: 848
Ten Roosen	−1235	3	MB 7: 449
Ter Hagen	1230	3	MB 7: 465
Thelouet	1124	7	AP 8: 308
Thetford	−ca. 1163x1180	2	WR, 230
Thicket	−1180	1	WR, 230

Name	Date	Archdiocese	Reference
la Thure	1244	3	MB 1: 478
Toul	ca. 970	4	GC 13: 978, 1068
Toulouse (= Longages)	1203	13	HGL 4: 697
Toulouse	−1247	13	Agathange, 49
Touvoie	ca. 1136	7	AP 8: 251[109]
Trainel	−1163	6	GC 7: 640
le Trésor	1227	5	AP 7: 67
Tunstall	ca. 1148x1160	2	WR, 230
Tusschenbeek	1147x1148[110]	3	MP 2: 424
Tusson	ca. 1112	9	Bienvenu, 107
Usk	−1236	2	MRH, 267
le Val d'Osne	1140x1145	3	AP 1: 143[111]
Val-de-Grace	−1183	6	GC 7: 574
le Val des Vignes	−1231	8	AP 12: 408
Valeys	−1279	10	DHGE 2: 621
Valnegre	−1206	13	HGL 4: 851
Valprofonde	ca. 1138[112]	6	MP 2: 475, 534–535
Valsauve	−1217	13	HGL 4: 869
Valvion	ca. 1124[113]	3	MP 2:544, 571
Vanault-les-Dames	1135[114]	3	MP 3: 110–111
Variville	ca. 1150	3	AP 18: 192
Vaupillon	1140	12	AP 3: 144
Vauxbons	ca. 1181	8	AP 12: 406
Verdun (St-Maur)	ca. 1020	4	GC 13: 1312–1313
Verdun (St-Louis)	ca. 1250	4	GC 13: 1262
Vergaville	966	4	GC 13: 936
le Verger	−1225	3	AP 14: 450
Vernaison	ca. 1150	11	AP 9: 121
Vernon	1260	5	GC 11: 662
Vielmur-sur-l'Agout	−1048	10	AP 4: 49
Vienne (St-André-le-Haut)	1031[115]	11	AP 9: 31
Vienne (Notre-Dame)	−1281	11	AP 9: 32
Vignats	ca. 1130	5	AP 7: 233
le Vignogoul	−1130	13	HGL 4: 827
Villarceaux	−1164	5	AP 7: 80[116]
la Villedieu	−1152	11	GC 16: 596
Villers-Canivet	1140	5	AP 7: 223
Villesalem	1089	9	AP 3: 253–254
Villiers-aux-Nonnains	ca. 1220	6	AP 6: 45
Vinets	1155	3	[117]
la Virginité	ca. 1220	7	AP 8: 161
Vitry-en-Perthois	ca. 1235	3	GC 9: 973–974
le Vivier (Arras)	1228	3	AP 14: 454
Vix	−1220	9	[118]
Voisins	1213	6	AP 1: 363
Waesmunster	1226	3	GC 5: 226
Wallingwells	ca. 1144	1	WR, 230
Waterbeach	1294	2	MRH, 287
Watton	1151x1153	1	WR, 230
Wauthier-Braine	ca. 1228	3	MB 4: 588–589
Westwood	1155x1158	2	WR, 230

Name	Date	Archdiocese	Reference
Wherwell	ca. 986	2	MRH, 267
Whiston	–1241	2	WR, 230
Wilberfoss	1147x1153	1	WR, 230
Willencourt	ca. 1200	3	AP 14: 457
Wilton	–933	2	MRH, 267; see Chapter 2
Winchester	ca. 900	2	MRH, 268
Wintney	–1154x1161	2	WR, 230
Wix	1123x1133	2	WR, 230
Woestine	–1217	3	GC 3: 537
Worcester	–1241	2	MRH, 288
Wothorpe	ca. 1160	2	WR, 230
Wroxhall	1123x1153	2	WR, 231
Wykeham	–1153	1	WR, 231
Yedingham	–1158	1	WR, 231
Yerres	1134	6	AP 1: 80
Zandvliet	1124[119]	3	MP 2: 265, 337
Zwijveke	–1223	3	MB 7: 476

NOTES TO APPENDIX A

1. For an early description, see Mary M. McLaughlin, "Looking for Medieval Women: An Interim Report on the Project 'Women's Religious Life and Communities, A.D. 500–1500,'" *Medieval Prosopography* 8 (1987): 61–91. The project is now archived at Mount Holyoke College under the name "Matrix." Katherine J. Gill of the Yale Divinity School is directing the transformation of Matrix into an Internet resource with databases, maps, and images accessible on the World Wide Web. The URL is http://matrix.divinity.yale.edu/Matrix WebData/matrix.html

2. MRH, 7. In revising Anselme Dimier's 1974 list of female Cistercian houses in France, the editor of Dimier's mélanges admitted that such a repertory "ne saurait . . . prétendre ni à l'exhaustivité ni à l'exactitude complète tant est délicate l'histoire des moniales" (Anselme Dimier, "Liste des abbayes cisterciennes féminines de France au Moyen-Age," in *Mélanges Anselme Dimier*, ed. Benoît Chauvin, 3 vols. [Arbois, 1984], 2: 591).

3. Anne-Marie Bautier, "De 'Prepositus' à 'Prior,' de 'Cella' à 'Prioratus': Evolution linguistique et genèse d'une institution (jusqu'à 1200)," in *Prieurs et prieurés dans l'Occident médiéval*, ed. Jean-Loup Lemaître (Geneva, 1987), 15–17.

4. Joseph Avril, "Le statut de prieurés d'après les conciles provinciaux et les statuts synodaux (fin XIIe–début XIVe siècles)" in *Prieurs et prieurés*, 74; Bautier, "De 'Prepositus' à 'Prior,'" 15.

5. Avril, "Le statut de prieurés," 74.

6. In addition to the articles cited above in notes 3 and 4, C. D. Du Cange, *Glossarium mediae et infimae latinitatis*, new ed. rev. Leopold Favre, 10 vols. (Niort, 1883–1887, repr. Paris, 1935), 6: 506, col. 1 contains the entry for "PRIORATUS, Obedientia, seu minus beneficium a majori Monasterio dependens." See also the same volume for "OBEDIENTIA." R. Naz, ed., *Dictionnaire de droit canonique*, 7 vols. (Paris, 1935–1965), 7: 213–214, notes the several meanings of *prieur* and *prieuré*. There is a full discussion of the word "prieuré" in the Introduction to the revision of Beaunier's eighteenth-century repertory in *Archives de la France monastique* 4 (1906), xii–xvi. "On ne peut pas donc conclure de la présence d'un prieuré en une localité quelconque à l'existence d'un monastère véritable" (xv–xvi). By

analogy, I have come to believe that a *priorissa* need not necessarily be the head of an independent community, but might, especially in the twelfth century, be an official in an abbey, subordinate to the abbess, responsible for managing a portion of the house's patrimony.

7. It seems unlikely that nuns would have made a practice of colonizing abbatial properties singly or in pairs, as monks appeared to have done frequently; see Avril, "Le statut des prieurés." For an example of a list more inclusive than mine, see Pierre-Roger Gaussin, "Les communautés féminines dans l'espace Languedocien de la fin du XIe à la fin du XIVe siècle," *Cahiers de Fanjeaux* 23 (1988): 299–332. Gaussin is readier than I to find communities of women, especially in eleventh-century Benedictine priories, some of which he describes as "vraisemblablement conventuel." Oddly, the tallies of figures for twelfth- and thirteenth-century foundations do not match the lists provided.

8. This usage usually indicates a document in which a secular or ecclesiastical lord participates or is noted; the dates are those during which he held the office. In compiling statistics, I have always used the latest date in order to arrive at a *terminus ante quem*.

9. An ancient house restored at this date after destruction during the period of invasions.

10. For about 30 years previously, a hospital served by men and women; transformed into a Cistercian nunnery about 1232.

11. An ancient foundation, restored after destruction during the time of invasions.

12. But mistakenly identified as a simple priory: for evidence of habitation, see Paul Marchegay, "Notes sur deux prieurés de l'abbaye de Nyoiseau," *Bulletin de la société archéologique de Nantes* 6 (1866), 223–224.

13. For the date, see Jean Charay, *Aubenas en Vivarais*, 2 vols. (Aubenas, 1950–1952), 2: 94–96.

14. For the date, see Louis Guibert, "Destruction de l'Ordre et de l'abbaye de Grandmont: Appendice," *Bulletin de la société archéologique et historique du Limousin* 25 (1877), 296–297.

15. A house of nuns was here in the tenth century. The ruins on the site were given to a group of Norbertine sisters about 1150 by a knightly family.

16. Originally a hospital served by men and women, with origins in the early twelfth century.

17. A hospital since about 1210.

18. This Premonstratensian community was composed of men and women at its founding; nothing is known of the fate of the sisters.

19. Legends that attribute this foundation to Carolingian times have no surviving documentary basis. The earliest charter is of 1180–1182; see *Cartulaire de l'abbaye de Cysoing*, 57.

20. For the date, see Laurent, *Cartulaires de l'abbaye de Molesme* 1: 264.

21. The house of Saint John in Amiens, Premonstratensian since 1124, moved its sisters to Bertricourt by 1148. There was also a very short-lived house of women at Valvion.

22. Founded as a male monastery ca. 1150.

23. For the date, see Parisse, "Les religieuses bénédictines de Lorraine," 267.

24. For the date, see Paul Marchegay, "Le prieuré de Bois-Goyer," *Annuaire départemental de la société d'émulation de la Vendée* 3 (1856), 257–258.

25. The Premonstratensian house of Belval, founded between 1120 and 1130, moved its sisters to Bois-les-Dames about 1137.

26. The Premonstratensian house of Septfontaines, established about 1140, moved its sisters to Bonlieu by 1174.

27. Men and women began to live at Saint Norbert's foundation of Prémontré in the early 1120s. The sisters were separated about 1138 and lived in two other places before settling at Bonneuil by 1148.

28. Founded on the site of a seventh-century male house destroyed in the ninth century.

29. The Premonstratensian house of Braine, founded in 1130, moved its sisters to Bruyères some ten years later.

30. A refoundation of a twelfth-century house of canons.

31. For the date, see Jean-Baptiste Déribier-du-Châtelet, *Dictionnaire statistique ou: Histoire, description et statistique du département du Cantal,* 5 vols. (Aurillac, 1852–1857), 3: 58.

32. The Premonstratensian house of Thenailles, founded in 1130, moved its sisters to Caumont between 1137 and 1143.

33. This community was at first a rural Benedictine house dedicated to Saint Marcellus. In 1327, Pope John XXII ordered the nuns to abandon their solitary monastery and move into the town of Cavaillon in order to serve in a hospital.

34. In this year a group of Benedictine nuns were replaced by Carthusian sisters from Sourribes.

35. See Bienvenu, "Les premiers temps de Fontevraud," 314.

36. For the date, see Edouard, *Fontevraud et ses monuments,* 2: 291.

37. See Ludovic de Vauzelles, *Histoire du prieuré de la Magdeleine-lez-Orléans* (Paris, 1873), 21, 212–213.

38. For the date, see ibid., 18–19.

39. For the date, see the foundation charter in the cartulary of Saint-Sulpice of Rennes: *Bulletin et mémoires de la société archéologique du département d'Ille-et-Vilaine* 35 (1906), 360.

40. About this time nuns began to live in what had been a monastery for monks founded in the early eleventh century.

41. For the date, see Edouard, *Fontevraud et ses monuments,* 2: 285.

42. For the date, see G. Clément-Simon, "Notice sur le couvent de Derses," *Bulletin de la société scientifique, historique et archéologique de la Corrèze* 11 (1889), 549–551.

43. The house of Saint Martin in Laon, inhabited by Premonstratensians since 1124, transferred its sisters to Dionne around 1130.

44. The Premonstratensian house of Clairefontaine, founded about 1126, moved its sisters to Dorengt by the thirteenth century.

45. A typographical error here moves the date of foundation back one century but notes the affiliation to the Cisterican Order in 1234.

46. The Premonstratensian house of Valchrétien, founded in 1124, moved its sisters to Dormans in the 1140s.

47. See Marchegay, "Notes sur deux prieurés de l'abbaye de Nyoiseau," 226, 228.

48. For the date, see Guibert, "Destruction de l'Ordre et de l'abbaye de Grandmont: Appendice," 297–298.

49. The Premonstratensian house of Tongerloo, founded about 1130, moved its sisters to Eewen sometime between 1156 and 1167.

50. For the date, see Bienvenu, 108–110.

51. For the date, see Henry Cardon, "La chapelle d'Epargnemaille à Saint-Quentin et l'abbaye de Notre-Dame de Soissons," *Mémoires de la société académique de Saint-Quentin* 4th ser., 11 (1891–1892), 127.

52. For the date, see Deladreue, "Histoire de l'abbaye de Saint-Paul-lès-Beauvais," 76.

53. The monastery was destroyed in the twelfth century, then rebuilt by King Philip II outside the city wall.

54. For the date, see Deladreue, "Histoire de l'abbaye de Saint-Paul-lès-Beauvais," 57–58.

55. The Premonstratensian house of Septfontaine, founded in 1129–1135, moved its sisters to Neuville in 1141, and then to Feuchère.

56. The Premonstratensian house of Dilo, founded about 1132, moved its sisters to Fossemore shortly afterward.

57. For the date, see a charter from the cartulary of Saint-Sulpice-la-Forêt: *Bulletin et mémoires de la société archéologique du département d'Ille-et-Vilaine* 35 (1905): 376–377.

58. The first charters of this house date only to the mid-thirteenth century, but there remain buildings of the eleventh and twelfth centuries. "By 1100" is a conservative estimate of the antiquity of the community.

59. For the date, see Bienvenu, 110.

60. The Premonstratensian house of Justemont, founded about 1130, moved its sisters to Hamewiller between 1153 and 1184.

61. The house of Vicogne was given to Premonstratensian men and women at this time; the sisters went to Harchies about 1140.

62. Legend has it that the nuns of a house at Eltisley moved to this site in the time of William the Conqueror, but the earliest evidence for the community at Hinchinbrooke dates to the late twelfth century.

63. Veurnes, a house of Augustinian canons founded in 1120, became a Premonstratensian community about 1135. Its sisters went to Hof ten Vrouwen in 1179.

64. There had been a hospital here since the early thirteenth century.

65. For the date, see GC 12, instr. 153.

66. The Premonstratensian house of Valsery, founded in 1124 or 1126, moved its sisters to Javages in 1148.

67. For the foundation charter of 1115, which shows that there were nuns in what shortly afterward became an all-male house, see GC 2: 200.

68. For the date, see Charles François Roussel, *Le diocèse de Langres: Histoire et statistique*, 4 vols. (Langres, 1873–1879), 3: 97.

69. For the date, see A. Lagier, "Abbaye de Notre-Dame de Laval-Bénite de Bressieux," *Bulletin d'histoire ecclésiastique et d'archéologie religieuse des diocèses de Valence, Digne, Gap, Grenoble, et Viviers* 3 (1882–1883), 234.

70. See Wischermann, *Marcigny-sur-Loire*, 506.

71. There was a house of nuns at this site in the seventh century, restored in late Anglo-Saxon times for secular canons, then given over to nuns again sometime before 1046, when Swein, the son of Earl Godwin, removed the abbess and raped her. The community subsequently dispersed.

72. For the date, see the charter ed. Paul Marchegay ("Cartularium prioratus Libaudi," *Archives historiques de Poitou* 1 [1872], 55–56.) Witnesses included Unsmiling Arnold (*Arnaudo Qui Non Ridet*) and Robert Bad Shrew (*Robertus Mala Sorex*).

73. For the date, see Celestin Port, *Dictionnaire historique, géographique et biographique de Maine et Loire*, rev. ed. (Angers, 1965–   ), 2: 527.

74. For the earliest charter, see Paul Pellot, "Le cartulaire du prieuré du Longueau," *Revue de Champagne et de Brie* 2d ser., 7 (1895), 161–162.

75. From about 1130, Premonstratensian men and women served at the house of Mont Saint Martin; the sisters moved to Macquincourt in 1212.

76. For the date, see the foundation charter in André Lesort, *Chroniques et chartes de l'abbaye de Saint-Mihiel* (Paris, 1909), 354–355.

77. This community, founded in the early fifth century, was restored at the end of the tenth century, nearly 100 years after the abbey was destroyed by Saracens. A new house, in a new place, was built around 1030. See Ferdinand André, *Histoire de l'abbaye des religieuses de Saint-Sauveur de Marseille* (Marseille, 1863), 16–17.

78. When the Premonstratensian canons moved away from the original house not long after 1133 because of flooding, they left the sisters there. The women's community appears to have lasted at least another century.

79. See Maurice Josselin, "Acte inédit du roi Louis VII (1178)," *Bibliothèque de l'Ecole des Chartes* 71 (1910), 466–467.

80. Vauzelles, *Histoire du prieuré de la Magdeleine-lez-Orléans*, 22–23, 221.

81. The Premonstratensian house of Valsecret, founded in 1133, moved its sisters to Monthodon shortly afterward.

82. In this year Duke Robert of Normandy rebuilt an old monastery that had been destroyed some time earlier.

83. A house of Premonstratensian sisters, adjacent to a male house, survived into the thirteenth century.

84. The Premonstratensian house of Grimbergen, founded about 1128, moved its sisters to Nieuwenrode about 1140.

85. About this time, women joined a community of canons, which subsequently left Odeghem to the sisters and went elsewhere.

86. The Premonstratensian house of Ninove, founded in 1137, moved its sisters to Pamel in 1188.

87. In this year, a house for monks founded in the late twelfth century was given to nuns.

88. The Premonstratensian house of Tronchiennes, founded in 1136, moved its sisters to Peteghem a few years later.

89. The Premonstratensian house of Jandeures, founded in 1143, moved its sisters to Plainemont shortly afterward.

90. On the history of this house, see Elkins, *Holy Women*, 13, 71–72.

91. For the date, see the charter of foundation printed in Quantin, *Cartulaire général de l'Yonne*, 1: 493–494.

92. For the date, see M. le Commandant du Broc de Sagagne, "Prieuré de Pontratier," *Bulletin de la société d'émulation du Bourbonnais* 16 (1908), 576.

93. For the date, see E. Leriche, "Excursion archéologique de la société de la Diana," *Bulletin de la Diana* 13 (1902–1903), 177–178. The monastery is thought to have been established in the twelfth century, but the earliest evidence is a legacy of Count Guy III of Forez, who died on crusade in 1202.

94. For the date, see Laurent, *Cartulaires de l'abbaye de Molesme*, 1: 265.

95. In this year the abbot of Montmajour gave this property to nuns from the house of Prébayon, which had become uninhabitable because of flooding. According to legend, the community of Prébayon dates to the early Middle Ages.

96. For the date, see J.-X. Carré de Busserolle, "Notice sur le prieuré de Ste-Marie de Rives," *Mémoires de la société archéologique de Touraine* 13 (1861), 182–183.

97. The Premonstratensian house of Bonne Esperance, founded in 1125 or 1126, moved its sisters to Rivreulle sometime between 1140 and 1182.

98. The Premonstratensians of Cuissy, founded in this year, sent their sisters to Gérigny between 1139 and 1145 and then to Rouez after 1148.

99. For the date, see Deladreue, "Histoire de l'abbaye de Saint-Paul-lès-Beauvais," 67–68.

100. A house for monks founded about 1168 was given to Cistercian nuns about this time.

101. See Gustave Ducos, *Sainte-Croix de Volvestre et son monastère* (Toulouse, 1937), 33–34.

102. For the date, see Gaussin, *L'abbaye de la Chaise-Dieu*, 335; the monastery was already in existence in the time of Abbot Robert of Chaise-Dieu.

103. For the date, see "Cartulaire de l'abbaye de Saint-Georges de Rennes," *Bulletin et mémoires de la société archéologique du département d'Ille-et-Vilaine* 9 (1875): 255.

104. For the date, see Gaussin, *L'abbaye de la Chaise-Dieu*, 336.

105. An early medieval nunnery, destroyed by Normans in the ninth century, was restored at this time by Bishop Drogo.

106. For the date, see Jean Verdon, "Recherches sur les monastères féminins dans la France du Sud au IXe–XIe siècles," *Annales du Midi* 88 (1976): 119.

107. For the date, see Etienne Faillon, *Monuments inédits sur l'apostolat de Sainte Marie-Madeleine en Provence*, 2 vols. (Paris, 1863–1865), 2: 687–688.

108. An eleventh-century foundation for men was transferred to women two centuries later.

109. For the date, see Bienvenu, "Les premiers temps de Fontevraud," 318.

110. Premonstratensian sisters from Peteghem first settled at Serskamp, but moved in 1256 to nearby Tusschenbeek after an invasion of reptiles made the place uninhabitable.

111. For the date, see Laurent, *Cartulaires de l'abbaye de Molesme,* 1: 262.

112. A Premonstratensian house in Auxerre, founded about 1138, moved its sisters to Val-profonde soon after.

113. See Bertricourt.

114. The Premonstratensian house of Saint Paul in Verdun, established in 1135, moved its sisters in 1148 to Vanault-les-Dames, nearby but in the diocese of Châlons-sur-Marne.

115. One of the oldest convents in Western Europe, destroyed by invading Saracens, was restored in this year.

116. For the date of the conventual priory, see Toussaint Duplessis, *Description géographique et historique de la haute Normandie,* 2 vols. (Paris, 1740), 2: 326.

117. See Laurent, *Cartulaires de l'abbaye de Molesme,* 1: 263.

118. See Johnson, *Equal in Monastic Profession,* 196.

119. The Premonstratensian house of Saint Michael in Antwerp, founded in 1124, moved its sisters to Zandvliet sometime between 1148 and 1155.

∂íocesan centeRs
an∂ otheR cíties

𝒲hat follows is a handlist of cities in the region under scrutiny in the central Middle Ages. About 80 percent of the list is composed of episcopal seats, the number and organization of which changed relatively little from the early medieval period to the fourteenth century; most of the exceptions to this rule are the English sees. Another thirty-five or so cities had attained prominence for commerce and/or secular administration and a population to match by the eleventh or twelfth century. My list of nondiocesan cities draws on the work of a number of scholars, and because it is notoriously difficult to guess population figures before the fourteenth century, it would be a mistake to construe it as some kind of imprimatur. However, I believe that no town of uncontested importance in this period has been omitted.

Sources

The maps and corresponding text in John Godfrey, *The Church in Anglo-Saxon England* (Cambridge, Eng., 1962) are particularly helpful for untangling the history of several sees, complicated as a result of successive reorganizations in the early tenth century and in the wake of the Norman Conquest. The Domesday Survey provides a relatively easy basis for identifying major nondiocesan cities; I have relied on the list provided by H. C. Darby, "Domesday England" in *A New Historical Geography of England,* ed. H. C. Darby (Cambridge, Eng., 1973), 67–71.

For the Continental realms a convenient list of medieval dioceses may be found in the *New Catholic Encyclopedia,* q.v. "France," which, with the exception of the omission of the dioceses of Riez and Fréjus from the archdiocese of Aix, is accurate. On the Continent, very little changed between the ninth century and the fourteenth. An idea of the relative antiquity of these Continental dioceses, many of which date to the fifth century or earlier, may be had from the entries in Pius Bonifacius Gams, *Series episcoporum ecclesiae catholicae* (Regensburg, 1873), although the lists of bishops are not to be relied upon. In supplementing the diocesan list, I have found two studies especially helpful: F.-L. Ganshof, *Etude sur le développement des villes entre Loire et Rhin au moyen âge* (Paris, 1943), and J. C. Russell, *Medieval Regions and Their Cities* (Newton Abbot, Eng., 1972).

CITIES IN THE CENTRAL MIDDLE AGES

+ Archdiocese (15 total)
* Nonepiscopal city (37 total)

Total number of cities: 165

Unless otherwise noted by a date in parentheses, diocesan cities were founded in the early Middle Ages.

Adge	Bayeux
Agen	Bayonne
Aire	Bazas
+Aix-en-Provence	Beauvais
Albi	Béziers
Amiens	*Blois
Angers	+Bordeaux
Angoulême	+Bourges
*Antwerp	*Bruges
Apt	*Brussels
+Arles	*Bury St Edmunds
Arras (1093)	*Caen
+Auch	Cahors
Autun	Cambrai
Auxerre	+Canterbury
Avignon	Carcassonne
Avranches	Carlisle (1133)
Bangor	Carpentras
*Bar-sur-Aube	Cavaillon
Bath (with Wells from 1090)	Châlon-sur-Saône

Châlons-sur-Marne
Chartres
*Chester[1]
Chichester (ca. 1078)[2]
Clermont
*Colchester
Comminges (St-Bertrand)
*Courtrai
Couserans (St-Lizier)
Coutances
Coventry (1102)[3]
Dax
Die
*Dijon
Dol
Dorchester[4]
*Douai
*Dunwich
Durham[5]
Elne
Elmham[6]
Ely (1109)
*Epernay
*Etampes
Evreux
Exeter (1050)[7]
Fréjus
Gap
*Ghent
*Gloucester
Grenoble
Hereford
*Huntingdon
*Lagny
Langres
Laon
Lectoure
Lescar
*Lewes
Lichfield[8]
*Lille
Limoges
Lincoln (1075)[9]
Lisieux
Llandaff
Lodève
London
*Louvain
+Lyon
Mâcon
Maguelonne
Le Mans

Marseille
Meaux
*Mechelen (Mâlines)
Metz
*Mons
*Montaubon
*Montpellier
*Nancy
Nantes
+Narbonne
Nevers
Nîmes
Norwich (from 1094)[10]
Noyon
Orange
Orléans
*Oxford
*Pamiers
Paris
Périgueux
*Perpignan
Poitiers
*Provins
Le Puy
Quimper
+Reims
Rennes
Riez
*La Rochelle
Rochester
Rodez
+Rouen
St Asaph
St-Brieuc
St Davids
St-Malo
*St-Omer
St-Paul-Trois-Châteaux
St-Pol-de-Léon
Saintes
Salisbury (ca. 1075)
Séez
Selsey[11]
Senlis
+Sens
Sherbourne[12]
Sisteron (at Forqualquier ca. 1080–1169)
Soissons
*Stamford
Tarbes
Thérouanne
*Thetford[13]

Toul
Toulon
Toulouse
Tournai (1148)
+Tours
Tréguier
+Trier
Troyes
Uzès
Vaison
Valence

Vannes
Verdun
+Vienne
Viviers
*Wallingford
Wells (909)
Winchester
Worcester
+York
*Ypres

NOTES TO APPENDIX B

1. The ancient see of Lichfield was transferred to Chester in 1075, then to Coventry in 1102. The town was of considerable importance in the period and the site of a royal mint.
2. The South Saxon diocese was tranferred from Selsey to Chichester after the Conquest.
3. See Chester and Lichfield.
4. From the late ninth century, this see combined the ancient dioceses of Lindsey, Leicester, and Dorchester into the largest bishopric in England. The episcopal center was transferred to Lincoln in 1075.
5. The final site of the Northumbrian see, which had been at Lindisfarne until Viking invasion forced a retreat to Chester-le-Street, where the bishops remained until 994, when they moved to nearby Durham.
6. The bishops of Dunwich vanished from view in the ninth century; their successors in East Anglia were at Elmham until shortly after the Conquest. The see was briefly at Thetford and then settled finally at Norwich in 1091.
7. From the early tenth century, the bishops of Cornwall were at St Germans, those of Devonshire at Crediton. Crediton, which had by then absorbed St Germans, was transferred to Exeter in 1050.
8. This ancient see was transferred to Chester in 1075 and to Coventry in 1102 but maintained a cathedral chapter and a palace as well as remaining the center of diocesan organization.
9. See Dorchester.
10. See Elmham.
11. The ancient episcopal seat was transferred to Chichester in the late 1070s.
12. This ancient diocese was joined to Ramsbury, a seat created in the tenth century, in 1058, and gave way to the new see of Salisbury in the 1070s.
13. An important town at the time of the Domesday Survey, it was also the seat of the East Anglian bishopric from ca. 1070 until 1094. See Elmham.

bíblíogRaphy

MANUSCRIPTS

Angers, Archives Départementales de Maine-et-Loire
   101 H 225 (Grand Cartulaire de Fontevraud, fragment)
   101 H 225bis (Charters of Fontevraud)
   171 H 6 (Cartulary of l'Espinasse)
   186 H 3 (Cartulary of Montazais)
   236 H 1 (Charters of Villesalem)
   243 H 1 (Charters of Amesbury)
   251 H 14 (Charters of les Lochereaux)
Caen, Archives Départementales de Calvados
   H, femmes, 160 (uncatalogued) (Charters of Villers-Canivet)
   H Ancienne bibliothèque capitulaire de Bayeux ms. 162 (Charters of Cordillon)
Paris, Archives Nationales
   L 1018, 1019 (Charters of Fontevraud)
   LL 1599 B (Cartulary of Yerres)
Paris, Bibliothèque Nationale
   Collection Languedoc, vol. 149
   Collection Picardie, vol. 93
   Collection Touraine et Anjou, vol. 5
   Ms.lat. 9885 (Cartulary of Crisenon)
   Ms.lat. 11002 (Cartulary of Senlis)
   Ms.nouv.acq.lat. 2414 (Grand Cartulaire de Fontevraud)
Poitiers, Bibliothèque Municipale
   Collection Fonteneau, vols. 18, 27 (Charters of Sainte-Croix and Sainte-Trinité, Poitiers)

Rouen, Archives Départementales de Seine-Maritime
   51 H (Charters of Bival)
   52 H (Charters of Bondeville)
   55 H 1 (Cartulary of Saint-Amand, Rouen)

Printed Sources

Some of the entries cited under Secondary Works are edited documents.

Abelard. *Historia calamitatum.* Edited by Jacques Monfrin. Paris, 1959.
[Abelard.] "Abelard's Rule for Religious Women," edited by T. P. McLaughlin. *Mediaeval Studies* 18 (1956): 241–292.
[Abelard and Heloise.] "The Letter of Heloise on Religious Life and Abelard's First Reply," edited by J. T. Muckle. *Mediaeval Studies* 17 (1955): 240–281.
Les actes de Guillaume le Conquérant et de la reine Mathilde pour les abbayes caennaises. Edited by Lucien Musset. Caen, 1967.
Alpert of Metz. *De diversitate temporum.* In MGH SS 4: 700–723.
Andreas. *Vita altera B. Roberti de Arbrisselo.* In PL 162: 1058–1078.
Andreas Capellanus. *Andreas Capellanus on Love.* Edited and translated by P. G. Walsh. London, 1982.
Anglo-Saxon Charters. Edited by A. J. Robertson. 2d ed. Cambridge, Eng., 1956.
The Anglo-Saxon Chronicle. Edited and translated by Dorothy Whitelock et al. London, 1961.
Anglo-Saxon Wills. Edited by Dorothy Whitelock. Cambridge, Eng., 1930.
[Asser.] *Asser's Life of King Alfred.* Edited by William H. Stevenson. London, 1904.
Baudry of Dol. *Vita prima B. Roberti de Arbrisello.* In PL 162: 1043–1058.
[Bernard of Clairvaux.] *Sancti Bernardi Opera.* Edited by J. Leclercq, C. H. Talbot, and H. Rochais. Rome, 1957– .
The Book of Saint Gilbert. Edited by Raymonde Foreville and Gillian Keir. Oxford, 1987.
Cartulaire de l'abbaye de Cysoing et de ses dépendances. Edited by Ignace de Coussemaker. Lille, 1886.
Cartulaire de l'abbaye de Maubuisson (Notre-Dame-la-Royale). Edited by A. Dutilleux and J. Depoin. Pontoise, 1890–1913.
Un cartulaire de l'abbaye de Notre-Dame de Bourbourg. Edited by Ignace de Coussemaker. Lille, 1891.
Cartulaire de l'abbaye de Saint-Bertin. Edited by Benjamin Guérard. Paris, 1840.
"Cartulaire de l'abbaye de Saint-Georges de Rennes," edited by Paul de la Bigne-Villeneuve. *Bulletin et mémoires de la société archéologique du département d'Ille-et-Vilaine* 9 (1875): 129–311 and 10 (1876): 3–327.
"Cartulaire de l'abbaye de Saint-Sulpice-la-Forêt," edited by Pierre Anger. *Bulletin et mémoires de la société archéologique du département d'Ille-et-Vilaine* 34 (1905): 164–262; 35 (1906): 325–388; 37 (1907): 3–160; 38 (1908): 205–280; 39 (1909): 1–207; 40, pt. 1 (1910): 33–192; and 40, pt. 2 (1910): 1–89.

Cartulaire de l'abbaye du Paraclet. Edited by Charles Lalore. Volume 2 of *Collection des principaux cartulaires du diocèse de Troyes.* Paris, 1878.

Cartulaire de l'abbaye du Ronceray d'Angers (1028–1184). Edited by Paul Marchegay and Bertrand de Broussillon. Paris, 1900.

Cartulaire de l'abbaye royale de Notre-Dame de Saintes de l'ordre de Saint Benoît. Edited by Th. Grasilier. Volume 2 of *Cartulaires inédits de la Saintonge.* Niort, 1871.

Le cartulaire de Marcigny-sur-Loire (1045–1144): Essai de reconstitution d'un manuscrit disparu. Edited by Jean Richard. Dijon, 1957.

"Cartulaire du prieuré de Jully-les-Nonnains," edited by Ernest Petit. *Bulletin de la société des sciences historiques et naturelles de l'Yonne* 3d ser., 2 (1880): 249–302.

"Le cartulaire du prieuré de Longueau," edited by Paul Pellot. *Revue de Champagne et de Brie* 2d ser., 7 (1895): 19–39, 161–190, 279–288, 337–350.

Cartulaire et archives des communes de l'ancien diocèse et de l'arrondissement administratif de Carcassonne. Edited by Alphonse Mahul. 6 volumes. Paris, 1857–1882.

Cartulaire général de l'Yonne. Edited by Maximilien Quantin. 2 volumes. Auxerre, 1854–1860.

Cartulaires de l'abbaye de Molesme, ancien diocèse de Langres, 916–1250. Edited by Jacques Laurent. 2 volumes. Paris, 1907–1911.

"Cartularium prioratus Libaudi," edited by Paul Marchegay. *Archives historiques de Poitou* 1 (1872): 53–75.

Cartularium Saxonicum. Edited by Walter de Gray Birch. 4 volumes. London, 1855–1899.

The Cartulary and Charters of Notre-Dame of Homblières. Edited by Theodore Evergates and Giles Constable. Cambridge, Mass., 1990.

Cartulary of St Mary Clerkenwell. Edited by William O. Hassall. London, 1949.

Charters and Custumals of the Abbey of Holy Trinity, Caen. Edited by Marjorie Chibnall. London, 1985.

Chartes de Notre-Dame de Bertaud. Edited by Paul Guillaume. Paris, 1888.

Chroniques et chartes de l'abbaye de Saint-Mihiel. Edited by André Lesort. Paris, 1909.

Councils and Synods with Other Documents Relating to the English Church. Edited by F. M. Powicke et al. Oxford, 1964– .

Documents Illustrative of the Social and Economic History of the Danelaw. Edited by F. M. Stenton. London, 1920.

English Episcopal Acta I: Lincoln, 1067–1185. Edited by David M. Smith. London, 1980.

English Historical Documents, Volume 1, c. 500–1042. Edited by Dorothy Whitelock et al. 2d ed. New York, 1979.

Epistolae pontificum Romanorum ineditae. Edited by Samuel Loewenfeld. Leipzig, 1885.

Geoffrey of Vendôme. *Epistola XLVII* [to Robert of Arbrissel]. In PL 157: 181–84.

Gerald of Wales. *Gemma Ecclesiastica.* Edited by John S. Brewer. Volume 2 of *Giraldi Cambrensis Opera,* edited by John S. Brewer. London, 1862.

Guibert of Nogent. *Autobiographie [De vita sua, sive monodiae].* Edited and translated by Edmond-René Labande. Paris, 1981.

[Guibert of Nogent.] *Self and Society in Medieval France: The Memoirs of Abbot Guibert of Nogent (1064?–c. 1125).* Edited by John F. Benton. New York, 1970.

Helgaud de Fleury. *Vie de Robert le Pieux.* Edited and translated by Robert-Henri Bautier. Paris, 1965.

Herman of Laon. *De miraculis S. Mariae Laudunensis.* In PL 156: 962–1018.

Jacques de Vitry. *The Historia Occidentalis of Jacques de Vitry.* Edited by John Frederick Hinnebusch. Fribourg, 1972.

John of St. Arnulf. *Vita Iohannis abbatis Gorziensis.* In MGH SS 4: 335–377.

The Letters of Abelard and Heloise. Translated by Betty Radice. Harmondsworth, Eng., 1974.

Liber Eliensis. Edited by E. O. Blake. London, 1962.

The Life of Christina of Markyate: A Twelfth-Century Recluse. Edited and translated by C. H. Talbot. Rev. ed. Oxford, 1987.

Marie de France. *Lais.* Edited by Alfred Ewert. Oxford, 1947.

Marie de France. *The Lais of Marie de France.* Translated by Robert Hanning and Joan Ferrante. Durham, N.C., 1978.

Memorials of Saint Dunstan. Edited by William Stubbs. London, 1874.

Les miracles de Saint Benoît. Edited by Eugène de Certain. Paris, 1858.

Monumenta Vizeliacensia: Textes relatifs à l'histoire de l'abbaye de Vézelay. Edited by R. B. C. Huygens. Turnhout, 1976.

Orderic Vitalis. *The Ecclesiastical History of Orderic Vitalis.* Edited and translated by Marjorie Chibnall. 6 volumes. Oxford, 1969–1980.

Les origines de l'abbaye de Bouxières-aux-Dames au diocèse de Toul: Reconstitution du chartrier et édition critique des chartes antérieures à 1200. Edited by Robert-Henri Bautier. Nancy, 1987.

The Paraclete Statutes: Institutiones Nostrae. Edited by Chrysogonus Waddell. Trappist, Ky., 1987.

Peter the Venerable. *The Letters of Peter the Venerable.* Edited by Giles Constable. 2 vol. Cambridge, Mass., 1967.

Recueil des actes de Henri II, roi d'Angleterre et duc de Normandie concernant les provinces françaises et les affaires de France. Edited by Léopold Delisle and Elie Berger. 3 volumes. Paris, 1916–1927.

Recueil des actes de Lothaire et de Louis V, rois de France (954–987). Edited by Louis Halphen and Ferdinand Lot. Paris, 1908.

Recueil des actes de Philippe Auguste. Edited by H.–F. Delaborde, Charles Petit-Dutaillis et al. 4 volumes. Paris, 1916–1979.

Recueil des chartes de l'abbaye royale de Montmartre. Edited by Edouard de Barthélemy. Paris, 1883.

Regularis Concordia. Edited and translated by Thomas Symons. London, 1953.

Rodolfus Glaber. *The Five Books of the Histories.* Edited and translated by John France. Oxford, 1989.

Rouleaux des morts du IXe au XVe siècle. Edited by Léopold Delisle. Paris, 1866.

Rotuli de dominabus et pueris et puellis de XII comitatibus. Edited by J. H. Round. London, 1913.

Sacrorum conciliorum nova et amplissima collectio. Edited by J. D. Mansi. 53 volumes. Venice, 1759–1798.

Sigebert of Gembloux. *Vita Deoderici episcopi Mettensis.* In MGH SS 4: 461–483.

Statuta capitulorum generalium ordinis Cisterciensis, Volume 1, *Ab anno 1116 ad annum 1220.* Edited by Josèphe-Marie Canivez. Louvain, 1933.

Suger. *Oeuvres complètes de Suger.* Edited by Albert Lecoy de la Marche. Paris, 1867.

William of Malmesbury. *Gesta pontificum Anglorum.* Edited by N. E. S. A. Hamilton. London, 1870.

William of Malmesbury. *Gesta regum Anglorum.* Edited by William Stubbs. 2 volumes. London, 1887–1889.

REPERTORIES, DICTIONARIES, ENCYCLOPEDIAS, AND ATLASES

AA Big Road Atlas: France, Belgium, and Luxembourg. Basingstoke, 1992.

Agathange de Paris, P. "L'origine et la fondation des monastères de clarisses en Aquitaine au XIIIe siècle." *Collectanea franciscana* 25 (1955): 5–52.

Backmund, Norbert. *Monasticon Praemonstratense.* 3 volumes. Straubing, 1948–1956.

Besse, Jean-Martial, et al. *Abbayes et prieurés de l'ancienne France.* Paris, 1905– . In *Archives de la France monastique* 1 (1905), 4 (1906), 7 (1909), 10 (1910), 12 (1911), 14 (1912), 15 (1913), 17 (1914), 19 (1920), 36 (1932), 37 (1933), 45 (1941) and in *Revue Mabillon,* hors serie, no. 241 (1970), nos. 243 and 245 (1971), nos. 247 and 249 (1972), nos. 251 and 253 (1973), nos. 255 and 257 (1974), no. 259 (1975), nos. 263 and 265 (1976), nos. 267 and 269 (1977), nos. 271 and 273 (1978), nos. 275 and 277 (1979), nos. 279 and 281 (1980), no. 283 (1981), nos. 299–304 (1985–1986), and nos. 315–318 (1989).

Constable, Giles. *Medieval Monasticism: A Select Bibliography.* Toronto, 1976.

Cottineau, Laurent-Henri. *Répertoire topo-bibliographique des abbayes et prieurés.* 3 volumes. Mâcon, 1935–1970.

Déribier-du-Châtelet, Jean-Baptiste. *Dictionnaire statistique ou: Histoire, description et statistique du département du Cantal.* 5 volumes. Aurillac, 1852–1857.

Devic, Claude, and Joseph Vaissete. *Histoire générale de Languedoc.* 16 volumes. Toulouse, 1872–1904.

Dictionary of the Middle Ages. 13 volumes. New York, 1982–1989.

Dictionnaire d'histoire et de géographie ecclésiastiques. Paris, 1912– .

Dimier, Anselme. "Liste des abbayes cisterciennes féminines de France au Moyen-Age." In *Mélanges Anselme Dimier,* edited by Benoît Chauvin. 3 volumes. Arbois, 1984, 2: 591–594.

Dubois, Jacques. "La carte des diocèses de France avant la Révolution." *Annales* 20 (1965): 680–691 with map insert.

Du Cange, C. D. *Glossarium mediae et infimae latinitatis.* New ed., revised by Léopold Favre. 10 volumes. Niort, 1883–1887 (repr. Paris, 1937–1938).

Emery, Richard W. *The Friars in Medieval France: A Catalogue of French Mendicant Convents, 1200–1550.* New York, 1962.

Gallia christiana in provincias ecclesiasticas distributa. 16 volumes. Paris, 1744–1877.

Gams, Pius Bonifacius. *Series episcoporum ecclesiae catholicae.* 2 volumes. Regensberg, 1873.

Gaussin, Pierre-Roger. "Les communautés féminines dans l'espace Languedocien de la fin du XIe à la fin du XIVe siècle." *Cahiers de Fanjeaux* 23 (1988): 299–332.

Jaffé, Philippe, et al. *Regesta pontificum Romanorum ab condita ecclesia ad annum post Christum natum 1198.* 2d ed. 2 volumes. Leipzig, 1885–1888.

Knowles, David, and R. Neville Hadcock. *Medieval Religious Houses: England and Wales.* 2d ed. London, 1971.

Longnon, Auguste. *Atlas historique de la France.* Paris, 1912.

Lusse, Jackie. "Les religieuses en Champagne jusqu'au XIIIe siècle." In *Les religieuses en France au XIIIe siècle*, edited by Michael Parisse, 11–26. Nancy, 1985.

Map of Monastic Britain, South Sheet. 2d ed. London, 1954.

Mayeur, Jean-Marie, et al. *Histoire du christianisme des origines à nos jours.* Volume 4, *Evêques, moines et empereurs (610–1054)*, and Volume 5, *Apogée de la papauté et expansion de la chrétieneté (1054–1274).* Paris, 1993.

McLaughlin, Mary M. "Looking for Medieval Woman: An Interim Report on the Project 'Women's Religious Life and Communities, A.D. 500–1500.'" *Medieval Prosopography* 8 (1987): 61–91.

Monasticon Belge. 8 volumes. Bruges; Liége, 1890–1993.

Moreau, Edouard de. *Histoire de l'église en Belgique.* 2d ed. 6 volumes. Brussels, 1945–1948.

Naz, R., ed. *Dictionnaire de droit canonique.* 7 volumes. Paris, 1935–1965.

The New Catholic Encyclopedia. 18 volumes. New York, 1967–1988.

Niermeyer, J. F. *Mediae latinitatis lexicon minus.* Leiden, 1984.

Port, Celestin. *Dictionnaire historique, géographique et biographique de Maine et Loire.* Rev. ed. Angers, 1965– .

Potthast, Auguste. *Regesta pontificum Romanorum inde ab a. post Christum natum 1198 ad a. 1304.* 2 volumes. Berlin, 1874–1875.

Sawyer, Peter H. *Anglo-Saxon Charters: An Annotated List and Bibliography.* London, 1968.

Stein, Henri. *Bibliographie générale des cartulaires français.* Paris, 1907.

Victoria County Histories. London, 1900–

SECONDARY WORKS

The original publication dates of translated works are indicated in brackets.

André, Ferdinand. *Histoire de l'abbaye des religieuses de Saint-Sauveur de Marseille.* Marseille, 1863.

Anger, Pierre. *Histoire de l'abbaye de Saint-Sulpice-la-Forêt.* Paris, 1920.

Avril, Joseph. "Les fondations, l'organisation et l'évolution des établissements de moniales dans le diocèse d'Angers (du XIe au XIIIe siècle)." In *Les religieuses en France au XIIIe siècle*, edited by Michel Parisse, 27–67. Nancy, 1985.

———. "Le statut de prieurés d'après les conciles provinciaux et les statuts synodaux (fin XIIe–début XIVe siècles)." In *Prieurs et prieurés dans l'Occident médiéval*, edited by Jean-Loup Lemaître, 71–93. Geneva, 1987.

Bachrach, Bernard S. *Fulk Nerra, the Neo-Roman Consul, 987–1040.* Berkeley, Calif., 1993.

Backmund, Norbert. *Geschichte des Prämonstratenserordens.* Grafenau, 1986.

Baker, Derek, ed. *Medieval Women.* Oxford, 1978.

Baldwin, John W. *The Government of Philip Augustus.* Berkeley, Calif., 1986.

Barrère, Joseph. *Histoire religieuse et monumentale du diocèse d'Agen.* 2 volumes. Agen, 1855–1856.

Barrière, Bernadette. "The Cistercian Convent of Coyroux in the Twelfth and Thirteenth Centuries." *Gesta* 31 (1992): 76–82.

Barstow, Anne Llewellyn. *Married Priests and the Reforming Papacy.* New York, 1982.

Barthélemy, Dominique. *L'ordre seigneurial, XIe–XIIe siècle.* Paris, 1990.

Bascher, Jacques de. "Villesalem: L'ermitage fontgombaldien et les origines du prieuré fontevriste." *Revue Mabillon* 61, nos. 307–308 (1987): 97–129.

Bautier, Anne-Marie. "De 'Prepositus' à 'Prior', de 'Cella' à 'Prioratus': Evolution linguistique et genèse d'une institution (jusqu'à 1200)." In *Prieurs et prieurés dans l'Occident médiéval,* edited by Jean-Loup Lemaître, 1–21. Geneva, 1987.

Bautier, Robert-Henri. "Paris au temps d'Abélard." In *Abélard en son temps,* 21–77. Paris, 1981.

Beech, George T. *A Rural Society in Medieval France: The Gâtine of Poitou in the Eleventh and Twelfth Centuries.* Baltimore, 1964.

Berlière, Ursmer. "Les monastères doubles aux XIIe et XIIIe siècles." *Mémoires de l'académie royale de Belgique, Classe des lettres et des sciences morales et politiques* 2d ser., 18 (1923): 3–32.

——. "Le nombre des moines dans les anciens monastères." *Revue bénédictine* 41 (1929): 231–261 and 42 (1930): 18–42.

Berman, Constance H. "Fashions in Monastic Patronage: The Popularity of Supporting Cistercian Abbeys for Women in Thirteenth-Century Northern France." *Proceedings of the Annual Meeting of the Western Society for French History* 17 (1990): 36–45.

——. *Medieval Agriculture, the Southern French Countryside, and the Early Cistercians.* Philadelphia, 1986.

——. "Men's Houses, Women's Houses: The Relationship between the Sexes in Twelfth-Century Monasticism." *Medieval Studies at Minnesota* 2 (1988): 43–52.

Biddle, Martin. "*Felix Urbs Winthonia*: Winchester in the Age of Monastic Reform." In *Tenth-Century Studies,* edited by David Parsons, 123–140. London, 1975.

Bienvenu, Jean-Marc. "Aux origines d'un ordre religieux: Robert d'Arbrissel et la fondation de Fontevraud." *Cahiers d'Histoire* 20 (1975): 227–251.

——. "Le conflit entre Ulger, évêque d'Angers, et Pétronille de Chemillé, abbesse de Fontevrault (vers 1140–1149)." *Revue Mabillon* 53, no. 248 (1972): 113–132.

——. *L'étonnant fondateur de Fontevraud, Robert d'Arbrissel.* Paris, 1981.

——. "Les premiers temps de l'ordre de Fontevraud (1101–1189). Naissance et évolution d'un ordre religieux." Thèse de doctorat d'Etat. University of Paris, Sorbonne, 1980.

Birch, Walter de Gray. *An Ancient Manuscript of the Eighth or Ninth Century.* London, 1889.

Bisson, T. N. "The Crisis of the Catalonian Franchises (1150–1200)." *Estudi General* 5–6 (1985–1986): 153–172.

——. "'The Feudal Revolution.'" *Past and Present* 142 (1994): 6–42.

——. "Nobility and Family in Medieval France: A Review Essay." *French Historical Studies* 16 (1990): 597–613.

Bitel, Lisa M. *Isle of the Saints: Monastic Settlement and Christian Community in Early Ireland.* Ithaca, N.Y., 1989.

Blanc, Colette. "Les pratiques de piété des laïcs dans les pays du Bas-Rhône aux XIe et XIIe siècles." *Annales du Midi* 72 (1960): 137–147.

Bloch, Marc. *Feudal Society.* Translated by L. A. Manyon. 2 volumes. Chicago, 1961 [1939–1940].

Bloch, R. Howard. *Medieval Misogyny and the Invention of Western Romantic Love.* Chicago, 1991.

Bois, Guy. *The Transformation of the Year One Thousand: The Village of Lournand from Antiquity to Feudalism.* Translated by Jean Birrell. New York, 1992 [1989].

Bolton, Brenda. "Mulieres Sanctae." In *Women in Medieval History,* edited by Susan Mosher Stuard, 141–158. Philadelphia, 1976.

Borderie, Arthur de la. "Chartes inédites de Locmaria de Quimper(1022–1336)" *Bulletin archéologique du Finistère* 24 (1897): 96–113.

Boswell, John. *The Kindness of Strangers: The Abandonment of Children in Western Europe from Late Antiquity to the Renaissance.* New York, 1988.

Bouchard, Constance B. "Community: Society and the Church in Medieval France." *French Historical Studies* 17 (1992): 1035–1047.

——. "Consangunity and Noble Marriages in the Tenth and Eleventh Centuries." *Speculum* 56 (1981): 268–287.

——. *Holy Entrepreneurs: Cistercians, Knights, and Economic Exchange in Twelfth-Century Burgundy.* Ithaca, N.Y., 1991.

——. "Merovingian, Carolingian, and Cluniac Monasticism: Reform and Renewal in Burgundy." *Journal of Ecclesiastical History* 41 (1990): 365–388.

——. *Spirituality and Administration: The Role of the Bishop in Twelfth-Century Auxerre.* Cambridge, Mass, 1979.

——. *Sword, Miter, and Cloister: Nobility and the Church in Burgundy, 980–1198.* Ithaca, N.Y., 1987.

Boussard, Jacques. "La vie en Anjou au XIe et XIIe siècles." *Le Moyen Age* 56 (1950): 29–68.

[Bouton, Jean de la Croix, ed.] *Les moniales cisterciennes.* Valence, 1986– .

Bouton, Jean de la Croix, Benoît Chauvin, and Elisabeth Grosjean. "L'abbaye de Tart et ses filiales au moyen âge." In *Mélanges Anselme Dimier,* edited by Benoît Chauvin. 3 volumes. Arbois, 1984, 3: 19–61.

Boyd, Catherine E. *A Cistercian Nunnery in Medieval Italy: The Story of Rifreddo in Saluzzo, 1220–1300.* Cambridge, Mass., 1943.

Broc de Sagagne, M. le Commandant du. "Prieuré de Pontratier." *Bulletin de la société d'émulation du Bourbonnais* 16 (1908): 573–590.

Bücher, Karl. *Die Frauenfrage im Mittelalter.* Tübingen, 1882.

Bull, Marcus. *Knightly Piety and the Lay Response to the First Crusade: The Limousin and Gascony, c. 970–c. 1130.* Oxford, 1993.

Bullough, D. A. "The Continental Background of the Reform." In *Tenth-Century Studies,* edited by David Parsons, 20–36. London, 1975.

Bur, Michel. *La formation du comté de Champagne, v. 950–v. 1150.* Nancy, 1977.

Burton, Janet. *Monastic and Religious Orders in Britain, 1000–1300.* Cambridge, Eng., 1994.

———. *The Yorkshire Nunneries in the Twelfth and Thirteenth Centuries.* Borthwick Papers, no. 56. York, 1979.

Bynum, Caroline Walker. *Holy Feast and Holy Fast: The Religious Significance of Food to Medieval Women.* Berkeley, Calif., 1987.

Cabré y Pairet, Montserrat. "'Deodicatae' y 'Deovotae.' La regulación de la religiosidad femenina en los condados catalanes, siglos IX–XI." In *Las mujeres en el cristianismo medieval,* edited by Angela Muñoz Fernández, 169–182. Madrid, 1989.

Caisso-Rivière, Denise. "Les origines de l'abbaye de la Trinité de Poitiers." *Bulletin de la société des antiquaires de l'Ouest* 3d ser., 4 (1955): 49–73.

Cardon, Henry. "La chapelle d'Epargnemaille à Saint-Quentin et l'abbaye de Notre-Dame de Soissons." *Mémoires de la société académique de Saint-Quentin* 4th ser., 11 (1891–1892): 120–167.

Carlier, Claude. *Histoire du duché de Valois.* 3 volumes. Paris, 1764.

Carré de Busserolle, J.-X. "Notice sur le prieuré de Ste-Marie de Rives." *Mémoires de la société archéologique de Touraine* 13 (1861): 182–187.

Charay, Jean. *Aubenas en Vivarais.* 2 volumes. Aubenas, 1950–1952.

Charrier, Charlotte. *Héloïse dans l'histoire et dans la légende.* Paris, 1933.

Chaussy, Yves, ed. *L'abbaye d'Almenèches-Argentan et Sainte Opportune, sa vie et son culte.* Paris, 1970.

Chédeville, André. *Chartres et ses campagnes (XIe–XIIIe siècle).* Paris, 1973.

Chettle, H. F. "The English Houses of the Order of Fontevraud." *Downside Review* 60 [= n.s. vol. 41] (1942): 33–55.

Clanchy, M. T. *From Memory to Written Record: England, 1066–1307.* 2d ed. Cambridge, Mass., 1993.

Clément-Simon, G. "Notice sur le couvent de Derses." *Bulletin de la société scientifique, historique et archéologique de la Corrèze* 11 (1889): 546–568.

Constable, Giles. "Aelred of Rievaulx and the Nun of Watton: An Episode in the Early History of the Gilbertine Order." In *Medieval Women,* edited by Derek Baker, 205–226. Oxford, 1978.

———. "The Diversity of Religious Life and Acceptance of Social Pluralism in the Twelfth Century." In *History, Society, and the Churches,* edited by Derek Beales and Geoffrey Best, 29–47. Cambridge, Eng., 1985.

Contamine, Philippe, et al. *L'économie médiévale.* Paris, 1993.

Cooke, Kathleen. "Donors and Daughters: Shaftesbury Abbey's Benefactors, Endowment and Nuns, c.1086–1130." *Anglo-Norman Studies* 12 (1990): 29–45.

Coussemaker, Edmond de. "Notice sur l'abbaye de Ravensberg." *Annales du comité flamand de France* 6 (1862): 223–282.

Cowdrey, H. E. J. *The Cluniacs and the Gregorian Reform.* Oxford, 1970.

———. Review of *The Papal Monarchy: The Western Church from 1050 to 1250. History: The Journal of the Historical Association* 75 (1990): 472–473.

Daichman, Graciela. *Wayward Nuns in Medieval Literature.* Syracuse, N.Y., 1986.

Dalarun, Jacques. *L'impossible sainteté: La vie retrouvée de Robert d'Arbrissel (v. 1045–1116), fondateur de Fontevraud.* Paris, 1985.

———. "Robert d'Arbrissel et les femmes." *Annales* 39 (1984): 1140–1160.

Dales, Douglas. *Dunstan: Saint and Statesman.* Cambridge, Eng., 1988.

Dameron, George W. *Episcopal Power and Florentine Society, 1000–1320.* Cambridge, Mass., 1991.

Darby, H. C. "Domesday England." In *A New Historical Geography of England,* edited by H. C. Darby. Cambridge, Eng., 1973.

Debord, André. *La société laïque dans les pays de la Charente, Xe–XIIe s.* Paris, 1984.

Deladreue, E. "Histoire de l'abbaye de Saint-Paul-lès-Beauvais." *Mémoires de la société académique de l'Oise* 6 (1865–1866): 36–218, 411–504.

Deshoulières, F. "Le prieuré d'Orsan en Berri." *Mémoires de la société des antiquaires du Centre* 25 (1901): 51–138.

Dessalles, Léon. *Histoire du Bugue.* Périgueux, 1857.

Devailly, Guy. *Le Berry du Xe au milieu du XIIIe siècle.* Paris, 1973.

Dimier, Anselme. "Chapitres généraux d'abbesses cisterciennes." *Cîteaux: Commentarii Cistercienses* 11 (1960): 268–275.

Dinzelbacher, Peter, and Dieter R. Bauer, eds. *Religiöse Frauenbewegung und mystische Frömmigkeit im Mittelalter.* Vienna, 1988.

Dobson, R. B., and Sara Donaghey. *The History of Clementhorpe Nunnery.* London, 1984.

Ducos, Gustave. *Sainte-Croix de Volvestre et son monastère.* Toulouse, 1937.

Dubois, Marc. "Chartreuse de Prébayon et de Saint-André-de-Ramières (611–1340)." *Revue Mabillon* 26 (1936): 43–62.

Duby, Georges. *The Chivalrous Society.* Translated by Cynthia Postan. Berkeley, Calif., 1977.

———. *The Early Growth of the European Economy: Warriors and Peasants from the Seventh to the Twelfth Century.* Translated by Howard B. Clarke. Ithaca, N.Y., 1974 [1973].

———. *The Knight, the Lady, and the Priest: The Making of Modern Marriage in Medieval France.* Translated by Barbara Bray. New York, 1983 [1981].

———. *Medieval Marriage: Two Models from Twelfth-Century France.* Translated by Elborg Forster. Baltimore, 1978.

———. *Rural Economy and Country Life in the Medieval West.* Translated by Cynthia Postan. London, 1968 [1962].

———. *La société aux XIe et XIIe siècles dans la région mâconnaise.* Paris, 1953.

Dunbabin, Jean. *France in the Making, 843–1180.* Oxford, 1985.

Duplessis, Toussaint. *Description géographique et historique de la haute Normandie.* 2 volumes. Paris, 1740.

Eckenstein, Lina. *Women under Monasticism.* Cambridge, Eng., 1896.

Edouard, J. *Fontevrault et ses monuments.* 2 volumes. Paris, 1873–1874.

Elkins, Sharon K. *Holy Women of Twelfth-Century England.* Chapel Hill, N.C., 1988.

Elliott, Dyan. *Spiritual Marriage: Sexual Abstinence in Medieval Wedlock.* Princeton, 1993.

Erens, A. "Les soeurs dans l'ordre de Prémontré." *Analecta Praemonstratensia* 5 (1929): 5–29.

Evergates, Theodore. *Feudal Society in the Bailliage of Troyes under the Counts of Champagne, 1152–1284.* Baltimore, 1975.

Faillon, Etienne. *Monuments inédits sur l'apostolat de Sainte Marie-Madeleine en Provence.* 2 volumes. Paris, 1863–1865.

Farmer, D. H. "The Progress of the Monastic Revival." In *Tenth-Century Studies,* edited by David Parsons, 10–19. London, 1975.

Fawtier, Robert. *The Capetian Kings of France: Monarchy and Nation (987–1328).* Translated by Lionel Butler and R. J. Adam. New York, 1960.

Faye, M. "Notice sur le monastère de Montazai, de l'ordre de Fontevrauld." *Mémoires de la société des antiquaires de l'Ouest* 20 (1853): 89–128.

Fisher, D. J. V. *The Anglo-Saxon Age, c. 400–1042.* London, 1973.

Fontette, Micheline de. *Les religieuses à l'âge classique du droit canon.* Paris, 1967.

Foreville, Raymonde. "Royaumes, métropolitains et conciles provinciaux." In *Le istituzioni ecclesiastiche della 'societas christiana' dei secoli XI–XII.* Miscellanea del Centro di Studi Medioevali 7. Milan, 1974, 272–313.

Fossier, Robert. *Enfance de l'Europe, Xe–XIIe siècle: Aspects économiques et sociaux.* 2d ed. 2 volumes. Paris, 1989.

———. *La terre et les hommes en Picardie jusqu'à la fin du XIIIe siècle.* 2 volumes. Paris, 1968.

Gaillard, Michèle. "Les fondations féminines dans le Nord et l'Est de la Gaule de la fin du VIe siècle." *Revue d'histoire de l'Eglise en France* 76 (1990): 5–20.

Galbraith, V. H. "Monastic Foundation Charters of the Eleventh and Twelfth Centuries." *Cambridge Historical Journal* 4 (1934): 205–222, 296–298.

Ganck, Roger de. "The Integration of Nuns in the Cistercian Order, Particularly in Belgium." *Cîteaux: Commentarii Cistercienses* 35 (1984): 235–247.

Ganshof, F.-L. *Etude sur le développement des villes entre Loire et Rhin au moyen âge.* Paris, 1943.

Gaussin, Pierre-Roger. *L'abbaye de la Chaise-Dieu (1043–1518).* Paris, 1962.

———. "Les religieuses de la congrégation de la Chaise-Dieu." In *Les religieuses en France au XIIIe siècle,* edited by Michel Parisse, 107–119. Nancy, 1985.

Gazeau, Roger. "La clôture des moniales au XIIe siècle en France." *Revue Mabillon* 58, no. 258 (1974): 289–308.

Gilchrist, Roberta. *Contemplation and Action: The Other Monasticism.* London, 1995.

———. *Gender and Medieval Culture: The Archaeology of Religious Women.* London, 1994.

Godfrey, John. *The Church in Anglo-Saxon England.* Cambridge, Eng., 1962.

Gold, Penny Schine. *The Lady and the Virgin: Image, Attitude, and Experience in Twelfth-Century France.* Chicago, 1985.

——. "Male/Female Cooperation: The Example of Fontevraud." In *Medieval Religious Women*, Volume 1, *Distant Echoes*, edited by John A. Nichols and Lillian Thomas Shank, 151–168. Kalamazoo, Mich., 1984.

Golding, Brian. *Gilbert of Sempringham and Gilbertine Order, c. 1130–c. 1300*. Oxford, 1995.

——. "Hermits, Monks, and Women in Twelfth-Century France and England: The Experience of Obazine and Sempringham." *Monastic Studies* 1 (1990): 127–145.

Graham, Rose. *S. Gilbert of Sempringham and the Gilbertines*. London, 1901.

Graves, Coburn. "English Cistercian Nuns in Lincolnshire." *Speculum* 54 (1979): 492–499.

Grundmann, Herbert. *Religiöse Bewegungen im Mittelalter*. 2d ed. Hildesheim, 1961.

Guibert, Louis. "Destruction de l'Ordre et de l'abbaye de Grandmont: Appendice." *Bulletin de la société archéologique et historique du Limousin* 25 (1877): 33–384.

Guillemain, Bernard. "Les origines des évêques en France au XIe et XIIe siècles." In *Le istituzioni ecclesiastiche della 'societas christiana' dei secoli XI–XII*. Miscellanea del Centro di Studi Medioevali 7. Milan, 1974, 374–407.

Gutsch, Milton R. "A Twelfth-Century Preacher: Fulk of Neuilly." In *The Crusades and Other Historical Essays*, edited by L. J. Paetow, 183–206. New York, 1928.

D'Haenens, Albert. "Quotidienneté et contexte: Pour un modèle d'interprétation de la réalité monastique médiévale (XIe–XIIe siècles)." In *Istituzioni monastiche e istituzioni canonicali in Occidente (1123–1215)*. Miscellanea del Centro di Studi Medioevali 9. Milan, 1980, 567–598.

Hallam, Elizabeth M. "Henry II as a Founder of Monasteries." *Journal of Ecclesiastical History* 28 (1977): 113–132.

Hallam, H. E. *Rural England, 1066–1348*. Sussex, 1981.

Herlihy, David. "Did Women Have a Renaissance?: A Reconsideration." *Medievalia et Humanistica* n.s. 13 (1985): 1–22.

——. *Medieval Households*. Cambridge, Mass., 1985.

——. "The Medieval Marriage Market." *Medieval and Renaissance Studies* 6 (1976): 3–27.

——. *Opera Muliebria: Women and Work in Medieval Europe*. New York, 1990.

Higounet, Charles. *Défrichements et villeneuves du bassin parisien (XIe–XIVe siècles)*. Paris, 1990.

Holdsworth, Christopher J. "Christina of Markyate." In *Medieval Women*, edited by Derek Baker, 185–204. Oxford, 1978.

Hollebeke, Léopold van. *L'abbaye de Nonnenbosche, 1101–1796*. Bruges, 1865.

Hollis, Stephanie. *Anglo-Saxon Women and the Church: Sharing a Common Fate*. Woodbridge, Eng., 1992.

Hunt, Noreen. *Cluny under Saint Hugh, 1049–1109*. London, 1967.

Iogna-Prat, Dominique. "La femme dans la perspective pénitentielle des ermites du Bas-Maine (fin XIe–début XIIe siècle)." *Revue d'histoire de la spiritualité* 53 (1977): 47–64.

Jessee, W. Scott. "Robert d'Arbrissel: Aristocratic Patronage and the Question of Heresy." *Journal of Medieval History* 20 (1994): 221–235.

Johnson, Penelope D. "Agnes of Burgundy: An Eleventh-Century Woman as Monastic Patron." *Journal of Medieval History* 15 (1989): 93–104.

——. *Equal in Monastic Profession: Religious Women in Medieval France.* Chicago, 1991.

——. *Prayer, Patronage, and Power: The Abbey of La Trinité, Vendôme, 1032–1187.* New York, 1981.

Josselin, Maurice. "Acte inédit du roi Louis VII (1178)." *Bibliothèque de l'Ecole des Chartes* 71 (1910): 466–467.

Kinder, T. N. "Blanche of Castille and the Cistercians: An Architectural Re-evaluation of Maubuisson Abbey." *Cîteaux: Commentarii Cistercienses* 27 (1976): 161–188.

Knowles, David. *The Monastic Order in England: A History of its Development from the Times of St. Dunstan to the Fourth Lateran Council, 943–1216.* Cambridge, Eng., 1950.

——. *The Religious Orders in England.* 3 volumes. Cambridge, Eng., 1960–1961.

——. "The Revolt of the Lay Brothers of Sempringham." *English Historical Review* 50 (1935): 465–487.

Lagier, A. "Abbaye de Notre-Dame de Laval-Bénite de Bressieux." *Bulletin d'histoire ecclésiastique et d'archéologie religieuse des diocèses de Valence, Digne, Gap, Grenoble, et Viviers* 3 (1882–1883): 233–245, 270–284.

Latzke, Therese. "Robert von Arbrissel, Ermengard und Eva." *Mittellateinisches Jahrbuch* 19 (1984): 116–154.

Lawrence, C. H. *Medieval Monasticism: Forms of Religious Life in Western Europe in the Middle Ages.* 2d ed. London, 1989.

Le Cacheux, Marie-Josèphe. *Histoire de l'abbaye de Saint-Amand de Rouen des origines à la fin du XIVe siècle.* Caen, 1937.

Leclercq, Jean. "La crise du monachisme aux XIe et XIIe siècles." *Bulletino dell'Istituto storico italiano per il medio evo* 70 (1958): 19–41.

——. *Women and Saint Bernard of Clairvaux.* Translated by Marie-Bernard Saïd. Kalamazoo, Mich., 1989.

Le Goff, Jacques. *La ville médiévale.* Paris, 1980.

Lekai, Louis J. *The Cistercians: Ideals and Reality.* Kent, Ohio, 1977.

Lemarignier, Jean-François. "Political and Monastic Structures in France at the End of the Tenth and the Beginning of the Eleventh Century." In *Lordship and Community in Medieval Europe,* edited by Fredric L. Cheyette, 100–127. New York, 1968.

Leriche, E. "Excursion archéologique de la société de la Diana." *Bulletin de la Diana* 13 (1902–1903): 171–205.

Le Roy Ladurie, Emmanuel. *Montaillou: The Promised Land of Error.* Translated by Barbara Bray. New York, 1978.

Leyser, Henrietta. *Hermits and the New Monasticism: A Study of Religious Communities in Western Europe, 1000–1150.* London, 1984.

Leyser, Karl J. *Rule and Conflict in an Early Medieval Society: Ottonian Saxony.* Bloomington, Ind., 1979.

L'Hermite-Leclercq, Paulette. *Le monachisme féminin dans la société de son temps: Le monastère de la Celle (XIe–début du XVIe siècle).* Paris, 1989.

Linière, R. de. "Le prieuré conventuel de la Fontaine-Saint-Martin." *Revue historique et archéologique du Maine* 58 (1905): 5–54, 162–211, 241–300.

Little, Lester K. *Religious Poverty and the Profit Economy in the Middle Ages.* Ithaca, N.Y., 1978.

Lopez, Robert S. *The Commercial Revolution of the Middle Ages, 950–1350.* Englewood Cliffs, N.J., 1971.

Lorçin, Marie-Thérèse. *Société et cadre de vie en France, Angleterre et Bourgogne (1050–1250).* Paris, 1985.

Luchaire, Achille. *Etudes sur les actes de Louis VII.* Paris, 1885.

———. *Louis VI le Gros.* Paris, 1890.

Lynch, J. E. "Marriage and Celibacy of the Clergy: The Discipline of the Western Church, an Historico-Canonical Synopsis." *The Jurist* 32 (1972): 14–38, 189–212.

Lynch, Joseph H. *Simoniacal Entry into the Religious Life from 1000 to 1260.* Columbus, Ohio, 1976.

McDonnell, Ernest W. *The Beguines and Beghards in Medieval Culture.* New Brunswick, N.J., 1954.

McLeod, Enid. *Héloïse: A Biography.* London, 1971.

McNamara, Jo Ann. "Victims of Progress: Women and the Twelfth Century." In *Female Power in the Middle Ages,* edited by Karen Glente and Lise Winther-Jensen, 26–37. Copenhagen, 1989.

McNamara, Jo Ann, and Suzanne Wemple. "The Power of Women through the Family in Medieval Europe, 500–1100." In *Clio's Consciousness Raised: New Perspectives on the History of Women,* edited by Mary S. Hartman and Lois Banner, 105–118. New York, 1974.

———. "Sanctity and Power: The Dual Pursuit of Medieval Women." In *Becoming Visible: Women in European History,* edited by Renate Bridenthal and Claudia Koonz, 92–118. Boston, 1977.

Magnou-Nortier, Elisabeth. "Formes féminines de vie consacrée dans les pays du Midi jusqu'au début du XIIe siècle." *Cahiers de Fanjeaux* 23 (1988): 193–216.

———. *La société laïque et l'église dans la province ecclésiastique de Narbonne.* Toulouse, 1974.

Marchegay, Paul. "L'abbaye de Nyoiseau." *Revue de l'Anjou et de Maine-et-Loire* 1st ser., 1, pt. 2 (1852): 77–88.

———. "Chartes de Fontevraud concernant l'Aunis et la Rochelle. *Bibliothèque de l'Ecole des Chartes* 19 [= 4th ser., vol. 4] (1858): 132–170, 321–347.

———. "Un enterrement au douzième siècle." *Revue de l'Anjou et de Maine-et-Loire* 1st ser., 1, pt. 2 (1852): 177–186.

———. "Notes sur deux prieurés de l'abbaye de Nyoiseau." *Bulletin de la société archéologique de Nantes* 6 (1866): 223–229.

———. "Le prieuré de Bois-Goyer." *Annuaire départemental de la société d'émulation de la Vendée* 3 (1856): 252–270.

———. "Recherches sur les cartulaires d'Anjou." In *Archives d'Anjou: Recueil de documents et mémoires inédits sur cette province*, edited by Paul Marchegay, 3 volumes. Angers, 1848–1854, 1:185–429.

Metz, René. "Le statut de la femme en droit canonique médiéval." *Recueils de la Société Jean Bodin* 12 (1962): 59–113.

Meyer, Marc Anthony. "Women and the Tenth-Century English Monastic Reform." *Revue bénédictine* 87 (1977): 34–61.

Miller, Edward, and John Hatcher. *Medieval England: Rural Society and Economic Change, 1086–1348.* London, 1978.

Miller, Maureen C. *The Formation of a Medieval Church: Ecclesiastical Change in Verona, 950–1150.* Ithaca, N.Y., 1993.

Millinger, Susan. "Humility and Power: Anglo-Saxon Nuns in Anglo-Norman Hagiography." In *Medieval Religious Women*, Volume 1, *Distant Echoes*, edited by John A. Nichols and Lillian Thomas Shank, 115–129. Kalamazoo, Mich., 1984.

Monsabert, P. de. "Documents inédits pour servir à l'histoire de l'abbaye de Sainte-Croix de Poitiers." *Revue Mabillon* 9 (1913–1914): 50–88, 259–282.

Moolenbroek, Jaap van. *Vital l'ermite, prédicateur itinérant, fondateur de l'abbaye normande de Savigny.* Translated by Anne-Marie Nambot. Assen, 1990.

Moore, R. I. "Family, Community, and Cult on the Eve of the Gregorian Reform." *Transactions of the Royal Historical Society* 5th ser., 30 (1980): 49–69.

———. *The Formation of a Persecuting Society: Power and Deviance in Western Europe, 950–1250.* Oxford, 1987.

———. "The Reconstruction of the Cartulary of Fontevraud." *Bulletin of the Institute of Historical Research* 41 (1968): 87–95.

Moorman, John. *A History of the Franciscan Order from Its Origins to the Year 1517.* Oxford, 1968.

Moreau, Marthe. *L'âge d'or des religieuses: Monastères féminins du Languedoc méditerranéen au Moyen Age.* Montpellier, 1988.

———. "Les moniales du diocèse de Maguelone au XIIIe siècle." *Cahiers de Fanjeaux* 23 (1988): 241–260.

Moret, J.-J. *Histoire de Saint-Menoux.* Moulins, 1907.

Morris, Colin. *The Papal Monarchy: The Western Church from 1050 to 1250.* Oxford, 1989.

Neel, Carol. "The Origins of the Beguines." *Signs* 14 (1989): 321–341.

Nelson, Janet L. "Society, Theodicy, and the Origins of Medieval Heresy." *Studies in Church History* 9 (1972): 65–77.

———. "Women and the Word in the Earlier Middle Ages." *Studies in Church History* 27 (1990): 53–78.

Newman, William Mendel. *Le domaine royal sous les premiers capétiens (987–1180).* Paris, 1937.

Nichols, John A., and Lillian Thomas Shank, eds. *Medieval Religious Women*, Volume 1, *Distant Echoes.* Kalamazoo, Mich., 1984.

Nicolas, David. *Medieval Flanders.* New York, 1992.

Oulmont, Charles. *Les débats du clerc et du chevalier*. Paris, 1907.

Pacaut, Marcel. *Louis VII et les élections épiscopales dans le royaume de France*. Paris, 1957.

——. *Les moines blancs: Histoire de l'ordre de Cîteaux*. Paris, 1993.

——. *L'ordre de Cluny (909–1789)*. Paris, 1986.

Paris, Louis. *Histoire de l'abbaye d'Avenay*. 2 volumes. Paris, 1879.

Parisse, Michel. "Le concile de Remiremont: Poème satirique du XIIe siècle." *Le Pays de Remiremont* 4 (1981): 10–15.

——. "Fontevraud, monastère double." In *Doppelklöster und andere Formen der Symbiose männlicher und weiblicher Religiosen im Mittelalter*, edited by Kasper Elm and Michel Parisse, 135–147. Berlin, 1992.

——. *La Lorraine monastique au Moyen Age*. Nancy, 1981.

——. "Les monastères de femmes en Saxe (XIe–XIIe siècles)." *Revue Mabillon* n.s. 2 [= 63] (1991): 5–48.

——. *Noblesse et chevalerie en Lorraine médiévale: Les familles nobles du XIe au XIIIe siècle*. Nancy, 1982.

——. *Les nonnes au Moyen Age*. Le Puy, 1983.

——. "Des prieurés de femmes." In *Prieurs et prieurés dans l'Occident médiéval*, edited by Jean-Loup Lemaître, 115–126. Geneva, 1987.

——. "Les religieuses bénédictines de Lorraine au temps de la réforme des XIe et XIIe siècle." *Revue Mabillon* 61, nos. 309–310 (1987): 257–279.

——, ed. *Les religieuses en France au XIIIe siècle*. Nancy, 1985.

Pasztor, Edith. "Il monachesimo femminile." In *Dall' eremo al cenobio: La civiltà monastica in Italia dalle origini all'età di Dante;* 155–180, Milan, 1987.

Perroy, Edouard. "Les plus anciennes chartes du prieuré de Jourcey." *Bulletin de la Diana* 28 (1943): 172–185.

Petigny, J. de. "Lettre inédite de Robert d'Arbrissel à la comtesse Ermengarde." *Bibliothèque de l'Ecole des Chartes* 3d ser., 5 (1854): 209–235.

Petit, François. *Norbert et l'origine des Prémontrés*. Paris, 1981.

Petroff, Elizabeth Alvilda. *Body and Soul: Essays on Medieval Women and Mysticism*. New York, 1994.

Picavet, François. *Roscelin: Philosophe et théologien*. Paris, 1911.

Piolin, Paul. *Histoire de l'église du Mans*. 3 volumes. Paris, 1851–1863.

——. "Le moine Raoul et le bienheureux Raoul de la Fustaye." *Revue des questions historiques* 42 (1887): 497–509.

Poirer-Coutansais, Françoise. *Les abbayes bénédictines du diocèse de Reims. Gallia monastica*, Volume 1, edited by Jean-François Lemarignier. Paris, 1974.

Poly, Jean-Pierre. *La Provence et la société féodale, 879–1166*. Paris, 1976.

Poly, Jean-Pierre, and Eric Bournazel. *The Feudal Transformation, 900–1200*. Translated by Caroline Higgitt. New York, 1991 [1980].

Postan, M. M. *The Medieval Economy and Society: An Economic History of Britain in the Middle Ages*. London, 1972.

Pounds, Norman J. G. *An Historical Geography of Europe, 450 B.C.–A.D. 1330*. Cambridge, Eng., 1973.

Power, Eileen. *Medieval English Nunneries, c. 1275–1535*. Cambridge, Eng., 1922.

——. "The Position of Women." In *The Legacy of the Middle Ages,* edited by G. C. Crump and E. F. Jacob, 401–433. Oxford, 1926.

Raison, L., and R. Niderst. "Le mouvement érémitique dans l'Ouest de la France (fin XIe-début XIIe siècles)." *Annales de Bretagne* 55 (1948): 1–46.

Les religieuses dans le cloître et dans le monde. Saint-Etienne, 1994.

Robert, Ulysse. *Etude sur les actes du pape Calixte II.* Paris, 1874.

Roisin, Simone. "L'efflorescence cistercienne et le courant féminin de piété au XIIIe siècle." *Revue d'histoire ecclésiastique* 39 (1942): 342–378.

Rosenwein, Barbara H. *Rhinoceros Bound: Cluny in the Tenth Century.* Philadelphia, 1982.

——. *To Be the Neighbor of Saint Peter: The Social Meaning of Cluny's Property, 909–1049.* Ithaca, N.Y., 1989.

Roussel, Charles François. *Le diocèse de Langres: Histoire et statistique.* 4 volumes. Langres, 1873–1879.

Russell, J. C. *Medieval Regions and Their Cities.* Newton Abbot, 1972.

——. "Population in Europe, 500–1500." In *The Fontana Economic History of Europe,* edited by Carlo M. Cipolla. Volume 1, *The Middle Ages,* 25–70. New York, 1976.

Sanfaçon, Roland. *Défrichements, peuplement et institutions seigneuriales en Haut-Poitou du Xe au XIIIe siècle.* Quebec, 1967.

Sassier, Yves. *Louis VII.* Paris, 1991.

Schmitz, Philibert. *Histoire de l'ordre de Saint Benoît.* Volume 7: *Les moniales.* Maredsous, 1956.

Schulenburg, Jane Tibbetts. "Sexism and the Celestial Gynaeceum from 500 to 1200." *Journal of Medieval History* 4 (1978): 117–133.

——. "Strict Active Enclosure and Its Effects on the Female Monastic Experience (ca. 500–1100)." In *Medieval Religious Women,* Volume 1, *Distant Echoes,* edited by John A. Nichols and Lillian Thomas Shank, 51–86. Kalamazoo, Mich., 1984.

——. "Women's Monastic Communities, 500–1100: Patterns of Expansion and Decline." *Signs* 14 (1989): 262–291.

Shahar, Shulamith. *The Fourth Estate: A History of Women in the Middle Ages.* Translated by Chaya Galai. London, 1983.

Simmons, Loraine. "The Abbey Church at Fontevraud in the Later Twelfth Century: Anxiety, Authority, and Architecture in the Female Spiritual Life." *Gesta* 31 (1992): 99–107.

Simons, Walter. "The Beguine Movement in the Southern Low Countries: A Reassessment." *Bulletin de l'Institut Historique Belge de Rome* 59 (1989): 63–105.

Sivéry, Gérard. *L'économie du royaume de France au siècle de Saint Louis (vers 1180–vers 1315).* Lille, 1984.

Skinner, Mary. "Benedictine Life for Women in Central France, 850–1100: A Feminist Revival." In *Medieval Religious Women.* Volume 1, *Distant Echoes,* edited by John A. Nichols and Lillian Thomas Shank, 87–113. Kalamazoo, Mich., 1984.

Smith, Jacqueline. "Robert of Arbrissel: *Procurator Mulierum.*" In *Medieval Women,* edited by Derek Baker, 175–184. Oxford, 1978.

Southern, R. W. *Western Society and the Church in the Middle Ages.* Harmondsworth, Eng. 1970.

Strayer, Joseph. *On the Medieval Origins of the Modern State.* Princeton, N.J., 1970.

Stuard, Susan Mosher, ed. *Women in Medieval History and Historiography.* Philadelphia, 1987.

Symons, Thomas. "*Regularis Concordia*: History and Derivation." In *Tenth-Century Studies*, edited by David Parsons, 37–59. London, 1975.

Thompson, Sally. "The Problem of the Cistercian Nuns in the Twelfth and Early Thirteenth Centuries." In *Medieval Women*, edited by Derek Baker, 227–252. Oxford, 1978.

———. *Women Religious: The Founding of English Nunneries after the Norman Conquest.* Oxford, 1991.

Tunc, Suzanne. "Après la mort de Robert d'Arbrissel: Le conflit entre l'abbesse et l'évêque." *Le Moyen Age* 98 (1992): 379–390.

———. *Les femmes au pouvoir: Deux abbesses de Fontevraud aux XIIe et XVII siècles.* Paris, 1993.

Van Damme, J.-B. "Les pouvoirs de l'abbé de Cîteaux aux XIIe et XIIIe siècle." *Analecta Cisterciensia* 24 (1968): 47–85.

Van Engen, John. "The Christian Middle Ages as an Historiographical Problem." *American Historical Review* 91 (1986): 519–552.

———. "The 'Crisis of Cenobitism' Reconsidered: Benedictine Monasticism in the Years 1050–1150." *Speculum* 61 (1986): 269–304.

Van Overstraeten, Daniel. *Inventaire des archives de l' abbaye de Ghislinghien.* Brussels, 1976.

Vauzelles, Ludovic de. *Histoire du prieuré de la Magdeleine-lez-Orléans de l'ordre de Fontevraud.* Paris, 1873.

Verdon, Jean. "Le monachisme en Poitou au Xe siècle." *Revue Mabillon* 59, no. 272 (1978): 235–253.

———. "Les moniales dans la France de l'Ouest aux XIe et XIIe siècles: Etude d'histoire sociale." *Cahiers de civilisation médiévale* 19 (1976): 247–264.

———. "Notes sur le rôle économique des monastères féminins en France dans la seconde moitié du IXe et au début du Xe siècle." *Revue Mabillon* 58, nos. 260–261 (1975): 329–343.

———. "Recherches sur les monastères féminins dans la France du Nord aux IXe–XIe siècles." *Revue Mabillon* 59, no. 266 (1976): 49–96.

———. "Recherches sur les monastères féminins dans la France du Sud aux IXe–XIe siècles." *Annales du Midi* 88 (1976): 117–138.

———. "Les sources de l'histoire de la femme en Occident aux Xe–XIIIe siècles." *Cahiers de civilisation médiévale* 20 (1977): 219–251.

Verhulst, Adriaan. *Histoire du paysage rural en Flandre de l'époque romaine au XVIIIe siècle.* Brussels, 1966.

Veronese, Allessandra, "Monasteri femminili in Italia settentrionale nell'alto medioevo: Confronto con i monasteri maschili attraverso un tentativo de analisi 'statistica.'" *Benedictina* 34 (1987): 355–416.

Vicaire, M.-H. "L'action de saint Dominique sur la vie régulière des femmes en Languedoc." *Cahiers de Fanjeaux* 23 (1988): 217–240.

Waldman, Thomas G. "Abbot Suger and the Nuns of Argenteuil." *Traditio* 61 (1985): 239–272.

Walter, Johannes von. *Die ersten Wanderprediger Frankreichs: Studien zur Geschichte des Mönchtums.* 2 volumes. Leipzig, 1903–1906.

Warren, Ann K. *Anchorites and Their Patrons in Medieval England.* Berkeley, Calif., 1985.

Warren, W. L. *Henry II.* Berkeley, Calif., 1973.

Wemple, Suzanne Fonay. *Women in Frankish Society: Marriage and the Cloister, 500 to 900.* Philadelphia, 1981.

Werner, Ernst. "Zur Frauenfrage und zum Frauenkult im Mittelalter: Robert v. Arbrissel und Fontevrault." *Forschungen und Fortschritte* 29 (1955): 269–276.

White, Stephen D. *Custom, Kinship, and Gifts to Saints: The Laudatio Parentum in Western France, 1050–1150.* Chapel Hill, N.C., 1988.

Wischermann, Elsa Maria. *Marcigny-sur-Loire: Gründungs-und Frühgeschichte des ersten Cluniacenserinnenpriorates (1055–1150).* Munich, 1986.

index of monastic houses

Note: Only houses mentioned in the text of the book are indexed; for a complete alphabetical listing of nunnery foundations, 900–1300, see Appendix A. Some houses listed here were founded before 900. Male monasteries are marked with an asterisk.

general index

abbesses and prioresses: Adela of Rennes, 38, 45; Adeline of les Blanches, 65; Aelfwyn of Chatteris, 26n; Aethelgifu of Shaftesbury, 17, 20–21; Agnes of Orsan, 61, 89, 96; Alimburgis of St-Geniès, 42; Ava of St-Maur, Verdun, 31; Edburga of Winchester, 22; Elizabeth of Vergy of Tart l'Abbaye, 73–74, 84; Ermengarde of Fervacques, 71; Godealde of Etival, 66; Helisende of Avenay, 169; Hermengarde of Ste-Croix, Poitiers, 32; Judith of St-Geniès, 42; Leoburga of Angers (La Ronceray), 37, 46; Longuebrune of Boulaur, 62; Lucy of Vauxbons, 151; Marsilia of St-Paul-lès-Beauvais, 149; Mathilda of La Trinité, Caen, 85–86; Raina of Rieunette, 124; Rothildis of Bouxières-aux-Dames, 30, 45; Thecia of St-Paul-lès-Beauvais, 149. See also Heloise; Hersende; Liutgarde; Petronilla of Chemillé

Abelard, Peter, 85, 120–121, 123; his rule for religious women, 121

Adela, daughter of William the Conquerer, 78, 98

Adela, sister of Liutgarde, 40–41

Adelaide, viscountess of Narbonne, 41–42

Aelred of Rievaulx, 166–167

Aethelfleda, mentor of Saint Dunstan, 25–26, 28

Aethelred, king of England, 21, 26

Aethelstan, king of England, 21–24

Alfred the Great, king of England, 9, 17, 19–22, 27

Alpert of Metz, 40–41

anchorites and recluses, 24, 44–45, 78–79, 99, 179–180; Aelfwyn, 78–79; Eadburh, 24; Eve, 77; Hervey, 77; Humbert, 45; Roger, 78. See also Aethelfleda; Christina of Markyate; nonregular religious life

Andegavina, nun of Montazais, 89, 91, 97n, 102, 115

Andreas, biographer of Robert of Arbrissel, 58n, 61, 96, 116

Andreas Capellanus, 165–166

Asser, 17, 19–21

Augustinian Rule, 15, 54n, 81

Baldwin IX, count of Flanders, 149

Baudry of Dol, 58, 96

beguines and beguinages, 91–92, 177–179. See also nonregular religious life

Benedictine Rule, 13, 15, 31–32, 54–55, 64, 72–73, 81–82, 121, 176

Bernard of Clairvaux, 13, 119, 185

Bertrade of Montfort, countess of Anjou, 75, 96, 98, 109

bishops. See councils; founders and patrons of nunneries

Carthusians, 15

Cassian, John, 7, 34

Charles the Good, count of Flanders, 127

charters, 3, 100, 104–107, 114, 119, 124, 143–151, 153–154, 185–186

Christina of Markyate, 4, 78–79, 84–86, 102, 115

Cistercians, 1, 7, 13–15, 53, 65, 68, 72–74, 80–81, 84, 105–107, 110, 112n, 118n,